SELECTED WRITINGS OF SYDNEY SMITH

Clive Hannon
August 2024

SELECTED WRITINGS OF
Sydney Smith

EDITED AND WITH AN INTRODUCTION BY

W. H. AUDEN

faber and faber

This edition first published in 2009
by Faber and Faber Ltd
Bloomsbury House, 74–77 Great Russell Street
London WC1B 3DA

A CIP record for this book is available from the British Library

ISBN 978-0-571-25275-6

CONTENTS

Introduction by W. H. Auden   vii

PART I

The Peter Plymley Letters   3
Methodism   75
Persecuting Bishops   101
Letter to the Bishop of London   119
What Is a Puseyite? (poem)   123
Letters to Archdeacon Singleton   124
Letter to Lord Lansdowne   187

PART II

Letter to Mrs. Beach   191
Two Letters to M. H. Beach   191
Letter to Francis Jeffrey   194
Letter to *The Farmer's Magazine*   195
Advice to Parishioners   196
A Little Moral Advice   199
Letter to Lady Georgianna Morpeth   201
A Nice Person   201
Letter to Messrs. Hunt & Clark, Booksellers   202
Letter to —— Bedford, Esq.   203
Letter to Vestry of Halberton   204
Letter to Lord John Russell   205

PART III

Game Laws   211
Spring Guns and Man Traps   226

Counsel for Prisoners   237
Too Much Latin and Greek   258
Female Education   271
The Society for the Suppression of Vice   287
Chimney Sweepers   298
"Locking In" on Railways (two letters)   311
Modern Changes   316

PART IV

Letter to Francis Jeffrey (extract)   321
Letter to John Allen (extract)   321
Letter to Lord Grey (extract)   322
Letter to Lady Grey (extract)   323
Letter to Mr. Swing   324
Four Speeches on the Reform Bill   325
Ballot   347

PART V

America   371
On American Debts   387

INTRODUCTION

Sydney Smith was born in 1771, two years after the invention of Watt's steam-engine and one year after Goldsmith's *Deserted Village,* that vivid description of the effects of land enclosure. It was still dangerous to walk through the streets of London after dark, there were no waterproof hats, no braces, no calomel, no quinine, no clubs, no savings banks, the government was completely in the hands of great landowners, and, in the best society, one third of the gentlemen were always drunk. He died in 1845, which was also the year in which Engels' *State of the Working Classes in England* was published and Newman was received into the Roman Catholic Church. The American Revolution, the French Revolution, the Napoleonic wars, the Romantic Movement had all occurred, there was gaslight in houses, there were railways through the country, the Victorian proprieties were firmly established (Bowdler's *Shakespeare* appeared in 1818) and public opinion had forced Parliament to soften the rigors of pure laisser-faire (the first Factory Act was passed in 1833).

Sydney Smith's mother, Maria Olier, came of French Huguenot stock; his father, Robert Smith, was an eccentric unstable character who left his bride at the church door and departed to America for several years, spent the rest of his life in travel and unsuccessful speculations, and insisted on his family sitting over the dinner table in the half-dark for hours. His children, however, did better for themselves: three of his sons went to India (the only daughter stayed, of course, at home), where one died young and the other two made fortunes; Sydney, his second son, ended up as a Canon of St. Paul's and the most famous wit of his generation.

Physically, he was swarthy, sturdy tending to stoutness and suffering in later life from gout. Mentally, like so many funny men, he had to struggle constantly against melancholia: he found it difficult to get up in the morning, he could not bear dimly lit rooms—"Better," he wrote, "to eat dry bread by the splendour of

gas than to dine on wild beef with wax-candles"—and music in a
minor key upset him. Writing to a friend who was similarly afflicted,
he gave his own recipe for combating low spirits.

1. Go into the shower-bath with a small quantity of water at a
   temperature low enough to give you a slight sensation of
   cold, 75° or 80°.
2. Short views of human life—not further than dinner or tea.
3. Be as busy as you can.
4. See as much as you can of those friends who respect and
   like you, and of those acquaintances who amuse you.
5. Attend to the effects tea and coffee produce upon you.
6. Avoid poetry, dramatic representations (except comedy),
   music, serious novels, sentimental people, and everything
   likely to excite feeling and emotion, not ending in active
   benevolence.
7. Keep good blazing fires.
8. Be firm and constant in the exercise of rational religion.

This illustrates well enough both the virtues of his mind and its
limitations. Such a man will always have an excellent grasp of the
concrete and the immediately possible, but one must not expect
from him profound speculative insights. Sydney Smith was perfectly sincere in his religious faith, but one is not surprised to find
that, as a young man, his ambition was to read for the Bar and
that it was only lack of money which compelled him instead to
take Holy Orders. In his admirable attacks on religious intolerance
the reader cannot but be conscious of a distrust of all theological
dogma until he wonders whether Sydney Smith could have explained just why he was an Anglican and not, say, a Unitarian.
His criticisms of the Methodists and the Puseyites are acute
enough but one cannot help feeling that it was religious "enthusiasm" as such, not merely the follies to which it is liable, which
aroused his scorn and distrust.

II

The finances of the Church Visible are always a fascinating subject.
As a State Church, the revenues of the Church of England are derived, partly from property which it owns, partly from taxation
but comparatively little from the alms of the faithful. Patronage
is not solely in the hands of the Crown; some livings are bestowed
by bishops, some by cathedral chapters and many by private
patrons. With its money it has to pay for the upkeep of churches

and parsonages and to secure for every parish, if it can, a vicar of good manners and education. Moreover, since most Anglican clergymen are married men, they will need enough money to support and educate their families.

In Sydney Smith's time, by his own calculations, the total revenues of the Church would, if equally divided, have been sufficient to give every minister excluding curates, an annual income of £250—"about the same as that enjoyed by the upper domestic of a nobleman." Needless to say, its revenues were not so divided, but ranged from rich sees like Canterbury, worth £25,000, to country livings worth no more than £150. In the competition for preferment, those who had sufficient private means to endure the rigors of their early clerical years and those with good social connections who could gain the ears of the disposers of patronage had, naturally, a great advantage. It was not, however, impossible for a person of humble birth to succeed. Sydney Smith paints the following picture of the ecclesiastical career of a baker's son:

> Young Crumpet is sent to school—takes to his books—spends the best years of his life, as all eminent Englishmen do, in making Latin verses—knows that the *crum* in crum-pet is long, and the *pet* short—goes to the University—gets a prize for an Essay on the Dispersion of the Jews—takes orders—becomes a Bishop's chaplain—has a young nobleman for his pupil— publishes an useless classic, and a serious call to the unconverted—and then goes through the Elysian transitions of Prebendary, Dean, Prelate, and the long train of purple, profit and power.

It is not hard to deduce from this description the personal qualities best fitted for a rise from obscurity to a mitre: an unoriginal brightness of intellect which is good at passing exams but not at thinking for itself, a proper respect for titles, a talent for flattery, a solemn mien and, above all, Tory political opinions.

Sydney Smith possessed none of these; intellectual ability he had in abundance but of a dangerously lively kind; though he came to number many titled and rich people among his friends, he was utterly without snobbery and incapable of flattery; he was continually making jokes and, worst of all, he was a convinced Whig. Yet, starting from the bottom—with an income of £100 a year and no influential friends—he rose, if not to a bishopric, to a residential canon of St. Paul's at a salary of £2000 a year. It may be not without interest to consider how he did it. His career began with a stroke of good luck: the local squire of the Wiltshire village where he was a young curate took a shine to him and asked him to accompany his son as a tutor on the Grand Tour. Sydney Smith recommended Weimar but the outbreak of war made it impossible and they went to Edinburgh instead. There he met Jeffrey, Brougham, and Francis Horner and started with them *The Edinburgh Review,* devoted to the criticism of contemporary literature and the furthering of Whig policies. The review was an instantaneous success and Smith began to be talked about. In 1800 he married for love and the marriage seems to have remained a singularly happy one. The only gift he had for his bride was six worn silver teaspoons and she, though she possessed some small means of her own, had presently to sell her mother's jewelry to meet expenses. In 1803 the couple moved to London, where he managed to live by preaching at the Foundling Hospital and lecturing on Moral Philosophy at The Royal Institution. Through his elder brother he was introduced into the Holland House circle, the center of Whig society, of which he quickly became a popular and admired member. He was still, however, too poor to afford an umbrella, far less a carriage; moreover, his new friends, while cultivated and rich, belonged to the party which was out of power and likely to remain so. Again, he had a stroke of luck for, after Pitt's death, the Whigs came into power for a few months, just long enough to appoint him to the living of Foston in Yorkshire, worth £500 a year. Foston had not had a resident vicar since the reign of Charles II and Smith had no intention of leaving the social amenities of London which he loved for the country which he regarded as "a healthy grave" and where it seemed to him as if "the whole creation were going to expire at tea-time." In 1808, however, a Tory government passed the Clergy Residence Bill and he was banished, at the age of thirty-eight, to a village "twelve miles from a lemon," its existing parsonage a brick-floored kitchen with one room above it, there to do duty for the next twenty years.

Any man might have quailed at the prospect but for an intellectual and man-about-town like Smith, anonymous author of *The Peter Plymley Letters* which had electrified the public and enraged the government, accustomed to the best tables, the best conversation, the most elegant ladies and gentlemen, it must have seemed the end, and a stranger might well have expected him to lapse into despondency and drink. He did nothing of the kind. He kept up his reading, his reviewing, and his large correspondence; he designed a new parsonage for himself and got the local carpenter to furnish it; he devised all sorts of ingenious gadgets—devices for added draft to the fires, devices to prevent smoky chimneys, lamps

burning mutton-fat to save the expense of candles, a special
scratcher pole for all his animals etc., and, far from neglecting his
parish duties, became one of the best county vicars of whom there
is record, and the idol of his parishioners. Church services were
only a small part of his ministrations: he started small vegetable
gardens, let out to the laborers at very low rents, to help them augment their food supply; he experimented with diets to discover
which were both cheap and nourishing; he acted as their doctor
and, as a local magistrate, saved many of them from going unjustly
to jail.

During the first half of his residence at Foston, he was never
free from financial anxiety—during the bad harvest year of 1816,
for instance, he could no more afford to buy white flour than
could his parishioners—but in 1820 an unexpected legacy from an
aunt lightened his burden and in 1828, as in 1808, a brief Coali-
tion Ministry including Whigs remembered him and procured him
a canonry at Bristol and the living of Combe Florey in Somerset
which, though it did not increase his income, was a step up in the
Ecclesiastical Hierarchy.

From then on his life was smooth sailing: two causes in which
he was a leader triumphed—the Catholic Emancipation act was
passed in 1829 and the Reform Bill in 1832,—his services were
rewarded in his sixty-first year by a canonry at St. Paul's, and then
his unmarried younger brother died, leaving him a third of his
very large fortune. He was now rich, popular, and famous. A letter
he wrote shortly before his death aptly describes the last fourteen
years of his life:

> Being Canon of St. Paul's in London, and a rector of a parish
> in the country, my time is divided equally between town and
> country. I am living among the best society in the Metropolis,
> and at ease in my circumstances; in tolerable health, a mild
> Whig, a tolerating Churchman, and much given to talking,
> laughing and noise. I dine with the rich in London, and physic
> the poor in the country; passing from the sauces of Dives to the
> sores of Lazarus. I am, upon the whole, a happy man, have
> found the world an entertaining place, and am thankful to
> Providence for the part alloted to me in it.

III

Many of Sydney Smith's wisecracks are widely known. Nowell
Smith's definitive edition of his letters (Oxford Press, 1953) must
already have convinced many readers that he is among the supreme

masters of the epistolary art, but his published writings still seem
to be little known. This is understandable because Smith was not
a poet or a novelist but from first to last a writer of polemics, as
pure an example as we have in English of *l'écrivain engagé*.
As a general rule it is the fate of the polemical writer to be forgotten when the cause for which he fought has been won or is no
longer a live issue, and it will always be difficult to persuade a later
generation that there can be exceptions, polemical writers, jour-
nalists if you will, of such brilliance and charm that they can be
read with delight and admiration by those to whom their subject
matter is in itself of little interest.

Literary criticism, too, is apt to avoid the polemical writer because there is little to say about him. Unlike the creator of "pure"
literature, the poet, the novelist, the dramatist etc., he rarely shows
"development," stylistic or ideological. His cast of mind, his way
of expressing himself are generally established early and any
variety that his work may show will come mostly from a variety
in the topics upon which he writes.

Nevertheless there are a few such authors who must be ranked
very high by any literary standard and first among such I would
place Hooker, Swift, Sydney Smith and Bernard Shaw. Milton in
his polemical works is too bad-mannered and abusive, and Junius,
for all his brilliance, too biased.

Of them all, Sydney Smith has, perhaps, the most exact sense
of the particular audience he is addressing on any given occasion,
and the widest variation of tone. He can equally well speak to the
average educated man—

> Is it necessary that the Archbishop of Canterbury should give
> feasts to Aristocratic London; and that the domestics of the
> Prelacy should stand with swords and bag-wigs round pig and
> turkey, and venison, to defend, as it were, the Orthodox gas-
> tronome from the fierce Unitarian, the fell Baptist, and all the
> famished children of Dissent.
>
> (*Letters to Archdeacon Singleton*)

to the unlettered rustic—

> I don't like that red nose, and those blear eyes, and that stupid,
> downcast look. You are a drunkard. Another pint, and one pint
> more; a glass of gin and water, rum and milk, cider and pepper,
> a glass of peppermint, and all the beastly fluids which drunkards
> pour down their throats. . . . It is all nonsense about not being
> able to work without ale, and gin, and cider, and fermented

liquors. Do lions and cart-horses drink ale? It is mere habit. . . .
I have no objection, you will observe, to a moderate use of ale,
or any other liquor you can *afford* to purchase. My objection is,
that you cannot afford it; that every penny you spend at the ale-
house comes out of the stomachs of the poor children, and strips
off the clothes of the wife—

(Advice to Parishioners)

and a child—

Lucy, dear child, mind your arithmetic. You know, in the first
sum of yours I ever saw, there was a mistake. You had carried
two (as a cab is licensed to do) and you ought, dear Lucy, to
have carried but one. Is this a trifle? What would life be without
arithmetic but a scene of horrors? . . . I now give you my part-
ing advice. Don't marry any body who has not a tolerable understanding and a thousand a year, and God bless you, dear
child.

Always lucid, well-informed and fair to his opponents, he is
equally at home with the long period and the short, the ornate
vocabulary and the plain, and is a master of every rhetorical effect,
the satirical inversion—

Their object is to preserve game; they have no objection to
preserve the lives of their fellow creatures also, if both can exist
at the same time; if not, the least worthy of God's creatures
must fall—the rustic without a soul—not the Christian partridge
—not the immortal pheasant—not the rational woodcock, or
the accountable hare.

the ironic description of shocking facts in tea-table terms—

One summer's whipping, only one: the thumb-screw for a short
season; a little light easy torturing between Lady-day and
Michaelmas.

the homely simile—

You may not be aware of it yourself, most reverend Abraham,
but you deny their freedom to the Catholics upon the same
principle that Sarah your wife refuses to give the receipt for a
ham or a gooseberry dumpling: she refuses her receipts, not because they secure to her a certain flavour, but because they remind her that her neighbours want it: a feeling laughable in a
priestess, shameful in a priest; venial when it witholds the
blessings of him, tyrannical and execrable when it narrows the
boon of religious freedom.

and the ringing peroration of righteous anger—

> If I lived at Hampstead upon stewed meats and claret; if I
> walked to church every Sunday before eleven young gentlemen
> of my own begetting with their faces washed, and their hair
> pleasingly combed; if the Almighty had blessed me with every
> earthly comfort—how awfully would I pause before I sent forth
> the flame and the sword over the cabins of the poor, brave,
> generous, open-hearted peasants of Ireland. . . . The vigour I
> love consists in finding out wherein subjects are aggrieved, in
> relieving them, in studying the temper and genius of a people,
> in consulting their prejudices, in selecting proper persons to
> lead and manage them, in the laborious, watchful, and difficult
> task of increasing public happiness by allaying each particular
> discontent. . . . But this, in the eyes of Mr. Percival, is imbecil-
> ity and meanness: houses are not broken open—women are
> not insulted—the people seem all to be happy; they are not
> rode over by horses, and cut by whips. Do you call this vigour?
> Is this government?

His command of comic effects is equally extensive and masterly.
Many of his impromptu puns are still remembered, such as his
remark on hearing two women screaming insults at each other
from upper stories on opposite sides of a narrow street in Edinburgh:

> Those two women will never agree: they are arguing from
> different premises.

His particular forte, perhaps, is the treatment of analogical
situations as identical; during the period of the Luddite riots he
wrote to a friend:

> What do you think of all these burnings? and have you heard
> of the new sort of burnings? Ladies' maids have taken to setting
> their mistresses on fire. Two dowagers were burned last week,
> and large rewards are offered! They are inventing little fire-
> engines for the toilet table, worked with lavender water!

Lastly, he can create pictures in what might be called the
ludicrous baroque style, as surely as Pope:

> Frequently did Lord John meet the destroying Bishops; much
> did he commend their daily heap of ruins; sweetly did they smile
> on each other, and much charming talk was there of meteor-
> ology and catarrh, and the particular cathedral they were pull-

ing down at the time; till one fine morning the Home Secretary, with a voice more bland, and a look more ardently affectionate, than that which the masculine mouse bestows on his nibbling female, informed them that the Government meant to take all the Church property into their own hands, to pay the rates out of it, and deliver the residue to the rightful possessors. Such an effect, they say, was never before produced by a *coup de théâtre*. The Commission was separated in an instant: London clenched his fist; Canterbury was hurried out by his chaplains, and put into a warm bed; a solemn vacancy spread itself over the face of Gloucester; Lincoln was taken out in strong hysterics.

IV

Sydney Smith is a perfect expression of the Whig mentality, of that English form of Liberalism which has always perplexed and sometimes enraged Continental observers both on the political Right and on the political Left. European liberalism, which has normally been anti-clerical, republican, and materialist, finds it bewildering that social reform in England should owe so much to religion—that the British Labour Party, for example, should be so closely associated with the Evangelical movement, and the increasing concern over juvenile delinquency and other cultural problems of urbanization with Anglo-Catholicism—and that the English Liberal who desires the abolition of the Crown or the House of Lords should be so rare a bird. Liberals like Godwin and H. G. Wells are a-typical, and much closer to the European mind.

For the European who knows a little history, it is all the more puzzling, since he is aware that Voltaire and the French Encyclopaedists of the Enlightenment who were the founders of continental Liberalism were inspired by and took many of their ideas from Locke, the Deists, and the Whig authors of the Glorious Revolution of 1688. If he is a pro-clerical monarchist, he is apt to conclude that the English Liberal is a materialist at heart who is only using religious sentiments as a smoke-screen, and to point to the ambiguities of the Thirty-Nine Articles as proof that an Anglican does not know what he believes; if he is an anti-clerical rationalist, he is apt to come to similar doubts about the Englishman's Liberal convictions, citing in evidence his devotion to irrational political institutions.

The clue to the difference is to be found in the difference in meaning of the word *Revolution* as applied to the events which took place in France in 1789 and as applied to the events which took place in England in 1688. In the former case it means a radical transformation, the birth of a new kind of society, in the latter it is an astronomical metaphor, meaning a restoration of balance. The radical transformation of English society which corresponds to the French Revolution was the work of the Tudors. The execution of Charles I was not, like the execution of Luis XVI, a revolutionary breach with the past but the restoration of a conservative, even medieval, idea, namely, that the ruler is not above but subject to Natural Law. Then, from their experiences under the Protectorate, Englishmen learned that the dangers of arbitrary power were not necessarily removed simply by the abolition of the Crown, for the claims of self-appointed saints to know by divine inspiration what the good life should be and to have the right to impose their notions on the ungodly could be as great a threat as the divine right of kings. The historical experience with which the Whigs of 1688 and their successors had to cope was a century and a half of bitter quarrels and drastic changes imposed upon the public by individuals or minorities. The most fundamental notion in English Liberalism, therefore, is the notion of limited sovereignty and its characteristic way of thinking goes something like this:

1. All people differ from each other in character and temperament so that any attempt to impose an absolute uniformity is a tyranny. On the other hand there can be no social life unless the members of a society hold certain beliefs in common, and behave in certain commonly accepted ways.

2. The beliefs which it is necessary to hold in common must therefor be so defined that differences of emphasis are possible and the laws which regulate social conduct must be such that they command common consent. In so far as conformity has to be inforced, this should be in matters of outward behavior not of private belief, firstly because there can be no doubt whether an individual does or does not conform, and secondly because men find behaving in a way with which they are not in complete sympathy more tolerable than being told to believe something they consider false. Thus, in the English Prayer Book the rules for conducting the Liturgy are precise, while the meaning of the Thirty-Nine Articles is purposely left vague.

3. The way in which a reform is effected is just as important as the reform itself. Violent change is as injurious to freedom as inertia.

4. Utopians are a public menace. Reformers must concern themselves with the concrete and the possible.

The authors of the French Enlightenment were confronted with a very different situation, a static society in which nothing had changed. To the French Liberal, therefor, nothing could seem to matter except that a radical change should occur and the threat to freedom was not absolute sovereignty as such but the imprisonment of the majority in an arbitrary social status. A Jacobin like St. Just could accept the notion of absolute sovereignty without question so long as it was taken from the Crown and given to the people. Materialism was a natural philosophy for French Liberalism to adopt since its enemy was the aristocrat who claimed privilege on biological grounds (Few of the English peerages in the eighteenth century were more than two hundred years old), and it was no less natural that this materialism should be militantly dogmatic since the philosophy European Liberalism associated with the *ancien régime,* the theology of the Roman Catholic Church, was itself rigid and uncompromising.

Sydney Smith is an example of English Liberalism at its best. He is never utopian or given to large generalizations but always attacks a specific abuse, and the reform he proposes is equally specific and always possible to realize. Further, he assumes that, though most people are selfish and many people are stupid, few are either lunatics or deliberate scoundrels impervious to rational argument.

Thus, in attacking the Game Laws, he avoids raising ultimate questions about the justice or injustice of private property and its unequal distribution, and sticks to the immediate issue of man-traps, spring-guns and the like. Assuming that no sane man will deny that they are cruel, he points out that they are unnecessary for the purpose for which they are intended; the prevention of poaching can be achieved by humane means, namely by giving every landlord, great or small, the right to kill game, by making game private property like geese or ducks and by allowing the owner to sell game to whom he chooses since, as long as the sale of game is forbidden and there are rich men who want it, a black market supplied by poachers is inevitable.

Knowing both the world of the rich and the world of the poor and an enemy of neither, he is aware that many injustices to the poor exist, not because the rich are intentionally unjust but because their own world has never felt them. In attacking the law which denied defense counsel to prisoners accused of a felony, a

leftover from feudal times when a defense of prisoners accused
by the Crown was felt to imply disloyalty, he explains very simply
why, though this feeling no longer existed, the law still remained
on the statute books.

> To ask why there are not petitions—why the evil is not more
> noticed, is mere parliamentary froth and ministerial juggling.
> Gentlemen are rarely hung. If they were so, there would be
> petitions without end for counsel.

There is a certain type of professional Liberal who assumes that
in every issue the liberal position must be on the Left. Sydney
Smith was never fooled in this way as a comparison of his two
principal set of pamphlets, the *Peter Plymley Letters* and the
Letters to Archdeacon Singleton, clearly demonstrates. In the former his opponent is the conservative. Laws prohibiting Roman
Catholics from voting or holding public offices which, when they
were originally passed may have had some justification—an attempt to bring back the Stuarts might have met with their support—were still in effect, long after any such danger had passed.
Sydney Smith assumes that the vast majority of those who opposed
their repeal were capable of seeing that they were unjust, if he can
demonstrate that there was no danger incurred by removing them.
With the inveterately stupid or demagogic minority, his argument
is different; he warns them of the unpleasant material consequences to themselves which will follow if they refuse to listen
to their conscience.

In the case of the Singleton letters, his enemies are not those who
refuse to make a needed reform but those who would impose a
necessary reform from above in a hasty and unjust manner. What
right, he asks, have the bishops to make changes without consulting
the lower clergy who will be most affected by them and whose experience of parochial life make them better equipped to make concrete judgements about abuses instead of generalisations. Further
he complains that much of the plan for reform was utopian, since
to do what it was intended to do would require a sum of money
which the Church did not possess.

In his opposition to secret ballot, later experience has shown
us that he was mistaken, because he did not foresee—neither, for
that matter, did his opponents—a day when there would arise one-
party governments prepared to use all the instruments of coercion
at their disposal to ensure an overwhelming vote in their favour.
Even so, he makes two points in his pamphlet which no liberal

democracy should forget; firstly, that the free voter must hold himself responsible for the consequence of his vote:

> Who brought that mischievous profligate villain into Parlia-
> ment? Let us see the names of his real supporters. Who stood
> out against the strong and uplifted arm of power? Who discov-
> ered this excellent and hitherto unknown person? . . . Is it not
> a dark and demoralising system to draw this veil over human
> actions, to say to the mass, be base, and you will not be de-
> spised; be victorious and you will not be honored—

and secondly that the free voter is the voter whose choice is deter-
minded by what he believes to be in the best interest of his country
and by nothing else.

> The Radicals are quite satisfied if a rich man of popular man-
> ners gains the votes and affections of his dependents; but why
> is not this as bad as intimidation? The real object is to vote for
> the good politician, not for the kind-hearted or agreeable man:
> the mischief is just the same to the country whether I am
> smiled into a corrupt choice, or frowned into a corrupt choice.

v

Today the Whig tradition which Sydney Smith represented is under
a cloud. It is under attack for being aesthetically unappealing and
psychologically or metaphysically shallow.

> *. . . what is Whiggery?*
> *A levelling, rancorous, rational sort of mind*
> *That never looked out of the eye of a saint*
> *Or out of a drunkard's eye.*

Yet, unattractive and shallow as one may feel so many liberals to
be, how rarely on any concrete social issue does one find the liberal position the wrong one. Again, how often, alas, do those very
philosophers and writers who have most astounded us by their
profound insights into the human heart and human existence, dismay us by the folly and worse of their judgments on the issues
of everyday life.

Liberalism is also under criticism for being ineffective and in so
far as we have to combat enemies with whom rational discussion
is impossible because the absolute pre-suppositions on both sides
are radically different, the criticism has some justification. Some
of us, however, seem in danger of forgetting that rational discus-

sion is desirable and that liberty is not just a value of which one approves in the abstract but, to be real must be embodied in one's own person and daily acts. Indeed, the more critical a situation, the less the opinions a man expresses matter in comparison with his behavior. On this, if nothing else, the sober Whig and the wild Existentialist will agree. What a challenge to a second Landor it would be to compose an Imaginary Conversation between the shades of the author of the *Letters to Archdeacon Singleton* and the author of *Attack on Christendom*.

I should not be surprised if they understood each other much better than one would naturally expect. They both disliked abstract systems, they were both strikingly original personalities and they could both be very funny. Kierkegaard, whose chief complaint against the bourgeois was that they were a parody of the Knight of Faith, would have appreciated, I think, Sydney Smith's use of bourgeois terms to define *A Nice Person:*

A nice person is neither too tall nor too short, looks clean and cheerful, has no prominent features, makes no difficulties, is never displaced, sits bodkin, is never foolishly affronted, and is void of affectations. . . . A nice person is clear of trumpery little passions, acknowledges superiority, delights in talent, shelters humility, pardons adversity, forgives deficiency, respects all men's rights, never stops the bottle, is never long and never wrong, always knows the day of the month, the name of everybody at table, and never gives pain to any human being. . . . A nice person never knocks over wine or melted butter, does not tread upon the dog's foot, or molest the family cat, eats soup without noise, laughs in the right place, and has a watchful and attentive eye.

W. H. AUDEN

PART I

THE PETER PLYMLEY LETTERS

Letters on the subject of the Catholics to my brother Abraham who lives in the country.—*Peter Plymley.*

LETTER I.

Dear Abraham,

A worthier and better man than yourself does not exist; but I have always told you from the time of our boyhood, that you were a bit of a goose. Your parochial affairs are governed with exemplary order and regularity; you are as powerful in the vestry as Mr. Perceval is in the House of Commons,—and, I must say, with much more reason; nor do I know any church where the faces and smock-frocks of the congregation are so clean, or their eyes so uniformly directed to the preacher. There is another point, upon which I will do you ample justice; and that is, that the eyes so directed towards you are wide open; for the rustic has, in general, good principles, though he cannot control his animal habits; and, however loud he may snore, his face is perpetually turned toward the fountain of orthodoxy.

Having done you this act of justice, I shall proceed, according to our ancient intimacy and familiarity, to explain to you my opinions about the Catholics, and to reply to yours.

In the first place, my sweet Abraham, the Pope is not landed—nor are there any curates sent out after him—nor has he been hid at St. Alban's by the Dowager Lady Spencer—nor dined privately at Holland House—nor been seen near Dropmore. If these fears exist (which I do not believe), they exist only in the mind of the Chancellor of the Exchequer; they emanate from his zeal for the Protestant interest; and, though they reflect the highest honour upon the delicate irritability of his faith, must certainly be considered as more ambiguous proofs of the sanity and vigour of his

3

understanding. By this time, however, the best informed clergy in
the neighbourhood of the metropolis are convinced that the rumour
is without foundation; and, though the Pope is probably hovering
about our coast in a fishing smack, it is most likely he will fall a
prey to the vigilance of our cruisers; and it is certain he has not yet
polluted the Protestantism of our soil.

Exactly in the same manner, the story of the wooden gods
seized at Charing Cross, by an order from the Foreign Office, turns
out to be without the shadow of a foundation: instead of the angels
and archangels, mention by the informer, nothing was discovered
but a wooden image of Lord Mulgrave, going down to Chatham,
as a head-piece for the Spanker gun-vessel: it was an exact resemblance of his Lordship in his military uniform; and *therefore* as
little like a god as can well be imagined.

Having set your fears at rest, as to the extent of the conspiracy
formed against the Protestant religion, I will now come to the
argument itself.

You say these men interpret the Scriptures in an unorthodox
manner, and that they eat their God.—Very likely. All this may
seem very important to you, who live fourteen miles from a market
town, and, from long residence upon your living, are become a
kind of holy vegetable; and, in a theological sense, it is highly important. But I want soldiers and sailors for the state; I want to
make a greater use than I now can do of a poor country full of
men; I want to render the military service popular among the
Irish; to check the power of France; to make every possible exertion for the safety of Europe, which in twenty years' time will be
nothing but a mass of French slaves: and then you, and ten other
such boobies as you, call out—"For God's sake, do not think of
raising cavalry and infantry in Ireland! . . . . They interpret the
Epistle to Timothy in a different manner from what we do! . . . .
They eat a bit of wafer every Sunday, which they call their God!"
. . . . I wish to my soul they would eat you, and such reasoners as
you are. What! when Turk, Jew, Heretic, Infidel, Catholic, Protestant, are all combined against this country; when men of every
religious persuasion, and no religious persuasion; when the population of half the globe is up in arms against us; are we to stand
examining our generals and armies as a bishop examines a candidate for holy orders? and to suffer no one to bleed for England
who does not agree with you about the 2nd of Timothy? You talk
about Catholics! If you and your brotherhood have been able to
persuade the country into a continuation of this grossest of all absurdities, you have ten times the power which the Catholic clergy

ever had in their best days. Louis XIV, when he revoked the Edict of Nantes, never thought of preventing the Protestants from fighting his battles; and gained accordingly some of his most splendid victories by the talents of his Protestant generals. No power in Europe, but yourselves, has ever thought for these hundred years past, of asking whether a bayonet is Catholic, or Presbyterian, or Lutheran; but whether it is sharp and well-tempered. A bigot delights in public ridicule; for he begins to think he is a martyr. I can promise you the full enjoyment of this pleasure, from one extremity of Europe to the other.

I am as disgusted with the nonsense of the Roman Catholic religion as you can be: and no man who talks such nonsense shall ever tithe the product of the earth, nor meddle with the ecclesiastical establishment in any shape;—but what have I to do with the speculative nonsense of his theology, when the object is to elect the mayor of a county town, or to appoint a colonel of a marching regiment? Will a man discharge the solemn impertinences of the one office with less zeal, or shrink from the bloody boldness of the other with greater timidity, because the blockhead believes in all the Catholic nonsense of the real presence? I am sorry there should be such impious folly in the world, but I should be ten times a greater fool than he is, if I refused, in consequence of this folly, to lead him out against the enemies of the state. Your whole argument is wrong: the state has nothing whatever to do with theological errors which do not violate the common rules of morality, and militate against the fair power of the ruler: it leaves all these errors to you, and to such as you. You have every tenth porker in your parish for refuting them; and take care that you are vigilant, and logical in the task.

I love the Church as well as you do; but you totally mistake the nature of an establishment, when you contend that it ought to be connected with the military and civil career of every individual in the state. It is quite right that there should be one clergyman to every parish interpreting the Scriptures after a particular manner, ruled by a regular hierarchy, and paid with a rich proportion of haycocks and wheatsheafs. When I have laid this foundation for a rational religion in the state—when I have placed ten thousand well educated men in different parts of the kingdom to preach it up, and compelled everybody to pay them, whether they hear them or not—I have taken such measures as I know must always procure an immense majority in favour of the Established Church; but I can go no further. I cannot set up a civil inquisition, and say to one, you shall not be a butcher, because you are not orthodox;

and prohibit another from brewing, and a third from administering the law, and a fourth from defending the country. If common justice did not prohibit me from such a conduct, common sense would. The advantage to be gained by quitting the heresy would make it shameful to abandon it; and men who had once left the Church would continue in such a state of alienation from a point of honour, and transmit that spirit to the latest posterity. This is just the effect your disqualifying laws have produced. They have fed Dr. Rees, and Dr. Kippis; crowded the congregation of the Old Jewry to suffocation; and enabled every sublapsarian, and superlapsarian, and semi-pelagian clergyman, to build himself a neat brick chapel, and live with some distant resemblance to the state of a gentleman.

You say the King's coronation oath will not allow him to consent to any relaxation of the Catholic laws.—Why not relax the Catholic laws as well as the laws against Protestant dissenters? If one is contrary to his oath, the other must be so too; for the spirit of the oath is, to defend the Church establishment, which the Quaker and the Presbyterian differ from as much or more than the Catholic; and yet his Majesty has repealed the Corporation and Test Act in Ireland, and done more for the Catholics of both kingdoms than had been done for them since the Reformation. In 1778, the ministers said nothing about the royal conscience; in 1793 * no conscience; in 1804 no conscience; the common feeling of humanity and justice then seem to have had their fullest influence upon the advisers of the Crown: but in 1807—a year, I suppose, eminently fruitful in moral and religious scruples (as some years are fruitful in apples, some in hops)—it is contended by the well-paid John Bowles, and by Mr. Perceval (who tried to be well paid), that that is now perjury which we had hitherto called policy and benevolence! Religious liberty has never made such a stride as under the reign of his present Majesty; nor is there any instance in the annals of our history, where so many infamous and damnable laws have been repealed as those against the Catholics which have been put an end to by him: and then, at the close of this useful policy, his advisers discover that the very measures of concession and indulgence, or (to use my own language) the measures of justice, which he has been pursuing through the whole of his reign, are contrary to the oath he takes at its commencement! That oath binds his Majesty not to consent to any measure con-

---

* These feelings of humanity and justice were at some periods a little quickened by the representations of 40,000 armed volunteers.

trary to the interest of the Established Church: but who is to judge of the tendency of each particular measure? Not the King alone: it can never be the intention of this law that the King, who listens to the advice of his Parliament upon a road bill, should reject it upon the most important of all measures. Whatever be his own private judgment of the tendency of any ecclesiastical bill, he complies most strictly with his oath, if he is guided in that particular point by the advice of his Parliament, who may be presumed to understand its tendency better than the King, or any other individual. You say, if Parliament had been unanimous in their opinion of the absolute necessity for Lord Howick's bill, and the King had thought it pernicious, he would have been perjured if he had not rejected it. I say, on the contrary, his Majesty would have acted in the most conscientious manner, and have complied most scrupulously with his oath, if he had sacrificed his own opinion to the opinion of the great council of the nation; because the probability was that such opinion was better than his own: and upon the same principle, in common life, you give up your opinion to your physician, your lawyer, and your builder.

You admit this bill did not compel the King to elect Catholic officers, but only gave him the option of doing so if he pleased; but you add, that the King was right in not trusting such dangerous power to himself or his successors. Now you are either to suppose that the King for the time being has a zeal for the Catholic establishment, or that he has not. If he has not, where is the danger of giving such an option? If you suppose that he may be influenced by such an admiration of the Catholic religion, why did his present Majesty, in the year 1804, consent to that bill which empowered the Crown to station ten thousand Catholic soldiers in any part of the kingdom, and placed them absolutely at the disposal of the Crown? If the King of England for the time being is a good Protestant, there can be no danger in making the Catholic *eligible* to anything: if he is not, no power can possibly be so dangerous as that conveyed by the bill last quoted; to which, in point of peril, Lord Howick's bill is a mere joke. But the real fact is, one bill opened a door to his Majesty's advisers for trick, jobbing, and intrigue; the other did not.

Besides, what folly to talk to me of an oath, which, under all possible circumstances, is to prevent the relaxation of the Catholic laws! for such a solemn appeal to God sets all conditions and contingencies at defiance. Suppose Bonaparte was to retrieve the only very great blunder he has made, and were to succeed, after repeated trials, in making an impression upon Ireland, do you think we should hear anything of the impediment of a coronation oath? or would the spirit of this country tolerate for an hour such ministers, and such unheard-of nonsense, if the most distant prospect existed of conciliating the Catholics by every species even of the most abject concession? And yet, if your argument is good for anything, the coronation oath ought to reject, at such a moment, every tendency to conciliation, and to bind Ireland for ever to the crown of France.

I found in your letter the usual remarks about fire, fagot, and bloody Mary. Are you aware, my dear Priest, that there were as many persons put to death for religious opinions under the mild Elizabeth as under the bloody Mary? The reign of the former was, to be sure, ten times as long, but I only mention the fact, merely to show you that something depends upon the age in which men live, as well as on their religious opinions. Three hundred years ago, men burnt and hanged each other for these opinions. Time has softened Catholic as well as Protestant: they both required it; though each perceives only his own improvement, and is blind to that of the other. We are all the creatures of circumstances. I know not a kinder and better man than yourself; but you (if you had lived in those times) would certainly have roasted your Catholic: and I promise you, if the first exciter of this religious mob had been as powerful then as he is now, you would soon have been elevated to the mitre. I do not go to the length of saying that the world has suffered as much from Protestant as from Catholic persecution; far from it: but you should remember the Catholics had all the power, when the idea first started up in the world that there could be two modes of faith; and that it was much more natural they should attempt to crush this diversity of opinion by great and cruel efforts, than that the Protestants should rage against those who differed from them, when the very basis of their system was complete freedom in all spiritual matters.

I cannot extend my letter any further at present, but you shall soon hear from me again. You tell me I am a party man. I hope I shall always be so, when I see my country in the hands of a pert London joker and a second-rate lawyer. Of the first, no other good is known than that he makes pretty Latin verses; the second seems to me to have the head of a country parson, and the tongue of an Old Bailey lawyer.

If I could see good measures pursued, I care not a farthing who is in power; but I have a passionate love for common justice, and for common sense, and I abhor and despise every man who builds up his political fortune upon their ruin.

God bless you, reverend Abraham, and defend you from the Pope, and all of us from that administration who seek power by opposing a measure which Burke, Pitt, and Fox all considered as absolutely necessary to the existence of the country.

LETTER II.

Dear Abraham,

The Catholic not respect an oath! why not? What upon earth has kept him out of Parliament, or excluded him from all the offices whence he is excluded, but his respect for oaths? There is no law which prohibits a Catholic to sit in Parliament. There could be no such law; because it is impossible to find out what passes in the interior of any man's mind. Suppose it were in contemplation to exclude all men from certain offices who contended for the legality of taking tithes: the only mode of discovering that fervid love of decimation which I know you to possess would be to tender you an oath against that damnable doctrine, that it is lawful for a spiritual man to take, abstract, appropriate, subduct, or lead away the tenth calf, sheep, lamb, ox, pigeon, duck, &c. &c. &c., and every other animal that ever existed, which of course the lawyers would take care to enumerate. Now this oath I am sure you would rather die than take; and so the Catholic is excluded from Parliament because he will not swear that he disbelieves the leading doctrines of his religion! The Catholic asks you to abolish some oaths which oppress him; your answer is, that he does not respect oaths. Then why subject him to the test of oaths? The oaths keep him out of Parliament; why, then, he respects them. Turn which way you will, either your laws are nugatory, or the Catholic is bound by religious obligations as you are: but no eel in the well-sanded fist of a cook-maid, upon the eve of being skinned, ever twisted and writhed as an orthodox parson does when he is compelled by the gripe of reason to admit anything in favour of a Dissenter.

I will not dispute with you whether the Pope be or be not the Scarlet Lady of Babylon. I hope it is not so; because I am afraid it will induce his Majesty's Chancellor of the Exchequer to introduce several severe bills against popery, if that is the case; and though he will have the decency to appoint a previous committee of inquiry as to the fact, the committee will be garbled and the report inflammatory. Leaving this to be settled as he pleases to settle it, I wish to inform you, that previously to the bill last passed in favour of the Catholics, at the suggestion of Mr. Pitt, and for his satisfaction, the opinions of six of the most celebrated of the foreign Catholic universities were taken as to the right of the Pope to interfere in the temporal concerns of any country. The answer cannot possibly leave the shadow of a doubt, even in the mind of Baron Maseres; and Dr. Rennel would be compelled to admit it, if three Bishops lay dead at the very moment the question were put to him. To this answer might be added also the solemn declaration and signature of all the Catholics in Great Britain.

I should perfectly agree with you, if the Catholics admitted such a dangerous dispensing power in the hands of the Pope; but they all deny it, and laugh at it, and are ready to abjure it in the most decided manner you can devise. They obey the Pope as the spiritual head of their church; but are you really so foolish as to be imposed upon by mere names?—What matters it the seven thousandth part of a farthing who is the spiritual head of any church? Is not Mr. Wilberforce at the head of the church of Clapham? Is not Dr. Letsom at the head of the Quaker church? Is not the General Assembly at the head of the church of Scotland? How is the government disturbed by these many-headed churches? or in what way is the power of the Crown augmented by this almost nominal dignity?

The King appoints a fast day once a year, and he makes the Bishops: and if the government would take half the pains to keep the Catholics out of the arms of France that it does to widen Temple Bar, or improve Snow Hill, the King would get into his hands the appointments of the titular Bishops of Ireland.—Both Mr. C——'s sisters enjoy pensions more than sufficient to place the two greatest dignitaries of the Irish Catholic Church entirely at the disposal of the Crown.—Everybody who knows Ireland knows perfectly well, that nothing would be easier, with the expenditure of a little money, than to preserve enough of the ostensible appointment in the hands of the Pope to satisfy the scruples of the Catholics, while the real nomination remained with the Crown. But, as I have before said, the moment the very name of Ireland is mentioned, the English seem to bid adieu to common feeling, common prudence, and common sense, and to act with the barbarity of tyrants, and the fatuity of idiots.

Whatever your opinion may be of the follies of the Roman Catholic religion, remember they are the follies of four millions of human beings, increasing rapidly in numbers, wealth, and intelligence, who, if firmly united with this country, would set at defiance the power of France, and if once wrested from their alliance with England, would in three years render its existence as an independent nation absolutely impossible. You speak of danger to the Establishment: I request to know when the Establishment was ever so much in danger as when Hoche was in Bantry Bay, and whether all the books of Bossuet, or the arts of the Jesuits, were half so terrible? Mr. Perceval and his parsons forgot all this, in their horror lest twelve or fourteen old women may be converted to holy water, and Catholic nonsense. They never see that, while they are saving these venerable ladies from perdition, Ireland may be lost, England broken down, and the Protestant Church, with all its deans, prebendaries, Percevals and Rennels, be swept into the vortex of oblivion.

Do not, I beseech you, ever mention to me again the name of Dr. Duigenan. I have been in every corner of Ireland, and have studied its present strength and condition with no common labour. Be assured Ireland does not contain at this moment less than five millions of people. There were returned in the year 1791 to the hearth tax 701,000 houses, and there is no kind of question that there were about 50,000 houses omitted in that return. Taking, however, only the number returned for the tax, and allowing the average of six to a house (a very small average for a potato-fed people), this brings the population to 4,200,000 people in the year 1791: and it can be shown from the clearest evidence (and Mr. Newenham in his book shows it), that Ireland for the last fifty years has increased in its population at the rate of 50,000 or 60,000 per annum; which leaves the present population of Ireland at about five millions, after every possible deduction for *existing circumstances, just and necessary wars, monstrous and unnatural rebellions,* and all other sources of human destruction. Of this population, two out of ten are Protestants; and the half of the Protestant population are Dissenters, and as inimical to the Church as the Catholics themselves. In this state of things, thumbscrews and whipping—admirable engines of policy, as they must be considered to be—will not ultimately avail. The Catholics will hang over you; they will watch for the moment, and compel you hereafter to give them ten times as much, against your will, as they would now be contented with, if it were voluntarily surrendered. Remember what happened in the American war; when Ireland compelled you to give her everything she asked, and to renounce, in the most explicit manner, your claim of sovereignty over her. God Almighty grant the folly of these present men may not bring on such another crisis of public affairs!

What are your dangers which threaten the Establishment?— Reduce this declamation to a point, and let us understand what you mean. The most ample allowance does not calculate that there would be more than twenty members who were Roman Catholics in one house, and ten in the other, if the Catholic emancipation were carried into effect. Do you mean that these thirty members would bring in a bill to take away the tithes from the Protestant, and to pay them to the Catholic clergy? Do you mean that a Catholic general would march his army into the House of Commons and purge it of Mr. Perceval and Dr. Duigenan? or, that the theological writers would become all of a sudden more acute and more learned, if the present civil incapacities were removed? Do you fear for your tithes, or your doctrines, or your person, or the English Constitution? Every fear, taken separately, is so glaringly absurd, that no man has the folly or the boldness to state it. Every one conceals his ignorance, or his baseness, in a stupid general panic, which, when called on, he is utterly incapable of explaining. Whatever you think of the Catholics, there they are—you cannot get rid of them; your alternative is, to give them a lawful place for stating their grievances, or an unlawful one: if you do not admit them to the House of Commons, they will hold their parliament in Potato-place, Dublin, and be ten times as violent and inflammatory as they would be in Westminster. Nothing would give me such an idea of security, as to see twenty or thirty Catholic gentlemen in Parliament, looked upon by all the Catholics as the fair and proper organ of their party. I should have thought it the height of good fortune that such a wish existed on their part, and the very essence of madness and ignorance to reject it. Can you murder the Catholics?—Can you neglect them? They are too numerous for both these expedients. What remains to be done is obvious to every human being—but to that man who, instead of being a Methodist preacher, is, for the curse of us and our children, and for the ruin of Troy, and the misery of good old Priam and his sons, become a legislator and a politician.

A distinction, I perceive, is taken, by one of the most feeble noblemen in Great Britain, between persecution and the deprivation of political power; whereas there is no more distinction between these two things than there is between him who makes the distinction and a booby. If I strip off the relic-covered jacket of a Catholic, and give him twenty stripes. . . . I persecute: if I say, Everybody in the town where you live shall be a candidate for lucrative and honourable offices but you, who are a Catholic. . . . I do not persecute!—What barbarous nonsense is this! as if degradation was not as great an evil as bodily pain, or as severe poverty: as if I could not be as great a tyrant by saying, You shall not enjoy—as by saying, You shall suffer. The English, I believe, are as truly religious as any nation in Europe; I know no greater blessing: but it carries with it this evil in its train—that any villain who will bawl out *"The Church is in danger!"* may get a place and a good pension; and that any administration who will do the same thing may bring a set of men into power who, at a moment of stationary and passive piety, would be hooted by the very boys in the streets. But it is not all religion; it is, in great part, the narrow and exclusive spirit which delights to keep the common blessings of sun, and air, and freedom, from other human beings. "Your religion has always been degraded; you are in the dust, and I will take care you never rise again. I should enjoy less the possession of an earthly good, by every additional person to whom it was extended." You may not be aware of it yourself, most reverend Abraham, but you deny their freedom to the Catholics upon the same principle that Sarah your wife refuses to give the receipt for a ham or a gooseberry dumpling: she values her receipts, not because they secure to her a certain flavour, but because they remind her that her neighbours want it:—a feeling laughable in a priestess, shameful in a priest; venial when it withholds the blessings of a ham, tyrannical and execrable when it narrows the boon of religious freedom.

You spend a great deal of ink about the character of the present prime minister. Grant you all that you write—I say, I fear he will ruin Ireland, and pursue a line of policy destructive to the true interest of his country: and then you tell me, he is faithful to Mrs. Perceval, and kind to the Master Percevals! These are, undoubtedly, the first qualifications to be looked to in a time of the most serious public danger; but somehow or another (if public and private virtues must always be incompatible), I should prefer that he destroyed the domestic happiness of Wood or Cockell, owed for the veal of the preceding year, whipped his boys, and saved his country.

The late administration did not do right; they did not build their measures upon the solid basis of facts. They should have caused several Catholics to have been dissected after death by surgeons of either religion, and the report to have been published with accompanying plates. If the viscera, and other organs of life, had been found to be the same as in Protestant bodies; if the provisions of nerves, arteries, cerebrum, and cerebellum, had been the same as we are provided with, or as the Dissenters are now known to possess; then, indeed, they might have met Mr. Perceval upon a proud eminence, and convinced the country at large of

the strong probability that the Catholics are really human creatures, endowed with the feelings of men, and entitled to all their
rights. But instead of this wise and prudent measure, Lord Howick, with his usual precipitation, brings forward a bill in their
favour, without offering the slightest proof to the country that they
were anything more than horses and oxen. The person who shows
the lama at the corner of Piccadilly has the precaution to write
up—*Allowed by Sir Joseph Banks to be a real quadruped:* so his
Lordship might have said—*Allowed by the Bench of Bishops to
be real human creatures.* . . . I could write you twenty letters upon
this subject; but I am tired, and so I suppose are you. Our friendship is now of forty years' standing: you know me to be a truly
religious man; but I shudder to see religion treated like a cockade,
or a pint of beer, and made the instrument of a party. I love the
King, but I love the people as well as the King; and if I am sorry
to see his old age molested, I am much more sorry to see four
millions of Catholics baffled in their just expectations. If I love
Lord Grenville and Lord Howick, it is because they love their
country: if I abhor * * * * * *, it is because I know there is but
one man among them who is not laughing at the enormous folly
and credulity of the country, and that he is an ignorant and mischievous bigot. As for the light and frivolous jester of whom it is
your misfortune to think so highly—learn, my dear Abraham,
that this political Killigrew, just before the breaking-up of the last
administration, was in actual treaty with them for a place; and
if they had survived twenty-four hours longer, he would have
been now declaiming against the cry of No Popery! instead of in-
flaming it.—With this practical comment on the baseness of human nature, I bid you adieu!

LETTER III

ALL that I have so often told you, Mr. Abraham Plymley,
is now come to pass. The Scythians, in whom you and the neigh-
bouring country gentlemen placed such confidence, are smitten hip
and thigh; their Benningsen put to open shame; their magazines of
train oil intercepted—and we are waking from our disgraceful
drunkenness to all the horrors of Mr. Perceval and Mr. Canning.
. . . We shall now see if a nation is to be saved by school-boy
jokes and doggerel rhymes, by affronting petulance, and by the
tones and gesticulations of Mr. Pitt. But these are not all the auxiliaries on which we have to depend; to these his colleague will
add the strictest attention to the smaller parts of ecclesiastical

government—to hassocks, to psalters, and to surplices; in the last agonies of England, he will bring in a bill to regulate Easter-offerings; and he will adjust the stipends of curates * when the flag of France is unfurled on the hills of Kent. Whatever can be done by very mistaken notions of the piety of a Christian, and by very wretched imitation of the eloquence of Mr. Pitt, will be done by these two gentlemen. After all, if they both really were what they both either wish to be or wish to be thought; if the one were an enlightened Christian, who drew from the Gospel the toleration, the charity, and the sweetness which it contains; and if the other really possessed any portion of the great understanding of his Nisus who guarded him from the weapons of the Whigs; I should still doubt if they could save us. But I am sure we are not to be saved by religious hatred and by religious trifling; by any pslamody, however sweet; or by any persecution, however sharp: I am certain the sounds of Mr. Pitt's voice, and the measure of his tones, and the movement of his arms, will do nothing for us; when these tones, and movements, and voice bring us always declamation without sense or knowledge, and ridicule without good humour or conciliation. Oh, Mr. Plymley, Mr. Plymley! this never will do. Mrs. Abraham Plymley, my sister, will be led away captive by an amorous Gaul; and Joel Plymley, your first-born, will be a French drummer.

"Out of sight, out of mind," seems to be a proverb which applies to enemies as well as friends. Because the French army was no longer seen from the cliffs of Dover; because the sound of cannon was no longer heard by the debauched London bathers on the Sussex coast; because the *Morning Post* no longer fixed the invasion sometimes for Monday, sometimes for Tuesday, sometimes (positively for the last time of invading) on Saturday; because all these causes of terror were suspended, you conceived the power of Bonaparte to be at an end, and were setting off for Paris, with Lord Hawkesbury the conqueror.—This is precisely the method in which the English have acted during the whole of the revolutionary war. If Austria or Prussia armed, doctors of divinity immediately printed those passages out of Habakkuk in which the destruction of the Usurper by General Mack and the Duke of Brunswick is so clearly predicted. If Bonaparte halted, there was a mutiny, or a dysentery. If any one of his generals was eaten up by the light troops of Russia, and picked (as their man-

---

* The Reverend the Chancellor of the Exchequer has, since this was written, found time in the heat of the session to write a book on the Stipends of Curates.

ner is) to the bone, the sanguine spirit of this country displayed itself in all its glory. What scenes of infamy did the Society for the Suppression of Vice lay open to our astonished eyes! tradesmen's daughters dancing; pots of beer carried out between the first and second lesson; and dark and distant rumours of indecent prints. Clouds of Mr. Canning's cousins arrived by the waggon; all the contractors left their cards with Mr. Rose; and every plunderer of the public crawled out of his hole, like slugs, and grubs, and worms, after a shower of rain.

If my voice could have been heard at the late changes, I should have said, "Gently; patience; stop a little; the time is not yet come; the mud of Poland will harden, and the bowels of the French grenadiers will recover their tone. When honesty, good sense, and liberality have extricated you out of your present embarrassment, then dismiss them as a matter of course; but you cannot spare them just now. Don't be in too great a hurry, or there will be no monarch to flatter and no country to pillage. Only submit for a little time to be respected abroad; overlook the painful absence of the tax-gatherer for a few years; bear up nobly under the increase of freedom and of liberal policy for a little time, and I promise you, at the expiration of that period, you shall be plundered, insulted, disgraced, and restrained to your heart's content. Do not imagine I have any intention of putting servility and canting hypocrisy permanently out of place, or of filling up with courage and sense those offices which naturally devolve upon decorous imbecility and flexible cunning: give us only a little time to keep off the hussars of France, and then the jobbers and jesters shall return to their birthright, and public virtue be called by its own name of fanaticism." * Such is the advice I would have offered to my infatuated countrymen; but it rained very hard in November, Brother Abraham, and the bowels of our enemies were loosened, and we put our trust in white fluxes and wet mud; and there is nothing now to oppose to the conqueror of the world but a small table wit, and the sallow Surveyor of the Meltings.

You ask me, if I think it possible for this country to survive the

---

* This is Mr. Canning's term for the detection of public abuses; a term invented by him, and adopted by that simious parasite who is always grinning at his heels. Nature descends down to infinite smallness. Mr. Canning has his parasites; and if you take a large buzzing blue-bottle fly, and look at it in a microscope, you may see 20 or 30 little ugly insects crawling about it, which doubtless think their fly to be the bluest, grandest, merriest, most important animal in the universe, and are convinced the world would be at an end if it ceased to buzz.

recent misfortunes of Europe?—I answer you, without the slightest degree of hesitation: that if Bonaparte lives, and a great deal is not immediately done for the conciliation of the Catholics, it does seem to me absolutely impossible but that we must perish; and take this with you, that we shall perish without exciting the slightest feeling of present or future compassion, but fall amidst the hootings and revilings of Europe, as a nation of blockheads, Methodists, and old women. If there were any great scenery, and heroic feelings, any blaze of ancient virtue, any exalted death, any termination of England that would be ever remembered, ever honoured in that western world, where liberty is now retiring, conquest would be more tolerable, and ruin more sweet; but it is doubly miserable to become slaves abroad, because we would be tyrants at home; to persecute, when we are contending against persecution; and to perish, because we have raised up worse enemies within, from our own bigotry, than we are exposed to without, from the unprincipled ambition of France. It is, indeed, a most silly and affecting spectacle to rage at such a moment against our own kindred and our own blood; to tell them they cannot be honourable in war, because they are conscientious in religion; to stipulate (at the very moment when we should buy their hearts and swords at any price) that they must hold up the right hand in prayer, and not the left; and adore one common God, by turning to the east rather than to the west.

What is it the Catholics ask of you? Do not exclude us from the honours and emoluments of the state, because we worship God in one way, and you worship him in another. In a period of the deepest peace, and the fattest prosperity, this would be a fair request: it should be granted, if Lord Hawkesbury had reached Paris, if Mr. Canning's interpreter had threatened the Senate in an opening Speech, or Mr. Perceval explained to them the improvements he meant to introduce into the Catholic religion; but to deny the Irish this justice now, in the present state of Europe, and in the summer months, just as the season for destroying kingdoms is coming on, is (beloved Abraham), whatever you may think of it, little short of positive insanity.

Here is a frigate attacked by a corsair of immense strength and size, rigging cut, masts in danger of coming by the board, four foot water in the hold, men dropping off very fast; in this dreadful situation how do you think the Captain acts (whose name shall be Perceval)? He calls all hands upon deck; talks to them of King, country, glory, sweethearts, gin, French prison, wooden shoes, Old England, and hearts of oak: they give three cheers, rush to their guns, and, after a tremendous conflict, succeed in beating off the enemy. Not a syllable of all this: this is not the manner in which the honourable Commander goes to work: the first thing he does is to secure 20 or 30 of his prime sailors who happen to be Catholics, to clap them in irons, and set over them a guard of as many Protestants; having taken this admirable method of defending himself against his infidel opponents, he goes upon deck, reminds the sailors, in a very bitter harangue, that they are of different religions; exhorts the Episcopal gunner not to trust to the Presbyterian quartermaster; issues positive orders that the Catholics should be fired at upon the first appearance of discontent; rushes through blood and brains, examining his men in the Catechism and 39 Articles, and positively forbids every one to sponge or ram who has not taken the Sacrament according to the Church of England. Was it right to take out a captain made of excellent British stuff, and to put in such a man as this? Is not he more like a parson, or a talking lawyer, than a thoroughbred seaman? And built as she is of heart of oak, and admirably manned, is it possible with such a captain, to save this ship from going to the bottom?

You have an argument, I perceive, in common with many others, against the Catholics, that their demands complied with would only lead to further exactions, and that it is better to resist them now, before anything is conceded, than hereafter, when it is found that all concessions are in vain. I wish the Chancellor of the Exchequer, who uses this reasoning to exclude others from their just rights, had tried its efficacy, not by his understanding, but by (what are full of much better things) his pockets. Suppose the person to whom he applied for the Meltings had withstood every plea of wife and fourteen children, no business, and good character, and refused him this paltry little office, because he might hereafter attempt to get hold of the revenues of the Duchy of Lancaster for life; would not Mr. Perceval have contended eagerly against the injustice of refusing moderate requests, because immoderate ones may hereafter be made? Would he not have said (and said truly), Leave such exorbitant attempts as these to the general indignation of the Commons, who will take care to defeat them when they do occur; but do not refuse me the Irons and the Meltings now, because I may totally lose sight of all moderation hereafter? Leave hereafter to the spirit and the wisdom of hereafter; and do not be niggardly now, from the apprehension that men as wise as you should be profuse in times to come.

You forget, Brother Abraham, that it is a vast art (where quarrels cannot be avoided) to turn the public opinion in your favour and to the prejudice of your enemy; a vast privilege to feel that you are in the right, and to make him feel that he is in the wrong: a privilege which makes you more than a man, and your antagonist less; and often secures victory, by convincing him who contends, that he must submit to injustice if he submits to defeat. Open every rank in the army and the navy to the Catholic; let him purchase at the same price as the Protestant (if either Catholic or Protestant can purchase such refined pleasures) the privilege of hearing Lord Castlereagh speak for three hours; keep his clergy from starving, soften some of the most odious powers of the tything-man, and you will for ever lay this formidable question to rest. But if I am wrong, and you must quarrel at last, quarrel upon just rather than unjust grounds; divide the Catholic, and unite the Protestant; be just, and your own exertions will be more formidable and their exertions less formidable; be just, and you will take away from their party all the best and wisest understandings of both persuasions, and knit them firmly to your own cause. "Thrice is he armed who has his quarrel just"; and ten times as much may he be taxed. In the beginning of any war, however destitute of common sense, every mob will roar, and every Lord of the Bedchamber address; but if you are engaged in a war that is to last for years, and to require important sacrifices, take care to make the justice of your case so clear and so obvious, that it cannot be mistaken by the most illiterate country gentleman who rides the earth. Nothing, in fact, can be so grossly absurd as the argument which says, I will deny justice to you now, because I suspect future injustice from you. At this rate, you may lock a man up in your stable, and refuse to let him out, because you suspect that he has an intention, at some future period, of robbing your henroost. You may horsewhip him at Lady-day, because you believe he will affront you at Midsummer. You may commit a greater evil, to guard against a less which is merely contingent, and may never happen. You may do what you have done a century ago in Ireland, made the Catholics worse than Helots, because you suspected that they might hereafter aspire to be more than fellow-citizens; rendering their sufferings certain from your jealousy, while yours were only doubtful from their ambition; an ambition sure to be excited by the very measures which were taken to prevent it.

The physical strength of the Catholics will not be greater because you give them a share of political power. You may by these means turn rebels into friends; but I do not see how you make rebels more formidable. If they taste of the honey of lawful power, they will love the hive from whence they procure it; if they will struggle with us like men in the same state for civil influence, we are safe. All that I dread is, the physical strength of four millions of men combined with an invading French army. If you are to quarrel at last with this enormous population, still put it off as long as you can; you must gain, and cannot lose, by the delay. The state of Europe cannot be worse; the conviction which the Catholics entertain of your tyranny and injustice cannot be more alarming, nor the opinions of your own people more divided. Time, which produces such effect upon brass and marble, may inspire one Minister with modesty, and another with compassion; every circumstance may be better; some certainly will be so, none can be worse; and, after all, the evil may never happen.

You have got hold, I perceive, of all the vulgar English stories respecting the hereditary transmission of forfeited property, and seriously believe that every Catholic beggar wears the terriers of his father's land next his skin, and is only waiting for better times to cut the throat of the Protestant possessor, and get drunk in the hall of his ancestors. There is one irresistible answer to this mistake, and that is, that the forfeited lands are purchased indiscriminately by Catholic and Protestant, and that the Catholic purchaser never objects to such a title. Now the land (so purchased by a Catholic) is either his own family estate, or it is not. If it is, you suppose him so desirous of coming into possession, that he resorts to the double method of rebellion and purchase; if it is not his own family estate of which he becomes the purchaser, you suppose him first to purchase, then to rebel, in order to defeat the purchase. These things may happen in Ireland; but it is totally impossible they can happen anywhere else. In fact, what land can any man of any sect purchase in Ireland, but forfeited property? In all other oppressed countries which I have ever heard of, the rapacity of the conqueror was bounded by the territorial limits in which the objects of his avarice were contained; but Ireland has been actually confiscated twice over, as a cat is twice killed by a wicked parish boy.

I admit there is a vast luxury in selecting a particular set of Christians, and in worrying them as a boy worries a puppy dog; it is an amusement in which all the young English are brought up from their earliest days. I like the idea of saying to men who use a different hassock from me, that till they change their hassock, they shall never be Colonels, Aldermen, or Parliament-men. While I am gratifying my personal insolence respecting religious forms,

I fondle myself into an idea that I am religious, and that I am doing my duty in the most exemplary (as I certainly am in the most easy) way. But then, my good Abraham, this sport, admirable as it is, is become, with respect to the Catholics, a little dangerous; and if we are not extremely careful in taking the amusement, we shall tumble into the holy water, and be drowned. As it seems necessary to your idea of an established Church to have somebody to worry and torment, suppose we were to select for this purpose William Wilberforce, Esq., and the patent Christians of Clapham. We shall by this expedient enjoy the same opportunity for cruelty and injustice, without being exposed to the same risks: we will compel them to abjure vital clergymen by a public test, to deny that the said William Wilberforce has any power of working miracles, touching for barrenness or any other infirmity; or that he is endowed with any preternatural gift whatever. We will swear them to the doctrine of good works, compel them to preach common sense, and to hear it; to frequent Bishops, Deans, and other high Church-men; and to appear (once in the quarter at the least) at some melodrame, opera, pantomime, or other light scenical representation; in short, we will gratify the love of insolence and power: we will enjoy the old orthodox sport of witnessing the impotent anger of men compelled to submit to civil degradation, or to sacrifice their notions of truth to ours. And all this we may do without the slightest risk, because their numbers are (as yet) not very considerable. Cruelty and injustice must, of course, exist: but why connect them with danger? Why torture a bull-dog, when you can get a frog or a rabbit? I am sure my proposal will meet with the most universal approbation. Do not be apprehensive of any opposition from ministers. If it is a case of hatred, we are sure that one man will defend it by the Gospel: if it abridges human freedom, we know that another will find precedents for it in the Revolution.

In the name of Heaven, what are we to gain by suffering Ireland to be rode by that faction which now predominates over it? Why are we to endanger our own Church and State, not for 500,000 Episcopalians, but for ten or twelve great Orange families, who have been sucking the blood of that country for these hundred years last past? and the folly of the Orangemen * in playing this game themselves, is almost as absurd as ours in playing it for them. They ought to have the sense to see that their

---

* This remark begins to be sensibly felt in Ireland. The Protestants in Ireland are fast coming over to the Catholic cause.

business now is to keep quietly the lands and beeves of which the
fathers of the Catholics were robbed in days of yore; they must
give to their descendants the sop of political power: by contending
with them for names, they will lose realities, and be compelled to
beg their potatoes in a foreign land, abhorred equally by the English, who have witnessed their oppression, and by the Catholic
Irish, who have smarted under them.

LETTER IV.

THEN comes Mr. Isaac Hawkins Brown (the gentleman
who danced † so badly at the Court of Naples,) and asks if it is
not an anomaly to educate men in another religion than your own?
It certainly is our duty to get rid of error, and above all of religious error; but this is not to be done *per saltum,* or the measure
will miscarry, like the Queen. It may be very easy to dance away
the royal embryo of a great kingdom; but Mr. Hawkins Brown
must look before he leaps, when his object is to crush an opposite
sect in religion; false steps aid the one effect, as much as they are
fatal to the other: it will require not only the lapse of Mr. Hawkins Brown, but the lapse of centuries, before the absurdities of
the Catholic religion are laughed at as much as they deserve to
be; but surely, in the meantime, the Catholic religion is better than
none; four millions of Catholics are better than four millions of
wild beasts; two hundred priests educated by our own government
are better than the same number educated by the man who means
to destroy us.

The whole sum now appropriated by Government to the religious education of four millions of Christians is 13,000*l.*; a sum
about one hundred times as large being appropriated in the same
country to about one eighth part of this number of Protestants.
When it was proposed to raise this grant from 8,000*l.* to 13,000*l.*,
its present amount, this sum was objected to by that most indulgent
of Christians, Mr. Spencer Perceval, as enormous; he himself having secured for his own eating and drinking, and the eating and

---

† In the third year of his present Majesty, and in the 30th of his own age,
Mr. Isaac Hawkins Brown, then upon his travels, danced one evening at
the the Court of Naples. His dress was a volcano silk with lava buttons.
Whether (as the Neapolitan wits said) he had studied dancing under St.
Vitus, or whether David, dancing in a linen vest, was his model, is not
known; but Mr. Brown danced with such inconceivable alacrity and vigour,
that he threw the Queen of Naples into convulsions of laughter, which
terminated in a miscarriage, and changed the dynasty of the Neapolitan
throne.

drinking of the Master and Miss Percevals, the reversionary sum of 21,000*l.* a year of the public money, and having just failed in a desperate and rapacious attempt to secure to himself for life the revenues of the Duchy of Lancaster: and the best of it is, that this Minister, after abusing his predecessors for their impious bounty to the Catholics, has found himself compelled, from the apprehension of immediate danger, to grant the sum in question; thus dissolving his pearl * in vinegar, and destroying all the value of the gift by the virulence and reluctance with which it was granted.

I hear from some persons in Parliament, and from others in the sixpenny societies for debate, a great deal about unalterable laws passed at the Revolution. When I hear any man talk of an unalterable law, the only effect it produces upon me is to convince me that he is an unalterable fool. A law passed when there was Germany, Spain, Russia, Sweden, Holland, Portugal, and Turkey; when there was a disputed succession: when four or five hundred acres were won and lost after ten years' hard fighting; when armies were commanded by the sons of kings, and campaigns passed in an interchange of civil letters and ripe fruit; and for these laws, when the whole state of the world is completely changed, we are now, according to my Lord Hawkesbury, to hold ourselves ready to perish. It is no mean misfortune, in times like these, to be forced to say anything about such men as Lord Hawkesbury, and to be reminded that we are governed by them; but as I am driven to it, I must take the liberty of observing, that the wisdom and liberality of my Lord Hawkesbury are of that complexion which always shrinks from the present exercise of these virtues, by praising the splendid examples of them in ages past. If he had lived at such periods, he would have opposed the Revolution by praising the Reformation, and the Reformation by speaking handsomely of the Crusades. He gratifies his natural antipathy to great and courageous measures, by playing off the wisdom and courage which have ceased to influence human affairs against that wisdom and courage which living men would employ for present happiness. Besides, it happens unfortunately for the Warden of the Cinque Ports, that to the principal incapacities under which the Irish suffer, they were subjected after that great and glorious Revolution, to which we are indebted for so many blessings, and his Lordship for the termination of so many periods. The Catholics were not excluded from the Irish House of Commons, or

---

* Perfectly ready at the same time to follow the other half of Cleopatra's example, and to swallow the solution himself.

military commands, before the 3rd and 4th of William and Mary, and the 1st and 2nd of Queen Anne.

If the great mass of the people, environed as they are on every side with Jenkinsons, Percevals, Melvilles, and other perils, were to pray for divine illumination and aid, what more could Providence in its mercy do than send them the example of Scotland? For what a length of years was it attempted to compel the Scotch to change their religion: horse, foot, artillery, and armed Prebendaries, were sent out after the Presbyterian parsons and their congregations. The Percevals of those days called for blood: this call is never made in vain, and blood was shed; but to the astonishment and horror of the Percevals of those days, they could not introduce the Book of Common Prayer, nor prevent that metaphysical people from going to heaven their true way, instead of our true way. With a little oatmeal for food, and a little sulphur for friction, allaying cutaneous irritation with the one hand, and holding his Calvinistical creed in the other, Sawney ran away to his flinty hills, sung his psalm out of tune his own way, and listened to his sermon of two hours long, amid the rough and imposing melancholy of the tallest thistles. But Sawney brought up his unbreeched offspring in a cordial hatred of his oppressors; and Scotland was as much a part of the weakness of England then, as Ireland is at this moment. The true and the only remedy was applied; the Scotch were suffered to worship God after their own tiresome manner, without pain, penalty, and privation. No lightning descended from heaven; the country was not ruined; the world is not yet come to an end; the dignitaries, who foretold all these consequences, are utterly forgotten, and Scotland has ever since been an increasing source of strength to Great Britain. In the six hundredth year of our empire over Ireland, we are making laws to transport a man, if he is found out of his house after eight o'clock at night. That this is necessary, I know too well; but tell me why it is necessary? It is not necessary in Greece, where the Turks are masters.

Are you aware that there is at this moment a universal clamour throughout the whole of Ireland against the Union? It is now one month since I returned from that country; I have never seen so extraordinary, so alarming, and so rapid a change in the sentiments of any people. Those who disliked the Union before are quite furious against it now; those who doubted doubt no more: those who were friendly to it have exchanged that friendship for the most rooted aversion: in the midst of all this (which is by far the most alarming symptom), there is the strongest disposition on the part of the Northern Dissenters to unite with the Catholics, irritated by the faithless

THE PETER PLYMLEY LETTERS

injustice with which they have been treated. If this combination does take place (mark what I say to you), you will have meetings all over Ireland for the cry of *No Union*; that cry will spread like wild-fire, and blaze over every opposition; and if this be the case, there is no use in mincing the matter, Ireland is gone, and the deathblow of England is struck; and this event may happen *instantly*—before Mr. Canning and Mr. Hookham Frere have turned Lord Howick's last speech into doggerel rhyme; before "*the near and dear relations*" have received another quarter of their pension, or Mr. Perceval conducted the Curates' Salary Bill safely to a third reading.—If the mind of the English people, cursed as they now are with that madness of religious dissension which has been breathed into them for the purposes of private ambition, can be alarmed by any remembrances, and warned by any events, they should never forget how nearly Ireland was lost to this country during the American war; that it was saved merely by the jealousy of the Protestant Irish towards the Catholics, then a much more insignificant and powerless body than they now are. The Catholic and the Dissenter have since combined together against you. Last war, the winds, those ancient and unsubsidised allies of England, the winds, upon which English ministers depend as much for saving kingdoms as washerwomen do for drying clothes; the winds stood your friends: the French could only get into Ireland in small numbers, and the rebels were defeated. Since then, all the remaining kingdoms of Europe have been destroyed; and the Irish see that their national independence is gone, without having received any single one of those advantages which they were taught to expect from the sacrifice. All good things were to flow from the Union; they have none of them gained anything. Every man's pride is wounded by it; no man's interest is promoted. In the seventh year of that Union, four million Catholics, lured by all kinds of promises to yield up the separate dignity and sovereignty of their country, are forced to squabble with such a man as Mr. Spencer Perceval for five thousand pounds with which to educate their children in their own mode of worship; he, the same Mr. Spencer, having secured to his own Protestant self a reversionary portion of the public money amounting to four times that sum. A senior Proctor of the University of Oxford, the head of a house, or the examining Chaplain to a Bishop, may believe these things can last: but every man of the world, whose understanding has been exercised in the business of life, must see (and see with a breaking heart) that they will soon come to a fearful termination.

Our conduct to Ireland, during the whole of this war, has been that of a man who subscribes to hospitals, weeps at charity sermons, carries out broth and blankets to beggars, and then comes home and beats his wife and children. We had compassion for the victims of all other oppression and injustice, except our own. If Switzerland was threatened, away went a Treasury Clerk with a hundred thousand pounds for Switzerland; large bags of money were kept constantly under sailing orders; upon the slightest demonstration towards Naples, down went Sir William Hamilton upon his knees, and begged for the love of St. Januarius they would help us off with a little money; all the arts of Machiavel were resorted to, to persuade Europe to borrow; troops were sent off in all directions to save the Catholic and Protestant world; the Pope himself was guarded by a regiment of English dragoons; if the Grand Lama had been at hand, he would have had another; every Catholic Clergyman who had the good fortune to be neither English nor Irish, was immediately provided with lodging, soap, crucifix, missal, chapel-beads, relics, and holy water; if Turks had landed, Turks would have received an order from the Treasury for coffee, opium, korans, and seraglios. In the midst of all this fury of saving and defending, this crusade for conscience and Christianity, there was a universal agreement among all descriptions of people to continue every species of internal persecution; to deny at home every just right that had been denied before; to pummel poor Dr. Abraham Rees and his Dissenters; and to treat the unhappy Catholics of Ireland as if their tongues were mute, their heels cloven, their nature brutal, and designedly subjected by Providence to their Orange masters.

How would my admirable brother, the Rev. Abraham Plymley, like to be marched to a Catholic chapel, to be sprinkled with the sanctified contents of a pump, to hear a number of false quantities in the Latin tongue, and to see a number of persons occupied in making right angles upon the breast and forehead? And if all this would give you so much pain, what right have you to march Catholic soldiers to a place of worship, where there is no aspersion, no rectangular gestures, and where they understand every word they hear, having first, in order to get him to enlist, made a solemn promise to the contrary? Can you wonder, after this, that the Catholic priest stops the recruiting in Ireland, as he is now doing to a most alarming degree?

The late question concerning military rank did not individually affect the lowest persons of the Catholic persuasion; but do you imagine they do not sympathise with the honour and disgrace of their superiors? Do you think that satisfaction and dissatisfaction do not travel down from Lord Fingal to the most potatoless Catholic in Ireland, and that the glory or shame of the sect is not felt by many more than these conditions personally and corporeally affect? Do you suppose that the detection of Sir H. M. and the disappointment of Mr. Perceval *in the matter* of the Duchy of Lancaster, did not affect every dabbler in public property? Depend upon it these things were felt through all the gradations of small plunderers, down to him who filches a pound of tobacco from the King's warehouses; while, on the contrary, the acquittal of any noble and official thief would not fail to diffuse the most heartfelt satisfaction over the larcenous and burglarious world. Observe, I do not say because the lower Catholics are affected by what concerns their superiors, that they are not affected by what concerns themselves. There is no disguising the horrid truth; *there must be some relaxation with respect to tithe:* this is the cruel and heart-rending price which must be paid for national preservation. I feel how little existence will be worth having, if any alteration, however slight, is made in the property of Irish rectors; I am conscious how much such changes must affect the daily and hourly comforts of every Englishman; I shall feel too happy if they leave Europe untouched, and are not ultimately fatal to the destinies of America; but I am madly bent upon keeping foreign enemies out of the British empire, and my limited understanding presents me with no other means of effecting my object.

You talk of waiting till another reign before any alteration is made; a proposal full of good sense and good nature, if the measure in question were to pull down St. James's Palace, or to alter Kew Gardens. Will Bonaparte agree to put off his intrigues, and his invasion of Ireland? If so, I will overlook the question of justice, and finding the danger suspended, agree to the delay. I sincerely hope this reign may last many years, yet the delay of a single session of Parliament may be fatal; but if another year elapse without some serious concession made to the Catholics, I believe, before God, that all future pledges and concessions will be made in vain. I do not think that peace will do you any good under such circumstances: if Bonaparte give you a respite, it will only be to get ready the gallows on which he means to hang you. The Catholic and the Dissenter can unite in peace as well as war. If they do, the gallows is ready; and your executioner, in spite of the most solemn promises, will turn you off the next hour.

With every disposition to please (where to please within fair and rational limits is a high duty), it is impossible for public men to be long silent about the Catholics; pressing evils are not got rid of, because they are not talked of. A man may command his family to say nothing more about the stone, and surgical operations: but the ponderous malice still lies upon the nerve, and gets so big, that the patient breaks his own law of silence, clamours for the knife, and expires under its late operation. Believe me, you talk folly, when you talk of suppressing the Catholic question. I wish to God the case admitted of such a remedy: bad as it is, it does not admit of it. If the wants of the Catholics are not heard in the manly tones of Lord Grenville, or the servile drawl of Lord Castlereagh, they will be heard ere long in the madness of mobs, and the conflicts of armed men.

I observe, it is now universally the fashion to speak of the first personage in the state as the great obstacle to the measure. In the first place, I am not bound to believe such rumours because I hear them; and in the next place, I object to such language, as unconstitutional. Whoever retains his situation in the ministry, while the incapacities of the Catholics remain, is the advocate for those incapacities; and to him, and to him only, am I to look for responsibility. But waive this question of the Catholics, and put a general case:— How is a minister of this country to act when the conscientious scruples of his Sovereign prevent the execution of a measure deemed by him absolutely necessary to the safety of the country? His conduct is quite clear—he should resign. But what is his successor to do?—Resign. But is the King to be left without ministers, and is he in this manner to be compelled to act against his own conscience? Before I answer this, pray tell me in my turn, what better defence is there against the machinations of a wicked, or the errors of a weak, Monarch, than the impossibility of finding a minister who will lend himself to vice and folly? Every English Monarch, in such a predicament, would sacrifice his opinions and views to such a clear expression of the public will; and it is one method in which the Constitution aims at bringing about such a sacrifice. You may say, if you please, the ruler of a state is forced to give up his object, when the natural love of place and power will tempt no one to assist him in its attainment. This may be force; but it is force without injury, and therefore without blame. I am not to be beat out of these obvious reasonings, and ancient constitutional provisions, by the term conscience. There is no fantasy, however wild, that a man may not persuade himself that he cherishes from motives of conscience; eternal war against impious France, or rebellious America, or Catholic Spain, may in times to come be scruples of conscience. One English Monarch may, from scruples of conscience, wish to abolish every trait of religious persecution; another Monarch may deem it his absolute and indispensable duty to make a slight provision for Dissenters out of the revenues of the Church of England. So that you see, Brother Abraham, there are cases where it would be the duty of the best and most loyal subjects to oppose the conscientious scruples of their Sovereign, still taking care that their actions were constitutional, and their modes respectful. Then you come upon me with personal questions, and say that no such dangers are to be apprehended now under our present gracious Sovereign, of whose good qualities we must be all so well convinced. All these sorts of discussions I beg leave to decline; what I have said upon constitutional topics, I mean of course for general, not for particular application. I agree with you in all the good you have said of the powers that be, and I avail myself of the opportunity of pointing out general dangers to the Constitution, at a moment when we are so completely exempted from their present influence. I cannot finish this letter without expressing my surprise and pleasure at your abuse of the servile addresses poured in upon the Throne; nor can I conceive a greater disgust to a Monarch, with a true English heart, than to see such a question as that of Catholic Emancipation argued, not with a reference to its justice or importance, but universally considered to be of no further consequence than as it affects his own private feelings. That these sentiments should be mine, is not wonderful; but how they came to be yours, does, I confess, fill me with surprise. Are you moved by the arrival of the Irish Brigade at Antwerp, and the amorous violence which awaits Mrs. Plymley?

LETTER V.

Dear Abraham,

I never met a parson in my life, who did not consider the Corporation and Test Acts as the great bulwarks of the Church; and yet it is now just sixty-four years since bills of indemnity to destroy their penal effects, or, in other words, to repeal them, have been passed annually as a matter of course.

Heu vatum ignarae mentes.

These bulwarks, without which no clergyman thinks he could sleep with his accustomed soundness, have actually not been in existence since any man now living has taken holy orders. Every year the Indemnity Act pardons past breaches of these two laws, and prevents any fresh actions of informers from coming to a conclusion before the period for the next indemnity bill arrives; so that these penalties, by which alone the Church remains in existence, have not had one moment's operation for sixty-four years. You will say the legislature, during the whole of this period, has reserved to itself the discretion of suspending, or not suspending. But had not the legislature the right of re-enacting, if it was necessary? And now when you have kept the rod over these people (with the most scandalous abuse of all principle) for sixty-four years, and not found it necessary to strike once, is not that the best of all reasons why the rod should be laid aside? You talk to me of a very valuable hedge running across your fields which you would not part with on any account. I go down, expecting to find a limit impervious to cattle, and highly useful for the preservation of property; but, to my utter astonishment, I find that the hedge was cut down half a century ago, and that every year the shoots are clipped the moment they appear above ground: it appears, upon further inquiry, that the hedge never ought to have existed at all; that it originated in the malice of antiquated quarrels, and was cut down because it subjected you to vast inconvenience, and broke up your intercourse with a country absolutely necessary to your existence. If the remains of this hedge serve only to keep up an irritation in your neighbours, and to remind them of the feuds of former times, good nature and good sense teach you that you ought to grub it up, and cast it into the oven. This is the exact state of these two laws; and yet it is made a great argument against concession to the Catholics, that it involves their repeal; which is to say, Do not make me relinquish a folly that will lead to my ruin; because, if you do, I must give up other follies ten times greater than this.

I confess, with all our bulwarks and hedges, it mortifies me to the very quick, to contrast with our matchless stupidity, and inimitable folly, the conduct of Bonaparte upon the subject of religious persecution. At the moment when we are tearing the crucifixes from the necks of the Catholics, and washing pious mud from the foreheads of the Hindoos; at that moment this man is assembling the very Jews at Paris, and endeavouring to give them stability and importance. I shall never be reconciled to mending shoes in America; but I see it must be my lot, and I will then take a dreadful revenge upon Mr. Perceval, if I catch him preaching within ten miles of me. I cannot for the soul of me conceive whence this man has gained his notions of Christianity: he has the most evangelical charity for errors in arithmetic, and the most inveterate malice against errors in conscience. While he rages against those whom in the true spirit of the Gospel he ought to indulge, he forgets the only instance of severity which that Gospel contains, and leaves the jobbers, and contractors, and money-changers at their seats, without a single stripe.

You cannot imagine, you say, that England will ever be ruined and conquered; and for no other reason that I can find, but because it seems so very odd it should be ruined and conquered. Alas! so reasoned, in their time, the Austrian, Russian, and Prussian Plymleys. But the English are brave: so were all these nations. You might get together a hundred thousand men individually brave; but without generals capable of commanding such a machine, it would be as useless as a first-rate man of war manned by Oxford clergymen, or Parisian shopkeepers. I do not say this to the disparagement of English officers: they have had no means of acquiring experience; but I do say it to create alarm; for we do not appear to me to be half alarmed enough, or to entertain that sense of our danger which leads to the most obvious means of self-defence. As for the spirit of the peasantry in making a gallant defence behind hedge-rows, and through plate-racks and hen-coops, highly as I think of their bravery, I do not know any nation in Europe so likely to be struck with the panic as the English; and this from their total unacquaintance with the science of war. Old wheat and beans blazing for twenty miles round; cart mares shot; sows of Lord Somerville's breed running wild over the country; the minister of the parish wounded sorely in his hinder parts; Mrs. Plymley in fits; all these scenes of war an Austrian or a Russian has seen three or four times over; but it is now three centuries since an English pig has fallen in a fair battle upon English ground, or a farm-house been rifled, or a clergyman's wife been subjected to any other proposals of love than the connubial endearments of her sleek and orthodox mate. The old edition of Plutarch's Lives, which lies in the corner of your parlour window, has contributed to work you up to the most romantic expectations of our Roman behaviour. You are persuaded that Lord Amherst will defend Kew Bridge like Cocles; that some maid of honour will break away from her captivity, and swim over the Thames; that the Duke of York will burn his capitulating hand; and little Mr. Sturges Bourne * give forty years' purchase for Moulsham Hall, while the French are encamped upon it. I hope we shall witness all this, if the French do come; but in the meantime I am so enchanted with the ordinary English behaviour of these invaluable persons, that I earnestly pray no opportunity may be given them for Roman valour, and for those very un-Roman pensions which they would all, of course, take especial care to claim in consequence. But whatever was our conduct, if every ploughman was as great a hero as he who was called from his oxen to save Rome from her enemies, I should still say, that at such a crisis you want the affections of all your subjects, in both islands: there is no spirit which you must alienate, no heart you must avert, every man must feel he has a country, and

---

* There is nothing more objectionable in Plymley's Letters than the abuse of Mr. Sturges Bourne, who is an honourable, able, and excellent person; but such are the malevolent effects of party spirit.

that there is an urgent and pressing cause why he should expose himself to death.

The effects of penal laws, in matters of religion, are never confined to those limits in which the legislature intended they should be placed: it is not only that I am excluded from certain offices and dignities because I am a Catholic, but the exclusion carries with it a certain stigma, which degrades me in the eyes of the monopolising sect, and the very name of my religion becomes odious. These effects are so very striking in England, that I solemnly believe blue and red baboons to be more popular here than Catholics and Presbyterians; they are more understood, and there is a greater disposition to do something for them. When a country squire hears of an ape, his first feeling is to give it nuts and apples; when he hears of a Dissenter, his immediate impulse is to commit it to the county jail, to shave its head, to alter its customary food, and to have it privately whipped. This is no caricature, but an accurate picture of national feelings, as they degrade and endanger us at this very moment. The Irish Catholic gentleman would bear his legal disabilities with greater temper, if these were all he had to bear—if they did not enable every Protestant cheese-monger and tide-waiter to treat him with contempt. He is branded on the forehead with a red-hot iron, and treated like a spiritual felon, because, in the highest of all considerations he is led by the noblest of all guides, his own disinterested conscience.

Why are nonsense and cruelty a bit the better because they are enacted? If Providence, which gives wine and oil, had blessed us with that tolerant spirit which makes the countenance more pleasant and the heart more glad than these can do; if our Statute book had never been defiled with such infamous laws, the sepulchral Spencer Perceval would have been hauled through the dirtiest horse-pond in Hampstead, had he ventured to propose them. But now persecution is good, because it exists; every law which originated in ignorance and malice, and gratifies the passions from whence it sprang, we call the wisdom of our ancestors: when such laws are repealed, they will be cruelty and madness; till they are repealed, they are policy and caution.

I was somewhat amused with the imputation brought against the Catholics by the University of Oxford, that they are enemies to liberty. I immediately turned to my History of England, and marked as an historical error that passage in which it is recorded that, in the reign of Queen Anne, the famous decree of the University of Oxford, respecting passive obedience, was ordered, by the House of Lords, to be burnt by the hands of the common hangman, as contrary to the liberty of the subject, and the law of the land. Nevertheless, I wish, whatever be the modesty of those who impute, that the imputation was a little more true, the Catholic cause would not be quite so desperate with the present Administration. I fear, however, that the hatred to liberty in these poor devoted wretches may ere long appear more doubtful than it is at present to the Vice-Chancellor and his Clergy, inflamed, as they doubtless are, with classical examples of republican virtue, and panting, as they always have been, to reduce the power of the Crown within narrower and safer limits. What mistaken zeal, to attempt to connect one religion with freedom and another with slavery! Who laid the foundations of English liberty? What was the mixed religion of Switzerland? What has the Protestant religion done for liberty in Denmark, in Sweden, throughout the North of Germany, and in Prussia? The purest religion in the world, in my humble opinion, is the religion of the Church of England: for its preservation (so far as it is exercised without intruding upon the liberties of others) I am ready at this moment to venture my present life, and but through that religion I have no hopes of any other; yet I am not forced to be silly because I am pious; nor will I ever join in eulogiums on my faith, which every man of common reading and common sense can so easily refute.

You have either done too much for the Catholics (worthy Abraham), or too little; if you had intended to refuse them political power, you should have refused them civil rights. After you had enabled them to acquire property, after you had conceded to them all that you did concede in '78 and '93, the rest is wholly out of your power: you may choose whether you will give the rest in an honourable or a disgraceful mode, but it is utterly out of your power to withhold it.

In the last year, land to the amount of *eight hundred thousand pounds* was purchased by the Catholics in Ireland. Do you think it possible to be-Perceval, and be-Canning, and be-Castlereagh, such a body of men as this out of their common rights, and their common sense? Mr. George Canning may laugh and joke at the idea of Protestant bailiffs ravishing Catholic ladies, under the 9th clause of the Sunset Bill; but if some better remedy be not applied to the distractions of Ireland than the jocularity of Mr. Canning, they will soon put an end to his pension, and to the pension of those "near and dear relatives," for whose eating, drinking, washing, and clothing, every man in the United Kingdoms now pays his two-pence or three-pence a year. You may call these observations coarse, if you please; but I have no idea that the Sophias and Carolines of any man breathing are to eat national veal, to drink public tea, to wear Treasury ribands, and then that we are to be told that it is coarse to animadvert upon this pitiful and eleemosynary splendour. If this is right, why not mention it? If it is wrong, why should not he who enjoys the ease of supporting his sisters in this manner bear the shame of it? Everybody seems hitherto to have spared a man who never spares anybody.

As for the enormous wax candles, and superstitious mummeries, and painted jackets of the Catholic priests, I fear them not. Tell me that the world will return again under the influence of the smallpox; that Lord Castlereagh will hereafter oppose the power of the Court; that Lord Howick and Mr. Grattan will do each of them a mean and dishonourable action; that anybody who has heard Lord Redesdale speak once will knowingly and willingly hear him again; that Lord Eldon has assented to the fact of two and two making four, without shedding tears, or expressing the smallest doubt or scruple; tell me any other thing absurd or incredible, but, for the love of common sense, let me hear no more of the danger to be apprehended from the general diffusion of Popery. It is too absurd to be reasoned upon; every man feels it is nonsense when he hears it stated, and so does every man while he is stating it.

I cannot imagine why the friends to the Church Establishment should entertain such a horror of seeing the doors of Parliament flung open to the Catholics, and view so passively the enjoyment of that right by the Presbyterians and by every other species of Dissenter. In their tenets, in their Church government, in the nature of their endowments, the Dissenters are infinitely more distant from the Church of England than the Catholics are; yet the Dissenters have never been excluded from Parliament. There are 45 members in one House, and 16 in the other, who always are Dissenters. There is no law which would prevent every member of the Lords and Commons from being Dissenters. The Catholics could not bring into Parliament half the number of the Scotch members; and yet one exclusion is of such immense importance, because it has taken place; and the other no human being thinks of, because no one is accustomed to it. I have often thought, if the *wisdom of our ancestors* had excluded all persons with red hair from the House of Commons, of the throes and convulsions it would occasion to restore them to their natural rights. What mobs and riots would it produce! To what infinite abuse and obloquy would the capillary patriot be exposed; what wormwood would distil from Mr. Perceval, what froth would drop from Mr. Canning; how (I will not say *my*, but *our* Lord Hawkesbury, for he belongs to us all)—how our Lord Hawkesbury would work away about the hair of King William and Lord Somers, and the authors of the great and glorious Revolution; how Lord Eldon would appeal to the Deity and his own virtues, and to the hair of his children: some would say that red-haired men were superstitious; some would prove they were atheists; they would be petitioned against as the friends of slavery, and the advocates for revolt; in short, such a corruptor of the heart and the understanding is the spirit of persecution, that these unfortunate people (conspired against by their fellow-subjects of every complexion), if they did not emigrate to countries where hair of another colour was persecuted, would be driven to the falsehood of perukes, or the hypocrisy of the Tricosian fluid.

As for the dangers of the Church (in spite of the staggering events which have lately taken place), I have not yet entirely lost my confidence in the power of commen sense, and I believe the Church to be in no danger at all; but if it is, that danger is not from the Catholics, but from the Methodists, and from that patent Christianity which has been for some time manufacturing at Clapham, to the prejudice of the old and admirable article prepared by the Church. I would counsel my lords the Bishops to keep their eyes upon that holy village, and its hallowed vicinity: they will find there a zeal in making converts far superior to anything which exists among the Catholics; a contempt for the great mass of English clergy, much more rooted and profound; and a regular fund to purchase livings for those groaning and garrulous gentlemen, whom they denominate (by a standing sarcasm against the regular Church) Gospel preachers, and vital clergymen. I am too firm a believer in the general propriety and respectability of the English clergy, to believe they have much to fear either from old nonsense, or from new; but if the Church must be supposed to be in danger, I prefer that nonsense which is grown half venerable from time, the force of which I have already tried and baffled, which at least has some excuse in the dark and ignorant ages in which it originated. The religious enthusiasm manufactured by living men before my own eyes disgusts my understanding as much, influences my imagination not at all, and excites my apprehensions much more.

I may have seemed to you to treat the situation of public affairs with some degree of levity; but I feel it deeply, and with nightly and daily anguish; because I know Ireland; I have known it all my life; I love it, and I foresee the crisis to which it will soon be exposed. Who can doubt but that Ireland will experience ultimately from France a treatment to which the conduct they have experienced from England is the love of a parent, or a brother? Who can doubt but that five years after he has got hold of the country, Ireland will be tossed away by Bonaparte as a present to some one of his ruffian generals, who will knock the head of Mr. Keogh against the head of Cardinol Troy, shoot twenty of the most noisy blockheads of the

Roman persuasion, wash his pug-dogs in holy water, and confiscate the salt butter of the Milesian Republic to the last tub? But what matters this? or who is wise enough in Ireland to heed it? or when had common sense much influence with my poor dear Irish? Mr. Perceval does not know the Irish; but I know them, and I know that at every rash and mad hazard, they will break the Union, revenge their wounded pride and their insulted religion, and fling themselves into the open arms of France, sure of dying in the embrace. And now what means have you of guarding against this coming evil, upon which the future happiness or misery of every Englishman depends? Have you a single ally in the whole world? Is there a vulnerable point in the French empire where the astonishing resources of that people can be attracted and employed? Have you a ministry wise enough to comprehend the danger, manly enough to believe unpleasant intelligence, honest enough to state their apprehensions at the peril of their places? Is there anywhere the slightest disposition to join any measure of love, or conciliation, or hope, with that dreadful bill which the distractions of Ireland have rendered necessary? At the very moment that the last Monarchy in Europe has fallen, are we not governed by a man of pleasantry, and a man of theology? In the six hundredth year of our empire over Ireland, have we any memorial of ancient kindness to refer to? any people, any zeal, any country on which we can depend? Have we any hope, but in the winds of heaven, and the tides of the sea? any prayer to prefer to the Irish, but that they should forget and forgive their oppressors, who, in the very moment that they are calling upon them for their exertions, solemnly assure them that the oppression shall still remain.

Abraham, farewell! If I have tired you, remember how often you have tired me and others. I do not think we really differ in politics so much as you suppose; or, at least, if we do, that difference is in the means, and not in the end. We both love the Constitution, respect the King, and abhor the French. But though you love the Constitution, you would perpetuate the abuses which have been engrafted upon it; though you respect the King, you would confirm his scruples against the Catholics; though you abhor the French, you would open to them the conquest of Ireland. My method of respecting my Sovereign is by protecting his honour, his empire, and his lasting happiness; I evince my love of the Constitution, by making it the guardian of all men's rights and the source of their freedom; and I prove my abhorrence of the French, by uniting against them the disciples of every church in the only remaining nation in Europe. As for the men of whom I have been compelled in this age of mediocrity to say so much, they cannot of themselves be worth a moment's consideration, to you, to me, or to anybody. In a year after their death, they will be forgotten as completely as if they had never been; and are now of no further importance, than as they are the mere vehicles of carrying into effect the common-place and mischievous prejudices of the times in which they live.

LETTER VI.

Dear Abraham,

What amuses me the most is to hear of the *indulgences* which the Catholics have received, and their exorbitance in not being satisfied with those indulgences: now if you complain to me that a man is obtrusive and shameless in his requests, and that it is impossible to bring him to reason, I must first of all hear the whole of your conduct towards him; for you may have taken from him so much in the first instance, that, in spite of a long series of restitution, a vast latitude for petition may still remain behind.

There is a village (no matter where) in which the inhabitants, on one day in the year, sit down to a dinner prepared at the common expense; by an extraordinary piece of tyranny (which Lord Hawkesbury would call the wisdom of the village ancestors), the inhabitants of three of the streets, about a hundred years ago, seized upon the inhabitants of the fourth street, bound them hand and foot, laid them upon their backs, and compelled them to look on while the rest were stuffing themselves with beef and beer: the next year the inhabitants of the persecuted street (though they contributed an equal quota of the expense) were treated precisely in the same manner. The tyranny grew into a custom; and (as the manner of our nature is) it was considered as the most sacred of all duties to keep these poor fellows without their annual dinner: the village was so tenacious of this practice, that nothing could induce them to resign it; every enemy to it was looked upon as a disbeliever in Divine Providence, and any nefarious churchwarden who wished to succeed in his election had nothing to do but to represent his antagonist as an abolitionist, in order to frustrate his ambition, endanger his life, and throw the village into a state of the most dreadful commotion. By degrees, however, the obnoxious street grew to be so well peopled, and its inhabitants so firmly united, that their oppressors, more afraid of injustice, were more disposed to be just. At the next dinner they are unbound, the year after allowed to sit upright, then a bit of bread and a glass of water; till at last, after a long series of concessions, they are emboldened to ask, in pretty plain terms, that they may be allowed to sit down at the bottom of the table, and to fill their bellies as well as the rest. Forthwith a general cry of shame and scandal: "Ten years ago, were you not laid upon your backs? Don't you remember what a great thing you thought it to get a piece of bread? How thankful you were for cheese-parings? Have you forgotten that memorable era when the lord of the manor interfered to obtain for you a slice of the public pudding? And now, with an audacity only equalled by your ingratitude, you have the impudence to ask for knives and forks, and to request, in terms too plain to be mistaken, that you may sit down to table with the rest, and be indulged even with beef and beer: there are not more than half a dozen dishes which we have reserved for ourselves; the rest has been thrown open to you in the utmost profusion; you have potatoes, and carrots, suet dumplings, sops in the pan, and delicious toast and water, in incredible quantities. Beef, mutton, lamb, pork, and veal are ours; and if you were not the most restless and dissatisfied of human beings, you would never think of aspiring to enjoy them."

Is not this, my dainty Abraham, the very nonsense and the very insult which is talked to and practised upon the Catholics? You are surprised that men who have tasted of partial justice should ask for perfect justice; that he who has been robbed of coat and cloak will not be contented with the restitution of one of his garments. He would be a very lazy blockhead if he were content, and I (who, though an inhabitant of the village, have preserved, thank God, some sense of justice), most earnestly counsel these half-fed claimants to persevere in their just demands, till they are admitted to a more complete share of a dinner for which they pay as much as the others; and if they see a little attenuated lawyer squabbling at the head of their opponents, let them desire him to empty his pockets, and to pull out all the pieces of duck, fowl, and pudding, which he has filched from the public feast, to carry home to his wife and children.

You parade a great deal upon the vast concessions made by this country to the Irish before the Union. I deny that any voluntary concession was ever made by England to Ireland. What did Ireland ever ask that was granted? What did she ever demand that was not refused? How did she get her Mutiny Bill—a limited parliament—a repeal of Poyning's Law—a constitution? Not by the concessions of England, but by her fears. When Ireland asked for all these things upon her knees, her petitions were rejected with Percevalism and contempt; when she demanded them with the voice of 60,000 armed men, they were granted with every mark of consternation and dismay. Ask of Lord Auckland the fatal consequences of trifling with such a people as the Irish. He himself was the organ of these refusals. As secretary to the Lord-Lieutenant, the insolence and the tyranny of this country passed through his hands. Ask him if he remembers the consequences. Ask him if he has forgotten that memorable evening, when he came down booted and mantled to the House of Commons, when he told the House he was about to set off for Ireland that night, and declared before God, if he did not carry with him a compliance with all their demands, Ireland was for ever lost to this country. The present generation have forgotten this; but I have not forgotten it; and I know, hasty and undignified as the submission of England then was, that Lord Auckland was right, that the delay of a single day might very probably have separated the two people for ever. The terms submission and fear are galling terms, when applied from the lesser nation to the greater; but it is the plain historical truth, it is the natural consequence of injustice, it is the predicament in which every country places itself which leaves such a mass of hatred and discontent by its side. No empire is powerful enough to endure it; it would exhaust the strength of China, and sink it with all its mandarins and tea-kettles to the bottom of the deep. By refusing them justice, now when you are strong enough to refuse them anything more than justice, you will act over again, with the Catholics, the same scene of mean and precipitate submission which disgraced you before America, and before the volunteers of Ireland. We shall live to hear. the Hampstead Protestant pronouncing such extravagant panegyrics upon holy water, and paying such fulsome compliments to the thumbs and offals of departed saints, that parties will change sentiments, and Lord Henry Petty and Sam Whitbread take a spell at No Popery. The wisdom of Mr. Fox was alike employed in teaching his country justice when Ireland was weak, and dignity when Ireland was strong. We are fast pacing round the same miserable circle of ruin and imbecility. Alas! where is our guide?

You say that Ireland is a millstone about our necks; that it would be better for us if Ireland were sunk at the bottom of the sea; that the Irish are a nation of irreclaimable savages and barbarians. How often have I heard these sentiments fall from the plump and thoughtless squire, and from the thriving English shopkeeper, who has never felt the rod of an Orange master upon his back. Ireland a millstone about your neck! Why is it not a stone of Ajax in your hand? I agree with you most cordially, that, governed as Ireland now is, it would be a vast accession of strength if the waves of the sea were to rise and engulf her to-morrow. At this moment, opposed as we are to all the world, the annihilation of one of the most fertile islands on the face of the globe, containing five millions of human creatures, would be one of the most solid advantages which could happen to this country. I doubt very much, in spite of all the just abuse which has been lavished upon Bonaparte, whether there is any one of his conquered countries the blotting out of which would be as beneficial to him as the destruction of Ireland would be to us: of countries I speak differing in language from the French, little habituated to their intercourse, and inflamed with all the resentments of a recently conquered people. Why will you attribute the turbulence of our people to any cause but the right—to any cause but your own scandalous oppression? If you tie your horse up to a gate, and beat him cruelly, is he vicious because he kicks you? If you have plagued and worried a mastiff dog for years, is he mad because he flies at you whenever he sees you? Hatred is an active, troublesome passion. Depend upon it, whole nations have always some reason for their hatred. Before you refer the turbulence of the Irish to incurable defects in their character, tell me if you have treated them as friends and equals? Have you protected their commerce? Have you respected their religion? Have you been as anxious for their freedom as your own? Nothing of all this. What then? Why you have confiscated the territorial surface of the country twice over: you have massacred and exported her inhabitants: you have deprived four fifths of them of every civil privilege: you have at every period made her commerce and manufactures slavishly subordinate to your own: and yet the hatred which the Irish bear to you is the result of an original turbulence of character, and of a primitive, obdurate wildness, utterly incapable of civilisation. The embroidered inanities and the sixth-form effusions of Mr. Canning are really not powerful enough to make me believe this; nor is there any authority on earth (always excepting the Dean of Christ Church) which could make it credible to me. I am sick of Mr. Canning. There is not a "ha'p'orth of bread to all this sugar and sack." I love not the cretaceous and incredible countenance of his colleague. The only opinion in which I agree with these two gentlemen is that which they entertain of each other; I am sure that the insolence of Mr. Pitt, and the unbalanced accounts of Melville, were far better than the perils of this new ignorance:—

Nonne fuit satius tristes Amaryllidis iras
Atque superba pati fastidia—nonne Menalcam
Quamvis ille *niger?*

In the midst of the most profound peace, the secret articles of the Treaty of Tilsit, in which the destruction of Ireland is resolved upon, induce you to rob the Danes of their fleet. After the expedition sailed comes the Treaty of Tilsit, containing no article,* public or private, alluding to Ireland. The state of the world, you tell me, justified us in doing this. Just God! do we think only of the state of the world when there is an opportunity for robbery, for murder, and for plunder; and do we forget the state of the world when we are called upon to be wise, and good, and just? Does the state of the world never remind us, that we have four millions of subjects whose injuries we ought to atone for, and whose affections we ought to conciliate? Does the state of the world never warn us to lay aside our infernal bigotry, and to arm every man who acknowledges a God and can grasp a sword? Did it never occur to this administration that they might virtuously get hold of a force ten times greater than the force of the Danish fleet? Was there no other way of protecting Ireland, but by bringing eternal shame upon Great Britain, and by making the earth a den of robbers? See what the men whom you have supplanted would have done. They would have rendered the invasion of Ireland impossible, by restoring to the Catholics their long-lost rights: they would have acted in such a manner that the French would neither have wished for invasion, nor dared to attempt it: they would have increased the permanent strength of the country while they preserved its reputation unsullied. Nothing of this kind your friends have done, because they are solemnly pledged to do nothing of this kind; because to tolerate all religions, and to equalise civil rights to all sects, is to oppose some of the worst passions of our nature—to plunder and to oppress is to gratify them all. They wanted the huzzas of mobs, and they have for ever blasted the fame of England to obtain them. Were the fleets of Holland, France, and Spain destroyed by larceny? You resisted the power of 150 sail of the line by sheer courage, and violated every principle of morals from the dread of 15 hulks, while the expedition itself cost you three times more than the value of the larcenous matter brought away. The French trample upon the laws of God and man, not for old cordage, but for kingdoms, and always take care to be well paid for their crimes. We contrive, under the present administration, to unite moral with intellectual deficiency, and to grow weaker and worse by the same action. If they had any evidence of the intended hostility of the Danes, why was it not pro-

---

* This is now completely confessed to be the case by ministers.

duced? Why have the nations of Europe been allowed to feel an indignation against this country beyond the reach of all subsequent information? Are these times, do you imagine, when we can trifle with a year of universal hatred, dally with the curses of Europe, and then regain a lost character at pleasure, by the parliamentary perspirations of the Foreign Secretary, or the solemn asseverations of the pecuniary Rose? Believe me, Abraham, it is not under such ministers as these that the dexterity of honest Englishmen will ever equal the dexterity of French knaves; it is not in their presence that the serpent of Moses will ever swallow up the serpents of the magician.

Lord Hawkesbury says that nothing is to be granted to the Catholics from fear. What! not even justice? Why not? There are four millions of disaffected people within twenty miles of your own coast. I fairly confess, that the dread which I have of their physical power, is with me a very strong motive for listening to their claims. To talk of not acting from fear is mere parliamentary cant. From what motive but fear, I should be glad to know, have all the improvements in our constitution proceeded? I question if any justice has ever been done to large masses of mankind from any other motive. By what other motives can the plunderers of the Baltic suppose nations to be governed in their intercourse *with each other?* If I say, give this people what they ask because it is just, do you think I should get ten people to listen to me? Would not the lesser of the two Jenkinsons be the first to treat me with contempt? the only true way to make the mass of mankind see the beauty of justice, is by showing to them in pretty plain terms the consequences of injustice. If any body of French troops land in Ireland, the whole population of that country will rise against you to a man, and you could not possibly survive such an event three years. Such from the bottom of my soul, do I believe to be the present state of that country; and so far does it appear to me to be impolitic and unstatesmanlike to concede anything to such a danger, that if the Catholics, in addition to their present just demands, were to petition for the perpetual removal of the said Lord Hawkesbury from his Majesty's councils, I think, whatever might be the effect upon the destinies of Europe, and however it might retard our own individual destruction, that the prayer of the petition should be instantly complied with. Canning's crocodile tears should not move me; the hoops of the maids of honour should not hide him. I would tear him from the banisters of the back stairs, and plunge him in the fishy fumes of the dirtiest of all his Cinque Ports.

LETTER VII.

Dear Abraham,

In the correspondence which is passing between us you are perpetually alluding to the Foreign Secretary; and in answer to the dangers of Ireland, which I am pressing upon your notice, you have nothing to urge but the confidence which you repose in the discretion and sound sense of this gentleman.* I can only say, that I have listened to him long and often, with the greatest attention; I have used every exertion in my power to take a fair measure of him, and it appears to me impossible to hear him upon any arduous topic without perceiving that he is eminently deficient in those solid and serious qualities upon which, and upon which alone, the confidence of a great country can properly repose. He sweats, and labours, and works for sense, and Mr. Ellis seems always to think it is coming, but it does not come; the machine can't draw up what is not to be found in the spring; Providence has made him a light, jesting, paragraph-writing man, and that he will remain to his dying day. When he is jocular he is strong, when he is serious he is like Samson in a wig: any ordinary person is a match for him: a song, an ironical letter, a burlesque ode, an attack in the Newspaper upon Nicoll's eye, a smart speech of twenty minutes, full of gross misrepresentations and clever turns, excellent language, a spirited manner, lucky quotation, success in provoking dull men, some half information picked up in Pall Mall in the morning: these are your friend's natural weapons; all these things he can do; here I allow him to be truly great: nay, I will be just, and go still further, if he would confine himself to these things, and consider the *facete* and the playful to be the basis of his character, he would for that species of man, be universally regarded as a person of a very good understanding; call him a legislator, a reasoner, and the conductor of the affairs of a great nation, and it seems to me as absurd as if a butterfly were to teach bees to make honey. That he is an extraordinary writer of small poetry, and a diner out of the highest lustre, I do most readily admit. After George Selwyn, and perhaps Tickell, there has been no such man for this half century.

---

* The attack upon virtue and morals in the debate upon Copenhagen is brought forward with great ostentation by this gentleman's friends. But is Harlequin less Harlequin because he acts well? I was present: he leaped about, touched facts with his wand, turned yes into no, and no into yes: it was a pantomime well played, but a pantomime: Harlequin deserves higher wages than he did two years ago: is he therefore fit for serious parts?

The Foreign Secretary is a gentleman, a respectable as well as a highly agreeable man in private life; but you may as well feed me with decayed potatoes as console me for the miseries of Ireland by the resources of his *sense* and his *discretion*. It is only the public situation which this gentleman holds which entitles me or induces me to say so much about him. He is a fly in amber, nobody cares about the fly: the only question is, How the Devil did it get there? Nor do I attack him for the love of glory, but from the love of utility, as a burgomaster hunts a rat in a Dutch dyke, for fear it should flood a province.

The friends of the Catholic question are, I observe, extremely embarrassed in arguing when they come to the loyalty of the Irish Catholics. As for me, I shall go straight forward to my object, and state what I have no manner of doubt, from an intimate knowledge of Ireland, to be the plain truth. Of the great Roman Catholic proprietors, and of the Catholic prelates, there may be a few, and but a few, who would follow the fortunes of England at all events: there is another set of men who, thoroughly detesting this country, have too much property and too much character to lose, not to wait for some very favourable event before they show themselves; but the great mass of Catholic population, upon the slightest appearance of a French force in that country, would rise upon you to a man. It is the most mistaken policy to conceal the plain truth. There is no loyalty among the Catholics: they detest you as their worst oppressors, and they will continue to detest you till you remove the cause of their hatred. It is in your power in six months' time to produce a total revolution of opinions among this people; and in some future letter I will show you that this is clearly the case. At present, see what a dreadful state Ireland is in. The common toast among the low Irish is, the feast of the *passover*. Some allusion to *Bonaparte,* in a play lately acted at Dublin, produced thunders of applause from the pit and the galleries; and a politician should not be inattentive to the public feelings expressed in theatres. Mr. Perceval thinks he has disarmed the Irish: he has no more disarmed the Irish than he has resigned a shilling of his own public emoluments. An Irish * peasant fills the barrel of his gun full of tow dipped in oil, butters up the lock, buries it in a bog, and allows the Orange bloodhound to ransack his cottage at pleasure. Be just and kind to the Irish, and you will indeed disarm them; rescue them from the degraded servitude in which they are

* No man who is not intimately acquainted with the Irish, can tell to what a curious extent this concealment of arms is carried. I have stated the exact mode in which it is done.

held by a handful of their own countrymen, and you will add four millions of brave and affectionate men to your strength. Nightly visits, Protestant inspectors, licences to possess a pistol, or a knife and fork, the odious vigour of the *evangelical* Perceval—acts of Parliament, drawn up by some English attorney, to save you from the hatred of four millions of people—the guarding yourselves from universal disaffection by a police; a confidence in the little cunning of Bow Street, when you might rest your security upon the eternal basis of the best feelings: this is the meanness and madness to which nations are reduced when they lose sight of the first elements of justice, without which a country can be no more secure than it can be healthy without air. I sicken at such policy and such men. The fact is, the Ministers know nothing about the present state of Ireland; Mr. Perceval sees a few clergymen, Lord Castlereagh a few general officers, who take care, of course, to report what is pleasant rather than what is true. As for the joyous and lepid consul, he jokes upon neutral flags and frauds, jokes upon Irish rebels, jokes upon northern, and western, and southern foes, and gives himself no trouble upon any subject: nor is the mediocrity of the idolatrous deputy of the slightest use. Dissolved in grins, he reads no memorials upon the state of Ireland, listens to no reports, asks no questions, and is the

"*Bourn* from whom no traveller returns."

The danger of an immediate insurrection is now, I *believe*,* blown over. You have so strong an army in Ireland, and the Irish are become so much more cunning from the last insurrection, that you may perhaps be tolerably secure just at present from that evil: but are you secure from the efforts which the French may make to throw a body of troops into Ireland? and do you consider that event to be difficult and improbable? From Brest Harbour to Cape St. Vincent, you have above three thousand miles of hostile sea coast, and twelve or fourteen harbours quite capable of containing a sufficient force for the powerful invasion of Ireland. The nearest of these harbours is not two days' sail from the southern coast of Ireland, with a fair leading wind; and the furthest not ten. Five ships of the line, for so very short a passage, might carry five or six thousand troops with cannon and ammunition; and Ireland presents to their attack a southern coast of more than 500 miles, abounding in deep bays, admirable harbours, and disaffected in-

---

* I know too much, however, of the state of Ireland, not to speak trem- blingly about this. I hope to God I am right.

habitants. Your blockading ships may be forced to come home for provisions and repairs, or they may be blown off in a gale of wind and compelled to bear away for their own coast;—and you will observe, that the very same wind which locks you up in the British Channel when you are got there, is evidently favourable for the invasion of Ireland. And yet this is called Government, and the people huzza Mr. Perceval for continuing to expose his country day after day to such tremendous perils as these; cursing the men who would have given up a question in theology to have saved us from such a risk. The British empire at this moment is in the state of a peach-blossom—if the wind blows gently from one quarter, it survives, if furiously from the other, it perishes. A stiff breeze may set in from the north, the Rochefort squadron will be taken, and the Minister will be the most holy of men: if it comes from some other point, Ireland is gone; we curse ourselves as a set of monastic madmen, and call out for the unavailing satisfaction of Mr. Perceval's head. Such a state of political existence is scarcely credible; it is the action of a mad young fool standing upon one foot, and peeping down the crater of Mount Ætna, not the conduct of a wise and sober people deciding upon their best and dearest interests: and in the name, the much-injured name, of Heaven, what is it all for that we expose ourselves to these dangers? Is it that we may sell more muslin? Is it that we may acquire more territory? Is it that we may strengthen what we have already acquired? No: nothing of all this; but that one set of Irishmen may torture another set of Irishmen—that Sir Phelim O'Callaghan may continue to whip Sir Toby M'Tackle, his next door neighbour, and continue to ravish his Catholic daughters; and these are the measures which the honest and consistent Secretary supports; and this is the Secretary, whose genius in the estimation of Brother Abraham is to extinguish the genius of Bonaparte. Pompey was killed by a slave, Goliath smitten by a stripling, Pyrrhus died by the hand of a woman; tremble, thou great Gaul, from whose head an armed Minerva leaps forth in the hour of danger; tremble, thou scourge of God, a pleasant man is come out against thee, and thou shalt be laid low by a joker of jokes, and he shall talk his pleasant talk against thee, and thou shalt be no more!

You tell me, in spite of all this parade of sea coast, Bonaparte has neither ships nor sailors; but this is a mistake. He has not ships and sailors to contest the empire of the seas with Great Britain, but there remains quite sufficient of the navies of France, Spain, Holland, and Denmark, for these short excursions and invasions. Do you think, too, that Bonaparte does not add to his navy every year? Do you suppose, with all Europe at his feet, that he can find any difficulty in obtaining timber, and that money will not procure for him any quantity of naval stores he may want? The mere machine, the empty ship, he can build as well, and as quickly, as you can; and though he may not find enough of practised sailors to man large fighting fleets—it is not possible to conceive that he can want sailors for such sort of purposes as I have stated. He is at present the despotic monarch of above twenty thousand miles of sea coast, and yet you suppose he cannot procure sailors for the invasion of Ireland. Believe, if you please, that such a fleet met at sea by any number of our ships at all comparable to them in point of force, would be immediately taken, let it be so; I count nothing upon their power of resistance, only upon their power of escaping unobserved. If experience has taught us anything, it is the impossibility of perpetual blockades. The instances are innumerable, during the course of this war, where whole fleets have sailed in and out of harbour in spite of every vigilance used to prevent it. I shall only mention those cases where Ireland is concerned. In December, 1796, seven ships of the line, and ten transports, reached Bantry Bay from Brest, without having seen an English ship in their passage. It blew a storm when they were off shore, and therefore England still continues to be an independent kingdom. You will observe that at the very time the French fleet sailed out of Brest Harbour, Admiral Colpoys was cruising off there with a powerful squadron, and still, from the particular circumstances of the weather, found it impossible to prevent the French from coming out. During the time that Admiral Colpoys was cruising off Brest, Admiral Richery, with six ships of the line, passed him, and got safe into the harbour. At the very moment when the French squadron was lying in Bantry Bay, Lord Bridport with his fleet was locked up by a foul wind in the Channel, and for several days could not stir to the assistance of Ireland. Admiral Colpoys, totally unable to find the French fleet, came home. Lord Bridport, at the change of the wind, cruised for them in vain, and they got safe back to Brest, without having seen a single one of those floating bulwarks, the possession of which we believe will enable us with impunity to set justice and common sense at defiance. Such is the miserable and precarious state of an anemocracy, of a people who put their trust in hurricanes, and are governed by wind. In August, 1798, three forty-gun frigates landed 1100 men under Humbert, making the passage from Rochelle to Killala without seeing any English ship. In October of the same year, four French frigates anchored in Killala Bay with 2000 troops; and though they did not land their troops, they returned to France in safety. In the same month, a line-of-battle ship, eight stout frigates, and a brig, all full of troops and stores, reached the coast of Ireland, and were fortunately, in sight of land, destroyed, after an obstinate engagement, by Sir John Warren.

If you despise the little troop which, in these numerous experiments, did make good its landing, take with you, if you please, this *précis* of its exploits: eleven hundred men, commanded by a soldier raised from the ranks, put to rout a select army of 6000 men, commanded by General Lake, seized their ordnance, ammunition, and stores, advanced 150 miles into a country containing an armed force of 150,000 men, and at last surrendered to the Viceroy, an experienced general, gravely and cautiously advancing, at the head of all his chivalry and of an immense army, to oppose him. You must excuse these details about Ireland; but it appears to me to be of all other subjects the most important. If we conciliate Ireland, we can do nothing amiss; if we do not, we can do nothing well. If Ireland was friendly, we might equally set at defiance the talents of Bonaparte, and the blunders of his rival, Mr. Canning; we could then support the ruinous and silly bustle of our useless expeditions, and the almost incredible ignorance of our commercial Orders in Council. Let the present administration give up but this one point, and there is nothing which I would not consent to grant them. Mr. Perceval shall have full liberty to insult the tomb of Mr. Fox, and to torment every eminent Dissenter in Great Britain; Lord Camden shall have large boxes of plums; Mr. Rose receive permission to prefix to his name the appellative of virtuous; and to the Viscount Castlereagh * a round sum of ready money shall be well and truly paid into his hand. Lastly, what remains to Mr. George Canning, but that he ride up and down Pall Mall glorious upon a white horse, and that they cry out before him, Thus shall it be done to the statesman who hath written "The Needy Knife-Grinder," and the German play? Adieu only for the present; you shall soon hear from me again; it is a subject upon which I cannot long be silent.

LETTER VIII.

Nothing can be more erroneous than to suppose that Ireland is not bigger than the Isle of Wight, or of more consequence

---

* This is a very unjust imputation on Lord Castlereagh.

than Guernsey or Jersey; and yet I am almost inclined to believe, from the general supineness which prevails here respecting the dangerous state of that country, that such is the rank which it holds in our statistical tables. I have been writing to you a great deal about Ireland, and perhaps it may be of some use to state to you concisely the nature and resources of the country which has been the subject of our long and strange correspondence. There were returned, as I have before observed, to the hearth tax, in 1791, 701,132 * houses, which Mr. Newenham shows, from unquestionable documents, to be nearly 80,000 below the real number of houses in that country. There are 27,457 square English miles in Ireland,† and more than five millions of people.

By the last survey it appears that the inhabited houses in England and Wales amount to 1,574,902; and the population to 9,343,578, which gives an average of 5⅞ to each house, in a country where the density of population is certainly less considerable than in Ireland. It is commonly supposed that two-fifths of the army and navy are Irishmen, at periods when political disaffection does not avert the Catholics from the service. The current value of Irish exports in 1807 was 9,314,854*l*. 17*s*. 7*d*.; a state of commerce about equal to the commerce of England in the middle of the reign of George II. The tonnage of ships entered inward and cleared outward in the trade of Ireland, in 1807, amounted to 1,567,430 tons. The quantity of home spirits exported amounted to 10,284 gallons in 1796, and to 930,800 gallons in 1804. Of the exports which I have stated, provisions amounted to four millions, and linen to about four millions and a half. There was exported from Ireland, upon an average of two years ending in January, 1804, 591,274 barrels of barley, oats, and wheat; and by weight 910,848 cwts. of flour, oatmeal, barley, oats, and wheat. The amount of butter exported in 1804, from Ireland, was worth, in money, 1,704,680*l*. sterling. The importation of ale and beer, from the immense manufactures now carrying on of these articles, was diminished to 3209 barrels, in the year 1804, from 111,920 barrels, which was the average importation per annum, taking from three years ending in 1792; and at present there is an export trade of porter. On an average of the three years ending March, 1783, there were imported into Ireland,

---

* The checks to population were very trifling from the rebellion. It lasted two months: of his Majesty's Irish forces there perished about 1600: of the rebels 11,000 were killed in the field, and 2000 hanged or exported: 400 loyal persons were assassinated.
† In England, 49,450.

of cotton wool, 3326 cwts., of cotton yarn, 5405 lbs.; but on an average of three years, ending January, 1803, there were imported, of the first article, 13,159 cwts., and of the latter, 628,406 lbs. It is impossible to conceive any manufacture more flourishing. The export of linen has increased in Ireland from 17,776,862 yards, the average in 1770, to 43,534,971 yards, the amount in 1805. The tillage of Ireland has more than trebled within the last twenty-one years. The importation of coals has increased from 230,000 tons, in 1783, to 417,030, in 1804; of tobacco, from 3,459,861 lbs. in 1783, to 6,611,543, in 1804; of tea, from 1,703,855 lbs. in 1783, to 3,358,256, in 1804; of sugar, from 143,117 cwts. in 1782, to 309,076, in 1804. Ireland now supports a funded debt of about 64 millions; and it is computed that more than three millions of money are annually remitted to Irish absentees resident in this country. In Mr. Foster's report, of 100 folio pages, presented to the House of Commons in the year 1806, the total expenditure of Ireland is stated at 9,760,013*l*. Ireland has increased about two-thirds in its population within twenty-five years; and yet, and in about the same space of time, its exports of beef, bullocks, cows, pork, swine, butter, wheat, barley, and oats, collectively taken, have doubled; and this in spite of two years' famine, and the presence of an immense army, that is always at hand to guard the most valuable appanage of our empire from joining our most inveterate enemies. Ireland has the greatest possible facilities for carrying on commerce with the whole of Europe. It contains, within a circuit of 750 miles, 66 secure harbours; and presents a western frontier against Great Britain, reaching from the Firth of Clyde, north, to the Bristol Channel, south, and varying in distance from 20 to 100 miles; so that the subjugation of Ireland would compel us to guard with ships and soldiers a new line of coast, certainly amounting, with all its sinuosities, to more than 700 miles—an addition of polemics, in our present state of hostility with all the world, which must highly gratify the vigorists, and give them an ample opportunity of displaying that foolish energy upon which their claims to distinction are founded. Such is the country which the Right Reverend the Chancellor of the Exchequer would drive into the arms of France; and for the conciliation of which we are requested to wait, as if it were one of those sinecure places which were given to Mr. Perceval snarling at the breast, and which cannot be abolished till his decease.

How sincerely and fervently have I often wished that the Emperor of the French had thought as Mr. Spencer Perceval does upon the subject of government; that he had entertained doubts

and scruples upon the propriety of admitting the Protestants to an
equality of rights with the Catholics, and that he had left in the
middle of his empire these vigorous seeds of hatred and disaffection! But the world was never yet conquered by a blockhead.
One of the very first measures we saw him recurring to was the
complete establishment of religious liberty: if his subjects fought
and paid as he pleased, he allowed them to believe as they pleased:
the moment I saw this, my best hopes were lost. I perceived in a
moment the kind of man we had to do with. I was well aware of
the miserable ignorance and folly of this country upon the subject
of toleration; and every year has been adding to the success of
that game which it was clear he had the will and the ability to
play against us.

You say Bonaparte is not in earnest upon the subject of religion, and that this is the cause of his tolerant spirit; but is it possible you can intend to give us such dreadful and unamiable notions of religion? Are we to understand that the moment a man is
sincere he is narrow-minded; that persecution is the child of belief;
and that a desire to leave all men in the quiet and unpunished
exercise of their own creed can only exist in the mind of an infidel? Thank God! I know many men whose principles are as firm
as they are expanded, who cling tenaciously to their own modification of the Christian faith, without the slightest disposition to
force that modification upon other people. If Bonaparte is liberal
in subjects of religion because he has no religion, is this a reason
why we should be illiberal because we are Christians? If he owes
this excellent quality to a vice, is that any reason why we may not
owe it to a virtue? Toleration is a great good, and a good to be
imitated, let it come from whom it will. If a sceptic is tolerant, it
only shows that he is not foolish in practice as well as erroneous
in theory. If a religious man is tolerant, it evinces that he is religious from thought and inquiry, because he exhibits in his conduct
one of the most beautiful and important consequences of a religious mind,—an inviolable charity to all the honest varieties of
human opinion.

Lord Sidmouth, and all the anti-Catholic people, little foresee
that they will hereafter be the sport of the antiquary; that their
prophecies of ruin and destruction from Catholic emancipation
will be clapped into the notes of some quaint history, and be
matter of pleasantry even to the sedulous housewife and the rural
dean. There is always a copious supply of Lord Sidmouths in the
world; nor is there one single source of human happiness, against
which they have not uttered the most lugubrious predictions.

Turnpike roads, navigable canals, inoculation, hops, tobacco, the Reformation, the Revolution—there are always a set of worthy and moderately-gifted men, who bawl out death and ruin upon every valuable change which the varying aspect of human affairs absolutely and imperiously requires. I have often thought that it would be extremely useful to make a collection of the hatred and abuse that all those changes have experienced, which are now admitted to be marked improvements in our condition. Such a history might make folly a little more modest, and suspicious of its own decisions.

Ireland, you say, since the Union, is to be considered as a part of the whole kingdom; and therefore, however Catholics may predominate in that particular spot, yet, taking the whole empire together, they are to be considered as a much more insignificant quota of the population. Consider them in what light you please, as part of the whole, or by themselves, or in what manner may be most consentaneous to the devices of your holy mind—I say in a very few words, if you do not relieve these people from the civil incapacities to which they are exposed, you will lose them; or you must employ great strength and much treasure in watching over them. In the present state of the world, you can afford to do neither the one nor the other. Having stated this, I shall leave you to be ruined, Puffendorf in hand (as Mr. Secretary Canning says), and to lose Ireland, just as you have found out what proportion the aggrieved people should bear to the whole population, before their calamities meet with redress. As for your parallel cases, I am no more afraid of deciding upon them than I am upon their prototype. If ever any one heresy should so far spread itself over the principality of Wales that the Established Church were left in a minority of one to four; if you had subjected these heretics to very severe civil privations; if the consequence of such privations were a universal state of disaffection among that caseous and wrathful people; and if at the same time you were at war with all the world, how can you doubt for a moment that I would instantly restore them to a state of the most complete civil liberty? What matters it under what name you put the same case? Common sense is not changed by appellations. I have said how I would act to Ireland, and I would act so to all the world.

I admit that, to a certain degree, the Government will lose the affections of the Orangemen by emancipating the Catholics; much less, however, at present, than three years past. The few men, who have ill-treated the whole crew, live in constant terror that the oppressed people will rise upon them and carry the ship into

Brest:—they begin to find that it is a very tiresome thing to sleep every night with cocked pistols under their pillows, and to breakfast, dine, and sup with drawn hangers. They suspect that the privilege of beating and kicking the rest of the sailors is hardly worth all this anxiety, and that if the ship does ever fall into the hands of the disaffected, all the cruelties which they have experienced will be thoroughly remembered and amply repaid. To a short period of disaffection among the Orangemen, I confess I should not much object: my love of poetical justice does carry me as far as that; one summer's whipping, only one: the thumb-screw for a short season; a little light easy torturing between Lady-day and Michaelmas; a short specimen of Mr. Perceval's rigour. I have malice enough to ask this slight atonement for the groans and shrieks of the poor Catholics, unheard by any human tribunal, but registered by the Angel of God against their Protestant and enlightened oppressors.

Besides, if you who count ten so often can count five, you must perceive that it is better to have four friends and one enemy than four eneimes and one friend; and the more violent the hatred of the Orangemen, the more certain the reconciliation of the Catholics. The disaffection of the Orangemen will be the Irish rainbow; when I see it, I shall be sure that the storm is over.

If those incapacities, from which the Catholics ask to be relieved, were to the mass of them only a mere feeling of pride, and if the question were respecting the attainment of privileges which could be of importance only to the highest of the sect, I should still say, that the pride of the mass was very naturally wounded by the degradation of their superiors. Indignity to George Rose would be felt by the smallest nummary gentleman in the king's employ; and Mr. John Bannister could not be indifferent to anything which happened to Mr. Canning. But the truth is, it is a most egregious mistake to suppose that the Catholics are contending merely for the fringes and feathers of their chiefs. I will give you a list, in my next Letter, of those privations which are represented to be of no consequence to anybody but Lord Fingal, and some twenty or thirty of the principal persons of their sect. In the meantime, adieu, and be wise.

L E T T E R   I X .

Dear Abraham,

No Catholic can be chief Governor or Governor of this Kingdom, Chancellor or Keeper of the Great Seal, Lord High

Treasurer, Chief of any of the Courts of Justice, Chancellor of the
Exchequer, Puisne Judge, Judge in the Admiralty, Master of the
Rolls, Secretary of State, Keeper of the Privy Seal, Vice-Treasurer
or his Deputy, Teller or Cashier of Exchequer, Auditor or Gen-
eral, Governor or Custos Rotulorum of Counties, Chief Governor's
Secretary, Privy Councillor, King's Counsel, Sergeant, Attorney,
Solicitor-General, Master in Chancery, Provost or Fellow of
Trinity College, Dublin, Postmaster-General, Master and Lieuten-
ant-General of Ordnance, Commander-in-Chief, General on the
Staff, Sheriff, Sub-Sheriff, Mayor, Bailiff, Recorder, Burgess, or
any other officer in a City, or a Corporation. No Catholic can be
guardian to a Protestant, and no priest guardian at all: no Catholic can be a gamekeeper, or have for sale, or otherwise, any arms
or warlike stores: no Catholic can present to a living, unless he
choose to turn Jew in order to obtain that privilege; the pecuniary
qualification of Catholic jurors is made higher than that of Protestants, and no relaxation of the ancient rigorous code is permitted, unless to those who shall take an oath prescribed by 13 & 14
Geo. III. Now if this is not picking the plums out of the pudding,
and leaving the mere batter to the Catholics, I know not what is.
If it were merely the Privy Council, it would be (I allow) nothing
but a point of honour for which the mass of Catholics were contending, the honour of being chief-mourners or pall-bearers to the
country; but surely no man will contend that every barrister may
not speculate upon the possibility of being a puisne Judge; and
that every shopkeeper must not feel himself injured by his exclusion from borough offices.

One of the greatest practical evils which the Catholics suffer
in Ireland is their exclusion from the offices of Sheriff and Deputy
Sheriff. Nobody who is unacquainted with Ireland can conceive
the obstacles which this opposes to the fair administration of justice. The formation of juries is now entirely in the hands of the
Protestants; the lives, liberties, and properties of the Catholics in
the hands of the juries; and this is the arrangement for the administration of justice in a country where religious prejudices are
inflamed to the greatest degree of animosity! In this country, if
a man be a foreigner, if he sell slippers, and sealing wax, and arti-
ficial flowers, we are so tender of human life that we take care half
the number of persons who are to decide upon his fate should be
men of similar prejudices and feelings with himself: but a poor
Catholic in Ireland may be tried by twelve Percevals, and destroyed according to the manner of that gentleman in the name
of the Lord, and with all the insulting forms of justice. I do not

go the length of saying that deliberate and wilful injustice is done. I have no doubt that the Orange Deputy Sheriff thinks it would be a most unpardonable breach of his duty if he did not summon a Protestant panel. I can easily believe that a Protestant panel may conduct themselves very conscientiously in hanging the gentlemen of the crucifix; but I blame the law which does not guard the Catholic against the probable tenor of those feelings which must unconsciously influence the judgments of mankind. I detest that state of society which extends unequal degrees of protection to different creeds and persuasions; and I cannot describe to you the contempt I feel for a man who, calling himself a statesman, defends a system which fills the heart of every Irishman with treason, and makes his allegiance prudence, not choice.

I request to know if the vestry taxes in Ireland are a mere matter of romantic feeling, which can affect only the Earl of Fingal? In a parish where there are four thousand Catholics and fifty Protestants, the Protestants may meet together in a vestry meeting, at which no Catholic has the right to vote, and tax all the lands in the parish 1s. 6d. per acre, or in the pound, I forget which, for the repairs of the church—and how has the necessity of these repairs been ascertained? A Protestant plumber has discovered that it wants new leading; a Protestant carpenter is convinced the timbers are not sound, and the glazier who hates holy water (as an accoucheur hates celibacy because he gets nothing by it) is employed to put in new sashes.

The grand juries in Ireland are the great scene of jobbing. They have a power of making a county rate to a considerable extent for roads, bridges, and other objects of general accommodation. "You suffer the road to be brought through my park, and I will have the bridge constructed in a situation where it will make a beautiful object to your house. You do my job, and I will do yours." These are the sweet and interesting subjects which occasionally occupy Milesian gentlemen while they are attendant upon this grand inquest of justice. But there is a religion, it seems, even in jobs; and it will be highly gratifying to Mr. Perceval to learn that no man in Ireland who believes in seven sacraments can carry a public road, or bridge, one yard out of the direction most beneficial to the public, and that nobody can cheat that public who does not expound the Scriptures in the purest and most orthodox manner. This will give pleasure to Mr. Perceval: but, from his unfairness upon these topics, I appeal to the justice and the proper feelings of Mr. Huskisson. I ask him if the human mind can experience a more dreadful sensation than to see its own jobs refused, and the jobs of another religion perpetually succeeding? I ask him his opinion of a jobless faith, of a creed which dooms a man through life to a lean and plunderless integrity. He knows that human nature cannot and will not bear it; and if we were to paint a political Tartarus, it would be an endless series of snug expectations, and cruel disappointments. These are a few of many dreadful inconveniences which the Catholics of all ranks suffer from the laws by which they are at present oppressed. Besides, look at human nature:—what is the history of all professions? Joel is to be brought up to the bar: has Mrs. Plymley the slightest doubt of his being Chancellor? Do not his two shrivelled aunts live in the certainty of seeing him in that situation, and of cutting out with their own hands his equity habiliments? And I could name a certain minister of the Gospel who does not, in the bottom of his heart, much differ from these opinions. Do you think that the fathers and mothers of the holy Catholic Church are not as absurd as Protestant papas and mammas? The probability I admit to be, in each particular case, that the sweet little blockhead will in fact never get a brief;—but I will venture to say, there is not a parent from the Giant's Causeway to Bantry Bay who does not conceive that his child is the unfortunate victim of the exclusion, and that nothing short of positive law could prevent his own dear pre-eminent Paddy from rising to the highest honours of the State. So with the army, and parliament; in fact, few are excluded; but, in imagination, all: you keep twenty or thirty Catholics out, and you lose the affections of four millions; and, let me tell you, that recent circumstances have by no means tended to diminish in the minds of men that hope of elevation beyond their own rank which is so congenial to our nature: from pleading for John Roe to taxing John Bull, from jesting for Mr. Pitt and writing in the Anti-Jacobin, to managing the affairs of Europe—these are leaps which seem to justify the fondest dreams of mothers and of aunts.

I do not say that the disabilities to which the Catholics are exposed amount to such intolerable grievances, that the strength and industry of a nation are overwhelmed by them: the increasing prosperity of Ireland fully demonstrates to the contrary. But I repeat again, what I have often stated in the course of our correspondence, that your laws against the Catholics are exactly in that state in which you have neither the benefits of rigour nor of liberality: every law which prevented the Catholic from gaining strength and wealth is repealed; every law which can irritate remains; if you were determined to insult the Catholics, you should have kept them weak; if you resolved to give them strength, you should have ceased to insult them;—at present your conduct is pure unadulterated folly.

Lord Hawkesbury says, We heard nothing about the Catholics till we began to mitigate the laws against them; when we relieved them in part from this oppression they began to be disaffected. This is very true; but it proves just what I have said, that you have either done too much, or too little; and as there lives not, I hope, upon earth, so depraved a courtier that he would load the Catholics with their ancient chains, what absurdity it is then not to render their dispositions friendly, when you leave their arms and legs free!

You know, and many Englishmen know, what passes in China; but nobody knows or cares what passes in Ireland. At the beginning of the present reign, no Catholic could realise property, or carry on any business; they were absolutely annihilated, and had no more agency in the country than so many trees. They were like Lord Mulgrave's eloquence and Lord Camden's wit; the legislative bodies did not know of their existence. For these twenty-five years last past, the Catholics have been engaged in commerce; within that period the commerce of Ireland has doubled;—there are four Catholics at work for one Protestant, and eight Catholics at work for one Episcopalian; of course, the proportion which Catholic wealth bears to Protestant wealth is every year altering rapidly in favour of the Catholics. I have already told you what their purchases of land were the last year: since that period, I have been at some pains to find out the actual state of the Catholic wealth: it is impossible, upon such a subject, to arrive at complete accuracy; but I have good reason to believe that there are at present 2000 Catholics in Ireland, possessing an income from 500l. upwards, many of these with incomes of one, two, three and four thousand, and some amounting to fifteen and twenty thousand per annum:—and this is the kingdom, and these the people, for whose conciliation we are to wait, Heaven knows when, and Lord Hawkesbury why! As for me, I never think of the situation of Ireland without feeling the same necessity for immediate interference as I should do if I saw blood flowing from a great artery. I rush towards it with the instinctive rapidity of a man desirous of preventing death, and have no other feeling but that in a few seconds the patient may be no more.

I could not help smiling in the times of No Popery, to witness the loyal indignation of many persons at the attempt made by the last ministry to do something for the relief of Ireland. The general cry in the country was, that they would not see their beloved

Monarch used ill in his old age, and that they would stand by him to the last drop of their blood. I respect good feelings, however erroneous be the occasions on which they display themselves; and therefore I saw in all this as much to admire as to blame. It was a species of affection, however, which reminded me very forcibly of the attachment displayed by the servants of the Russian ambassador, at the beginning of the last century. His Excellency happened to fall down in a kind of apoplectic fit, when he was paying a morning visit in the house of an acquaintance. The confusion was of course very great, and messengers were despatched, in every direction, to find a surgeon; who, upon his arrival, declared that his Excellency must be immediately blooded, and prepared himself forthwith to perform the operation: the barbarous servants of the embassy, who were there in great numbers, no sooner saw the surgeon prepared to wound the arm of their master with a sharp shining instrument, than they drew their swords, put themselves in an attitude of defence, and swore in pure Sclavonic, "that they would murder any man who attempted to do him the slightest injury: he had been a very good master to them, and they would not desert him in his misfortunes, or suffer his blood to be shed while he was off his guard, and incapable of defending himself." By good fortune, the secretary arrived about this period of the dispute, and his Excellency, relieved from superfluous blood and perilous affection, was, after much difficulty, restored to life.

There is an argument brought forward with some appearance of plausibility in the House of Commons, which certainly merits an answer: You know that the Catholics now vote for members of parliament in Ireland, and that they outnumber the Protestants in a very great proportion; if you allow Catholics to sit in parliament, religion will be found to influence votes more than property, and the greater part of the 100 Irish members who are returned to parliament will be Catholics.—Add to these the Catholic members who are returned in England, and you will have a phalanx of heretical strength which every minister will be compelled to respect, and occasionally to conciliate by concessions incompatible with the interests of the Protestant Church. The fact is, however, that you are at this moment subjected to every danger of this kind which you can possibly apprehend hereafter. If the spiritual interests of the voters are more powerful than their temporal interests, they can bind down their representatives to support any measures favourable to the Catholic religion, and they can change the objects of their choice till they have found Protestant members (as they easily may do) perfectly obedient to their wishes. If the superior possessions of the Protestants prevent the Catholics from uniting for a common political object, then the danger you fear cannot exist: if zeal, on the contrary, gets the better of acres, then the danger at present exists, from the right of voting already given to the Catholics, and it will not be increased by allowing them to sit in parliament. There are, as nearly as I can recollect, thirty seats in Ireland for cities and counties, where the Protestants are the most numerous, and where the members returned must of course be Protestants. In the other seventy representations, the wealth of the Protestants is opposed to the number of the Catholics; and if all the seventy members returned were of the Catholic persuasion, they must still plot the destruction of our religion in the midst of 588 Protestants. Such terrors would disgrace a cookmaid, or a toothless aunt—when they fall from the lips of bearded and senatorial men, they are nauseous, antiperistaltic, and emetical.

How can you for a moment doubt of the rapid effects which would be produced by the emancipation?—In the first place, to my certain knowledge, the Catholics have long since expressed to his Majesty's ministers their perfect readiness *to vest in his Majesty, either with the consent of the Pope, or without it if it cannot be obtained, the nomination of the Catholic prelacy.* The Catholic prelacy in Ireland consists of twenty-six bishops and the warden of Galway, a dignitary enjoying Catholic jurisdiction. The number of Roman Catholic priests in Ireland exceeds one thousand. The expenses of his peculiar worship are, to a substantial farmer or mechanic, five shillings per annum; to a labourer (where he is not entirely excused) one shilling per annum; this includes the contribution of the whole family, and for this the priest is bound to attend them when sick, and to confess them when they apply to him: he is also to keep his chapel in order, to celebrate divine service, and to preach on Sundays and holydays. In the northern district a priest gains from 30*l.* to 50*l.*; in the other parts of Ireland from 60*l.* to 90*l.* per ann. The best paid Catholic bishops receive about 400*l.* per ann.; the others from 300*l.* to 350*l.* My plan is very simple; I would have 300 Catholic parishes at 100*l.* per ann., 300 at 200*l.* per ann., and 400 at 300*l.* per ann.; this, for the whole thousand parishes, would amount to 190,000*l.* To the prelacy I would allot 20,000*l.* in unequal proportions, from 1000*l.* to 500*l.*; and I would appropriate 40,000*l.* more for the support of Catholic schools, and the repairs of Catholic churches; the whole amount of which sum is 250,000*l.*, about the expense of three days of one of our genuine, good, English, *just and nec-*

essary wars. The clergy should all receive their salaries at the Bank of Ireland, and I would place the whole patronage in the hands of the Crown. Now, I appeal to any human being, except Spencer Perceval, Esq., of the parish of Hampstead, what the disaffection of a clergy would amount to, gaping after this graduated bounty of the Crown, and whether Ignatius Loyola himself, if he were a living blockhead, instead of a dead saint, could withstand the temptation of bouncing from 100*l.* a year at Sligo, to 300*l.* in Tipperary? This is the miserable sum of money for which the merchants, and landowners, and nobility of England are exposing themselves to the tremendous peril of losing Ireland. The sinecure places of the Roses and the Percevals, and the "dear and near relations," put up to auction at thirty years' purchase, would almost amount to the money.

I admit that nothing can be more reasonable than to expect that a Catholic priest should starve to death, genteelly and pleasantly, for the good of the Protestant religion; but is it equally reasonable to expect that he should do so for the Protestant pews, and Protestant brick and mortar? On an Irish Sabbath, the bell of a neat parish church often summons to church only the parson and an occasionally conforming clerk; while, two hundred yards off, a thousand Catholics are huddled together in a miserable hovel, and pelted by all the storms of heaven. Can anything be more distressing than to see a venerable man pouring forth sublime truths in tattered breeches, and depending for his food upon the little offal he gets from his parishioners? I venerate a human being who starves for his principles, let them be what they may; but starving for anything is not at all to the taste of the honourable flagellants: strict principles, and good pay, is the motto of Mr. Perceval: the one he keeps in great measure for the faults of his enemies, the other for himself.

There are parishes in Connaught in which a Protestant was never settled, nor even seen: in that province, in Munster, and in parts of Leinster, the entire peasantry for sixty miles are Catholics; in these tracts the churches are frequently shut for want of a congregation, or opened to an assemblage of from six to twenty persons. Of what Protestants there are in Ireland, the greatest part are gathered together in Ulster, or they live in towns. In the country of the other three provinces the Catholics see no other religion but their own, and are at the least as fifteen to one Protestant. In the diocese of Tuam they are sixty to one; in the parish of St. Mullins, diocese of Leghlin, there are four thousand Catholics and *one Protestant;* in the town of Grasgenamana, in the county of

Kilkenny, there are between four and five hundred Catholic houses, and three Protestant houses. In the parish of Allen, county Kildare, there is no Protestant, though it is very populous. In the parish of Arlesin, Queen's County, the proportion is one hundred to one. In the whole county of Kilkenny, by actual enumeration, it is seventeen to one; in the diocese of Kilmacduagh, province of Connaught, fifty-two to one, by ditto. These I give you as a few specimens of the present state of Ireland!—and yet there are men impudent and ignorant enough to contend that such evils require no remedy, and that mild family man who dwelleth in Hampstead can find none but the cautery and the knife,

———— omne per ignem
Excoquitur vitium.

I cannot describe the horror and disgust which I felt at hearing Mr. Perceval call upon the then ministry for measures of vigour in Ireland. If I lived at Hampstead upon stewed meats and claret; if I walked to church every Sunday before eleven young gentlemen of my own begetting, with their faces washed, and their hair pleasingly combed: if the Almighty had blessed me with every earthly comfort—how awfully would I pause before I sent forth the flame and the sword over the cabins of the poor, brave, generous, open-hearted peasants of Ireland! How easy it is to shed human blood—how easy it is to persuade ourselves that it is our duty to do so—and that the decision has cost us a severe struggle —how much in all ages have wounds and shrieks and tears been the cheap and vulgar resources of the rulers of mankind—how difficult and how noble it is to govern in kindness and to found an empire upon the everlasting basis of justice and affection!—But what do men call vigour? To let loose hussars and to bring up artillery, to govern with lighted matches, and to cut, and push, and prime—I call this, not vigour, but the *sloth of cruelty and ignorance*. The vigour I love consists in finding out wherein subjects are aggrieved, in relieving them, in studying the temper and genius of a people, in consulting their prejudices, in selecting proper persons to lead and manage them, in the laborious, watchful, and difficult task of increasing public happiness by allaying each particular discontent. In this way Hoche pacified La Vendée—and in this way only will Ireland ever be subdued. But this, in the eyes of Mr. Perceval, is imbecility and meanness: houses are not broken open—women are not insulted—the people seem all to be happy; they are not rode over by horses, and cut by whips. Do you call this vigour?—Is this government?

LETTER X. AND LAST.

You must observe that all I have said of the effects which will be produced by giving salaries to the Catholic Clergy, only proceeds upon the supposition that the emancipation of the laity is effected:—without that, I am sure there is not a clergyman in Ireland who would receive a shilling from government; he could not do so, without an entire loss of credit among the members of his own persuasion.

What you say of the moderation of the Irish Protestant Clergy in collecting tithes, is, I believe, strictly true. Instead of collecting what the law enables them to collect, I believe they seldom or ever collect more than two thirds; and I entirely agree with you, that the abolition of agistment tithe in Ireland by a vote of the Irish House of Commons, and without any remuneration to the Church, was a most scandalous and Jacobinical measure. I do not blame the Irish clergy; but I submit to your common sense, if it be possible to explain to an Irish peasant upon what principle of justice, or common sense, he is to pay every tenth potato in his little garden to a clergyman in whose religion nobody believes for twenty miles around him, and who has nothing to preach to but bare walls. It is true, if the tithes are bought up, the cottager must pay more rent to his landlord; but the same thing done in the shape of rent, is less odious than when it is done in the shape of tithe. I do not want to take a shilling out of the pockets of the clergy, but to leave the substance of things, and to change their names. I cannot see the slightest reason why the Irish labourer is to be relieved from the real onus, or from anything else but the name of tithe. At present he rents only nine tenths of the produce of the land; which is all that belongs to the owner; this he has at the market price; if the landowner purchase the other tenth of the Church, of course he has a right to make a correspondent advance upon his tenant.

I very much doubt, if you were to lay open all civil offices to the Catholics, and to grant salaries to their clergy, in the manner I have stated, if the Catholic laity would give themselves much trouble about the advance of their Church; for they would pay the same tithes under one system that they do under another. If you were to bring the Catholics into the daylight of the world, to the high situations of the army, the navy, and the bar, numbers of them would come over to the Established Church, and do as other people do; instead of that, you set a mark of infamy upon them, rouse every passion of our nature in favour of their creed, and then wonder that men are blind to the follies of the Catholic religion. There are hardly any instances of old and rich families among the Protestant Dissenters: when a man keeps a coach, and lives in good company, he comes to church, and gets ashamed of the meeting-house; if this is not the case with the father, it is almost always the case with the son. These things would never be so, if the Dissenters were in *practice* as much excluded from all the concerns of civil life, as the Catholics are. If a rich young Catholic were in parliament, he would belong to White's and to Brookes's, would keep racehorses, would walk up and down Pall Mall, be exonerated of his ready money and his constitution, become as totally devoid of morality, honesty, knowledge, and civility as Protestant loungers in Pall Mall, and return home with a supreme contempt for Father O'Leary and Father O'Callaghan. I am astonished at the madness of the Catholic clergy, in not perceiving that Catholic emancipation is Catholic infidelity; that to entangle their people in the intrigues of a Protestant parliament, and a Protestant Court, is to insure the loss of every man of fashion and consequence in their community. The true receipt for preserving their religion, is Mr. Perceval's receipt for destroying it: it is to deprive every rich Catholic of all the objects of secular ambition, to separate him from the Protestant, and to shut him up in his castle with priests and relics.

We are told, in answer to all our arguments, that this is not a fit period,—that a period of universal war is not the proper time for dangerous innovations in the constitution: this is as much as to say, that the worst time for making friends is the period when you have made many enemies; that it is the greatest of all errors to stop when you are breathless, and to lie down when you are fatigued. Of one thing I am quite certain: if the safety of Europe is once completely restored, the Catholics may for ever bid adieu to the slightest probability of effecting their object. Such men as hang about a court not only are deaf to the suggestions of mere justice, but they despise justice; they detest the word *right;* the only word which rouses them is *peril;* where they can oppress with impunity, they oppress for ever, and call it loyalty and wisdom.

I am so far from conceiving the legitimate strength of the Crown would be diminished by those abolitions of civil incapacities in consequence of religious opinions, that my only objection to the increase of religious freedom is, that it would operate as a diminution of political freedom: the power of the Crown is so overbearing at this period, that almost the only steady opposers of its fatal influence are men disgusted by religious intolerance. Our establishments are so enormous, and so utterly disproportioned to our population, that every second or third man you meet in society gains something from the public; my brother the commissioner,— my nephew the police justice,—purveyor of small beer to the army in Ireland,—clerk of the mouth,—yeoman to the left hand,— these are the obstacles which common sense and justice have now to overcome. Add to this, that the King, old and infirm, excites a principle of very amiable generosity in his favour; that he has led a good, moral, and religious life, equally removed from profligacy and methodistical hypocrisy; that he has been a good husband, a good father, and a good master; that he dresses plain, loves hunting and farming, hates the French, and is, in all his opinions and habits, quite English:—these feelings are heightened by the present situation of the world, and the yet unexploded clamour of Jacobinism. In short, from the various sources of interest, personal regard, and national taste, such a tempest of loyalty has set in upon the people that the 47th proposition in Euclid might now be voted down with as much ease as any proposition in politics; and therefore if Lord Hawkesbury hates the abstract truths of science as much as he hates concrete truth in human affairs, now is his time for getting rid of the multiplication table, and passing a vote of censure upon the pretensions of the *hypothenuse*. Such is the history of English parties at this moment: you cannot seriously suppose that the people care for such men as Lord Hawkesbury, Mr. Canning, and Mr. Perceval, on their own account; you cannot really believe them to be so degraded as to look for their safety to a man who proposes to subdue Europe by keeping it without Jesuits' Bark. The people, at present, have one passion, and but one—

A Jove principium, Jovis omnia plena.

They care no more for the ministers I have mentioned, than they do for those sturdy royalists who for 60*l.* per annum stand behind his Majesty's carriage, arrayed in scarlet and gold. If the present ministers opposed the Court instead of flattering it, they would not command twenty votes.

Do not imagine by these observations that I am not loyal: without joining in the common cant of the best of kings, I respect the King most sincerely as a good man. His religion is better than the religion of Mr. Perceval, his old morality very superior to the old morality of Mr. Canning, and I am quite certain he has a safer understanding than both of them put together. Loyalty within the bounds of reason and moderation, is one of the greatest instruments of English happiness; but the love of the King may easily become more strong than the love of the kingdom, and we may lose sight of the public welfare in our exaggerated admiration of him who is appointed to reign only for its promotion and support. I detest Jacobinism; and if I am doomed to be a slave at all, I would rather be the slave of a king than a cobbler. God save the King, you say, warms your heart like the sound of a trumpet. I cannot make use of so violent a metaphor; but I am delighted to hear it, when it is the cry of genuine affection; I am delighted to hear it, when they hail not only the individual man, but the outward and living sign of all English blessings. These are noble feelings, and the heart of every good man must go with them; but God save the King, in these times, too often means God save my pension and my place, God give my sisters an allowance out of the privy purse,—make me clerk of the irons, let me survey the meltings, let me live upon the fruits of other men's industry, and fatten upon the plunder of the public.

What is it possible to say to such a man as the Gentleman of Hampstead, who really believes it feasible to convert the four million Irish Catholics to the Protestant religion, and considers this as the best remedy for the disturbed state of Ireland? It is not possible to answer such a man with arguments; we must come out against him with beads, and a cowl, and push him into an hermitage. It is really such trash, that it is an abuse of the privilege of reasoning to reply to it. Such a project is well worthy the statesman who would bring the French to reason by keeping them without rhubarb, and exhibit to mankind the awful spectacle of a nation deprived of neutral salts. This is not the dream of a wild apothecary indulging in his own opium; this is not the distempered fancy of a pounder of drugs, delirious from smallness of profits: but it is the sober, deliberate, and systematic scheme of a man to whom the public safety is entrusted, and whose appointment is considered by many as a masterpiece of political sagacity. What a sublime thought, that no purge can now be taken between the Weser and the Garonne; that the bustling pestle is still, the canorous mortar mute, and the bowels of mankind locked up for fourteen degrees of latitude! When, I should be curious to know, were all the powers of crudity and flatulence fully explained to his Majesty's ministers? At what period was this great plan of conquest and constipation fully developed? In whose mind was the idea of destroying the pride and the plasters of France first engendered? Without castor oil they might, for some months, to be sure, have carried on a lingering war; but can they do without bark? Will the people live under a government where antimonial powders cannot be procured? Will they bear the loss of mercury? "There's the rub." Depend upon it, the absence of the materia medica will soon bring them to their senses, and the cry of *Bourbon and bolus* burst forth from the Baltic to the Mediterranean.

You ask me for any precedent in our history where the oath of supremacy has been dispensed with. It was dispensed with to the Catholics of Canada in 1774. They are only required to take a simple oath of allegiance. The same, I believe, was the case in Corsica. The reason of such exemption was obvious; you could not possibly have retained either of these countries without it. And what did it signify, whether you retained them or not? In cases where you might have been foolish without peril, you were wise; when nonsense and bigotry threaten you with destruction, it is impossible to bring you back to the alphabet of justice and common sense. If men are to be fools, I would rather they were fools in little matters than in great; dulness turned up with temerity, is a livery all the worse for the facings; and the most tremendous of all things is the magnanimity of a dunce.

It is not by any means necessary, as you contend, to repeal the Test Act if you give relief to the Catholic; what the Catholics ask for is to be put on a footing with the Protestant Dissenters, which would be done by repealing that part of the law which compels them to take the oath of supremacy and to make the declaration against transubstantiation: they would then come into parliament as all other Dissenters are allowed to do, and the penal laws to which they were exposed for taking office would be suspended every year, as they have been for this half century past towards Protestant Dissenters. Perhaps, after all, this is the best method, —to continue the persecuting law, and to suspend it every year,— a method which, while it effectually destroys the persecution itself, leaves to the great mass of mankind the exquisite gratification of supposing that they are enjoying some advantage from which a particular class of their fellow-creatures are excluded. We manage the Corporation and Test Acts at present much in the same manner as if we were to persuade parish boys who had been in the habit of beating an ass to spare the animal, and beat the skin of an ass stuffed with straw; this would preserve the semblance of tormenting without the reality, and keep boy and beast in good humour.

How can you imagine that a provision for the Catholic clergy affects the 5th article of the Union? Surely I am preserving the

Protestant Church in Ireland, if I put it in a better condition than that in which it now is. A tithe proctor in Ireland collects his tithes with a blunderbuss, and carries his tenth hay-cock by storm, sword in hand: to give him equal value in a more pacific shape cannot, I should imagine, be considered as injurious to the Church of Ireland; and what right has that Church to complain, if parliament chooses to fix upon the empire the burthen of supporting a double ecclesiastical establishment? Are the revenues of the Irish Protestant clergy in the slightest degree injured by such provision? On the contrary, is it possible to confer a more serious benefit upon that Church, than by quieting and contenting those who are at work for its destruction?

It is impossible to think of the affairs of Ireland without being forcibly struck with the parallel of Hungary. Of her seven millions of inhabitants, one half were Protestants, Calvinists, and Lutherans, many of the Greek Church, and many Jews; such was the state of their religious dissensions, that Mahomet had often been called in to the aid of Calvin, and the crescent often glittered on the walls of Buda and of Presburg. At last, in 1791, during the most violent crisis of disturbance, a diet was called, and by a great majority of voices a decree was passed, which secured to all the contending sects the fullest and freest exercise of religious worship and education; ordained (let it be heard in Hampstead) that churches and chapels should be erected for all on the most perfectly equal terms; that the Protestants of both confessions should depend upon their spiritual superiors alone; liberated them from swearing by the usual oath, "the holy Virgin Mary, the saints, and chosen of God"; and then the decree adds, "that *public offices and honours, high or low, great or small, shall be given to natural-born Hungarians who deserve well of their country, and possess the other qualifications, let their religion be what it may.*" Such was the line of policy pursued in a diet consisting of four hundred members, in a state whose form of government approaches nearer to our own than any other, having a Roman Catholic establishment of great wealth and power, and under the influence of one of the most bigoted Catholic Courts in Europe. This measure has now the experience of eighteen years in its favour; it has undergone a trial of fourteen years of revolution such as the world never witnessed, and more than equal to a century less convulsed: What have been its effects? When the French advanced like a torrent within a few days' march of Vienna, the Hungarians rose in a mass; they formed what they called the sacred insurrection, to defend their sovereign, their rights, and liberties, now common to all; and the apprehension of their approach dictated to the reluctant Bonaparte the immediate signature of the treaty of *Leoben.* The Romish hierarchy of Hungary exists in all its former splendour and opulence; never has the slightest attempt been made to diminish it; and those revolutionary principles, to which so large a portion of civilised Europe has been sacrificed, have here failed in making the smallest successful inroad.

The whole history of this proceeding of the Hungarian Diet is so extraordinary, and such an admirable comment upon the Protestantism of Mr. Spencer Perceval, that I must compel you to read a few short extracts from the law itself:—"The Protestants of both confessions shall, in religious matters, depend upon their own spiritual superiors alone. The Protestants may likewise retain their trivial and grammar schools. The Church dues which the Protestants have hitherto paid to the Catholic parish priests, schoolmasters, or other such officers, either in money, productions, or labour, shall in future entirely cease, and after three months from the publishing of this law, be no more anywhere demanded. In the building or repairing of churches, parsonage-houses, and schools, the Protestants are not obliged to assist the Catholics with labour, nor the Catholics the Protestants. The pious foundations and donations of the Protestants which already exist, or which in future may be made for their churches, ministers, schools and students, hospitals, orphan-houses and poor, cannot be taken from them under any pretext, nor yet the care of them; but rather the unimpeded administration shall be entrusted to those from among them to whom it legally belongs, and those foundations which may have been taken from them under the last government, shall be returned to them without delay. All affairs of marriage of the Protestants are left to their own consistories; all landlords and masters of families, under the penalty of public persecution, are ordered not to prevent their subjects and servants, whether they be Catholic or Protestant, from the observance of the festivals and ceremonies of their religion," &c. &c. &c.—By what strange chances are mankind influenced! A little Catholic barrister of Vienna might have raised the cry of *No Protestantism,* and Hungary would have panted for the arrival of a French army as much as Ireland does at this moment; arms would have been searched for; Lutheran and Calvinist houses entered in the dead of the night; and the strength of Austria exhausted in guarding a country from which, under the present liberal system, she may expect, in a moment of danger, the most powerful aid: and let it be remembered, that this memorable example of political wisdom took place at a period when many great monarchies were yet unconquered in Europe; in a country where the two religious parties were equal in number; and where it is impossible to suppose indifference in the party which relinquished its exclusive privileges. Under all these circumstances, the measure was carried in the Hungarian Diet by a majority of 280 to 120. In a few weeks, we shall see every concession denied to the Catholics by a much larger majority of Protestants, at a moment when every other power is subjugated but ourselves, and in a country where the oppressed are four times as numerous as their oppressors. So much for the wisdom of our ancestors—so much for the nineteenth century—so much for the superiority of the English over all the nations of the Continent.

Are you not sensible, let me ask you, of the absurdity of trusting the lowest Catholics with offices correspondent to their situation in life, and of denying such privilege to the higher? A Catholic may serve in the militia, but a Catholic cannot come into Parliament; in the latter case you suspect combination, and in the former case you suspect no combination; you deliberately arm ten or twenty thousand of the lowest of the Catholic people;—and the moment you come to a class of men whose education, honour, and talents seem to render all mischief less probable, then you see the danger of employing a Catholic, and cling to your investigating tests and disabling laws. If you tell me you have enough of members of Parliament, and not enough of militia, without the Catholics, I beg leave to remind you that, by employing the physical force of any sect, at the same time when you leave them in a state of utter disaffection, you are not adding strength to your armies, but weakness and ruin.—If you want the vigour of their common people, you must not disgrace their nobility, and insult their priesthood.

I thought that the terror of the Pope had been confined to the limits of the nursery, and merely employed as a means to induce young master to enter into his small-clothes with greater speed, and to eat his breakfast with greater attention to decorum. For these purposes, the name of the Pope is admirable; but why push it beyond? Why not leave to Lord Hawkesbury all further enumeration of the Pope's powers? For a whole century, you have been exposed to the enmity of France, and your succession was disputed in two rebellions; what could the Pope do at the period when there was a serious struggle, whether England should be Protestant or Catholic, and when the issue was completely doubtful? Could the Pope induce the Irish to rise in 1715? Could he induce them to rise in 1745? You had no Catholic enemy when half this island was in arms; and what did the Pope attempt in the last rebellion in Ireland? But if he had as much power over the minds of the Irish as Mr. Wilberforce has over the mind of a young Methodist converted the preceding quarter, is this a reason why we are to disgust men, who may be acted upon in such a manner by a foreign power? or is it not an additional reason why we should raise up every barrier of affection and kindness against the mischief of foreign influence? But the true answer is, the mischief does not exist. Gog and Magog have produced as much influence upon human affairs as the Pope has done for this half century past; and by spoiling him of his possessions, and degrading him in the eyes of all Europe, Bonaparte has not taken quite the proper method of increasing his influence.

But why not a Catholic king, as well as a Catholic member of Parliament, or of the Cabinet?—Because it is probable that the one would be mischievous, and the other not. A Catholic king might struggle against the Protestantism of the country, and if the struggle were not successful, it would at least be dangerous; but the efforts of any other Catholic would be quite insignificant, and his hope of success so small, that it is quite improbable the effort would ever be made: my argument is, that in so Protestant a country as Great Britain, the character of her parliaments and her cabinet could not be changed by the few Catholics who would ever find their way to the one or the other. But the power of the Crown is immeasurably greater than the power which the Catholics could obtain from any other species of authority in the state; and it does not follow, because the lesser degree of power is innocent, that the greater should be so too. As for the stress you lay upon the danger of a Catholic chancellor, I have not the least hesitation in saying, that his appointment would not do a ten thousandth part of the mischief to the English Church that might be done by a Methodistical chancellor of the true Clapham breed; and I request to know, if it is really so very necessary that a chancellor should be of the religion of the Church of England, how many chancellors you have had within the last century who have been bred up in the Presbyterian religion?—And again, how many you have had who notoriously have been without any religion at all?

Why are you to suppose that eligibility and election are the same thing, and that all the cabinet *will* be Catholics whenever all the cabinet *may* be Catholics? You have a right, you say, to suppose an extreme case, and to argue upon it—so have I: and I will suppose that the hundred Irish members will one day come down in a body, and pass a law compelling the King to reside in Dublin. I will suppose that the Scotch members, by a similar stratagem, will lay England under a large contribution of meal and sulphur: no measure is without objection, if you sweep the whole horizon for danger; it is not sufficient to tell me of what may happen, but you must show me a rational probability that it will happen: after all, I might, contrary to my real opinion, admit all your dangers to exist; it is enough for me to contend, that all other dangers taken together are not equal to the danger of losing Ireland from disaffection and invasion.

I am astonished to see you, and many good and well-meaning clergymen beside you, painting the Catholics in such detestable colours; two thirds, at least, of Europe are Catholics,—they are Christians, though mistaken Christians; how can I possibly admit that any sect of Christians, and above all, that the oldest and the most numerous sect of Christians, are incapable of fulfilling the common duties and relations of life: though I do differ from them in many particulars, God forbid I should give such a handle to infidelity, and subscribe to such blasphemy against our common religion!

Do you think mankind never change their opinions without formally expressing and confessing that change? When you quote the decisions of ancient Catholic councils, are you prepared to defend all the decrees of English convocations and universities since the reign of Queen Elizabeth? I could soon make you sick of your uncandid industry against the Catholics, and bring you to allow that it is better to forget times past, and to judge and be judged by present opinions and present practice.

I must beg to be excused from explaining and refuting all the mistakes about the Catholics made by my Lord Redesdale; and I must do that nobleman the justice to say, that he has been treated with great disrespect. Could anything be more indecent than to make it a morning lounge in Dublin to call upon his Lordship, and to cram him with Arabian-night stories about the Catholics? Is this proper behaviour to the representative of Majesty, the child of Themis, and the keeper of the conscience in West Britain? Whoever reads the Letters of the Catholic Bishops, in the Appendix to Sir John Hippesly's very sensible book, will see to what an excess this practice must have been carried with the pleasing and Protestant nobleman whose name I have mentioned, and from thence I wish you to receive your answer about excommunication, and all the trash which is talked against the Catholics.

A sort of notion has, by some means or another, crept into the world, that difference of religion would render men unfit to perform together the offices of common and civil life: that Brother Wood and Brother Grose could not travel together the same circuit if they differed in creed, nor Cockell and Mingay be engaged in the same cause if Cockell was a Catholic and Mingay a Muggletonian. It is supposed that Huskisson and Sir Harry Englefield would squabble behind the Speaker's chair about the Council of Lateran, and many a turnpike bill miscarry by the sarcastical controversies of Mr. Hawkins Brown and Sir John Throckmorton upon the real presence. I wish I could see some of these symptoms of earnestness upon the subject of religion; but it really seems to me that, in the present state of society, men no more think about inquiring concerning each other's faith than they do concerning the colour of each other's skins. There may have been times in England when the quarter sessions would have been disturbed by theological polemics: but now, after a Catholic justice had once been seen on the bench and it had been clearly ascertained that he spoke English, had no tail, only a single row of teeth, and that he loved port wine,—after all the scandalous and infamous reports of his physical conformation had been clearly proved to be false,—he would be reckoned a jolly fellow, and very superior in flavour to a sly Presbyterian. Nothing, in fact, can be more uncandid and unphilosophical * than to say that a man has a tail, because you cannot agree with him upon religious subjects; it appears to be ludicrous: but I am convinced it has done infinite mischief to the Catholics, and made a very serious impression upon the minds of many gentlemen of large landed property.

In talking of the impossibility of Catholic and Protestant living together with equal privilege under the same government, do you forget the Cantons of Switzerland? You might have seen there a Protestant congregation going into a church which had just been quitted by a Catholic congregation; and I will venture to say that the Swiss Catholics were more bigoted to their religion than any people in the whole world. Did the kings of Prussia ever refuse to employ a Catholic? Would Frederick the Great have rejected an able man on this account? We have seen Prince Czartorinski, a Catholic secretary of state in Russia; in former times, a Greek patriarch and an apostolic vicar acted together in the most perfect harmony in Venice; and we have seen the Emperor of Germany in modern times entrusting the care of his person and the command of his guard to a Protestant Prince, Ferdinand of Wirtemberg. But what are all these

---

* *Vide* Lord Bacon, Locke, and Descartes.

things to Mr. Perceval? He has looked at human nature from the top of Hampstead Hill, and has not a thought beyond the little sphere of his own vision. "The snail," say the Hindoos, "sees nothing but his own shell, and thinks it the grandest palace in the universe."

I now take a final leave of this subject of Ireland; the only difficulty in discussing it is a want of resistance, a want of something difficult to unravel, and something dark to illumine. To agitate such a question is to beat the air with a club, and cut down gnats with a scimitar; it is a prostitution of industry, and a waste of strength. If a man say, I have a good place, and I do not choose to lose it, this mode of arguing upon the Catholic question I can well understand; but that any human being with an understanding two degrees elevated above that of an Anabaptist preacher, should conscientiously contend for the expediency and propriety of leaving the Irish Catholics in their present state, and of subjecting us to such tremendous peril in the present condition of the world, it is utterly out of my power to conceive. Such a measure as the Catholic question is entirely beyond the common game of politics; it is a measure in which all parties ought to acquiesce, in order to preserve the place where and the stake for which they play. If Ireland is gone, where are jobs? where are reversions? where is my brother, Lord Arden? where are my dear and near relations? The game is up, and the Speaker of the House of Commons will be sent as a present to the menagerie at Paris. We talk of waiting from particular considerations, as if centuries of joy and prosperity were before us: in the next ten years our fate must be decided; we shall know, long before that period, whether we can bear up against the miseries by which we are threatened, or not: and yet, in the very midst of our crisis, we are enjoined to abstain from the most certain means of increasing our strength, and advised to wait for the remedy till the disease is removed by death or health. And now, instead of the plain and manly policy of increasing unanimity at home, by equalising rights and privileges, what is the ignorant, arrogant, and wicked system which has been pursued? Such a career of madness and of folly was, I believe, never run in so short a period. The vigour of the ministry is like the vigour of a grave-digger,—the tomb becomes more ready and more wide for every effort which they make. There is nothing which it is worth while either to take or to retain, and a constant train of ruinous expeditions have been kept up. Every Englishman felt proud of the integrity of his country; the character of the country is lost for ever. It is of the utmost consequence to a commercial people at war with the greatest part of Europe, that there should be a free entry of

neutrals into the enemy's ports; the neutrals who carried our manufactures we have not only excluded, but we have compelled them to
declare war against us. It was our interest to make a good peace, or
convince our own people that it could not be obtained; we have not
made a peace, and we have convinced the people of nothing but of
the arrogance of the Foreign Secretary: and all this has taken place
in the short space of a year, because a King's Bench barrister and a
writer of epigrams, turned into Ministers of State, were determined to
show country gentlemen that the late administration had no vigour.
In the meantime commerce stands still, manufactures perish, Ireland
is more and more irritated, India is threatened, fresh taxes are accumulated upon the wretched people, the war is carried on without
it being possible to conceive any one single object which a rational
being can propose to himself by its continuation; and in the midst
of this unparalleled insanity we are told that the Continent is to be
reconquered by the want of rhubarb and plums.* A better spirit
than exists in the English people never existed in any people in the
world; it has been misdirected, and squandered upon party purposes
in the most degrading and scandalous manner; they have been led
to believe that they were benefiting the commerce of England by destroying the commerce of America, that they were defending their
Sovereign by perpetuating the bigoted oppression of their fellow-
subjects; their rulers and their guides have told them that they would
equal the vigour of France by equalling her atrocity; and they have
gone on wasting that opulence, patience, and courage, which, if husbanded by prudent and moderate counsels, might have proved the
salvation of mankind. The same policy of turning the good qualities
of Englishmen to their own destruction, which made Mr. Pitt omnipotent, continues his power to those who resemble him only in his
vices; advantage is taken of the loyalty of Englishmen to make them
meanly submissive; their piety is turned into persecution, their courage into useless and obstinate contention; they are plundered because
they are ready to pay, and soothed into asinine stupidity because they
are full of virtuous patience. If England must perish at last, so let it
be; that event is in the hands of God; we must dry up our tears and
submit. But that England should perish swindling and stealing; that
it should perish waging war against lazar houses, and hospitals; that
it should perish persecuting with monastic bigotry; that it should
calmly give itself up to be ruined by the flashy arrogance of one
man, and the narrow fanaticism of another; these events are within

---

* Even Allen Park (accustomed as he has always been to be delighted
by all administrations) says it is too bad; and Hall and Morris are said
to have actually blushed in one of the divisions.

the power of human beings, and I did not think that the magnanimity of Englishmen would ever stoop to such degradations.

Longum vale!

PETER PLYMLEY.

METHODISM

This book * is the production of an honest man, possessed of a fair
share of understanding. He cries out lustily (and not before it is
time) upon the increase of Methodism; proposes various remedies
for the diminution of this evil; and speaks his opinions with a freedom which does him great credit, and convinces us that he is a respectable man. The clergy are accused of not exerting themselves.
What temporal motive, Mr. Ingram asks, have they for exertion?
Would a curate, who had served thirty years upon a living in the
most exemplary manner, secure to himself by such a conduct, the
slightest right or title to promotion in the Church? What can you
expect of a whole profession, in which there is no more connection
between merit and reward than between merit and beauty, or merit
and strength? This is the substance of what Mr. Ingram says upon
this subject; and he speaks the truth. We regret, however, that this
gentleman has thought fit to use against the dissenters the exploded
clamour of Jacobinism; or that he deems it necessary to call in to
the aid of the Church the power of intolerant laws in spite of the
odious and impolitic tests to which the dissenters are still subjected.
We believe them to be very good subjects; and we have no doubt
but that any further attempt upon their religious liberties, without
reconciling them to the Church, would have a direct tendency to
render them disaffected to the State.

Mr. Ingram (whose book, by the bye, is very dull and tedious)
has fallen into the common mistake of supposing his readers to be
as well acquainted with his subject as he is himself; and has talked
a great deal about dissenters, without giving us any distinct notions
of the spirit which pervades these people—the objects they have in
view—or the degree of talent which is to be found among them. To
remedy this very capital defect, we shall endeavour to set before the
eyes of the reader, a complete section of the tabernacle; and to present him with a near view of those sectaries, who are at present at
work upon the destruction of the orthodox churches, and are des-

---

* Causes of the Increase of Methodism and Dissension. *By Robert Aklem
Ingram, B.D.*

tined hereafter, perhaps, to act as conspicuous a part in public affairs, as the children of Sion did in the time of Cromwell.

The sources from which we shall derive our extracts are the Evangelical and Methodist Magazines for the year 1807;—works which are said to be circulated to the amount of 18,000 or 20,000 each, every month; and which contain the sentiments of Arminian and Calvinistic Methodists, and of the *evangelical* clergymen of the Church of England. We shall use the general term of Methodism, to designate these three classes of fanatics, not troubling ourselves to point out the finer shades and nicer discriminations of lunacy, but treating them all as in one general conspiracy against common sense, and rational orthodox Christianity.

In reading these very curious productions, we seemed to be in a new world, and to have got among a set of beings, of whose existence we had hardly before entertained the slightest conception. It has been our good fortune to be acquainted with many truly religious persons, both in the Presbyterian and Episcopalian churches; and from their manly, rational, and serious characters, our conceptions of true practical piety have been formed. To these confined habits, and to our want of proper introductions among the children of light and grace, any degree of surprise is to be attributed, which may be excited by the publications before us; which, under opposite circumstances, would (we doubt not) have proved as great a source of instruction and delight to the Edinburgh reviewers, as they are to the most melodious votaries of the tabernacle.

It is not wantonly, or with the most distant intention of trifling upon serious subjects, that we call the attention of the public to these sorts of publications. Their circulation is so enormous, and so increasing,—they contain the opinions, and display the habits of so many human beings,—that they cannot but be objects of curiosity and importance. The common and the middling classes of people are the purchasers; and the subject is religion,—though not that religion certainly which is established by law, and encouraged by national provision. This may lead to unpleasant consequences, or it may not; but it carries with it a sort of aspect, which ought to insure to it serious attention and reflection.

It is impossible to arrive at any knowledge of a religious sect, by merely detailing the settled articles of their belief: it may be the fashion of such a sect to insist upon some articles very slightly; to bring forward others prominently; and to consider some portion of their formal creed as obsolete. As the knowledge of the jurisprudence of any country can never be obtained by the perusal of volumes which contain some statutes that are daily enforced, and others that have been silently antiquated: in the same manner, the practice, the preaching, and the writing of sects, are comments absolutely necessary to render the perusal of their creed of any degree of utility.

It is the practice, we believe, with the orthodox, both in the Scotch and the English churches, to insist very rarely, and very discreetly, upon the particular instances of the interference of Divine Providence. They do not contend that the world is governed only by general laws—that a Superintending Mind never interferes for particular purposes; but such purposes are represented to be of a nature very awful and sublime,—when a guilty people are to be destroyed —when an oppressed nation is to be lifted up, and some remarkable change introduced into the order and arrangement of the world. With this kind of theology we can have no quarrel; we bow to its truth; we are satisfied with the moderation which it exhibits; and we have no doubt of the salutary effect which it produces upon the human heart. Let us now come to those special cases of the interference of Providence as they are exhibited in the publications before us:

An interference with respect to the Rev. James Moody

"Mr. James Moody was descended from pious ancestors, who resided at Paisley:—his heart was devoted to music, dancing, and theatrical amusements: of the latter he was so fond, that he used to meet with some men of a similar cast to rehearse plays, and used to entertain a hope that he should make a figure upon the stage. To improve himself in music, he would rise very early, even in severely cold weather, and practise on the German flute: by his skill in music and singing, with his general powers of entertaining, he became a desirable companion: he would sometimes venture to profane the day of God, by turning it into a season of carnal pleasure, and would join in excursions on the water, to various parts of the vicinity of London. But the time was approaching, *when the Lord, who had designs of mercy for him, and for many others by his means, was about to stop him in his vain career of sin and folly.* There were two professing servants in the house where he lived; one of these was a porter, who, in brushing his clothes, would say, 'Master James, this will never do—you must be otherwise employed—you must be a minister of the gospel.' This worthy man, earnestly wishing his conversion, put into his hands that excellent book which God hath so much owned, *Alleine's Alarm to the Unconverted.*

"About this time it pleased God to visit him with a disorder in his eyes, occasioned, as it was thought, by his sitting up in the night to improve himself in drawing. The apprehension of losing his sight occasioned many serious reflections; his mind was impressed with the importance and necessity of seeking the salvation of his soul, and he was induced to attend the preaching of the gospel. The first sermon that he heard with a desire to profit was at Spa-fields Chapel; a place which he had formerly frequented, when it was a temple of vanity and dissipation. Strong convictions of sin fixed on his mind; and he continued to attend the preached word, particularly at Tottenham-Court Chapel. Every sermon increased his sorrow and grief that he had not earlier sought the Lord. It was a considerable time before he found comfort from the gospel. He has stood in the free part of the chapel hearing, with such emotion, that the tears have flowed from his eyes in torrents; and when he has returned home, he has continued a great part of the night on his knees, praying over what he had heard.

"The change effected by the power of the Holy Spirit on his heart now became visible to all. Nor did he halt between two opinions, as some persons do; he became at once a decided character, and gave up for ever all his vain pursuits and amusements; devoting himself with as much resolution and diligence to the service of God, as he had formerly done to folly." (*Evangelical Magazine,* page 194.)

An interference respecting cards

"A clergyman not far distant from the spot on which these lines were written, was spending an evening—not in his closet, wrestling with his Divine Master for the communication of that grace which is so peculiarly necessary for the faithful discharge of the ministerial function—not in his study, searching the sacred oracles of divine truth for materials wherewith to prepare for his public exercises and feed the flock under his care,—not in pastoral visits to that flock, to inquire into the state of their souls, and endeavour, by his pious and affectionate conversation, to conciliate their esteem, and promote their edification,—but at the *card table.*"— After stating that when it was his turn to ˙deal, he dropt down dead, "It is worthy of remark (says the writer), that within a very few years this was the third character in the neighbourhood which had been summoned from the card table to the bar of God." (*Evangelical Magazine,* page 262.)

Interference respecting swearing,—a bee the instrument

"A young man is stung by a bee, upon which he buffets the bees
with his hat, uttering at the same time the most dreadful oaths
and imprecations. In the midst of his fury, one of these little com-
batants stung him upon the tip of that unruly member (his tongue),
which was then employed in blaspheming his Maker. Thus can
the Lord engage one of the meanest of His creatures in reprov-
ing the bold transgressor who dares to take His name in vain."
(*Evangelical Magazine*, page 363.)

*Interference with respect to David Wright, who was cured of
atheism and scrofula by one sermon of Mr. Coles*

This case is too long to quote in the language and with the evi-
dences of the writers. The substance of it is what our title implies.
David Wright was a man with scrofulous legs and atheistical principles;—being with difficulty persuaded to hear one sermon from
Mr. Coles, he limped to the church in extreme pain, and arrived
there after great exertions;—during church time he was entirely converted, walked home with the greatest ease, and never after experienced the slightest return of scrofula or infidelity. (*Evangelical Magazine,* page 444.)

*The displeasure of Providence is expressed at Captain Scott's
going to preach in Mr. Romaine's Chapel*

The sign of this displeasure is a violent storm of thunder and
lightning just as he came into town. (*Evangelical Magazine,* page
537.)

*Interference with respect to an Innkeeper, who was destroyed
for having appointed a cock-fight at the very time that the
service was beginning at the Methodist Chapel*

" 'Never mind,' says the innkeeper, "I'll get a greater congregation
than the Methodist parson;—we'll have a cock-fight.' But what
is man! how insignificant his designs, how impotent his strength,
how ill-fated his plans, when opposed to that Being who is infinite
in wisdom, boundless in power, terrible in judgment, and who
frequently reverses, and suddenly renders abortive, the projects
of the wicked! A few days after the avowal of his intention, the
innkeeper sickened," &c. &c. And then the narrator goes on to

state, that his corpse was carried by the meeting-house "*on the day and exactly at the time*, the deceased had fixed for the cock-fight." (*Methodist Magazine*, page 126.)

In page 167 a father, mother, three sons, and a sister, are destroyed by particular interposition.

In page 222 a dancing-master is destroyed for irreligion,—another person for swearing at a cock-fight,—and a third for pretending to be deaf and dumb. These are called *recent and authentic accounts* of God's avenging providence.

So much for the miraculous interposition of Providence in cases where the Methodists are concerned. We shall now proceed to a few specimens of the energy of their religious feelings:

Mr. Roberts's feelings in the month of May, 1793

"But, all this time, my soul was stayed upon God: my desires increased, and my mind was kept in a sweet praying frame, a going out of myself, as it were, and taking shelter in him. Every breath I drew, ended in a prayer. I felt myself helpless as an infant, dependent upon God for all things. I was in a constant daily expectation of receiving all I wanted; and, on Friday, May 31st, under Mr. Rutherford's sermon, though entirely independent of it (for I could not give any account of what he had been preaching about), I was given to feel that God was waiting to be very gracious to me; the spirit of prayer and supplication was given me, and such an assurance that I was accepted in the Beloved, as I cannot describe, but which I shall never forget." (*Methodist Magazine*, page 35.)

Mrs. Elizabeth Price and her attendants hear sacred music on a sudden

"A few nights before her death, while some neighbours and her husband were sitting up with her, a sudden and joyful sound of music was heard by all present, *although some of them were carnal people;* at which time she thought she saw her crucified Saviour before her, speaking these words with power to her soul, 'Thy sins are forgiven thee, and I love thee freely.' After this she never doubted of her acceptance with God; and on Christmas day following was taken to celebrate the Redeemer's birth in the Paradise of God. MICHAEL COUSIN." (*Methodist Magazine*, page 137.)

T. L., a sailor on board the Stag frigate, has a special revelation from our Saviour

"October 26th, being the Lord's day, he had a remarkable manifestation of God's love to his soul. That blessed morning he was much grieved by hearing the wicked use profane language, when Jesus revealed himself to him, and impressed on his mind these words, 'Follow Me.' This was a precious day to him." (*Methodist Magazine*, page 140.)

The manner in which Mr. Thomas Cook was accustomed to accost S. B.

"Whenever he met me in the street, his salutation used to be 'Have you free and lively intercourse with God to-day? Are you giving your whole heart to God?' I have known him on such occasions speak in so pertinent a manner, that I have been astonished at his knowledge of my state. Meeting me one morning, he said, 'I have been praying for you; you have had a sore conflict, though all is well now.' At another time he asked, 'Have you been much exercised these few days, for I have been led to pray that you might especially have suffering grace?' " (*Methodist Magazine*, page 247.)

Mr. John Kestin on his death-bed

" 'Oh, my dear, I am now going to glory, happy, happy, happy. I am going to sing praises to God and the Lamb: I am going to Abraham, Isaac, and Jacob. I think I can see my Jesus without a glass between. I can, I feel I can, discern "my title clear to mansions in the skies." Come, Lord Jesus, come! why are thy chariot-wheels so long delaying?' " (*Evangelical Magazine,* page 124.)

The Rev. Mr. Mead's sorrow for his sins

"This wrought him up to temporary desperation; his inexpressible grief poured itself forth in groans: 'Oh that I had never sinned against God! I have a hell here upon earth, and there is a hell for me in eternity!' One Lord's day, very early in the   orning, he was awoke by a tempest of thunder and lightning; and, imagining it to be the end of the world, his agony was great, supposing the great day of divine wrath was come, and he unprepared; but happy to find it not so." (*Evangelical Magazine*, page 147.)

Similar case of Mr. John Robinson

"About two hours before he died, he was in great agony of body and mind: it appeared that the enemy was permitted to struggle with him; and being greatly agitated, he cried out, 'Ye powers of darkness begone!' This, however, did not last long: 'the prey was taken from the mighty, and the lawful captive delivered,' although he was not permitted to tell of his deliverance, but lay quite still and composed." (*Evangelical Magazine*, page 177.)

The Reverend William Tennant in a heavenly trance

" 'While I was conversing with my brother,' said he, 'on the state of my soul, and the fears I had entertained for my future welfare, I found myself in an instant in another state of existence, under the direction of a superior being, who ordered me to follow him. I was accordingly wafted along, I know not how, till I beheld at a distance an ineffable glory, the impression of which on my mind it is impossible to communicate to mortal man. I immediately reflected on my happy change; and thought, Well, blessed be God! I am safe at last, notwithstanding all my fears. I saw an innumerable host of happy beings surrounding the inexpressible glory in acts of adoration and joyous worship; but I did not see any bodily shape or representation in the glorious appearance. I heard things unutterable. I heard their songs and hallelujahs of thanksgiving and praise with unspeakable rapture. I felt joy unutterable, and full of glory. I then applied to my conductor and requested leave to join the happy throng.' " (*Evangelical Magazine*, page 251.)

The following we consider to be one of the most shocking histories we ever read. God only knows how many such scenes take place in the gloomy annals of Methodism:

"A young man of the name of S—— C——, grandson to a late eminent dissenting minister, and brought up by him, came to reside at K——g, about the year 1803. He attended at the Baptist place of worship, not only on the Lord's day, but frequently at the week-day lectures and prayer meetings. He was supposed by some to be seriously inclined; but his opinion of himself was, that he had never experienced that divine change, without which no man can be saved.

"However that might be, there is reason to believe he had been for some years under powerful convictions of his miserable condition as a sinner. In June, 1806, these convicitons were observed to increase, and that in a more than common degree. From that time he went into no company, but, when he was not at work, kept in his chamber, where he was employed in singing plaintive hymns, and bewailing his lost and perishing state.

"He had about him several religious people; but could not be induced to open his mind to them, or to impart to any one the cause of his distress. Whether this contributed to increase it or not, it did increase, till his health was greatly affected by it, and he was scarcely able to work at his business.

"While he was at meeting on Lord's day, Sepembter 14th, he was observed to labour under very great emotion of mind, especially when he heard the following words: 'Sinner, if you die without an interest in Christ, you will sink into the regions of eternal death.'

"On the Saturday evening following, he intimated to the mistress of the house where he lodged, that some awful judgment was about to come upon him; and as he should not be able to be at meeting next day, requested that an attendant might be procured to stay with him. She replied that she would herself stay at home, and wait upon him: which she did.

"On the Lord's day he was in great agony of mind. His mother was sent for, and some religious friends visited him; but all was of no avail. That night was a night dreadful beyond conception. The horror which he endured brought on all the symptoms of raging madness. He desired the attendants not to come near him, lest they should be burnt. He said that 'the bed curtains were in flames,—that he smelt the brimstone,—that devils were come to fetch him,—that there was no hope for him, for that he had sinned against light and conviction, and that he should certainly go to hell.' It was with difficulty he could be kept in bed.

"An apothecary being sent for, as soon as he entered the house, and heard his dreadful howlings, he inquired if he had not been bitten by a mad dog. His appearance, likewise, seemed to justify such a suspicion, his countenance resembling that of a wild beast more than that of a man.

"Though he had no feverish heat, yet his pulse beat above 150 in a minute. To abate the *mania,* a quantity of blood was taken from him, a blister was applied, his head was shaved, cold water was copiously poured over him, and fox-glove was administered. By these means his fury was abated; but his mental agony continued, and all the symptoms of madness, which his bodily strength, thus reduced, would allow, till the following Thursday. On that day he seemed to have recovered his reason, and to be calm in his mind. In the evening he sent for the apothecary, and wished

to speak with him by himself. The latter, on his coming, desired
every one to leave the room, and thus addressed him: 'C——,
have you not something on your mind?'—'Ay,' answered he, '*that
is it!*' He then acknowledged that, early in the month of June, he
had gone to a fair in the neighbourhood, in company with a number of wicked young men; that they drank at a public house together, till he was in a measure intoxicated; and that from thence
they went into other company, where he was criminally connected
with a harlot. 'I have been a miserable creature,' continued he,
'ever since; but during the last three days and three nights, I have
been in a state of desperation.' He intimated to the apothecary,
that he could not bear to tell this story to the minister: 'But,' said
he, 'do you inform him that I shall not die in despair: for light
has broken in upon me: I have been led to the great Sacrifice for
sin, and I now hope in him for salvation.'

"From this time his mental distress ceased, his countenance became placid, and his conversation, instead of being taken up as
before with fearful exclamations concerning devils and the wrath
to come, was now confined to the dying love of Jesus! The apothecary was of opinion, that if his strength had not been so much
exhausted, he would now have been in a state of religious transport. His nervous system, however, had received such a shock,
that his recovery was doubtful; and it seemed certain, that if he
did recover, he would sink into a state of idiocy. He survived this
interview but a few days." (*Evangelical Magazine,* pages 412,
413.)

A religious observer stands at a turnpike-gate on a Sunday, to
witness the profane crowd passing by; he sees a man driving very
clumsily in a gig; the inexperience of the driver provokes the following pious observations:

" 'What (I said to myself) if a single untoward circumstance should
happen! Should the horse take fright, or the wheel on either side
get entangled, or the gig upset,—in either case what can preserve
them? And should a morning so fair and promising bring on evil
before night,—should death on his pale horse appear,—what follows?' My mind shuddered at the images I had raised." (*Evangelical Magazine,* pages 558, 559.)

Miss Louisa Cook's rapturous state

"From this period she lived chiefly in retirement, either in reading the sacred volume on her knees, or in pouring out her soul in

prayer to God. While thus employed, she was not unfrequently indulged with visits from her gracious Lord; and sometimes felt herself to be surrounded, as it were, by his glorious presence. After her return to Bristol, her frame of mind became so heavenly, that she seemed often to be dissolved in the love of God her Saviour." (*Evangelical Magazine*, pages 576, 577.)

Objection to almanacks

"Let those who have been partial to such vain productions only read Isaiah xlvii. 13, and Daniel ii. 27; and they will there see what they are to be accounted of, and in what company they are to be found; and let them learn to despise their equivocal and artful insinuations, which are too frequently blended with profanity; for is it not profanity in them to attempt to palm their frauds upon mankind by Scripture quotations, which they seldom fail to do, especially Judges v. 20, and Job xxxviii, 31? neither of which teaches nor warrants any such practice. Had Baruch or Deborah consulted the stars? No such thing." (*Evangelical Magazine*, page 600.)

This energy of feeling will be found occasionally to meddle with and disturb the ordinary occupations and amusements of life, and to raise up little qualms of conscience, which, instead of exciting respect, border, we fear, somewhat too closely upon the ludicrous.

A Methodist footman

"A gentleman's servant, who has left a good place because he was ordered to deny his master when actually at home, wishes something on this subject may be introduced into this work, that persons who are in the habit of denying themselves in the above manner may be convinced of its evils." (*Evangelical Magazine*.)

Doubts if it is right to take any interest for money

"*Usury.*—Sir, I beg the favour of you to insert the following case of conscience. I frequently find in Scripture, that *Usury* is particularly condemned; and that it is represented as the character of a good man, that 'he hath not given forth upon usury, neither hath taken any increase,' Ezek. xviii, 8., &c. I wish, therefore, to know how such passages are to be understood; and whether the taking of interest for money, as is universally practised among us, can be reconciled with the word and will of God? Q." (*Evangelical Magazine,* page 74.)

Dancing ill-suited to a creature on trial for eternity

"If dancing be a waste of time; if the precious hours devoted to it may be better employed; if it be a species of trifling ill-suited to a creature on trial for eternity, and hastening towards it on the swift wings of time; if it be incompatible with genuine repentance, true faith in Christ, supreme love to God, and a state of entire devotedness to him,—then is dancing a practice utterly opposed to the whole spirit and temper of Christianity, and subversive of the best interest of the rising generation." (*Methodist Magazine,* pages 127, 128.)

The Methodists consider themselves as constituting a chosen and separate people, living in a land of atheists and voluptuaries. The expressions by which they designate their own sects, are the *dear people*—the *elect*—the *people of God.* The rest of mankind are *carnal people—the people of this world,* &c. &c. The children of Israel were not more separated, through the favour of God, from the Egyptians, than the Methodists are, in their own estimation, from the rest of mankind. We had hitherto supposed that the disciples of the Established churches in England and Scotland had been Christians; and that after baptism duly performed by the appointed minister, and participation in the customary worship of these two churches, Christianity was the religion of which they were to be considered as members. We see, however, in these publications, men of twenty or thirty years of age first called to a knowledge of Christ *under a sermon* by the Rev. Mr. Venn,—or first admitted into the church of Christ *under a sermon* by the Rev. Mr. Romaine. The apparent admission turns out to have been a mere mockery; and the pseudo-christian to have had no religion at all, till the business was really and effectually done under these sermons by Mr. Venn and Mr. Romaine.

An awful and general departure from the Christian faith in the Church of England

"A second volume of Mr. Cooper's sermons is before us, stamped with the same broad seal of truth and excellence as the former. Amidst the awful and general departure from the faith, as once delivered to the saints in the Church of England, and sealed by the blood of our Reformers, it is pleasing to observe that there is a remnant, according to the election of grace, who continue rising up to testify the gospel of the grace of God, and to call back their fellows to the consideration of the great and leading doctrines on which the Reformation was built, and the Church of England by law established. The author of these sermons, avoiding all matters of more doubtful disputation, avowedly attaches himself to the great fundamental truths; and on the two substantial pillars, the Jachin and Boaz of the living temple, erects his superstructure. 1. Justification by faith, without works, free and full, by grace alone, through the redemption which is in Jesus Christ, stands at the commencement of the first volume; and on its side rises in the beauty of holiness," &c. (*Evangelical Magazine,* page 79.)

Mr. Robinson called to the knowledge of Christ under Mr. Venn's sermon

"Mr. Robinson was called in early life to the knowledge of Christ, under a sermon at St. Dunstan's, by the late Rev. Mr. Venn, from Ezek. xxxvi. 25, 26; the remembrance of which greatly refreshed his soul upon his deathbed." (*Evangelical Magazine,* page 176.)

Christianity introduced into the parish of Launton near Bicester, in the year 1807

"A very general spirit of inquiry having appeared for some time in the village of Launton, near Bicester, some serious persons were excited to communicate to them the word of life." (*Evangelical Magazine,* page 380.)

We learn in page 128, *Methodist Magazine,* that twelve months had elapsed from the time of Mrs. Cocker's joining *the people of God,* before she obtained a clear sense of forgiveness.

A religious hoy sets off every week for Margate

"*Religious Passengers accommodated.—To the Editor.*—Sir, it afforded me considerable pleasure to see upon the cover of your Magazine for the present month, an advertisement, announcing the establishment of a packet, to sail weekly between Lon-

don and Margate, during the season, which appears to have
been set on foot for the accommodation of religious characters;
and in which 'no profane conversation is to be allowed.'

"To those among the followers of a crucified Redeemer, who
are in the habit of visiting the Isle of Thanet in the summer,
and who, for the sea air, or from other considerations, prefer
travelling by water, such a conveyance must certainly be a *de-
sideratum,* especially if they have experienced a mortification
similar to that of the writer, in the course of the last summer,
when shut up in a cabin with a mixed multitude, who spake almost all languages but that of Canaan. Totally unconnected with
the concern, and personally a stranger to the worthy owner, I
take the liberty of recommending this vessel to the notice of
my fellow-Christians; persuaded that they will think themselves
bound to patronise and encourage an undertaking that has the
honour of the dear Redeemer for its professed object. It ought
ever to be remembered, that every talent we possess, whether
large or small, is given us in trust to be laid out for God;—and
I have often thought that Christians act inconsistently with their
high profession, when they omit, even in their most common
and trivial expenditures, to give a decided preference to the
friends of their Lord. I do not, however, anticipate any such
ground of complaint in this instance, but rather believe, that
the religious world in general will cheerfully unite with me,
while I most cordially wish success to the Princess of Wales
Yacht, and pray that she may ever sail under the divine protection and blessing;—that the humble followers of Him who
spoke the storm into a calm, when crossing the lake of Genne-
sareth, may often feel their hearts glowing with sacred ardour
while in her cabins they enjoy sweet communion with their Lord
and with each other;—and that strangers, who may be provi-
dentially brought among them, may see so much of the beauty
and excellency of the religion of Jesus exemplified in their conduct and conversation, that they may be constrained to say, 'We
will go with you, for we perceive that God is with you.—Your
God shall be our God, and his people shall henceforth be our
chosen companions and associates.' I am, Mr. Editor, your
obliged friend and sister in the gospel, E. T." (*Evangelical
Magazine,* page 268.)

*A religious newspaper is announced in the Evangelical Maga-
zine for September.*—It is said of common newspapers, "that *they
are absorbed in temporal concerns, while the consideration of*

those which are eternal is postponed: the business of this life has superseded the claims of immortality; and the monarchs of the world have engrossed an attention which would have been more properly devoted to the Saviour of the universe." It is then stated, "that the columns of this paper (*The Instructor, price* 6*d.*) will be supplied by pious reflections; suitable comments to improve the dispensations of providence will be introduced; and the whole conducted with an eye to our spiritual, as well as temporal welfare. The work will contain the latest news up to four o'clock on the day of publication, together with the most recent religious occurrences. The prices of stock, and correct market-tables, will also be accurately detailed."—*Evangelical Magazine, September Advertisement.* The Eclectic Review is also understood to be carried on upon Methodistical principles.

Nothing can evince more strongly the influence which Methodism now exercises upon common life, and the fast hold it has got of the people, than the advertisements which are circulated every month in these very singular publications. On the cover of a single number, for example, we have the following:—

"Wanted, by Mr. Turner, shoemaker, a steady apprentice; he will have the privilege of attending the ministry of the gospel;— a premium expected, p. 3.—Wanted, a serious young woman, as a servant of all work, 3.—Wanted a man of serious character, who can shave, 3.—Wanted, a serious woman, to assist in a shop, 3.—A young person in the millinery line wishes to be in a serious family, 4.—Wants a place, a young man who has brewed in a serious family, 4.—Ditto, a young woman of evangelical principles, 4.—Wanted, an active serious shopman, 5.— To be sold, an eligible residence, with 60 acres of land; gospel preached in three places within half a mile, 5.—A single gentleman may be accommodated with lodging in a small serious family, 5.—To let, a genteel first floor in an airy situation near the Tabernacle, 6.—Wanted, a governess, of evangelical principles and corresponding character, 10."

The religious vessel we have before spoken of, is thus advertised:—

"The Princess of Wales Yacht, J. Chapman, W. Bourn, master, by divine permission, will leave Ralph's Quay every Friday, 11." &c. &c. (*Evangelical Magazine,* July.)

After the specimens we have given of these people, anything which is said of their activity can very easily be credited. The army and navy appear to be particular objects of their attention.

"*British Navy.*—It is with peculiar pleasure we insert the following extract of a letter from the pious chaplain of a man-of-war, to a gentleman at Gosport, intimating the power and grace of God manifested towards our brave seamen. '*Off Cadiz, Nov.* 26, 1806.—My dear friend—A fleet for England found us in the night, and is just going away. I have only time to tell you that the work of God seems to prosper. Many are under convictions;—some, I trust, are converted. I preach every night, and am obliged to have a private meeting afterwards with those who wish to speak about their souls. But my own health is suffering much, nor shall I probably be able long to bear it. The ship is like a tabernacle; and really there is much external reformation. Capt. ———— raises no objection. I have near a hundred hearers every night at six o'clock. How unworthy am I!—Pray for us.' " (*Evangelical Magazine,* page 84.)

The testimony of a profane officer to the worth of pious sailors

"Mr. Editor—In the mouth of two or three witnesses a truth shall be established. I recently met with a pleasing confirmation of a narrative stated some time since in your Magazine. I was surprised by a visit from an old acquaintance of mine, the other day, who is now an officer of rank in his Majesty's navy. In the course of conversation, I was shocked at the profane oaths that perpetually interrupted his sentences; and took an opportunity to express my regret that such language should be so common among so valuable a body of men. 'Sir,' said he, still interspersing many solemn imprecations, 'an officer cannot live at sea without swearing; not one of my men would mind a word without an oath; it is common sea-language. If we were not to swear, the rascals would take us for lubbers, stare in our faces, and leave us to do our commands ourselves. I never knew but one exception; and that was extraordinary. I declare, believe me 'tis true (suspecting that I might not credit it); there was a set of fellows called *Methodists,* on board the Victory, Lord Nelson's ship (to be sure he was rather a religious man himself!) and those men never wanted swearing at. The dogs were the best seamen on board. Every man *knew* his duty, and every man *did* his duty. They used to meet together and sing hymns; and nobody dared molest them. The commander would not have suffered it, had they attempted it. They were allowed a mess by themselves; and never mixed with the other men. I have often heard them singing away myself; and 'tis true, I assure you, but not one of them was either killed or wounded at the battle of Trafalgar, though they did their duty as well as any men. No, not one of the psalm-singing gentry was even hurt; and there the fellows are swimming away in the Bay of Biscay at this very time, singing like the d——. They are now under a new commander; but still are allowed the same privileges, and mess by themselves. These were the only fellows that I ever knew do their duty without swearing; and I will do them the justice to say they do it.' J. C." (*Evangelical Magazine,* pages 119, 120.)

These people are spread over the face of the whole earth in the shape of missionaries.—Upon the subject of missions we shall say very little or nothing at present, because we reserve it for another article in a subsequent Number. But we cannot help remarking the magnitude of the collections made in favour of the missionaries at the Methodistical chapels, when compared with the collections for any common object of charity in the orthodox churches and chapels.

"*Religious Tract Society.*—A most satisfactory Report was presented by the Committee; from which it appeared, that, since the commencement of the Institution in the year 1799, upwards of *Four Millions* of Religious Tracts have been issued under the auspices of the Society; and that considerably more than one fourth of that number have been sold during the last year." (*Evangelical Magazine,* page 284.)

These tracts are dropped in villages by the Methodists, and thus every chance for conversion afforded to the common people. There is a proposal in one of the numbers of the volumes before us, that travellers, for every pound they spent upon the road, should fling one shilling's worth of these tracts out of the chaise window;— thus taxing his pleasures at 5 *per cent.* for the purposes of doing good.

"Every Christian who expects the protection and blessing of God, ought to take with him as many *shillings' worth,* at least, of cheap Tracts to throw on the road and leave at inns, as he takes out pounds to expend on himself and family. This is really but a trifling sacrifice. It is a highly reasonable one; and one which God will accept." (*Evangelical Magazine,* page 405.)

It is part of their policy to have a great change of Ministers.

"Same day, the Rev. W. Haward, from Hoxton Academy, was ordained over the independent church at Rendham, Suffolk. Mr. Pickles, of Walpole, began with prayer and reading: Mr. Price, of Woodbridge, delivered the introductory discourse, and asked the questions; Mr. Dennant, of Halesworth, offered the ordination prayer; *Mr. Shufflebottom, of Bungay, gave the charge* from Acts, xx. 28; Mr. Vincent, of Deal, the general prayer; and Mr. Walford, of Yarmouth, preached to the people from 2 Phil. ii. 16." (*Evangelical Magazine,* page 429.)

"*Chapels opened.*—Hambledon, Bucks, Sept. 22.—Eighteen months ago, this parish was destitute of the gospel: the people have now one of the Rev. G. Collison's students, the Rev. Mr. Eastmead, settled among them. Mr. English of Wooburn, and Mr. Frey, preached on the occasion; and Mr. Jones, of London, Mr. Churchill, of Henley, Mr. Redford, of Windsor, and Mr. Barratt, now of Petersfield, prayed." (*Evangelical Magazine,* page 533.)

Methodism in his Majesty's ship Tonnant—a letter from the sailmaker.

"It is with great satisfaction that I can now inform you God has deigned, in a yet greater degree, to own the weak efforts of his servant to turn many from Satan to himself. Many are called here, as is plain to be seen, by their pensive looks and deep sighs. And if they would be obedient to the heavenly call instead of grieving the Spirit of grace, I dare say we should soon have near half the ship's company brought to God. I doubt not, however, but, as I have cast my bread upon the waters, it will be found after many days. Our 13 are now increased to upwards of 30. Surely the Lord delighteth not in the death of him that dieth." (*Methodist Magazine,* page 188.)

It appears also from page 193, *Methodist Magazine,* that the same principles prevail on board his Majesty's ship *Sea-horse,* 44 guns. And in one part of the *Evangelical Magazine* great hopes are entertained of the 25th regiment. We believe this is the number: but we quote this fact from memory.

We must remember, in addition to these trifling specimens of their active disposition, that the Methodists have found a powerful party in the House of Commons, who, by the neutrality which

they affect, and partly adhere to, are courted both by ministers
and opposition; that they have gained complete possession of the
India House; and under the pretence, or perhaps with the serious
intention, of educating young people for India, will take care to
introduce (as much as they dare without provoking attention)
their own particular tenets. In fact, one thing must always be
taken for granted respecting these people,—that, wherever they
gain a footing, or whatever be the institutions to which they give
birth, *proselytism will be their main object;* everything else is a
mere instrument—this is their principal aim. When every proselyte
is not only an addition to their temporal power, but when the act
of conversion which gains a vote, saves (as they suppose) a soul
from destruction,—it is quite needless to state, that every faculty
of their minds will be dedicated to this most important of all temporal and eternal concerns.

Their attack upon the Church is not merely confined to publications; it is generally understood that they have a very considerable
fund for the purchase of livings, to which of course, ministers of
their own profession are always presented.

Upon the foregoing facts, and upon the spirit evinced by these
extracts, we shall make a few comments.

1. It is obvious, that this description of Christians entertain
   very erroneous and dangerous notions of the present judgments of God. A belief that Providence interferes in all the
   little actions of our lives, refers all merit and demerit to bad
   and good fortune; and causes the successful man to be always considered as a good man, and the unhappy man as the
   object of divine vengeance. It furnishes ignorant and design-
   ing men with a power which is sure to be abused:—the cry
   of, a *judgment,* a *judgment,* it is always easy to make, but not
   easy to resist. It encourages the grossest superstitions; for if
   the Deity rewards and punishes on every slight occasion, it
   is quite impossible, but that such a helpless being as man
   will set himself at work to discover the will of Heaven in the
   appearances of outward nature, and to apply all the phe-
   nomena of thunder, lightning, wind, and every striking appearance to the regulation of his conduct; as the poor Methodist, when he rode into Piccadilly in a thunder storm, and
   imagined that all the uproar of the elements was a mere hint
   to him not to preach at Mr. Romaine's chapel. Hence a great
   deal of error, and a great deal of secret misery. This doctrine of a theocracy must necessarily place an excessive

power in the hands of the clergy; it applies so instantly and
so tremendously to men's hopes and fears, that it must make
the priest omnipotent over the people, as it always has done
where it has been established. It has a great tendency to
check human exertions, and to prevent the employment of
those secondary means of effecting an object which Providence has placed in our power. The doctrine of the immediate, and perpetual interference of Divine Providence, is
not true. If two men travel the same road, the one to rob,
the other to relieve a fellow-creature who is starving; will
any but the most fanatic contend, that they do not both
run the same chance of falling over a stone, and breaking
their legs? and is not matter of fact, that the robber often
returns safe, and the just man sustains the injury? Have not
the soundest divines of both churches always urged this unequal distribution of good and evil, in the present state, as
one of the strongest natural arguments for a future state
of retribution? Have not they contended, and well, and admirably contended, that the supposition of such a state is
absolutely necessary to our notion of the justice of God,—
absolutely necessary to restore order to that moral confusion
which we all observe and deplore in the present world? The
man who places religion upon a false basis is the greatest
enemy to religion. If victory is always to the just and good,—
how is the fortune of impious conquerors to be accounted
for? Why do they erect dynasties, and found families which
last for centuries? The reflecting mind whom you have instructed in this manner, and for present effect only, naturally
comes upon you hereafter with difficulties of this sort; he
finds he has been deceived; and you will soon discover that,
in breeding up a fanatic, you have unwittingly laid the foundation of an atheist. The honest and the orthodox method is
to prepare young people for the world, as it actually exists;
to tell them that they will often find vice perfectly successful,
virtue exposed to a long train of afflictions; that they must
bear this patiently, and look to another world for its rectifi-
cation.

2. The second doctrine which it is necessary to notice among
the Methodists is, the doctrine of inward impulse and emo-
tions, which, it is quite plain, must lead, if universally insisted
upon, and preached among the common people, to every
species of folly and enormity. When a human being believes
that his internal feelings are the monitions of God, and that

these monitions must govern his conduct; and when a great
stress is purposely laid upon these inward feelings in all the
discourses from the pulpit; it is, of course, impossible to say
to what a pitch of extravagance mankind may not be carried,
under the influence of such dangerous doctrines.

3. The Methodists hate pleasure and amusements; no theatre,
no cards, no dancing, no punchinello, no dancing dogs, no
blind fiddlers;—all the amusements of the rich and of the poor
must disappear, wherever these gloomy people get a footing. It is not the abuse of pleasure which they attack, but the
interspersion of pleasure, however much it is guarded by
good sense and moderation;—it is not only wicked to hear
the licentious plays of Congreve, but wicked to hear *Henry
the Fifth,* or *The School for Scandal;*—it is not only dissi-
pated to run about to all the parties in London and Edinburgh,—but dancing is not *fit for a being who is preparing
himself for Eternity. Ennui,* wretchedness, melancholy,
groans and sighs, are the offerings which these unhappy men
make to a Deity who has covered the earth with gay colours,
and scented it with rich perfumes; and shown us, by the
plan and order of his works, that he has given to man something better than a bare existence, and scattered over his
creation a thousand superfluous joys which are totally unnecessary to the mere support of life.

4. The Methodists lay very little stress upon practical righteousness. They do not say to their people, Do not be deceitful;
do not be idle; get rid of your bad passions; or at least (if
they do say these things) they say them very seldom. Not
that they preach faith without works; for if they told the
people that they might rob and murder with impunity, the
civil magistrate must be compelled to interfere with such
doctrine:—but they say a great deal about faith, and very
little about works. What are commonly called the mysterious parts of our religion are brought into the fore-ground,
much more than the doctrines which lead to practice;—and
this among the lowest of the community.

The Methodists have hitherto been accused of dissenting
from the Church of England. This, as far as relates to mere
subscription to articles, is not true; but they differ in their
choice of the articles upon which they dilate and expand,
and to which they appear to give a preference, from the
stress which they place upon them. There is nothing heretical
in saying that God *sometimes* intervenes with his special

providence; but these people differ from the Established
Church, in the degree in which they insist upon this doctrine.
In the hands of a man of sense and education, it is a safe
doctrine; in the management of the Methodists, we have
seen how ridiculous and degrading it becomes. In the same
manner, a clergyman of the Church of England would not
do his duty if he did not insist upon the necessity of faith
as well as of good works; but as he believes that it is much
more easy to give credit to doctrines than to live well, he
labours most in those points where human nature is the *most*
liable to prove defective. Because he does so, he is accused
of giving up the articles of his faith, by men who have their
partialities also in doctrine; but partialities, not founded upon
the same sound discretion, and knowledge of human nature.

5. The Methodists are always desirous of making men more
   religious than it is possible, from the constitution of human
   nature, to make them. If they could succeed as much as they
   wish to succeed, there would be at once an end of delving
   and spinning, and of every exertion of human industry. Men
   must eat, and drink, and work; and if you wish to fix upon
   them high and elevated notions, as the *ordinary* furniture of
   their minds, you do these two things;—you drive men of
   warm temperaments mad,—and you introduce, in the rest
   of the world, a low and shocking familiarity with words and
   images, which every real friend to religion would wish to
   keep sacred. *The friends of the dear Redeemer who are in
   the habit of visiting the Isle of Thanet*—(as in the extract
   we have quoted)—Is it possibile that this mixture of the
   most awful, with the most familiar images, so common
   among Methodists now, and with the enthusiasts in the time
   of Cromwell, must not, in the end, divest religion of all the
   deep and solemn impressions which it is calculated to produce? In a man of common imagination (as we have before
   observed), the terror, and the feeling which it first excited,
   must necessarily be soon separated: but, where the fervour
   of impression is long preserved, piety ends in Bedlam. Accordingly, there is not a madhouse in England, where a considerable part of the patients have not been driven to insanity by the extravagance of these people. We cannot enter
   such places without seeing a number of honest artisans,
   covered with blankets, and calling themselves angels and
   apostles, who, if they had remained contented with the instruction of men of learning and education, would still have

been sound masters of their own trade, sober Christians, and useful members of society.

6. It is impossible not to observe how directly all the doctrine of the Methodists is calculated to gain power among the poor and ignorant. To say, that the Deity governs this world by general rules, and that we must wait for another and a final scene of existence, before vice meets with its merited punishment, and virtue with its merited reward; to preach this up daily would not add a single votary to the Tabernacle, nor sell a number of the Methodistical Magazine:—but, to publish an account of a man who was cured of scrofula by a single sermon—of Providence destroying the innkeeper at Garstang for appointing a cock-fight near the Tabernacle;—this promptness of judgment and immediate execution is so much like human justice, and so much better adapted to vulgar capacities, that the system is at once admitted, as soon as any one can be found who is impudent or ignorant enough to teach it; and, being once admitted, it produces too strong an effect upon the passions to be easily relinquished. The case is the same with the doctrine of inward impulse, or, as they term it, experience. If you preach up to ploughmen and artisans, that every singular feeling which comes across them is a visitation of the Divine Spirit—can there be any difficulty, *under* the influence of this nonsense, in converting these simple creatures into active and mysterious fools, and making them your slaves for life? It is not possible to raise up any dangerous enthusiasm, by telling men to be just, and good, and charitable; but keep this part of Christianity out of sight—and talk long and enthusiastically, before ignorant people, of the mysteries of our religion, and you will not fail to attract a crowd of followers:—verily the Tabernacle loveth not that which is simple, intelligible, and leadeth to good sound practice.

Having endeavoured to point out the spirit which pervades these people, we shall say a few words upon the causes, the effects, and the cure of this calamity.—The fanaticism so prevalent in the present day, is one of those evils from which society is never wholly exempt, but which bursts out at different periods, with peculiar violence, and sometimes overwhelms everything in its course. The last eruption took place about a century and a half ago, and destroyed both Church and Throne with its tremendous force. Though irresistible, it was short: enthusiasm spent its force—the usual reaction took place; and England was deluged with ribaldry and indecency, because it had been worried with fanatical restrictions. By degrees, however, it was found out, that orthodoxy and loyalty might be secured by other methods than licentious conduct and immodest conversation. The public morals improved; and there appeared as much good sense and moderation upon the subject of religion as ever can be expected from mankind in large masses. Still, however, the mischief which the Puritans had done was not forgotten; a general suspicion prevailed of the dangers of religious enthusiasm; and the fanatical preacher wanted his accustomed power among a people recently recovered from a religious war, and guarded by songs, proverbs, popular stories, and the general tide of humour and opinon, against all excesses of that nature. About the middle of the last century, however, the character of the genuine fanatic was a good deal forgotten; and the memory of the civil wars worn away; the field was clear for extravagance in piety; and causes, which must always produce an immense influence upon the mind of man, were left to their own unimpeded operations. Religion is so noble and powerful a consideration—it is so buoyant and so insubmergible—that it may be made, by fanatics, to carry with it any degree of error and of perilous absurdity. In this instance Messrs. Whitfield and Wesley happened to begin. They were men of considerable talents; they observed the common decorums of life, they did not run naked into the streets, or pretend to the prophetical character;—and therefore they were not committed to Newgate. They preached with great energy to weak people; who first stared—then listened—then believed—then felt the inward feeling of grace, and became as foolish as their teachers could possibly wish them to be:—in short, folly ran its ancient course,—and human nature evinced itself to be what it always has been under similar circumstances. The great and permanent cause, therefore, of the increase of Methodism, is the cause which has given birth to fanaticism in all ages,—*the facility of mingling human errors with the fundamental truths of religion.* The formerly imperfect residence of the clergy may, perhaps, in some trifling degree, have aided this source of Methodism. But unless a man of education, and a gentleman, could stoop to such disingenuous arts as the Methodist preachers,—unless he hears heavenly music all of a sudden, and enjoys *sweet experiences,*—it is quite impossible that he can contend against such artists as these. More active than they are at present the clergy might perhaps be; but the calmness and moderation of an Establishment can never possibly be a match for sectarian activity.—If the common people are *ennui'd* with the fine acting of Mrs. Siddons, they go to Sadler's Wells. The subject is too serious for ludicrous comparisons:— but the Tabernacle really is to the Church, what Sadler's Wells is to the Drama. There, popularity is gained by vaulting and tumbling,—by low arts, which the regular clergy are not too idle to have recourse to, but too dignified:—their institutions are chaste and severe,—they endeavour to do that which, *upon the whole, and for a great number of years,* will be found to be the most admirable and the most useful: it is no part of their plan to descend to small artifices, for the sake of present popularity and effect. The religion of the common people under the government of the Church may remain as it is for ever;—enthusiasm must be progressive, or it will expire.

It is probable that the dreadful scenes which have lately been acted in the world, and the dangers to which we are exposed, have increased the numbers of the Methodists. To what degree will Methodism extend in this country?—This question is not easy to answer. That it has rapidly increased within these few years, we have no manner of doubt; and we confess we cannot see what is likely to impede its progress. The party which it has formed in the Legislature; and the artful neutrality with which they give respectability to their small number,—the talents of some of this party, and the unimpeached excellence of their characters, all make it probable that fanaticism will increase rather than diminish. The Methodists have made an alarming inroad into the Church, and they are attacking the army and navy. The principality of Wales, and the East India Company they have already acquired. All mines and subterraneous places belong to them; they creep into hospitals and small schools, and so work their way upwards. It is the custom of the religious neutrals to beg all the little livings, particularly in the north of England, from the minister for the time being; and from these fixed points they make incursions upon the happiness and common sense of the vicinage. We most sincerely deprecate such an event; but it will excite in us no manner of surprise, if a period arrives when the churches of the sober and orthodox part of the English clergy are completely deserted by the middling and lower classes of the community. We do not prophesy any such event; but we contend that it is not impossible, —hardly improbable. If such, in future, should be the situation of this country, it is impossible to say what political animosities may not be ingrafted upon this marked and dangerous division of mankind into the *godly* and the *ungodly.* At all events, we are quite sure that happiness will be destroyed, reason degraded, sound

religion banished from the world; and that when fanaticism becomes too foolish and too prurient to be endured (as is at last
sure to be the case), it will be succeeded by a long period of the
grossest immorality, atheism, and debauchery.

We are not sure that this evil admits of any cure,—or of any
considerable palliation. We most sincerely hope that the government of this country will never be guilty of such indiscretion as to
tamper with the Toleration Act, or to attempt to put down these
follies by the intervention of the law. If experience has taught us
anything, it is the absurdity of controlling men's notions of eternity
by acts of Parliament. Something may perhaps be done, in the way
of ridicule, towards turning the popular opinion. It may be as
well to extend the privileges of the dissenters to the members of
the Church of England; for, as the law now stands, any man who
dissents from the Established Church may open a place of worship
where he pleases. No orthodox clergyman can do so, without the
consent of the parson of the parish,—who always refuses, because
he does not choose to have his monopoly disturbed; and refuses,
in parishes where there are not accommodations for one half of
the persons who wish to frequent the Church of England, and in
instances where he knows that the chapels from which he excludes
the established worship will be immediately occupied by sectaries.
It may be as well to encourage in the early education of the clergy,
as Mr. Ingram recommends, a better and more animated method
of preaching; and it may be necessary, hereafter, if the evil gets to
a great height, to relax the articles of the English Church, and to
admit a greater variety of Christians within the pale. The greatest
and best of all remedies, is perhaps the education of the poor;—
we are astonished, that the Established Church in England is not
awake to this mean of arresting the progress of Methodism. Of
course, none of these things will be done; nor is it *clear,* if they
were done, that they would do *much* good. Whatever happens, we
are for common sense and orthodoxy. Insolence, servile politics,
and the spirit of persecution, we condemn and attack, whenever
we observe them; but to the learning, the moderation, and the
rational piety of the Establishment, we most earnestly wish a decided victory over the nonsense, the melancholy, and the madness
of the Tabernacle.*

God send that our wishes be not in vain.

---

* There is one circumstance to which we have neglected to advert in the
proper place,—the dreadful pillage of the earnings of the poor which is
made by the Methodists. A case is mentioned in one of the numbers of
these two magazines for 1807, of a poor man with a family, earning only
twenty-eight shillings a week, *who has made two donations of ten guineas
each to the missionary fund!*

PERSECUTING BISHOPS

It is a great point in any question to clear away encumbrances, and to make a naked circle about the object in dispute, so that there may be a clear view of it on every side. In pursuance of this disencumbering process, we shall first acquit the Bishop * of all wrong intentions. He has a very bad opinion of the practical effects of high Calvinistic doctrines upon the common people; and he thinks it his duty to exclude those clergymen who profess them from his diocese. There is no moral wrong in this. He has accordingly devised no fewer than *eighty-seven* interrogatories, by which he thinks he can detect the smallest taint of Calvinism that may lurk in the creed of the candidate; and in this also, whatever we may think of his reasoning, we suppose his purpose to be blameless. He believes, finally, that he has legally the power so to interrogate and exclude; and in this, perhaps, he is not mistaken. His intentions, then, are good, and his conduct, perhaps, not amenable to the law. All this we admit in his favour: but against him we must maintain, that his conduct upon the points in dispute has been singularly injudicious, extremely harsh, and, in its effects (though not in its intentions), very oppressive and vexatious to the Clergy.

We have no sort of intention to avail ourselves of an anonymous publication to say unkind, uncivil, or disrespectful things to

* (1) *An Appeal to the Legislature and Public; or, the Legality of the Eighty-Seven Questions proposed by Dr. Herbert Marsh, the Bishop of Peterborough, to Candidates for Holy Orders, and for Licences, within that diocese, considered.* 2nd Edition. London, Seeley, 1821. (2) *A Speech, delivered in the House of Lords, on Friday, June 7, 1822, by Herbert, Lord Bishop of Peterborough, on the Presentation of a Petition against his Examination Questions; with Explanatory Notes, a Supplement, and a copy of the Questions.* London, Rivington, 1822. (3) *The Wrongs of the Clergy of the Diocese of Peterborough stated and illustrated.* By the Rev. T. S. Grimshawe, M.A., Rector of Burton, Northamptonshire; and Vicar of Biddenham, Bedfordshire. London, Seeley, 1822. (4) *Episcopal Innovation; or, the Test of Modern Orthodoxy, in Eighty-Seven Questions, imposed, as Articles of Faith, upon Candidates for Licences and for Holy Orders, in the Diocese of Peterborough; with a Distinct Answer to each Question, and General Reflections relative to their Illegal Structure and Pernicious Tendency.* London, Seeley, 1820. (5) *Official Correspondence between the Right Reverend Herbert, Lord Bishop of Peterborough, and the Rev. John Green, respecting his Nomination, to the Curacy of Blatherwycke, in the Diocese of Peterborough, and County of Northampton: Also, between His Grace Charles, Lord Archbishop of Canterbury, and the Rev. Henry William Neville, M.A., Rector of Blatherwycke, and of Cottesmore in the County of Rutland.* 1821.

a man of rank, learning, and character—we hope to be guilty of
no such impropriety; but we cannot believe we are doing wrong in
ranging ourselves on the weaker side, in the cause of propriety and
justice. The Mitre protects its wearer from indignity; but it does
not secure impunity.

It is a strong presumption that a man is wrong, when all his
friends, whose habits naturally lead them to coincide with him,
think him wrong. If a man were to indulge in taking medicine till
the apothecary, the druggist, and the physician, all called upon
him to abandon his philocathartic propensities—if he were to
gratify his convivial habits till the landlord demurred, and the
waiter shook his head—we should naturally imagine that advice so
wholly disinterested was not given before it was wanted, and that
it merited some little attention and respect. Now, though the Bench
of Bishops certainly love power, and love the Church, as well
as the Bishop of Peterborough, yet not one defended him—not
one rose to say, "I have done, or I would do, the same thing."
It was impossible to be present at the last debate on this question,
without perceiving that his Lordship stood alone—and this in a
very gregarious profession, that habitually combines and butts
against an opponent with a very extended front. If a lawyer is
wounded, the rest of the profession pursue him, and put him to
death. If a churchman is hurt, the others gather round for his protection, stamp with their feet, push with their horns, and demolish
the dissenter who did the mischief.

The Bishop has at least done a very unusual thing in his Eighty-
seven Questions. The two Archbishops, and we believe every other
Bishop, and all the Irish hierarchy, admit curates into their dioceses without any such precautions. The necessity of such severe
and scrupulous inquisition, in short, has been apparent to nobody
but the Bishop of Peterborough; and the authorities by which he
seeks to justify it are anything but satisfactory. His Lordship
states, that forty years ago he was himself examined by written
interrogatories, and that he is not the only Bishop who has done it;
but he mentions no names; and it was hardly worth while to state
such extremely slight precedents for so strong a deviation from
the common practice of the Church.

The Bishop who rejects a curate upon the Eighty-seven Questions is necessarily and inevitably opposed to the Bishop who ordained him. The Bishop of Gloucester ordains a young man of
twenty-three years of age, not thinking it necessary to put to him
these interrogatories, or putting them, perhaps, and approving of
answers diametrically opposite to those that are required by the

Bishop of Peterborough. The young clergyman then comes to the last-mentioned Bishop; and the Bishop, after *putting him to the Question,* says, "You are unfit for a clergyman,"—though, ten days before, the Bishop of Gloucester has made him one! It is bad enough for ladies to pull caps, but still worse for Bishops to pull mitres. Nothing can be more mischievous or indecent than such scenes; and no man of common prudence, or knowledge of the world, but must see that they ought immediately to be put a stop to. If a man is a captain in the army in one part of England, he is a captain in all. The general who commands north of the Tweed does not say, "You shall never appear in my district, or exercise the functions of an officer, if you do not answer eighty-seven questions on the art of war, according to my notions." The same officer who commands a ship of the line in the Mediterranean, is considered as equal to the same office in the North Seas. The sixth commandment is suspended, by one medical diploma, from the north of England to the south. But, by this new system of interrogation, a man may be admitted into orders at Barnet, rejected at Stevenage, readmitted at Brogden, kicked out as a Calvinist at Witham Common, and hailed as an ardent Arminian on his arrival at York.

It matters nothing to say that sacred things must not be compared with profane. In their importance, we allow, they cannot; but in their order and discipline they may be so far compared as to say, that the discrepancy and contention which would be disgraceful and pernicious in worldly affairs, should, in common prudence be avoided in the affairs of religion. Mr. Greenough has made a map of England, according to its geological varieties;— blue for the chalk, green for the clay, red for the sand, and so forth. Under this system of Bishop Marsh, we must petition for the assistance of the geologist in the fabrication of an ecclesiastical map. All the Arminian districts must be purple. Green for one theological extremity—sky-blue for another—as many colours as there are Bishops—as many shades of these colours as there are Archdeacons—a tailor's pattern card—the picture of vanity, fashion, and caprice.

The Bishop seems surprised at the resistance he meets with; and yet, to what purpose has he read ecclesiastical history, if he expect to meet with anything but the most determined opposition? Does he think that every sturdy supralapsarian bullock whom he tries to sacrifice to the Genius of Orthodoxy, will not kick, and push, and toss; that he will not, if he *can,* shake the axe from his neck, and hurl his mitred butcher into the air? His Lordship has undertaken a task of which he little knows the labour or the end. We know these men fully as well as the Bishop; he has not a chance of success against them. If one motion in Parliament will not do, they will have twenty. They will ravage, roar, and rush, till the very chaplains, and the Masters and Misses Peterborough request his Lordship to desist. He is raising up a storm in the English Church of which he has not the slightest conception; and which will end, as it ought to end, in his Lordship's disgrace and defeat.

The longer we live, the more we are convinced of the justice of the old saying, that an *ounce of mother wit is worth a pound of clergy;* that discretion, gentle manners, common sense, and good nature, are, in men of high ecclesiastical station, of far greater importance than the greatest skill in discriminating between sublapsarian and supralapsarian doctrines. Bishop Marsh should remember, that all men wearing the mitre work by character, as well as doctrine; that a tender regard to men's rights and feelings, a desire to avoid sacred squabbles, a fondness for quiet, and an ardent wish to make everybody happy, would be of far more value to the Church of England than all his learning and vigilance of inquisition. The Irish Tithes will probably fall next session of Parliament; the common people are regularly receding from the Church of England—baptizing, burying, and confirming for themselves. Under such circumstances, what would the worst enemy of the English Church require?—a bitter, bustling, theological Bishop, accused by his clergy of tyranny and oppression—the cause of daily petitions and daily debates in the House of Commons—the idoneous vehicle of abuse against the Establishment—a stalking-horse to bad men for the introduction of revolutionary opinions, mischievous ridicule, and irreligious feelings. Such will be the advantages which Bishop Marsh will secure for the English Establishment in the ensuing session. It is inconceivable how such a prelate shakes all the upper works of the Church, and ripens it for dissolution and decay. Six such Bishops, multiplied by eighty-seven, and working with five hundred and twenty-two questions, would fetch everything to the ground in less than six months. But what if it pleased Divine Providence to afflict every prelate with the spirit of putting eighty-seven queries, and the two Archbishops with the spirit of putting twice as many, and the Bishop of Sodor and Man with the spirit of putting only forty-three queries?—there would then be a grand total of two thousand three hundred and thirty-five interrogations flying about the English Church; and sorely vexed would the land be with Question and Answer.

We will suppose this learned Prelate, without meanness or un-due regard to his worldly interests, to feel that fair desire of rising in his profession, which any man, in any profession, may feel with-out disgrace. Does he forget that his character in the ministerial circles will soon become that of a violent impracticable man—whom it is impossible to place in the highest situations—who has been trusted with too much already, and must be trusted with no more? Ministers have something else to do with their time, and with the time of Parliament, than to waste them in debating squab-bles between Bishops and their Clergy. They naturally wish, and, on the whole, reasonably expect, that everything should go on silently and quietly in the Church. They have no objection to a learned Bishop; but they deprecate one atom more of learning than is compatible with moderation, good sense, and the soundest discretion. It must be the grossest ignorance of the world to sup-pose that the Cabinet has any pleasure in watching Calvinists.

The Bishop not only puts the questions, but he actually assigns the limits within which they are to be answered. Spaces are left in the paper of interrogations, to which limits the answer is to be confined;—two inches to original sin: an inch and a half to justifi-cation; three quarters to predestination; and to free will only a quarter of an inch. But if his Lordship gives them an inch, they will take an ell. His Lordship is himself a theological writer, and by no means remarkable for his conciseness. To deny space to his brother theologians, who are writing on the most difficult subjects, not from choice, but necessity; not for fame, but for bread; and to award rejection as the penalty of prolixity, does appear to us no slight deviation from Christian gentleness. The tyranny of calling for such short answers is very strikingly pointed out in a letter from Mr. Thurtell to the Bishop of Peterborough; the style of which pleads, we think, very powerfully in favour of the writer.

"Beccles, Suffolk, August 28*th,* 1821.

"My Lord,

"I ought, in the first place, to apologise for delaying so long to answer your Lordship's letter: but the difficulty in which I was involved, by receiving another copy of your Lordship's Questions, with positive directions to give short answers, may be sufficient to account for that delay.

"It is my sincere desire to meet your Lordship's wishes, and to obey your Lordship's directions in every particular; and I would therefore immediately have returned answers, without any 'restrictions or modifications,' to the Questions which your

Lordship has thought fit to send me, if, in so doing, I could have discharged the obligations of my conscience, by showing what my opinions really are. But it appears to me, that the Questions proposed to me by your Lordship are so constructed as to elicit only two sets of opinions; and that, by answering them in so concise a manner, I should be representing myself to your Lordship as one who believes in either of two particular creeds, to neither of which I do *really* subscribe. For instance, to answer Question I. chap. ii. in the manner your Lordship desires, I am reduced to the alternative of declaring, either that 'mankind are a mass of *mere* corruption,' which expresses more than I intend, or of leaving room for the inference, that they are only *partially* corrupt, which is opposed to the plainest declarations of the Homilies; such as these, 'Man is *altogether* spotted and defiled' (Hom. on Nat.), 'without a *spark* of goodness in him' (Serm. on Mis. of Man, &c.).

"Again, by answering the Questions comprised in the chapter on 'Free Will,' according to your Lordship's directions, I am compelled to acknowledge, either that man has such a share in the work of his own salvation as to exclude the *sole* agency of God, or that he has no share whatever; when the Homilies for Rogation Week and Whitsunday positively declare, that God is the 'only Worker,' or, in other words, *sole* Agent; and at the same time assign to man a certain share in the work of his own salvation. In short, I could, with your Lordship's permission, point out twenty Questions, involving doctrines of the utmost importance, which I am unable to answer, so as to convey my real sentiments, without more room for explanation than the printed sheet affords.

"In this view of the subject, therefore, and in the most deliberate exercise of my judgment, I deem it indispensable to my acting with that candour and truth with which it is my wish and duty to act, and with which I cannot but believe your Lordship desires I should act, to state my opinions in that language which expresses them most fully, plainly, and unreservedly. This I have endeavoured to do in the answers now in the possession of your Lordship. If any further explanation be required, I am most willing to give it, even to a minuteness of opinion beyond what the Articles require. At the same time, I would humbly and respectfully appeal to your Lordship's candour, *whether it is not hard to demand my decided opinion upon points which have been the themes of volumes; upon which the most pious and learned men of the Church have conscientiously differed;*

*and upon which the Articles, in the judgment of Bishop Burnet,
have pronounced no definite sentence.* To those Articles, my
Lord, I have already subscribed; and I am willing again to subscribe to every one of them, 'in its literal and grammatical
sense,' according to His Majesty's declaration prefixed to them.
"I hope, therefore, in consideration of the above statement,
that your Lordship will not compel me, by the conciseness of
my answers, to assent to doctrines which I do not believe, or
to expose myself to inferences which do not fairly and legiti-
mately follow from my opinions.

"I am, my Lord, &c. &c."

We are not much acquainted with the practices of courts of
justice; but, if we remember right, when a man is going to be
hanged, the judge lets him make his defence in his own way,
without complaining of its length. We should think a Christian
Bishop might be equally indulgent to a man who is going to be
ruined. The answers are required to be clear, concise, and correct—short, plain, and positive. In other words, a poor curate,
extremely agitated at the idea of losing his livelihood, is required
to write with brevity and perspicuity on the following subjects:—
Redemption by Jesus Christ—Original Sin—Free Will—Justification—Justification in reference to its Cause—Justification in reference to the time when it takes place—Everlasting Salvation—
Predestination—Regeneration on the New Birth—Renovation,
and the Holy Trinity. As a specimen of these questions, the answer to which is required to be so brief and clear, we shall insert
the following quotation:—

"Section II.—Of Justification, in reference to its cause.

"1. Does not the eleventh Article declare, that we are 'justified
by Faith *only?'*

"2. Does not the expression 'Faith only' derive additional
strength from the negative expression in the same Article
'and *not* for our own works?'

"3. Does not therefore the eleventh Article *exclude* good works
from all share in the office of Justifying? Or can we so construe the term 'Faith' in that Article, as to make it *include*
good works?

"4. Do not the twelfth and thirteenth Articles *further* exclude
them, the one by asserting that good works *follow after*
Justification, the other by maintaining that they *cannot
precede* it?

"5. Can that which never precedes an effect be reckoned among the *causes* of that effect?

"6. Can we then, consistently with our Articles, reckon the performance of good works among the *causes* of Justification, whatever qualifying epithet be used with the term *cause?*"

We entirely deny that the Calvinistical Clergy are bad members of their profession. We maintain that as many instances of good, serious, and pious men—of persons zealously interesting themselves in the temporal and spiritual welfare of their parishioners, are to be found among them, as among the clergy who put an opposite interpretation on the Articles. The Articles of Religion are older than Arminianism, *co nomine.* The early Reformers leant to Calvinism; and would, to a man, have answered the Bishop's questions in a way which would have induced him to refuse them ordination and curacies; and those who drew up the Thirty-nine Articles, if they had not prudently avoided all precise interpretation of their Creed on free will, necessity, absolute decrees, original sin, reprobation, and election, would have, in all probability, given an interpretation of them like that which the Bishop considers as a disqualification for Holy Orders. Laud's Lambeth Articles were illegal, mischievous, and are generally condemned. The Irish Clergy in 1641 drew up one hundred and four articles as the creed of their Church; and these are Calvinistic and not Arminian. They were approved and signed by Usher, and never abjured by him; though dropt as a test or qualification. Usher was promoted (even in the days of Arminianism) to bishoprics and archbishoprics—so little did a Calvinistic interpretation of the Articles in a man's own breast, or even an avowal of Calvinism beyond what was required by the Articles, operate even then as a disqualification for the cure of souls, or any other office in the Church. Throughout Charles II. and William III.'s time, the best men and greatest names of the Church not only allowed latitude in interpreting the Articles, but thought it would be wise to diminish their number, and render them more lax than they are; and be it observed that these latitudinarians leant to Arminianism rather than to high Calvinism; and thought, consequently, that the Articles, if objectionable at all, were exposed to the censure of being "too Calvinistic," rather than too Arminian. How preposterous, therefore, to twist them, and the subscription to them required by law, by the machinery of a long string of explanatory questions, into a barrier against Calvinists, and to give the Arminians a monopoly in the Church!

Archbishop Wake, in 1716, after consulting all the Bishops then attending Parliament, thought it incumbent on him *"to employ the authority which the ecclesiastical laws then in force, and the custom and laws of the realm vested in him"* in taking care that *"no unworthy person might hereafter be admitted into the sacred Ministry of the Church";* and he drew up twelve recommendations to the Bishops of England, in which he earnestly exhorts them not to ordain persons of bad conduct or character, or incompetent learning; but he does not require from the candidates for Holy Orders or preferment any explanation whatever of the Articles which they had signed.

The Correspondence of the same eminent Prelate with Professor Turretin in 1718, and with Mr. Le Clerc and the Pastors and Professors of Geneva in 1719, printed in London, 1782, recommends union among Protestants, and the omission of controverted points in Confessions of Faith, as a means of obtaining that union; and a constant reference to the practice of the Church of England is made, in elucidation of the charity and wisdom of such policy. Speaking of men who act upon a contrary principle he says, *O quantum potuit insana* φιλαυτια!

These passages, we think, are conclusive evidence of the practice of the Church till 1719. For Wake was not only at the time Archbishop of Canterbury, but both in his circular recommendations to the Bishops of England, and in his correspondence with foreign Churches, was acting in the capacity of metropolitan of the Anglican Church. He, a man of prudence and learning, publicly boasts to Protestant Europe, that his Church does *not* exact, and that he *de facto* has never avowed, and never will, his opinions on those very points upon which Bishop Marsh obliges every poor curate to be explicit, upon pain of expulsion from the Church.

It is clear, then, the practice was to extract subscription, and nothing else, as the test of orthodoxy—to that Wake is an evidence. As far as he is authority on a point of opinion, it is his conviction that this practice was wholesome, wise, and intended to preserve peace in the Church; that it would be wrong at least, if not illegal, to do otherwise; and that the observance of this forbearance is the only method of preventing schism. The Bishop of Peterborough, however, is of a different opinion; he is so thoroughly convinced of the pernicious effects of Calvinistic doctrines, that he does what no other Bishop does, or ever did do, for their exclusion. This may be either wise or injudicious, but it is at least zealous and bold; it is to encounter rebuke, and opposition, from a sense of duty. It is impossible to deny this merit to his Lordship.

And we have no doubt, that, in pursuance of the same theological gallantry, he is preparing a set of interrogatories for those clergymen who are presented to benefices in his diocese. The patron will have his action of *Quare impedit,* it is true; and the judge and jury will decide whether the Bishop has the right of interrogation at all; and whether Calvinistical answers to his interrogatories disqualify any man from holding preferment in the Church of England. If either of these points are given against the Bishop of Peterborough, he is in honour and conscience bound to give up his examination of curates. If Calvinistic ministers are, in the estimation of the Bishops, so dangerous as curates, they are, of course, much more dangerous as rectors and vicars. He has as much right to examine one as the other. Why, then, does he pass over the greater danger, and guard against the less? Why does he not show his zeal when he would run some risk, and where the excluded person (if excluded unjustly) could appeal to the laws of his country? If his conduct be just and right, has he anything to fear from that appeal? What should we say of a police officer, who acted in all cases of petty larceny, where no opposition was made, and let off all persons guilty of felony who threatened to knock him down? If the Bishop value his own character, he is bound to do less,—or to do more. God send his choice may be right! The law, as it stands at present, certainly affords very unequal protection to rector and to curate; but if the Bishop will not act so as to improve the law, the law must be so changed as to improve the Bishop; an action of *Quare impedit* must be given to the curate also—and then the fury of interrogation will be calmed.

We are aware that the Bishop of Peterborough, in his speech, disclaims the object of excluding the Calvinists by this system of interrogation. We shall take no other notice of his disavowal than expressing our sincere regret that he ever made it; but the question is not at all altered by the intention of the interrogator. Whether he aim at the Calvinists only, or includes them with other heterodox respondents—the fact is, they *are* included in the proscription, and excluded from the Church, the practical effect of the practice being that men are driven out of the Church who have as much right to exercise the duties of clergymen as the Bishop himself. If heterodox opinions are the great objects of the Bishop's apprehensions, he has his Ecclesiastical Courts, where regular process may bring the offender to punishment, and from whence there is an appeal to higher courts. This would be the fair thing to do. The curate and the Bishop would be brought into the light of day, and subjected to the wholesome restraint of public opinion.

His Lordship boasts that he has excluded only two curates. So the Emperor of Hayti boasted that he had only cut off two persons' heads for disagreeable behaviour at his table. In spite of the paucity of the visitors executed, the example operated as a considerable impediment to conversation; and the intensity of the punishment was found to be a full compensation for its rarity. How many persons have been deprived of curacies which they might have enjoyed but for the tenour of these interrogatories? How many respectable clergymen have been deprived of the assistance of curates connected with them by blood, friendship, or doctrine, and compelled to choose persons for no other qualification than that they could pass through the eye of the Bishop's needle? Violent measures are not to be judged of merely by the number of times they have been resorted to, but by the terror, misery, and restraint which the severity is likely to have produced.

We never met with any style so entirely clear of all redundant and vicious ornament as that which the ecclesiastical Lord of Peterborough has adopted towards his clergy. It, in fact, may be all reduced to these few words—"Reverend Sir, I shall do what I please. Peterborough."—Even in the House of Lords, he speaks what we must call very plain language. Among other things, he says that the allegations of the petitions are *false*. Now, as every Bishop is, besides his other qualities, a gentleman; and as the word *false* is used only by laymen who mean to hazard their lives by the expression; and as it cannot be supposed that foul language is ever used because it can be used with personal impunity, his Lordship must therefore be intended to mean not *false,* but *mistaken*—not a wilful deviation from truth, but an accidental and unintended departure from it.

His Lordship talks of the drudgery of wading through ten pages of answers to his eighty-seven questions. Who has occasioned this drudgery, but the person who means to be so much more active, useful, and important, than all other Bishops, by proposing questions which nobody has thought to be necessary but himself? But to be intolerably strict and harsh to a poor curate, who is trying to earn a morsel of hard bread, and then to complain of the drudgery of reading his answers, is much like knocking a man down with a bludgeon, and then abusing him for splashing you with his blood, and pestering you with his groans. It is quite monstrous, that a man who inflicts eighty-seven new questions in Theology upon his fellow-creatures, should talk of the drudgery of reading their answers.

A Curate—there is something which excites compassion in the very name of a Curate ! ! ! How any man of Purple, Palaces, and Preferment, can let himself loose against this poor working man of God, we are at a loss to conceive,—a learned man in an hovel, with sermons and saucepans, lexicons and bacon, Hebrew books and ragged children—good and patient—a comforter and a preacher—the first and purest pauper in the hamlet, and yet showing, that, in the midst of his worldly misery, he has the heart of a gentleman, and the spirit of a Christian, and the kindness of a pastor; and this man, though he has exercised the duties of a clergyman for twenty years—though he has most ample testimonies of conduct from clergymen as respectable as any Bishop— though an Archbishop add his name to the list of witnesses, is not good enough for Bishop Marsh; but is pushed out in the street, with his wife and children, and his little furniture, to surrender his honour, his faith, his conscience, and his learning—or to starve!

An obvious objection to these innovations is, that there can be no end to them. If eighty-three questions are assumed to be necessary by one Bishop, eight hundred may be considered as the minimum of interrogation by another. When once the ancient faith-marks of the Church are lost sight of and despised, any misled theologian may launch out on the boundless sea of polemical vexation.

The Bishop of Peterborough is positive, that the Arminian interpretation of the Articles is the right interpretation, and that Calvinists should be excluded from it; but the country gentlemen who are to hear these matters debated in the Lower House, are to remember, that other Bishops have written upon these points before the Bishop of Peterborough, and have arrived at conclusions diametrically opposite. When curates are excluded because their answers are Calvinistical, a careless layman might imagine that this interpretation of the Articles had never been heard of before in the Church—that it was a gross and palpable perversion of their sense, which had been scouted by all writers on Church matters, from the day the Articles were promulgated, to this hour —that such an unheard-of monster as a Calvinistical Curate had never leapt over the pale before, and been detected browsing in the sacred pastures.

The following is the testimony of Bishop Sherlock:—

" 'The Church has left a latitude of sense to prevent schisms and breaches upon every different opinion. It is evident the Church of England has so done in some Articles, which are most liable to the hottest disputes; which yet are penned with that temper as to be willingly subscribed by men of different apprehensions in those matters.' "—(SHERLOCK's *Defence of Stillingfleet's Unreasonableness of Separation.*)

Bishop Cleaver, describing the difficulties attending so great an undertaking as the formation of a national creed, observes:—

" 'These difficulties, however, do not seem to have discouraged the great leaders in this work from forming a design as wise as it was liberal, that of framing a confession, which in the enumeration and method of its several articles, should meet the approbation, and engage the consent of the whole reformed world. " 'If upon trial it was found that a comprehension so extensive could not be reduced to practice, still as large a comprehension as could be contrived, within the narrower limits of the kingdom, became, for the same reasons which first suggested the idea, at once an object of prudence and duty in the formation and government of the English Church.'

"After dwelling on the means necessary to accomplish this object, the Bishop proceeds to remark:—'Such evidently appears to have been the origin, and such the actual complexion of the confession comprised in the Articles of our Church; *the true scope and design of which will not, I conceive, be correctly apprehended in any other view than that of one drawn up and adjusted with an intention to comprehend the assent of all, rather than to exclude that of any who concurred in the necessity of a reformation.*

" 'The means of comprehension intended were, not any general ambiguity or equivocation of terms, *but a prudent forbearance in all parties not to insist on the full extent of their opinions in matters not essential or fundamental; and in all cases to waive, as much as possible, tenets which might divide, where they wish to unite.'* " (Remarks on the Design and Formation of the Articles of the Church of England, by WILLIAM, Lord Bishop of Bangor, 1802.—pp. 23-25.)

We will finish with Bishop Horsley.

"It has been the fashion of late to talk about Arminianism as the system of the Church of England, and of Calvinism as some-

thing opposite to it, to which the Church is hostile. That I may
not be misunderstood in what I have stated, or may have occasion further to say upon this subject, I must here declare, that
I use the words Arminianism and Calvinism in that restricted
sense in which they are now generally taken, to denote the doc-
trinal part of each system, as unconnected with the principles
either of Arminians or Calvinists, upon Church discipline and
Church government. This being premised, I assert, what I often
have before asserted, and by God's grace I will persist in the
assertion to my dying day, that so far is it from the truth that
the Church of England is decidedly Arminian, and hostile to
Calvinism, that the truth is this, *that upon the principal points
in dispute between the Arminians and the Calvinists—upon all
the points of doctrine characteristic of the two sects, the Church
of England maintains an absolute neutrality; her Articles explicitly assert nothing but what is believed both by Arminians
and by Calvinists.* The Calvinists indeed hold some opinions
relative to the same points, which the Church of England has
not gone the length of asserting in her Articles; but neither has
she gone the length of explicitly contradicting those opinions;
insomuch, that *there is nothing to hinder the Arminian and the
highest supralapsarian Calvinist from walking together in the
Church of England and Ireland as friends and brothers, if they
both approve the discipline of the Church, and both are willing
to submit to it.* Her discipline has been approved; it has been
submitted to; it has been in former times most ably and zealously
defended by the highest supralapsarian Calvinists. Such was the
great Usher; such was Whitgift; such were many more, burning
and shining lights of our Church in her early days (when first
she shook off the Papal tyranny), long since gone to the resting-
place of the spirits of the just."—(*Bishop* HORSLEY's *Charges*,
p. 216—pp. 25, 26.)

So that these unhappy Curates are turned out of their bread for
an exposition of the Articles which such men as Sherlock, Cleaver,
and Horsley think may be fairly given of their meaning. We do
not quote their authority, to show that the right interpretation is
decided, but that it is doubtful—that there is a balance of authorities—that the opinion which Bishop Marsh has punished with
poverty and degradation, has been considered to be legitimate by
men at least as wise and learned as himself. In fact, it is to us
perfectly clear, that the Articles were originally framed to prevent
the very practices which Bishop Marsh has used for their protec-

tion—they were purposely so worded, that Arminians and Calvinists could sign them without blame. They were intended to combine both these descriptions of Protestants, and were meant principally for a bulwark against the Catholics.

"Thus," says Bishop Burnet, "was the doctrine of the Church cast into a short and plain form; in which they took care both to establish the positive articles of religion and to cut off the errors formerly introduced in the time of Popery, or of late broached by the Anabaptists and enthusiasts of Germany; *avoiding the niceties of schoolmen, or the peremptoriness of the writers of controversy; leaving, in matters that are more justly controvertible, a liberty to divines to follow their private opinions without thereby disturbing the peace of the Church."*—(History of the Reformation, Book I. part ii. p. 168, folio edition.)

The next authority is that of Fuller.

"In the Convocation now sitting, wherein Alexander Nowel, Dean of St. Paul's, was Prolocutor, the nine-and-thirty Articles were composed. For the main they agree with those set forth in the reign of King Edward the Sixth, though in some particulars allowing more liberty to dissenting judgments. For instance, in this King's Articles it is said, that it is to be believed that Christ went down to hell (to preach to the spirits there); which last clause is left out in these Articles, and men left to a latitude concerning the cause, time, and manner of his descent.
"Hence some have unjustly taxed the composers for too much favour extended in their large expressions, clean through the contexture of these Articles, which should have tied men's consciences up closer, in more strict and particularising propositions, *which indeed proceeded from their commendable moderation.* Children's clothes ought to be made of the biggest, because afterwards their bodies will grow up to their garments. Thus the Articles of this English Protestant Church, in the infancy thereof, they thought good to draw up in general terms, foreseeing that posterity would grow up to fill the same: I mean these holy men did prudently prediscover, that differences in judgments would unavoidably happen in the Church, *and were loath to unchurch any, and drive them off from an ecclesiastical communion, for such petty differences, which made them pen the Articles in comprehensive words, to take in all who, differing in the branches, meet in the root of the same religion.*

"Indeed most of them had formerly been sufferers themselves, and cannot be said, in compiling these Articles, (an acceptable service, no doubt,) to offer to God what cost them nothing, some having paid imprisonment, others exile, all losses in their estates, for this their experimental knowledge in religion, *which made them the more merciful and tender in stating those points,* seeing such who themselves have been most patient in bearing, will be most pitiful in burdening the consciences of others."— (See FULLER'S *Church History,* book ix. p. 72, folio edit.)

But this generous and pacific spirit gives no room for the display of zeal and theological learning. The gate of admission has been left too widely open. I may as well be without power at all, if I cannot force my opinions upon other people. What was purposely left indefinite, I must make finite and exclusive. Questions of contention and difference must be laid before the servants of the Church, and nothing like neutrality in theological metaphysics allowed to the ministers of the Gospel. *I come not to bring peace,* &c.

The Bishop, however, seems to be quite satisfied with himself, when he states, that he has a *right to do* what he has done—just as if a man's character with his fellow-creatures depended upon legal rights alone, and not upon a discreet exercise of those rights. A man may persevere in doing what he has a right to do, till the Chancellor shuts him up in Bedlam, or till the mob pelt him as he passes. It must be presumed, that all men whom the law has invested with rights, Nature has invested with common sense to use those rights. For these reasons, children have no rights till they have gained some common sense, and old men have no rights after they lose their common sense. All men are at all times accountable to their fellow-creatures for the discreet exercise of every right they possess.

Prelates are fond of talking of *my* see, *my* clergy, *my* diocese, as if these things belonged to them, as their pigs and dogs belonged to them. They forget that the clergy, the diocese, and the Bishops themselves, all exist only for the public good; that the public are a third, and principal party in the whole concern. It is not simply the tormenting Bishop *versus* the tormented Curate, but the public against the system of tormenting; as tending to bring scandal upon religion and religious men. By the late alteration in the laws, the labourers in the vineyard are given up to the power of the inspectors of the vineyard. If he have the meanness and malice to do so, an inspector may worry and plague to death any labourer against whom he may have conceived an antipathy. As often as such cases are detected, we believe they will meet, in either House of Parliament, with the severest reprehension. The noblemen and gentlemen of England will never allow their parish clergy to be treated with cruelty, injustice, and caprice, by men who were parish clergymen themselves yesterday, and who were trusted with power for very different purposes.

The Bishop of Peterborough complains of the insolence of the answers made to him. This is certainly not true of Mr. Grimshawe, Mr. Neville, or of the author of the Appeal. They have answered his Lordship with great force, great manliness, but with perfect respect. Does the Bishop expect that humble men, as learned as himself, are to be driven from their houses and homes by his new theology, and then to send him letters of thanks for the kicks and cuffs he has bestowed upon them? Men of very small incomes, be it known to his Lordship, have very often very acute feelings; and a Curate trod on feels a pang as great as when a Bishop is refuted.

We shall now give a specimen of some answers, which, we believe, would exclude a curate from the diocese of Peterborough, and contrast these answers with the Articles of the Church to which they refer. The 9th Article of the Church of England is upon Original Sin. Upon this point his Lordship puts the following question:—

"Did the fall of Adam produce such an effect on his posterity, that mankind became thereby a mass of mere corruption, or of absolute and entire depravity? Or is the effect only such, that we are very *far gone* from original righteousness, and of our own nature *inclined* to evil?"

Excluding Answer.

"The fall of Adam produced such an effect on his posterity, that mankind became thereby a mass of mere corruption, or of absolute and entire depravity."

The Ninth Article.

"Original sin standeth not in the following of Adam (as the Pelagians do vainly talk); but it is the fault or corruption of the nature of every man, that naturally is engendered of the offspring of Adam, whereby man is very far gone from original righteousness, and is of his own nature inclined to evil, so that the flesh lusteth always contrary to the spirit; and therefore, in every person born into the world, it deserveth God's wrath and damnation."

The 9th Question, Cap. 3rd, on Free Will, is as follows:—"Is it not contrary to Scripture to say, that man has no share in the work of his salvation?"

Excluding Answer.

"It is quite agreeable to Scripture to say, that man has no share in the work of his own salvation."

Tenth Article.

"The condition of man after the fall of Adam is such, that he cannot turn and prepare himself, by his own natural strength and good works, to faith, and calling upon God. Wherefore, we have no power to do good works pleasant and acceptable to God, without the grace of God by Christ preventing us, that we may have a good will, and working with us when we have that good will."

On Redemption, his Lordship has the following question, Cap. 1st, Question 1st:—"Did Christ die for all men, or did he die only for a chosen few?"

Excluding Answer.

"Christ did not die for all men, but only for a chosen few."

Part of Article Seventh.

"Predestination to life is the everlasting purpose of God, whereby (before the foundations of the world were laid) he hath constantly decreed by his counsel, secret to us, to deliver from curse and damnation those whom he hath chosen in Christ out of mankind, and to bring them by Christ unto everlasting salvation, as vessels made to honour."

Now, whether these answers are right or wrong, we do not presume to decide; but we cannot help saying, there appears to be some little colour in the language of the Articles for the errors of the respondent. It does not appear at first sight to be such a deviation from the plain, literal, and grammatical sense of the Articles, as to merit rapid and ignominious ejectment from the bosom of the Church.

Now we have done with the Bishop. We give him all he asks as to his legal right; and only contend, that he is acting a very indiscreet and injudicious part—fatal to his quiet—fatal to his reputation as a man of sense—blamed by Ministers—blamed by all the Bench of Bishops—vexatious to the Clergy, and highly injurious to the Church. We mean no personal disrespect to the Bishop; we are as ignorant of him as of his victims. We should have been heartily glad if the debate in Parliament had put an end to these blamable excesses; and our only object, in meddling with the question, is to restrain the arm of Power within the limits of moderation and justice—one of the great objects which first led to the establishment of this Journal [*The Edinburgh Review*] and which, we hope, will always continue to characterise its efforts.

Letter to the BISHOP OF LONDON

    A few words more, my dear Lord, before we part, after a controversy of four years:

In reading your speech, I was a good deal amused by your characteristic indignation at the idea of any man, or any body of men, being competent to offer you advice; at the same time I have a sort of indistinct recollection of your name, as defendant in courts of justice, where it appeared, not only to the judges who decided against you, but to your best friends also, that you would have made rather a better figure if you had begged a few contributions of wisdom and temper from those who had any to share: till these cases are erased from our legal reports, it would perhaps be expedient to admit for yourself a small degree of fallibility, and to leave the claim of absolute wisdom to Alderman Wood.

You say that you always consult your archdeacon and rural dean; this I believe to be quite true—but then you generally consult them after the error, and not before. Immediately after this aspernation of all human counsel, I came to the following sentence,—such a sentence as I believe mortal and mitred man never spoke before, and the author of which, as it seems to me, should be loaded with four atmospheres of advice instead of one, and controlled regularly by that number of cathedral councils. In speaking of the 3,000 clergymen who have petitioned against the destruction of the church, you say:

"I could easily get as many to petition upon any subject connected with the church. The mode by which in the present case a great proportion of these signatures have been obtained is as follows:—the Archdeacon, who has always great influence with the parochial clergy, and justly so, as visiting them every year, and as being in habits of more familiar intercourse with them than their Bishop, and who is moreover considered by them as acting, in some degree, with the sanction of the Bishop, circulates printed forms of petition against the bill amongst the Rural Deans; the Rural Dean goes with them to the parochial clergy; and he must be a bold or a very well-informed man who refuses to sign a petition so recommended by his immediate ecclesiastical superiors."

Now I am afraid you will be very angry with me, but for the life of me I cannot discover in this part of your speech any of those marks of unerring and unassistable wisdom—that perfect useless-ness of counsellors to the Bishop of London of which you seem to be so intimately convinced; and this, remember, is not a lapse to be forgiven in the fervour of speaking, but a cold printed insult; or what is the plain English of the passage? "Archdeacons and rural deans are a set of base and time-serving instruments, whom their superiors can set on for any purpose to abuse their power and in-fluence over the lower clergy, and the lower clergy themselves are either in such a state of intellectual destitution that they cannot com-prehend what they sign, or they are so miserably enthralled by their ecclesiastical superiors that they dare not dissent. I could put this depraved machinery in action for any church purpose I wished to carry." If Lord Melbourne, in the exercise of his caprice, had offered me a bishopric, and I had been fool enough to have accepted it, this insult upon the whole body of the parochial clergy should not have been passed over with the silent impunity with which it was received in the House of Lords. You call me in the speech your facetious friend, and I hasten with gratitude in this letter to denominate you my solemn friend; but you and I must not run into commonplace errors; you must not think me necessarily foolish because I am face-tious, nor will I consider you necessarily wise because you are grave; but whether foolish or facetious or what not, I admire and respect you too much not to deplore this passage in your speech; and, in spite of all your horror of being counselled by one of your own canons, I advise you manfully to publish another edition of your speech, and to expunge with the most ample apology this indecent aggression upon the venerable instructors of mankind.

In our future attacks upon the Catholics let us wisely omit our customary sarcasms on their regard for oaths. The only persons who appear to me to understand the doctrine of oaths are the two honest sheriffs whom Lord John put into prison for respecting them.

In the eighth page of your speech you say—"I am continually brought into contact, in the discharge of my official duties, with vast masses of my fellow-creatures living without God in the world. I traverse the streets of this crowded city with deep and solemn thoughts of the spiritual condition of its inhabitants. I pass the mag-nificent church which crowns the metropolis, and is consecrated to the noblest of objects, the glory of God, and I ask of myself, in what

degree it answers that object. I see there a dean and three residentiaries, with incomes amounting in the aggregate to between £ 10,000
and £ 12,000 a year. I see, too, connected with the cathedral 29
clergymen, whose offices are all but sinecures, with an annual income of about £ 12,000 at the present moment, and likely to be
very much larger after the lapse of a few years. I proceed a mile or
two to the E. and N.E., and find myself in the midst of an immense
population in the most wretched state of destitution and neglect,
artisans, mechanics, labourers, beggars, thieves, to the number of
at least 300,000."

This stroll in the metropolis is extremely well contrived for your
Lordship's speech; but suppose, my dear Lord, that instead of going
E. and N.E., you had turned about, crossed London Bridge, and, re-
solving to make your walk as impartial as possible, had proceeded
in a S.W. direction, you would soon in that case have perceived a
vast palace, containing, not a dean, three residentiaries, and 29
clergymen, but one attenuated prelate with an income enjoyed by
himself alone, amount to £ 30,000 per annum, twice as great as
that of all these confiscated clergymen put together; not one penny
of it given up by act of Parliament during his life to that spiritual
destitution which he so deeply deplores, and £ 15,000 per annum
secured to his successor: though all the duties of the office might be
most effectually performed for one-third of the salary.

Having refreshed yourself, my dear Lord, by the contemplation
of this beautiful and consistent scene, and recovered a little from
those dreadful pictures of spiritual destitution which have been ob-
truded upon you by the sight of St. Paul's, you must continue our
religious promenade to the banks of the Thames; but, as the way is
long, let us rest ourselves for a few minutes in your palace in St.
James's Square, no scene certainly of carnal and secular destitution.
Having halted for a few minutes in this mansion of humility, we
shall now be able to reach your second palace of Fulham, where I
think your animal spirits will be restored, and the painful theme of
spiritual destitution be for the moment put to sleep. £ 20,000 per
annum to the present possessor increasing in value every hour, not
a shilling legally given up during life to 'the masses who are living
without God', and £ 10,000 per annum secured to the successor.
I know that you are both of you generous and munificent men, but
£ 2,000 or £ 3,000 subscribed, though much more observed, is
much more economical also, than a fixed and legal diminution of an
income, now out of all character and proportion, for those who feel
the spiritual destitution so deeply. But these feelings upon spiritual
destitution, my Lord, are of the most singular description; they

seem to be under the most perfect control when bishops are to be provided for, and of irresistible plenitude and power when prebends are to be destroyed; such charity is the charity of my poor dear friend, old Lady C——, who was so powerfully affected (she said) by my sermon, that she borrowed a sovereign of some gentleman in the pew and put it in the plate.

My Lord, you are a very able, honest, and good man, but I pray you, as one of your council, be a little more discreet. You have taught the enemies of the church a fearful lesson, and they are very good scholars. In the midst of your ecclesiastical elegies upon spiritual destitution, take care they do not turn upon you and say, "We can place the bench of Bishops in a position by which their usefulness will be materially increased, and £60,000 per annum be saved for the spiritual destitution of the church." . . .

It is very easy, my Lord, to swing about in the House of Lords, and to be brave five years after the time, and to point out to their Lordships the clear difference between moral and physical fear, and to be nodded to by the Duke of Wellington, but I am not to be paid by such coin. I believe that the old-fashioned, orthodox, hand-shaking, bowel-disturbing passion of fear had a good deal to do with the whole reform. You choose to forget it, but I remember the period when the Bishops never remained unpelted; they were pelted going, coming, riding, walking, consecrating, and carousing; the Archbishop of Canterbury, in the town of Canterbury, at the period of his visitation, was only saved from the mob by the dexterity of his coachman. If you were not frightened by all this, I was, and would have given half my preferment to save the rest; but then I was not a Commissioner, and had no great interests committed to my charge. If such had been my lot, I would have looked severely into my own soul.

You have laid yourself open to some cruel replies and retorts in various parts of your pamphlet speech; but the law is past, and the subject is at an end.

You are fast hastening on, with the acclamations and gratitude of the Whigs, to Lambeth, and I am hastening, after a life of 70 years, with gout and asthma, to the grave. I am most sincere, therefore, when I say, that in the management of this businesss you have (in my opinion) made a very serious and fatal mistake: you have shaken the laws of property, and prepared the ruin of the church by lowering the character of its members, and encouraging the aggressions of its enemies. That your error has been the error of an upright, zealous, and honest man, I have not the most remote doubt. I have fought you lustily for four years, but I admire your talents, and re-

spect your character as sincerely as I lament the mistakes into which
you have been hurried by the honest and headlong impetuosity of
your nature.

I remain, my Lord, your obedient, humble servant,

SYDNEY SMITH

The Times
5 September 1840

WHAT IS A PUSEYITE?

"At a recent trial Lord Justice Knight Bruce asked if any of the learned
counsel could define a Puseyite, but none of the learned gentlemen attempted a definition."—*vide Morning Herald.*

I

Pray tell me what's a Puseyite? 'Tis puzzling to describe
This ecclesiastic genus of a pious, hybrid tribe.
At Lambeth and the Vatican he's equally at home,
Altho' 'tis said he rather gives the preference to Rome.

II

Voracious as a book-worm is his antiquarian maw,
The "Fathers" are his text-book, the "Canons" are his law,
He's mighty in the Rubrics, and well up in the Creeds,
But he only quotes the "Articles" just as they suit his needs.

III

The Bible is to him almost a sealèd Book,
Reserve is on his lips and mystery in his look;
The sacramental system is the torch to illumine his night,
He loves the earthly candlestick more than the heavenly light.

IV

He's great in punctilios, where he bows and where he stands,
In the cutting of his surplice, and the hemming of his bands,
Each saint upon the Calendar he knows by heart at least,
He always dates his letters on a "Vigil" or a "Feast."

V

But hark! With what a nasal twang, betwixt a whine and groan,
He doth our noble liturgy most murderously intone;
Cold are his prayers and praises, his preaching colder still,
Inanimate and passionless; his very look does chill.

VI

He talketh much of discipline, yet when the shoe doth pinch,
This most obedient, duteous son will not give way an inch;
Pliant and obstinate by turns, whate'er may be the whim,
He's only for the Bishop when the Bishop is for him.

VII

Others as weak, but more sincere, who rather feel than think,
Encouraging he leads to Popery's dizzy brink,
And when they take the fatal plunge, he walks back quite content
To his snug birth at Mother Church, and wonders why they went.

VIII

Such, and much worse, aye, worse! had I time to write,
Is a faint sketch, your worship, of a thorough Puseyite,
Whom even Rome repudiates, as she laughs within her sleeve,
At the sacerdotal mimic, the solemn Would-Believe.

IX

Oh, well it were for England, if her Church were rid of those
Half-Protestant, half-Papist, who are less her friends than foes.
Give me the open enemy, not the hollow friend;
With God, and with our Bible, we will the truth defend.

Letters to ARCHDEACON SINGLETON

LETTER I.

MY DEAR SIR,

As you do me the honour to ask my opinion respecting the
constitution and proceedings of the Ecclesiastical Commission, and
of their conduct to the Dignitaries of the Church, I shall write to
you without any reserve upon this subject.

The first thing which excited my surprise, was the Constitution of
the Commission. As the reform was to comprehend every branch
of Churchmen, Bishops, Dignitaries and Parochial Clergymen, I
cannot but think it would have been much more advisable to have
added to the Commission some members of the two lower orders of
the Church—they would have supplied that partial knowledge which
appears in so many of the proceedings of the Commissioners to have
been wanting—they would have attended to those interests (not episcopal) which appear to have been so completely overlooked—and

they would have screened the Commission from those charges of injustice and partiality which are now so generally brought against it. There can be no charm in the name of Bishop—the man who was a Curate yesterday is a Bishop to-day. There are many Prebendaries, many Rectors, and many Vicars, who would have come to the Reform of the Church with as much integrity, wisdom, and vigour, as any Bishop on the Bench; and, I believe, with a much stronger recollection that all the orders of the Church were not to be sacrificed to the highest; and that to make their work respectable, and lasting, it should, in all (even its minutest provisions), be founded upon justice.

All the interests of the Church in the Commutation of Tithes are entrusted to one parochial clergyman *; and I have no doubt, from what I hear of him, that they will be well protected. Why could not one or two such men have been added to the Commission, and a general impression been created, that Government in this momentous change had a parental feeling for all orders of men whose interests might be affected by it? A Ministry may laugh at this, and think if they cultivate Bishops, that they may treat the other orders of the Church with contempt and neglect; but I say, that to create a general impression of justice, if it be not what common honesty requires from any Ministry, is what common sense points out to them. It is strength and duration—it is the only power which is worth having —in the struggle of parties it gives victory, and is remembered, and goes down to other times.

A mixture of different orders of Clergy in the Commission would at least have secured a decent attention to the representations of all; for of seven communications made to the Commission by Cathedrals, and involving very serious representations respecting high interests, six were totally disregarded, and the receipt of the papers not even acknowledged.

I cannot help thinking that the Commissioners have done a great deal too much. Reform of the Church was absolutely necessary—it cannot be avoided, and ought not to be postponed; but I would have found out what really gave offence, have applied a remedy, removed the nuisance, and done no more. I would not have operated so largely on an old, and (I fear) a decaying building. I would not, in days of such strong political excitement, and amidst such a disposition to universal change, have done one thing more than was absolutely necessary, to remove the odium against the Establishment, the only

---

* The Rev. Mr. Jones is the Commissioner appointed by the Archbishop of Canterbury to watch over the interests of the Church.

sensible reason for issuing any Commission at all; and the means which I took to effect this should have agreed as much as possible with institutions already established. For instance, the public were disgusted with the spectacle of rich Prebendaries enjoying large incomes, and doing little or nothing for them. The real remedy for this would have been to have combined wealth and labour; and as each of the present Prebendaries fell off, to have annexed the stall to some large and populous parish. A Prebendary of Canterbury or of St. Paul's, in his present state, may make the Church unpopular; but place him as Rector of a Parish, with 8000 or 9000 people, and in a Benefice of little or no value, he works for his wealth, and the odium is removed. In like manner the Prebends, which are not the property of the Residentiaries, might have been annexed to the smallest livings of the neighbourhood where the Prebendal estate was situated. The interval which has elapsed since the first furious demand for Reform would have enabled the Commissioners to adopt a scheme of much greater moderation than might perhaps have been possible at the first outbreak of popular indignation against the Church; and this sort of distribution would have given much more general satisfaction than the plan adopted by Commissioners; for though money, in the estimation of philosophers, has no ear mark, it has a very deep one in the opinion of the multitude. The riches of the Church of Durham were most hated in the neighbourhood of Durham; and there such changes as I have pointed out would have been most gladly received, and would have conciliated the greatest favour to the Church. The people of Kent cannot see why their Kentish Estates, given to the Cathedral of Canterbury, are to augment livings in Cornwall. The Citizens of London see some of their ministers starving in the city, and the profits of the extinguished Prebends sent into Northumberland. These feelings may be very unphilosophical, but they are the feelings of the mass; and to the feelings of the mass the Reforms of the Church ought to be directed. In this way the evil would have been corrected where it was most seen and noticed. All patronage would have been left as it was. One order of the Church would not have plundered the other. Nor would all the Cathedrals in England have been subjected to the unconciliating empire, and unwearied energy of one man.

Instead of this quiet and cautious mode of proceeding, all is change, fusion, and confusion. New Bishops, new Dioceses, confiscated Prebends—Clergymen changing Bishops, and Bishops Clergymen—mitres in Manchester, Gloucester turned into Bristol. Such a scene of revolution and commutation as has not been seen since the days of Ireton and Cromwell! and the singularity is, that all this has

been effected by men selected from their age, their dignity, and their
known principles, and from whom the considerate part of the community expected all the caution and calmness which these high req-
uisites seemed to promise, and ought to have secured.

The plea of making a fund is utterly untenable—the great object
was not to make a fund; and there is the mistake into which the
Commission have fallen: the object was not to add 10*l*. or 20*l*.
per annum to a thousand small livings, and to diminish inequalities
in a ratio so trifling that the public will hardly notice it; a very proper
thing to do if higher interests were not sacrificed to it, but the great
object was to remove the causes of hatred from the Church, by lessening such incomes as those of Canterbury, Durham, and London,
exorbitantly and absurdly great—by making idleness work—and by
these means to lessen the envy of laymen. It is impossible to make
a fund which will raise the smaller livings of the Church into anything like a decent support for those who possess them. The whole
income of the Church, episcopal, prebendal, and parochial, divided
among the Clergy, would not give to each Clergyman an income
equal to that which is enjoyed by the upper domestic of a great nobleman. The method in which the Church has been paid, and must continue to be paid, is by unequal divisions. All the enormous changes
which the Commission is making will produce a very trifling difference in the inequality, while it will accustom more and more those
enemies of the Church, who are studying under their Right Rev.
Masters, to the boldest revolutions in Ecclesiastical affairs. Out of
10,478 benefices, there are 297 of about 40*l*. per annum value,
1629 at about 75*l*., and 1602 at about 125*l*.: to raise all these
benefices to 200*l*. per annum would require an annual sum of
371,293*l*.; and upon 2878 of those benefices there are no houses;
and upon 1728 no houses fit for residence. What difference in the
apparent inequality of the Church would this sum of 371,293*l*.
produce, if it could be raised? or in what degree would it lessen the
odium which that inequality creates? The case is utterly hopeless;
and yet with all their confiscations the Commissioners are so far
from being able to raise the annual sum of 371,000*l*. that the utmost they expect to gain is 130,000*l*. per annum.

It seems a paradoxical statement; but the fact is, that the respectability of the Church, as well as of the Bar, is almost entirely preserved
by the unequal division of their revenues. A Bar of one hundred
lawyers travel the Northern Circuit, enlightening provincial ignorance, curing local partialities, diffusing knowledge, and dispensing
justice in their route: it is quite certain that all they gain is not equal
to all that they spend: if the profits were equally divided there would

not be six and eight-pence for each person, and there would be no
Bar at all. At present, the success of the leader animates them all—
each man hopes to be a Scarlett or a Brougham—and takes out his
ticket in a lottery by which the mass must infallibly lose, trusting
(as mankind are so apt to do) to his good fortune, and believing
that the prize is reserved for him—disappointment and defeat for
others. So it is with the clergy; the whole income of the Church, if
equally divided, would be about 250*l.* for each minister. Who would
go into the Church and spend 1200*l.* or 1500*l.* upon his education, if such were the highest remuneration he could ever look to?
At present, men are tempted into the Church by the prizes of the
Church, and bring into that Church a great deal of capital, which
enables them to live in decency, supporting themselves, not with the
money of the public, but with their own money, which, but for this
temptation, would have been carried into some retail trade. The
offices of the Church would then fall down to men little less coarse
and ignorant than agricultural labourers—the clergyman of the parish would soon be seen in the squire's kitchen; and all this would
take place in a country where poverty is infamous.

In fact, nothing can be more unjust and idle than the reasoning of
many laymen upon Church matters. You choose to have an Establishment—God forbid you should choose otherwise! and you wish
to have men of decent manners and good education as the Ministers
of that Establishment: all this is very right: but are you willing to
pay them as such men ought to be paid? Are you willing to pay to
each Clergyman, confining himself to one spot, and giving up all his
time to the care of one parish, a salary of 500*l.* per annum? To do
this would require three millions to be added to the present revenues of the Church; and such an expenditure is impossible! What
then remains, if you will have a Clergy, and will not pay them equi-
tably and separately, than to pay them unequally and by lottery?
and yet this very inequality, which secures to you a respectable
Clergy upon the most economical terms, is considered by laymen as
a gross abuse. It is an abuse, however, which they have not the spirit
to extinguish by increased munificence to their Clergy, nor justice
to consider as the only other method by which all the advantages of
a respectable Establishment can be procured; but they use it at the
same time as a topic for sarcasm and a source of economy.

This, it will be said, is a Mammonish view of the subject: it is
so, but those who make this objection forget the immense effect
which Mammon produces upon religion itself. Shall the Gospel be
preached by men paid by the State? shall these men be taken from
the lower orders, and be meanly paid? shall they be men of learning

and education? and shall there be some magnificent endowments to allure such men into the Church? Which of these methods is the best for diffusing the rational doctrines of Christianity? Not in the age of the Apostles, not in the abstract, timeless, nameless, placeless land of the philosophers, but in the year 1837, in the porter-brewing, cotton-spinning, tallow-melting kingdom of Great Britain, bursting with opulence, and flying from poverty as the greatest of human evils. Many different answers may be given to these questions; but they are questions which, not ending in Mammon, have a powerful bearing on real religion, and deserve the deepest consideration from its disciples and friends. Let the comforts of the Clergy go for nothing. Consider their state only as religion is affected by it. If upon this principle I am forced to allot to some an opulence which my clever friend the Examiner would pronounce to be unapostolical, I cannot help it; I must take this people with all their follies, and prejudices, and circumstances, and carve out an establishment best suited for them, however unfit for early Christianity in barren and conquered Judea.

Not only will this measure of the Commission bring into the Church a lower and worse educated set of men, but it will have a tendency to make the Clergy fanatical. You will have a set of ranting, raving Pastors, who will wage war against all the innocent pleasures of life, vie with each other in extravagance of zeal, and plague your heart out with their nonsense and absurdity: cribbage must be played in caverns, and sixpenny whist take refuge in the howling wilderness. In this way, low men, doomed to hopeless poverty, and galled by contempt, will endeavour to force themselves into station and significance.

There is an awkward passage in the memorial of the Church of Canterbury, which deserves some consideration from him to whom it is directed. The Archbishop of Canterbury, at his consecration, takes a solemn oath that he will maintain the rights and liberties of the Church of Canterbury; as Chairman, however, of the New Commission, he seizes the patronage of that Church, takes two-thirds of its Revenues, and abolishes two-thirds of its Members. That there is an answer to this I am very willing to believe, but I cannot at present find out what it is; and this attack upon the Revenues and Members of Canterbury is not obedience to an Act of Parliament, but the very Act of Parliament, which takes away, is recommended, drawn up, and signed by the person who has sworn he will never take away; and this little apparent inconsistency is not confined to the Archbishop of Canterbury, but is shared equally by all the Bishop Commissioners, who have all (unless I am grievously mistaken) taken similar oaths for the preservation of their respective Chapters. It would be more easy to see our way out of this little embarrassment, if some of the embarrassed had not unfortunately, in the parliamentary debates on the Catholic Question, laid the greatest stress upon the King's oath, applauded the sanctity of the monarch to the skies, rejected all comments, called for the oath in its plain meaning, and attributed the safety of the English Church to the solemn vow made by the King at the altar to the Archbishops of Canterbury and York, and the other Bishops. I should be very sorry if this were not placed on a clear footing, as fools will be imputing to our Church the *pia et religiosa Calliditas*, which is so commonly brought against the Catholics.

Urbem quam dicunt Romam, Melibœe, putavi
Stultus ego huic nostræ similem.

The words of Henry VIII, in endowing the Cathedral of Canterbury, are thus given in the translation:—"We therefore, dedicating the aforesaid close, site, circle, and precinct to the honour and glory of the Holy and undivided Trinity, Father, Son, and Holy Spirit, have decreed that a certain Cathedral and Metropolitan Church, with one Dean, Presbyter, and Twelve Prebendaries Presbyters; these verily and for ever to serve Almighty God shall be created, set up, settled, and established; and the same aforesaid Cathedral and Metropolitan Church, with one Dean, Presbyter, and Twelve Prebendaries Presbyters, with other Ministers necessary for divine worship, by the tenor of these presents in reality, and plenitude of force, we do create, set up, settle, and establish, and do command to be established and to be in perpetuity, and inviolably maintained and upheld by these presents." And this is the Church, the rights and liberties of which the Archbishop at his consecration swears to maintain. Nothing can be more ill-natured among politicians, than to look back into Hansard's Debates, to see what has been said by particular men upon particular occasions, and to contrast such speeches with present opinions—and therefore I forbear to introduce some inviting passages upon taking oaths in their plain and obvious sense, both in debates on the Catholic Question and upon that fatal and *Mezentian* oath which binds the Irish to the English Church.

It is quite absurd to see how all the Cathedrals are to be trimmed to an exact *Procrustes* pattern;—*quieta movere* is the motto of the Commission:—there is to be everywhere a Dean and four Residentiaries; but St. Paul's and Lincoln have at present only three Residentiaries and a Dean, who officiates in his turn as a

Canon:—a fourth must be added to each. Why? nobody wants more Prebendaries; St. Paul's and Lincoln go on very well as they are. It is not for the lack of Prebendaries, it is for idleness, that the Church of England is unpopular; but in the lust of reforming, the Commission cut and patch property as they would cut figures in pasteboard. This little piece of wanton change, however, gives to two of the Bishops, who are Commissioners as well as Bishops, patronage of a thousand a year each; and though I am willing not to consider this as the cause of the recommendation, yet I must observe it is not very common that the same persons should bring in the verdict and receive the profits of the suit. No other Archdeacons are paid in such a manner, and no other Bishops out of the Commission have received such a bonus.*

I must express my surprise that nothing in this Commission of Bishops, either in the Bill which has passed, or in the Report which preceded it, is said of the duties of Bishops. A Bishop is not now forced by law to be in his diocese, or to attend his duty in Parliament —he may be entirely absent from both; nor are there wanting instances within these six years where such has been the case. It would have been very easy to have placed the repairs of Episcopal Palaces (as the concurrent leases of Bishops are placed) under the superintendence of Deans and Chapters; but though the Bishop's bill was accompanied by another bill, containing the strictest enactments for the residence of the Clergy, and some very arbitrary and unjust rules for the repair of their houses, it did not appear upon the face of the law that the Bishops had any such duties to perform; and yet I remember the case of a bishop, dead not six years ago, who was scarcely ever seen in the House of Lords, or in his diocese; and I remember well also the indignation with which the inhabitants of a great Cathedral town spoke of the conduct of another Bishop (now also deceased), who not only never entered his palace, but turned his horses into the garden. When I mention these instances, I am not setting myself up as the satirist of Bishops. I think, upon the whole, they do their duty in a very exemplary manner; but they are not, as the late bills would have us to suppose, *impeccable*. The Church Commissioners should not have suffered their reports and recommendations to paint the other branches of the Church as such slippery transgredient mortals, and to leave the world to imagine that Bishops may be safely trusted to their own goodness without enactment or control.

---

*This extravagant pay of Archdeacons is taken, remember, from that fund for the augmentation of small Livings, for the establishment of which all the divisions and confiscations have been made.

This squabble about patronage is said to be disgraceful. Those who mean to be idle, and insolent, because they are at peace, may look out of the window and say, "This is a disgraceful squabble between Bishops and Chapters"; but those who mean to be just should ask, *Who begins?* the *real* disgrace of the squabble is in the attack, and not in the defence. If any man put his hand into my pocket to take my property, am I disgraced if I prevent him? Churchmen are ready enough to be submissive to their superiors; but were they to submit to a spoliation so gross, accompanied with ignominy, and degradation, and to bear all this in submissive silence;—to be accused of Nepotism by Nepotists, who were praising themselves indirectly by the accusation, and benefiting themselves directly by the confiscation founded on it;—the real disgrace would have been to have submitted to this: and men are to be honoured, not disgraced, who come forth contrary to their usual habits, to oppose those masters, whom, in common seasons, they would willingly obey; but who, in this matter, have tarnished their dignity, and forgotten what they owe to themselves and to us.

It is a very singular thing that the law always suspects Judges, and never suspects Bishops. If there be any way in which the partialities of the Judge may injure laymen, the subject is fenced round with all sorts of jealousies, and enactments, and prohibitions—all partialities are guarded against, and all propensities watched. Where Bishops are concerned, acts of Parliament are drawn up for beings who can never possibly be polluted by pride, prejudice, passion, or interest. Not otherwise would be the case with Judges, if they, like the heads of the Church, legislated for themselves.

Then comes the question of patronage: can anything be more flagrantly unjust, than that the patronage of Cathedrals should be taken away and conferred upon the Bishops? I do not want to go into a long and tiresome history of Episcopal Nepotism; but it is notorious to all, that Bishops confer their patronage upon their sons, and sons-in-law, and all their relations; and it is really quite monstrous in the face of the world, who see this every day, and every hour, to turn round upon Deans and Chapters, and to say to them, "We are credibly informed that there are instances in your Chapters where preferment has not been given to the most learned men you can find, but to the sons and brothers of some of the Prebendaries. These things must not be—we must take these Benefices into our own keeping"; and this is the language of men swarming themselves with sons and daughters, and who, in enumerating the advantages of their stations, have always spoken of the opportunities of providing for their families as the greatest and most important. It is, I admit, the duty of every man, and of everybody, to present the best man that can be found to any living of which he is the Patron; but if this duty has been neglected, it has been neglected by Bishops quite as much as by Chapters; and no man can open the "Clerical Guide," and read two pages of it, without seeing that the Bench of Bishops are the last persons from whom any remedy of this evil is to be expected.

The legislature has not always taken the same view of the comparative trustworthiness of Bishops and Chapters as is taken by the Commission. Bishops' leases for years are for twenty-one years, renewable every seven. When seven years are expired, if the present tenant will not renew, the Bishop may grant a concurrent lease. How does his Lordship act on such occasions? He generally asks two years' income for the renewal, when Chapters, not having the privilege of granting such concurrent leases, ask only a year and a half; and if the Bishop's price is not given, he puts a son, or a daughter, or a trustee, into the estate, and the price of the lease deferred is money saved for his family. But unfair and exorbitant terms may be asked by his Lordship, and the tenant may be unfairly dispossessed; therefore, the legislature enacts that all those concurrent leases must be countersigned by the Dean and Chapter of the diocese—making them the safeguards against Episcopal rapacity; and, as I hear from others, not making them so in vain. These sort of laws do not exactly correspond with the relative views taken of both parties by the Ecclesiastical Commission. This view of Chapters is of course overlooked by a Commission of Bishops, just as all mention of bridles would be omitted in a meeting of horses; but in this view Chapters might be made eminently useful. In what profession, too, are there no gradations? Why is the Church of England to be nothing but a collection of Beggars and Bishops—the Right Reverend Dives in the palace, and Lazarus in orders at the gate, doctored by dogs, and comforted with crumbs?

But to take away the patronage of existing Prebendaries is objectionable for another class of reasons. If it is right to take away the patronage of my Cathedral and to give it to the Bishop, it is at least unjust to do so with my share of it during my life. Society have a right to improve, or to do what they think an improvement, but then they have no right to do so suddenly, and hastily to my prejudice! After securing to me certain possessions by one hundred statutes passed in six hundred years—after having clothed me in fine garments, and conferred upon me pompous names, they have no right to turn round upon me all of a sudden, and to say, You are not a Dean nor a Canon-Residentiary, but a vagabond and an outcast, and a morbid excrescence upon society. This would not be a reform, but the grossest tyranny and oppression. If a man cannot live under the canopy of ancient law, where is he safe? how can he see his way, or lay out his plan of life?

Dubitant homines serere atque impendere curas.

You tolerated for a century the wicked traffic in slaves, legislated for that species of property, encouraged it by premiums, defended it in your Courts of Justice—West Indians bought, and sold, trusting (as Englishmen always ought to trust) in Parliaments. Women went to the altar, promised that they should be supported by that property; and children were born to it, and young men were educated with it: but God touched the hearts of the English people, and they would have no slaves. The scales fell from their eyes, and they saw the monstrous wickedness of the traffic; but then they said, and said magnificently, to the West Indians, "We mean to become wiser and better, but not at your expense; the loss shall be ours, and we will not involve you in ruin, because we are ashamed of our former cruelties, and have learnt a better lesson of humanity and wisdom." And this is the way in which improving nations ought to act, and this is the distinction between reform and revolution.

Justice is not changed by the magnitude or minuteness of the subject. The old Cathedrals have enjoyed their patronage for seven hundred years, and the new ones since the time of Henry VIII; which latter period even gives a much longer possession than ninety-nine out of a hundred of the legislators, who are called upon to plunder us, can boast of for their own estates. And these rights, thus sanctioned, and hallowed by time, are torn from their present possessors without the least warning or preparation, in the midst of all that fever of change which has seized upon the people, and which frightens men to the core of their hearts; and this spoliation is made, not by low men rushing into the plunder of the Church and State, but by men of admirable and unimpeached character in all the relations of life—not by rash men of new politics, but by the ancient conservators of ancient law—by the Archbishops and Bishops of the land, high official men, invented and created, and put in palaces to curb the lawless changes and the mutations, and the madness of mankind; and, to crown the whole, the ludicrous is added to the unjust, and what they take from the other branches of the Church they confer upon *themselves*.

Never dreaming of such sudden revolutions as these, a Prebendary brings up his son to the Church, and spends a large sum of money in his education, which perhaps he can ill afford. His hope is (wicked wretch!) that according to the established custom of the body to which he (immoral man!) belongs, the chapter will (when his turn arrives), if his son be of fair attainments and good character, attend to his nefarious recommendation, and confer the living upon the young man; and in an instant all his hopes are destroyed, and he finds his preferment seized upon, under the plea of public good, by a stronger churchman than himself. I can call this by no other name than that of tyranny and oppression. I know very well that this is not the theory of patronage; but who does better?—do individual patrons?—do Colleges who give in succession?—and as for Bishops, lives there the man so weak, and foolish, so little observant of the past, as to believe (when this tempest of purity and perfection has blown over) that the name of Blomfield will not figure in those benefices from which the names of Copleston, Blomberg, Tate, and Smith, have been so virtuously excluded? I have no desire to make odious comparisons between the purity of one set of patrons and another, but they are forced upon me by the injustice of the Commissioners. I must either make such comparisons, or yield up, without remonstrance, those rights to which I am fairly entitled.

It may be said that the Bishops will do better in future; that now the *public eye* is upon them, they will be shamed into a more lofty and antinepotic spirit; but, if the argument of past superiority be given up, and the hope of future amendment resorted to, why may *we* not improve as well as our masters? but the Commission say, "These excellent men (meaning themselves) have promised to do better, and we have an implicit confidence in their word: we must have the patronage of the Cathedrals." In the meantime we are ready to promise as well as the Bishops.

With regard to that common newspaper phrase *the public eye*—there's nothing (as the Bench well know) more wandering and slippery than the *public eye*. In five years hence the public eye will no more see what description of men are promoted by Bishops, than it will see what Doctors of Law are promoted by the Turkish Uhlema; and at the end of this period (such is the example set by the Commission), the *public eye* turned in every direction may not be able to see any Bishops at all.

In many instances, Chapters are better patrons than Bishops, because their preferment is not given exclusively to one species of Incumbents. I have a diocese now in my private eye which has undergone the following changes. The first of three Bishops whom I remember was a man of careless easy temper, and how patronage went in those early days may be conjectured by the following letters—which are not his, but serve to illustrate a system:

THE BISHOP TO LORD A——.

My dear Lord,

I have noticed with great pleasure the behaviour of your Lordship's second son, and am most happy to have it in my power to offer to him the living of . . . He will find it of considerable value; and there is, I understand, a very good house upon it, &c. &c.

This is to confer a living upon a man of real merit out of the family; into which family, apparently sacrificed to the public good, the living is brought back by the second letter:

THE SAME TO THE SAME A YEAR AFTER

My dear Lord,

Will you excuse the liberty I take in soliciting promotion for my grandson? He is an officer of great skill and gallantry, and can bring the most ample testimonials from some of the best men in the profession: the Arethusa frigate is, I understand, about to be commissioned; and if, &c. &c.

Now I am not saying that hundreds of Prebendaries have not committed such enormous and stupendous crimes as this (a declaration which will fill the Whig Cabinet with horror); all that I mean to contend for is, that such is the practice of Bishops quite as much as it is of inferior Patrons.

The second Bishop was a decided enemy of Calvinistical doctrines, and no Clergyman so tainted had the slightest chance of preferment in his diocese.

The third Bishop could endure no man whose principles were not strictly Calvinistic, and who did not give to the Articles that kind of interpretation. Now here were a great mass of Clergy naturally alive to the emoluments of their profession, and not knowing which way to look or stir, because they depended so entirely upon the will of one person. Not otherwise is it with a very Whig Bishop, or a very Tory Bishop: but the worst case is that of a superannuated Bishop: here the preferment is given away, and must be given away by wives and daughters, or by sons, or by butlers, perhaps, and valets, and the poor dying Patron's paralytic hand is guided to the signature of papers, the contents of which he is utterly unable to comprehend. In all such cases as these, the superiority of Bishops as Patrons will not assist that violence which the Commissioners have committed upon the patronage of Cathedrals.

I never heard that Cathedrals had sold the patronage of their preferment; such a practice, however, is not quite unknown among the higher orders of the Church. When the Archbishop of Canterbury consecrates an inferior Bishop, he marks some piece of preferment in the gift of the Bishop as his own. This is denominated an *option;* and when the preferment falls, it is not only in the gift of the Archbishop, if he is alive, but in the gift of his representatives if he is not. It is an absolute chattel, which, like any other chattel, is part of the Archbishop's assets; and if he died in debt, might be taken, and sold, for the benefit of his creditors—and within the memory of man such options have been publicly sold by auction—and if the present Archbishop of Canterbury were to die in debt to-morrow, such might be the fate of his options. What Archbishop Moore did with his options I do not know, but the late Archbishop Sutton very handsomely and properly left them to the present—a bequest, however, which would not have prevented such options from coming to the hammer, if Archbishop Sutton had not cleared off, before his death, those incumbrances which at one period of his life sat so heavily upon him.

What the present Archbishop means to do with them, I am not informed. They are not alluded to in the Church Returns, though they must be worth some thousand pounds. The Commissioners do not seem to know of their existence—at least they are profoundly silent on the subject; and the bill which passed through Parliament in the summer for the regulation of the Emoluments of Bishops does not make the most distant allusion to them. When a parallel was drawn between two species of patrons—which ended in the confiscation of the patronage of Cathedrals—when two Archbishops helped to draw the parallel, and profited by the parallel, I have a perfect right to state this corrupt and unabolished practice of their own sees—a practice which I never heard charged against Deans and Chapters.*

I do not mean to imply, in the most remote degree, that either of the present Archbishops have sold their options, or ever thought of it. Purer and more high-minded gentlemen do not exist, nor men more utterly incapable of doing anything unworthy of their high station; and I am convinced the Archbishop of Canterbury †

---

* Can anything be more shabby in a Government legislating upon Church abuses, than to pass over such scandals as these existing in high places? Two years have passed, and they are unnoticed.

† The options of the Archbishop of York are comparatively trifling. I never heard, at any period, that they have been sold; but they remain, like those of Canterbury, in the absolute possession of the Archbishop's representa-

will imitate or exceed the munificence of his predecessor: but when
twenty-four public bodies are to be despoiled of their patronage, we
must look not only to present men, but historically, to see how it has
been administered in times of old, and in times also recently past;
and to remember, that at this moment, when Bishops are set up as
the most admirable dispensers of patronage—as the only persons
fit to be intrusted with it—as Marvels, for whom law, and justice,
and ancient possessions, ought to be set aside, that this patronage
(very valuable because selected from the whole diocese) of the two
heads of the Church is liable to all the accidents of succession—
that it may fall into the hands of a superannuated wife, of a profligate son, of a weak daughter, or a rapacious creditor,—that it
may be brought to the hammer, and publicly bid for at an auction,
like all the other chattels of the palace; and that such have been
the indignities to which this optional patronage has been exposed,
from the earliest days of the Church to this moment. Truly, men
who live in houses of glass (especially where the panes are so
large) ought not to fling stones; or if they do, they should be especially careful at whose head they are flung.

And then the patronage which is not seized—the patronage
which the Chapter is allowed to present to its own body—may be
divided without their consent. Can anything be more thoroughly
lawless, or unjust, than this—that my patronage during my life
shall be divided without my consent? How do my rights during
my life differ from those of a lay patron, who is tenant for life?
and upon what principle of justice or common sense is his patronage protected from the Commissioners' dividing power to
which mine is subjected? That one can sell, and the other cannot
sell, the next presentation, would be bad reasoning if it were good
law; but it is not law, for an Ecclesiastical Corporation, aggregate
or sole, can sell a next presentation as legally as a lay life-tenant
can do. They have the same power of selling as laymen, but they
never do so; that is, they dispense their patronage with greater
propriety and delicacy, which, in the estimate of the Commissioners, seems to make their right weaker, and the reasons for taking
it away more powerful.

Not only are laymen guarded by the same act which gives the
power of dividing livings to the Commissioners, but Bishops are
also guarded. The Commissioners may divide the livings of Chapters without their consent; but before they can touch the living of

tives after his death. I will answer for it that the present Archbishop will
do everything with them which becomes his high station and high character.
They ought to be abolished by Act of Parliament.

a Bishop, his consent must be obtained. It seems, after a few of those examples, to become a little clearer, and more intelligible, why the appointment of any other Ecclesiastics than Bishops was so disagreeable to the Bench.

The reasoning then is this: If a good living be vacant in the patronage of a Chapter, they will only think of conferring it on one of their body or their friends. If such a living fall to the gift of a Bishop, he will totally overlook the interests of his sons and daughters, and divide the living into small portions for the good of the public; and with these sort of anilities, Whig leaders, whose interest it is to lull the Bishops into a reform, pretend to be satisfied; and upon this intolerable nonsense they are not ashamed to justify spoliation.*

A division is set up between public and private patronage, and it is pretended that one is holden in trust for the public, the other is private property. This is mere theory—a slight film thrown over convenient injustice. Henry VIII. gave to the Duke of Bedford much of his patronage. Roger de Hoveden gave to the Church of St. Paul's much of their patronage before the Russells were in existence. The Duke has the legal power to give his preferment to whom he pleases—so have we. We are both under the same moral and religious restraint to administer that patronage properly—the trust is precisely the same to both: and if the public good require it, the power of dividing livings without the consent of patrons should be given in all instances, and not confined as a mark of infamy to Cathedrals alone. This is not the real reason of the difference: Bishops are the active Members of the Commission— they do not choose that their own patronage should be meddled with, and they know that the Laity would not allow for a moment that their livings should be pulled to pieces by Bishops; and that if such a proposal were made, there would be more danger of the Bishop being pulled to pieces than the living. The real distinction is, between the weak and the strong—between those who have power to resist encroachments, and those who have not. This is the reason why we are selected for experiment, and so it is with all the bill from beginning to end. There is purple and fine linen in every line of it.

Another strong objection to the dividing power of the Commission is this: According to the printed bill brought forward last session, if the living be not taken by some members of the body,

---

* These reasonings have had their effect, and many early acts of injustice of the Commission have been subsequently corrected.

it lapses to the Bishop. Suppose then the same person to be Bishop and Commissioner, he breaks the living into little pieces as a Commissioner, and after it is rejected in its impoverished state by the Chapter, he gives it away as Bishop of the diocese. The only answer that is given to such objections is, the *impeccability of Bishops;* and upon this principle the whole bill has been constructed: and here is the great mistake about Bishops. They are, upon the whole, very good and worthy men; but they are not (as many ancient ladies suppose) wholly exempt from human infirmities: they have their malice, hatred, uncharitableness, persecution, and interest like other men; and an Administration who did not think it more magnificent to laugh at the lower Clergy than to protect them, should suffer no Ecclesiastical bill to pass through Parliament without seriously considering how its provisions may affect the happiness of poor Clergymen pushed into living tombs, and pining in solitude—

> Vates procul atque in sola relegant
> Pascua, post montem oppositum, et trans
> flumina lata.

There is a practice among some Bishops, which may as well be mentioned here as anywhere else, but which I think cannot be too severely reprobated. They send for a Clergyman, and insist upon his giving evidence respecting the character and conduct of his neighbour. Does he hunt? Does he shoot? Is he in debt? Is he temperate? Does he attend to his parish? &c. &c. Now what is this but to destroy for all Clergymen the very elements of social life—to put an end to all confidence between man and man—and to disseminate among gentlemen, who are bound to live in concord, every feeling of resentment, hatred, and suspicion? but the very essence of tyranny is to act as if the finer feelings, like the finer dishes, were delicacies only for the rich and great, and that little people have no taste for them and no right to them. A good and honest Bishop (I thank God there are many who deserve that character!) ought to suspect himself, and carefully to watch his own heart. He is all of a sudden elevated from being a tutor, dining at an early hour with his pupil, (and occasionally, it is believed, on cold meat,) to be a spiritual Lord; he is dressed in a magnificent dress, decorated with a title, flattered by Chaplains, and surrounded by little people looking up for the things which he has to give away; and this often happens to a man who has had no opportunities of seeing the world, whose parents were in very humble life, and who has given up all his thoughts to the Frogs of Aris-

tophanes and the Targum of Onkelos. How is it possibile that
such a man should not lose his head? that he should not swell? that
he should not be guilty of a thousand follies, and worry and tease
to death (before he recovers his common sense) a hundred men
as good, and as wise, and as able as himself? *

The history of the division of Edmonton has, I understand, been
repeatedly stated in the Commission—and told as it has been by
a decided advocate, and with no sort of evidence called for on the
other side of the question, has produced an unfair impression
against Chapters. The history is shortly this:—Besides the Mother
Church of Edmonton, there are two Chapels—Southgate and
Winchmore Hill Chapel. Winchmore Hill Chapel was built by the
Society for building Churches, upon the same plan as the portions
of Marylebone are arranged: the Clergyman was to be remuner-
ated by the lease of the pews, and if Curates with talents for
preaching had been placed there, they might have gained 200*l.*
per annum. Though men of perfectly respectable and honourable
character, they were not endowed with this sort of talent, and
they gained no more than from 90*l.* to 100*l.* per annum. The
Bishop of London applied to the Cathedral of St. Paul's to consent
to 250*l.* per annum, in addition to the proceeds from the letting
of the pews, or that proportion of the whole of the value of the living should be allotted to the chapel of Winchmore; and at the same
time we received an application from the chapel at Southgate,
that another considerable portion, I forget what, but I believe it to
have been rather less (perhaps 200*l.*), should be allotted to them,
and the whole living severed into three parishes. Now the living of
Edmonton is about 1350*l.* per annum, besides surplice fees; but
this 1350*l.* depends upon a Corn Rent of 10*s.* 3*d.* per bushel,
present valuation, which at the next valuation would, in the opinion of eminent land surveyors, whom we consulted, be reduced to
about 6*s.* per bushel, so that the living, considering the reduction
also of all voluntary offerings to the Church, would be reduced
one half, and this half was to be divided into three, and one or
two Curates (two Curates by the present bill) to be kept by the
Vicar of the old Church; and thus three clerical beggars were,
by the activity of the Bishop of London, to be established in a
district where the extreme dearness of all provisions is the plea for
making the See of London double in value to that of any Bishopric

---

* Since writing this, and after declining the living for myself, I have had
the pleasure of seeing it presented in an undivided state to my amiable and
excellent friend, Mr. Tate, who, after a long life of moods and tenses, has
acquired (as he has deserved) ease and opulence in his old age.

in the country. To this we declined to agree; and this, heard only on one side, with the total omission of the changing value of the Benefice from the price of corn, has most probably been the parent of the clause in question. The right cure for this and all similar cases would be, to give the Bishop a power of allotting to such Chapels as high a salary as to any other Curate in the diocese, taking, as part of that salary, whatever was received from the lease of the pews, and to this no reasonable man could or would object: but this is not enough—all must bow to one man—"Chapters must be taught submission. No pamphlets, no meeting of independent Prebendaries, to remonstrate against the proceedings of their superiors—no opulence and ease but mine."

Some effect was produced also upon the Commission, by the evidence of a Prelate who is both Dean and Bishop,* and who gave it as his opinion, that the patronage of Bishops was given upon better principles than that of Chapters, which, translated into fair English, is no more than this—that the said witness, not meaning to mislead, but himself deceived, has his own way entirely in his diocese, and can only have it partially in his Chapter.

There is a rumour that these reasonings, with which they were assailed from so many quarters in the last Session of Parliament, have not been without their effect, and that it is the intention of the Commissioners only to take away the patronage from the Cathedrals exactly in proportion as the numbers of their Members are reduced. Such may be the intention of the Commissioners; but as that intention has not been publicly notified, it depends only upon report; and the Commissioners have changed their minds so often, that they may alter their intentions twenty times again before the meeting of Parliament. The whole of my observations in this letter are grounded upon their *bills of last year*—which Lord John Russell stated his intention of re-introducing at the beginning of this Session. If they have any new plans, they ought to have published them three months ago—and to have given to the Clergy an ample opportunity of considering them; but this they take the greatest care never to do. The policy of the Government and the Commissioners is to hurry their bills through with such rapidity, that very little time is given to those who suffer by them for consideration and remonstrance, and we must be prepared for the worst beforehand. You are cashiered and confiscated before you can look about you—if you leave home for six weeks, in

---

* This prelate stated it as his opinion to the Commission, that in future all Prelates ought to declare that they held their patronage in trust for the public.

these times, you find a Commissioner in possession of your house and office.

A report has reached my ears, that though all other Cathedrals are to retain patronage exactly equal to their reduced numbers, a separate measure of justice is to be used for St. Paul's; that our numbers are to be augmented by a fifth; and our patronage reduced by a third; and this immediately on the passing of the bill. That the Bishop of Exeter, for instance, is to receive his augmentation of patronage only in proportion as the Prebendaries die off, and the Prebendaries themselves will, as long as they live, remain in the same proportional state as to patronage; and that when they are reduced to four (their stationary number), they will retain one-third of all the patronage the twelve now possess. Whether this be wise or not, is a separate question, but at least it is just; the four who remain cannot with any colour of justice complain that they do not retain all the patronage which was divided among twelve; but at St. Paul's not only are our numbers to be augmented by a fifth, but the patronage of fifteen of our best livings is to be instantly conferred upon the Bishop of London. This little *episode of plunder* involves three separate acts of gross injustice: in the first place, if only our numbers had been augmented by a fifth (in itself a mere bonus to Commissioners), our patronage would have been reduced one fifth in value. Secondly, one third of the preferment is to be taken away immediately, and these two added together make eight fifteenths, or more than one half of our whole patronage. So that when all the Cathedrals are reduced to their reformed numbers, each Cathedral will enjoy precisely the same proportion of patronage as it now does, and each member of every other Cathedral will have precisely the same means of promoting men of merit or men of his own family, as is now possessed; while less than half of these advantages will remain to St. Paul's. Thirdly, if the Bishop of London were to wait (as all the other Bishops by this arrangement must wait) till the present patrons die off, the injustice would be to the future body; but by this scheme, every present incumbent of St. Paul's is instantly deprived of eight fifteenths of his patronage; while every other member of every other Cathedral (as far as patronage is concerned) remains precisely in the same state in which he was before. Why this blow is levelled against St. Paul's I cannot conceive; still less can I imagine why the Bishop of London is not to wait, as all other Bishops are forced to wait, for the death of the present Patrons. There is a reason, indeed, for not waiting, by which (had I to do with a person of less elevated character than the Bishop of

London) I would endeavour to explain this precipitate seizure of
patronage—and that is, that the livings assigned to him in this remarkable scheme are all very valuable, and the incumbents all
very old. But I shall pass over this scheme as a mere supposition,
invented to bring the Commission into disrepute, a scheme to
which it is utterly impossible the Commissioners should ever affix
their names.

I should have thought, if the love of what is just had not excited
the Commissioner-Bishops, that the ridicule of men voting such
comfortable things to themselves as the Prebendal patronage,
would have alarmed them; but they want to sacrifice with other
men's hecatombs, and to enjoy, at the same time, the character of
great disinterestedness, and the luxury of unjust spoliation. It was
thought necessary to make a fund; and the Prebends in the gift of
the Bishops * were appropriated to that purpose. The Bishops who
consented to this have then made a great sacrifice:—true, but they
have taken more out of our pockets than they have disbursed from
their own. Where then is the sacrifice? They must either give back
the patronage or the martyrdom: if they choose to be martyrs—
which I hope they will do—let them give us back our patronage:
if they prefer the patronage, they must not talk of being martyrs—
they cannot effect this double sensuality and combine the sweet
flavour of rapine with the aromatic odour of sanctity.

We are told, if you agitate these questions among yourselves,
you will have the democratic Philistines come down upon you, and
sweep you all away together. Be it so; I am quite ready to be swept
away when the time comes. Everybody has their favourite death:
some delight in apoplexy, and others prefer marasmus. I would infinitely rather be crushed by democrats, than, under the plea of the
public good, be mildly and blandly absorbed by Bishops.

I met the other day, in an old Dutch Chronicle, with a passage
so apposite to this subject, that, though it is somewhat too light
for the occasion, I cannot abstain from quoting it. There was a
great meeting of all the Clergy at Dordrecht, and the Chronicler
thus describes it, which I give in the language of the translation:—
"And there was great store of Bishops in the town, in their robes

---

* The Bishops have, however, secured for themselves all the Livings which
were in the separate gifts of Prebendaries and Deans, and they have received from the Crown a very large contribution of valuable patronage;
why or wherefore is known only to the unfathomable wisdom of Ministers.
The glory of martyrdom can be confined only at best to the Bishops of the
old Cathedrals, for there are scarcely any separate Prebends in the new
Cathedrals.

goodly to behold, and all the great men of the State were there, and folks poured in in boats on the Meuse, the Merve, the Rhine, and the Linge, coming from the Isle of Beverlandt and Isselmond, and from all quarters in the Bailiwick of Dort; Arminians and Gomarists, with the friends of John Barneveldt and of Hugh Grote. And before my Lords the Bishops, Simon of Gloucester, who was a Bishop in those parts, disputed with Vorstius and Leoline the Monk, and many texts of Scripture were bandied to and fro; and when this was done, and many propositions made, and it waxed towards twelve of the clock, my Lords the Bishops prepared to set them down to a fair repast, in which was great store of good things—and among the rest a roasted peacock, having in lieu of a tail the arms and banners of the Archbishop, which was a goodly sight to all who favoured the Church—and then the Archbishop would say a grace, as was seemly to do, he being a very holy man; but ere he had finished, a great mob of townspeople and folks from the country who were gathered under the window, cried out, *Bread! bread!* for there was a great famine, and wheat had risen to three times the ordinary price of the *sleich*; * and when they had done crying *Bread! bread!* they called out *No Bishops!*—and began to cast up stones at the windows. Whereat my Lords the Bishops were in a great fright, and cast their dinner out of the window to appease the mob, and so the men of that town were well pleased, and did devour the meats with a great appetite; and then you might have seen my Lords standing with empty plates, and looking wistfully at each other, till Simon of Gloucester, he who disputed with Leoline the Monk, stood up among them and said, *'Good my Lords, is it your pleasure to stand here fasting, and that those who count lower in the Church than you do should feast and fluster? Let us order to us the dinner of the Deans and Canons, which is making ready for them in the chamber below.'* And this speech of Simon of Gloucester pleased the Bishops much; and so they sent for the host, one William of Ypres, and told him it was for the public good, and he, much fearing the Bishops, brought them the dinner of the Deans and Canons; and so the Deans and Canons went away without dinner, and were pelted by the men of the town, because they had not put any meat out of the window like the Bishops; and when the Count came to hear of it, he said it was a pleasant conceit, *and that the Bishops were right cunning men, and had ding'd the Canons well."*

---

* A measure in the Bailiwick of Dort containing two gallons one pint English dry measure.

When I talk of sacrifices, I mean the sacrifices of the Bishop-Commissioners, for we are given to understand that the great mass of Bishops were never consulted at all about these proceedings; that they are contrary to everything which consultations at Lambeth, previous to the Commission, had led them to expect; and that they are totally disapproved of by them. The voluntary sacrifice, then (for it is no sacrifice if it be not voluntary), is in the Bishop-Commissioners only; and besides the indemnification which they have voted to themselves out of the patronage of the Cathedrals, they will have all that never-ending patronage which is to proceed from the working of the Commission, and the endowments bestowed upon different livings. So much for episcopal sacrifices!

And who does not see the end and meaning of all this? The Lay Commissioners, who are members of the Government, cannot and will not attend—the Archbishops of York and Canterbury are quiet and amiable men, going fast down in the vale of life—some of the members of the Commission are expletives—some must be absent in their dioceses—the Bishop of London is passionately fond of labour, has certainly no aversion to power, is of quick temper, great ability, thoroughly versant in ecclesiastical law, and always in London. He will become the Commission, and when the Church of England is mentioned, it will only mean *Charles James of London,* who will enjoy a greater power than has ever been possessed by any Churchman since the days of Laud, and will become the *Church of England here upon earth.* As for the Commission itself, there is scarcely any power which is not given to it. They may call for every paper in the world, and every human creature who possesses it, and do what they like to one or the other. It is hopeless to contend with such a body; and most painful to think that it has been established under a Whig Government.* A Commission of Tory Churchmen, established for such purposes, should have been framed with the utmost jealousy, and with the most cautious circumspection of its powers, and with the most earnest wish for its extinction when the purposes of its creation were answered. The Government have done everything in their power to make it vexatious, omnipotent, and everlasting. This immense power, flung into the hands of an individual, is one of the many foolish consequences which proceed from the centralisation of the bill, and the unwillingness to employ the local knowl-

* I am speaking here of the permanent Commission established by Act of Parliament in 1835. The Commission for reporting had come to an end six months before this letter was written.

edge of the Bishops in the process of annexing dignified to parochial preferment.

There is a third bill concocted by the Commission-Bishops, in
which the great principle of increasing the power of the Bench has
certainly not been lost sight of:—A brother Clergyman falls ill
suddenly in the country, and he begs his clerical neighbour to do
duty for him in the afternoon, thinking it better that there should
be single service in two churches, than two services in one, and
none in the other. The Clergyman who accedes to this request is
liable to a penalty of 5*l.* There is a harshness and ill nature in this
—a gross ignorance of the state of the poorer Clergy—a hard-
heartedness produced by the long enjoyment of wealth and power,
which makes it quite intolerable. I speak of it as it stands in the
bill of last year.*

If a Clergyman has a living of 400*l.* per annum, and a population of two thousand persons, the Bishop can compel him to
keep a Curate to whom he can allot any salary which he may allot
to any other Curate; in other words, he may take away half the
income of the Clergyman, and instantly ruin him—and this without any complaint from the Vestry; with every testimonial of the
most perfect satisfaction of the Parish in the labours of a Minister,
who may, perhaps, be dedicating his whole life to their improvement. I think I remember that the Bishop of London once attempted this before he was a Commissioner, and was defeated. I
had no manner of doubt that it would speedily become the law,
after the Commission had begun to operate. The Bishop of London is said to have declared, after this trial, that *if it was not law
it should soon be law:* † and *law* you will see it will become. In
fact, he can slip into any Ecclesiastical Act of Parliament anything
he pleases. There is nobody to heed or to contradict him; provided the power of Bishops is extended by it, no Bishop is so un-
genteel as to oppose the Act of his Right Reverend Brother; and
there are not many men who have knowledge, eloquence, or force
of character to stand up against the Bishop of London, and, above
all, of industry to watch him. The Ministry, and the Lay Lords,
and the House of Commons, care nothing about the matter; and
the Clergy themselves, in a state of the greatest ignorance as to
what is passing in the world, find their chains heavier and heavier,

---

* This is also given up.

† The Bishop of London denies that he ever said this; but the Bishop of
London affects short sharp sayings, seasoned, I am afraid, sometimes with
a little indiscretion; and these sayings are not necessarily forgotten because
he forgets them.

without knowing who or what has produced the additional encumbrance. A good honest Whig Minister should have two or three stout-hearted parish priests in his train to watch the Bishops' bills, and to see that they were constructed on other principles than that *Bishops can do no wrong, and cannot have too much power.* The Whigs do nothing of this, and yet they complain that they are hated by the Clergy, and that in all elections the Clergy are their bitterest enemies. Suppose they were to try a little justice, a little notice, and a little protection. It would take more time than quizzing, and contempt, but it might do some good.

The Bishop puts a great number of questions to his Clergy, which they are to be compelled, by this new law of the Commission, to answer, under a penalty, and if they do answer them, they incur, perhaps, a still heavier penalty. "Have you had two services in your Church all the year?"—"I decline to answer."—"Then I fine you 20*l.*"—"I have only had one service."—"Then I fine you 250*l.*" In what other profession are men placed between this double fire of penalties, and compelled to criminate themselves? It has been disused in England, I believe, ever since the time of Laud and the Star Chamber.*

By the same bill, as it first emanated from the Commission, a Bishop could compel a Clergyman to expend three years' income upon a house in which he had resided perhaps fifty years, and in which he had brought up a large family. With great difficulty, some slight modification of this enormous power was obtained, and it was a little improved in the amended bill.† In the same way an attempt was made to try delinquent Clergymen by a jury of Clergymen, nominated by the Bishop; but this was too bad, and was not

---

* This attempt upon the happiness and independence of the Clergy has been abandoned.
† I perceive that the Archbishop of Canterbury borrows money for the improvement of his palace, and pays the principal off in forty years. This is quite as soon as a debt incurred for such public purposes ought to be paid off, and the Archbishop has done rightly to take that period. In process of time I think it very likely that this indulgence will be extended to country Clergymen, who are compelled to pay off the debts for buildings (which they are compelled to undertake) in twenty years; and by the new bill, not yet passed, this indulgence is extended to thirty years. Why poor Clergymen have been compelled for the last five years to pay off the encumbrances at the rate of one twentieth per annum, and are now compelled to pay them off, or will, when the bill passes, be so compelled, at the rate of one thirtieth per annum, when the Archbishop takes forty years to do the same thing, and has made that bargain in the year 1831, I really cannot tell. A Clergyman who does not reside is forced to pay off his building debt in ten years.

endured for an instant; still it showed the same love of power and
the same principle of *impeccability,* for the bill is expressly confined to all suits and complaints against persons *below the dignity
and degree of Bishops.* The truth is, that there are very few men
in either House of Parliament (Ministers or any one else), who
ever think of the happiness and comfort of the working Clergy, or
bestow one thought upon guarding them from the increased and
increasing power of their encroaching masters. What is called taking care of the Church is taking care of the Bishops; and all bills
for the management of the Clergy are left to the concoction of
men who very naturally believe they are improving the Church
when they are increasing their own power. There are many Bishops
too generous, too humane, and too Christian, to oppress a poor
Clergyman; but I have seen (I am sorry to say) many grievous instances of partiality, rudeness, and oppression.* I have seen Clergymen treated by them with a violence and contempt which the
lowest servant in the Bishop's establishment would not have endured for a single moment; and if there be a helpless, friendless,
wretched being in the community, it is a poor Clergyman in the
country, with a large family. If there be an object of compassion,
he is one. If there be any occasion in life where a great man should
lay aside his office, and put on those kind looks, and use those
kind words which raise the humble from the dust, these are the
occasions when those best parts of the Christian character ought
to be displayed.

I would instance the unlimited power which a Bishop possesses
over a Curate, as a very unfair degree of power for any man to
possess. Take the following dialogue, which represents a real
event.

Bishop.—Sir, I understand you frequent the Meetings of the
Bible Society?

Curate.—Yes, my Lord, I do.

Bishop.—Sir, I tell you plainly, if you continue to do so, I shall
silence you from preaching in my diocese.

Curate.—My Lord, I am very sorry to incur your indignation,
but I frequent that Society upon principle, because I think it eminently serviceable to the cause of the Gospel.

Bishop.—Sir, I do not enter into your reasons, but tell you
plainly, if you continue to go there you shall be silenced.

The young man did go, and was silenced;—and as Bishops have

---

* What Bishops like best in their Clergy is a dropping-down-deadness of
manner.

always a great deal of clever machinery at work of testimonials and *bene-decessits,* and always a lawyer at their elbow, under the name of a secretary, a Curate excluded from one diocese is excluded from all. His remedy is an appeal to the Archbishop from the Bishop: his worldly goods, however, amount to ten pounds: he never was in London: he dreads such a tribunal as an Archbishop: he thinks, perhaps, in time the Bishop may be softened: if he is compelled to restore him, the enmity will be immortal. It would be just as rational to give to a frog or a rabbit, upon which the physician is about to experiment, an appeal to the Zoological Society, as to give to a country Curate an appeal to the Archbishop against his purple oppressor.

The errors of the bill are a public concern—the injustice of the bill is a private concern. Give us our patronage for life.* Treat the Cathedrals all alike, with the same measure of justice. Don't divide livings in the patronage of present Incumbents without their consent—or do the same with all livings. If these points be attended to in the forthcoming bill, *all complaint of unfairness and injustice will be at an end.* I shall still think, that the Commissioners have been very rash and indiscreet, that they have evinced a contempt for existing institutions, and a spirit of destruction which will be copied to the life hereafter, by Commissioners of a very different description. Bishops live in high places with high people, or with little people who depend upon them. They walk delicately, like Agag. They hear only one sort of conversation, and avoid bold reckless men, as a lady veils herself from rough breezes. I am half inclined to think sometimes, that the Bishop-Commissioners really think that they are finally settling the Church; that the House of Lords will be open to the Bench for ages; and that many Archbishops in succession will enjoy their fifteen thousand pounds a year in Lambeth. I wish I could do for the Bishop-Commissioners what his mother did for Æneas, in the last days of Troy:—

> Omnem quæ nunc obducta tuenti
> Mortales hebetat visus tibi, et humida circum
> Caligat, nubem eripiam.
> Apparent diræ facies, &c. &c.

It is ominous for liberty when Sydney and Russell cannot agree; but when Lord John Russell, in the House of Commons, said, that we showed no disposition to make any sacrifices for the good

---

* This has now been given to us.

of the Church, I took the liberty to remind that excellent person that he must first of all *prove* it to be for the good of the Church that our patronage should be taken away by the Bishops, and then he might find fault with us for not consenting to the sacrifice.

I have little or no personal nor pecuniary interest in these things, and have made all possible exertion (as two or three persons in power well know) that they should not come before the public. I have no son nor son-in-law in the Church, for whom I want any patronage. If I were young enough to survive any incumbent of St. Paul's, my own preferment is too agreeably circumstanced to make it at all probable I should avail myself of the opportunity. I am a sincere advocate for Church Reform; but I think it very possible, and even very easy, to have removed all odium from the Establishment, in a much less violent and revolutionary manner, without committing or attempting such flagrant acts of injustice, and without leaving behind an odious Court of Inquisition, which will inevitably fall into the hands of a single individual, and will be an eternal source of vexation, jealousy, and change. I give sincere credit to the Commissioners for good intentions. How can such men have intended anything but good? And I firmly believe that they are hardly conscious of the extraordinary predilection they have shown for Bishops in all their proceedings: it is like those errors in tradesmen's bills of which the retail arithmetician is really unconscious, but which somehow or another always happen to be in his own favour. Such men as the Commissioners do not say this patronage belongs justly to the Cathedrals, and we will take it away unjustly for ourselves; but after the manner of human nature a thousand weak reasons prevail, which would have no effect, if self-interest were not concerned: they are practising a deception on themselves, and sincerely believe they are doing right. When I talk of spoil and plunder, I do not speak of the intention, but of the effect, and the precedent.

Still the Commissioners are on the eve of entailing an immense evil upon the country, and unfortunately they have gone so far, that it is necessary they should ruin the Cathedrals to preserve their character for consistency. They themselves have been frightened a great deal too much by the mob; have overlooked the chances in their favour produced by delay; have been afraid of being suspected (as Tories) of not doing enough; and have allowed themselves to be hurried on by the constitutional impetuosity of one man, who cannot be brought to believe that wisdom often consists in leaving alone, standing still and doing nothing. From the joint operation of all these causes, all the Cathedrals of

England will in a few weeks be knocked about our ears. You, Mr. Archdeacon Singleton, will sit like Caius Marius on the ruins, and we shall lose for ever the wisest scheme for securing a well-educated Clergy upon the most economical terms, and for preventing that low fanaticism which is the greatest curse upon human happiness, and the greatest enemy of true religion. We shall have all the evils of an Establishment, and none of its good.

You tell me I shall be laughed at as a rich and overgrown Churchman. Be it so. I have been laughed at a hundred times in my life, and care little or nothing about it. If I am well provided for now—I have had my full share of the blanks in the lottery as well as the prizes. Till thirty years of age I never received a farthing from the Church; then 50l. per annum for two years—then nothing for ten years—then 500l. per annum, increased for two or three years to 800l., till, in my grand climacteric, I was made Canon of St. Paul's; and before that period, I had built a Parsonage-house with farm offices for a large farm, which cost me 4000l., and had reclaimed another from ruins at the expense of 2000l. A Lawyer, or a Physician in good practice, would smile at this picture of great Ecclesiastical wealth; and yet I am considered as a perfect monster of Ecclesiastical prosperity.

I should be very sorry to give offence to the dignified Ecclesiastics who are in the Commission: I hope they will allow for the provocation, if I have been a little too warm in the defence of St. Paul's, which I have taken a solemn oath to defend. I was at school and college with the Archbishop of Canterbury: fifty-three years ago he knocked me down with the chess-board for checkmating him—and now he is attempting to take away my patronage. I believe these are the only two acts of violence he ever committed in his life: the interval has been one of gentleness, kindness, and the most amiable and high-principled courtesy to his Clergy. For the Archbishop of York I feel an affectionate respect—the result of that invariable kindness I have received from him: and who can see the Bishop of London without admiring his superior talents—being pleased with his society—without admitting that, *upon the whole,* * the public is benefited by his ungovernable passion for business; and without receiving the constant workings of a really good heart, as an atonement for the occasional excesses of an impetuous disposition? I am quite sure if the tables had been turned,

---

* I have heard that the Bishop of London employs eight hours per day in the government of his diocese—in which no part of Asia, Africa, or America is included. The world is, I believe, taking one day with another, governed in about a third of that time.

and if it had been his lot, as a Canon, to fight against the encroachments of Bishops, that he would have made as stout a defence as I have done—the only difference is, that he would have done it with much greater talent.

As for my friends the Whigs, I neither wish to offend them nor anybody else. I consider myself to be as good a Whig as any amongst them. I was a Whig before many of them were born—and while some of them were Tories and Waverers. I have always turned out to fight their battles, and when I saw no other Clergyman turn out but myself—and this in times before liberality was well recompensed, and therefore in fashion, and when the smallest appearance of it seemed to condemn a Churchman to the grossest obloquy, and the most hopeless poverty. It may suit the purpose of the Ministers to flatter the Bench; it does not suit mine. I do not choose in my old age to be tossed as a prey to the Bishop; I have not deserved this of my Whig friends. I know very well there can be no justice for Deans and Chapters, and that the momentary Lords of the earth will receive our statement with derision and *persiflage*—the great principle which is now called in for the government of mankind. Nobody admires the general conduct of the Whig Administration more than I do. They have conferred, in their domestic policy, the most striking benefits on the country. To say that there is no risk in what they have done is mere nonsense: there is great risk; and all honest men must balance to counteract it—holding back as firmly down hill as they pulled vigorously up hill. Still, great as the risk is, it was worth while to incur it in the Poor Law Bill, in the Tithe Bill, in the Corporation Bill, and in the circumscription of the Irish Protestant Church. In all these matters, the Whig Ministry, after the heat of party is over, and when Joseph Hume and Wilson Croker * are powdered into the dust of death, will gain great and deserved fame. In the question of the Church Commission they have behaved with the grossest injustice; delighted to see this temporary delirium of Archbishops and Bishops, scarcely believing their eyes, and carefully suppressing their laughter, when they saw these eminent Conservatives laying about them with the fury of Mr. Tyler or Mr. Straw; they have taken the greatest care not to disturb them, and to give them no offence: "Do as you like, my Lords, with the Chapters and the Parochial Clergy; you will find some pleasing morsels in the ruins of the Cathedrals. Keep for your-

---

* I meant no harm by the comparison, but I have made two bitter enemies by it.

selves anything you like—whatever is agreeable to you cannot
be unpleasant to us." In the meantime, the old friends of, and the
old sufferers for, liberty, do not understand this new meanness,
and are not a little astonished to find their leaders prostrate on
their knees before the Lords of the Church, and to receive no
other answer from them than that, if they are disturbed in their
adulation, they will immediately resign!

LETTER II.

MY DEAR SIR,

IT is a long time since you have heard from me, and in
the mean time the poor Church of England has been trembling,
from the Bishop who sitteth upon the throne, to the Curate who
rideth upon the hackney horse. I began writing on the subject to
avoid bursting from indignation; and as it is not my habit to recede, I will go on till the Church of England is either up or down
—semianimous on its back, or vigorous on its legs.

Two or three persons have said to me—"Why, after writing an
entertaining and successful letter to Archdeacon Singleton, do
you venture upon another, in which you may probably fail, and be
weak or stupid?" All this I utterly despise: I write upon these matters not to be entertaining, but because the subjects are very important, and because I have strong opinions upon them. If what
I write is liked, so much the better; but liked or not liked, sold
or not sold, Wilson Crokered or not Wilson Crokered, I will write.
If you ask me who excites me—I answer you, it is that Judge who
stirs good thoughts in honest hearts—under whose warrant I impeach the wrong, and by whose help I hope to chastise it.

There are in most Cathedrals two sorts of Prebendaries—the
one resident, the other non-resident. It is proposed by the Church
Commission to abolish all the Prebendaries of the latter and many
of the former class; and it is the Prebendaries of the former class,
the Resident Prebendaries, whom I wish to save.

The Non-resident Prebendaries never come near the Cathedral;
they are just like so many country gentlemen: the difference is,
that their appointments are elective, not hereditary. They have
houses, manors, lands, and every appendage of territorial wealth
and importance. Their value is very different. I have one, Neasdon,
near Willesdon, which consists of a quarter of an acre of land,
worth a few shillings per annum, but animated by the burden of
repairing a bridge, which sometimes costs the unfortunate Prebendary fifty or sixty pounds. There are other Non-resident Preb-

endaries, however, of great value; and one, I believe, which would be worth, if the years or lives were run out, from 40,000l. to 60,000l. per annum.

Not only do these Prebendaries do nothing, and are never seen, but the existence of the preferment is hardly known; and the abolition of the preferment, therefore, would not in any degree lessen the temptation to enter into the Church, while the mass of these preferments would make an important fund for the improvement of small livings. The Residentiary Prebendaries, on the contrary, perform all the services of the Cathedral Church; their existence is known, their preferment coveted, and to get a stall, and to be preceded by men with silver rods, is the bait which the ambitious squire is perpetually holding out to his second son. What Prebendary is next to come into residence is as important a topic to the Cathedral town, and ten miles round it, as what the evening or morning star may be to the astronomer. I will venture to say, that there is not a man of good humour, sense, and worth, within ten miles of Worcester, who does not hail the rising of Archdeacon Singleton in the horizon as one of the most agreeable events of the year. If such sort of preferments are extinguished, a very serious evil (as I have often said before) is done to the Church—the service becomes unpopular, further spoliation is dreaded, the whole system is considered to be altered and degraded, capital is withdrawn from the Church, and no one enters into the profession but the sons of farmers and little tradesmen, who would be footmen if they were not vicars—or figure on the coach-box if they were not lecturing from the pulpit.

But what a practical rebuke to the Commissioners, after all their plans and consultations and carvings of Cathedral preferment, to leave it integral, and untouched! It is some comfort, however, to me, to think, that the persons of all others to whom this preservation of Cathedral property would give the greatest pleasure are the Ecclesiastical Commissioners themselves. Can any one believe that the Archbishop of Canterbury or the Bishop of London really wish for the confiscation of any Cathedral property, or that they were driven to it by anything but fear, mingled, perhaps, with a little vanity of playing the part of great Reformers? They cannot, of course, say for themselves what I say for them; but of what is really passing in the ecclesiastical minds of these great personages, I have no more doubt than I have of what passes in the mind of the prisoner when the prosecutor recommends and relents, and the Judge says he shall attend to the recommendation.

What harm does a Prebend do, in a politico-economical point of view? The alienation of the property for three lives, or twenty-one years, and the almost certainty that the tenant has of renewing, give him sufficent interest in the soil for all purposes of cultivation,* and a long series of elected clergymen is rather more likely to produce valuable members of the community than a long series of begotten squires. Take, for instance, the Cathedral of Bristol, the whole estates of which are about equal to keeping a pack of fox-hounds. If this had been in the hands of a country gentleman, instead of Precentor, Succentor, Dean, and Canons, and Sexton, you would have had huntsman, whipper in, dog-feeders and stoppers of earths; the old squire, full of foolish opinions, and fermented liquids, and a young gentleman of gloves, waistcoats, and pantaloons: and how many generations might it be before the fortuitous concourse of noodles would produce such a man as Professor Lee, one of the Prebendaries of Bristol, and by far the most eminent Oriental scholar in Europe? The same argument might be applied to every Cathedral in England. How many hundred coveys of squires would it take to supply as much knowledge as is condensed in the heads of Dr. Copplestone, or Mr. Tate, of St. Paul's? and what a strange thing it is that such a man as Lord John Russell, the Whig leader, should be so squirrel-minded as to wish for a movement without object or end! Saving there can be none, for it is merely taking from one Ecclesiastic to give it to another; public clamour, to which the best men must sometimes yield, does not require it; and so far from doing any good, it would be a source of infinite mischief to the Establishment.

If you were to gather a Parliament of Curates on the hottest Sunday in the year, after all the services, sermons, burials, and baptisms of the day, were over, and to offer them such increase of salary as would be produced by the confiscation of the Cathedral property, I am convinced they would reject the measure, and prefer splendid hope, and the expectation of good fortune in advanced life, to the trifling improvement of poverty which such a fund could afford. Charles James, of London, was a Curate; the Bishop of Winchester was a Curate; almost every rose-and-shovelman has been a Curate in his time. All Curates hope to draw great prizes.

---

* The Church, it has been urged, do not plant—they do not extend their woods; but almost all Cathedrals possess woods, and regularly plant a succession, so as to keep them up. A single evening of dice and hazard does not doom their woods to sudden destruction; a life-tenant does not cut down all the timber to make the most of his estate; the woods of ecclesiastical bodies are managed upon a fixed and settled plan, and considering the sudden prodigalities of Laymen, I should not be afraid of a comparison.

I am surprised it does not strike the mountaineers how very much the great emoluments of the Church are flung open to the lowest ranks of the community. Butchers, bakers, publicans, schoolmasters, are perpetually seeing their children elevated to the mitre. Let a respectable baker drive through the city from the west end of the town, and let him cast an eye on the battlements of Northumberland House; has his little muffin-faced son the smallest chance of getting in among the Percies, enjoying a share of their luxury and splendour, and of chasing the deer with hound and horn upon the Cheviot Hills? But let him drive his alum-steeped loaves a little further, till he reaches St. Paul's Churchyard, and all his thoughts are changed when he sees that beautiful fabric; it is not impossible that his little penny roll may be introduced into that splendid oven. Young Crumpet is sent to school—takes to his books—spends the best years of his life, as all eminent Englishmen do, in making Latin verses—knows that the *crum* in crumpet is long, and the *pet* short—goes to the University—gets a prize for an Essay on the Dispersion of the Jews—takes orders—becomes a Bishop's chaplain—has a young nobleman for his pupil —publishes an useless classic, and a serious call to the unconverted—and then goes through the Elysian transitions of Prebendary, Dean, Prelate, and the long train of purple, profit, and power.

It will not do to leave only four persons in each Cathedral upon the supposition that such a number will be sufficient for all the men of real merit who ought to enjoy such preferment; we ought to have a steady confidence that the men of real merit will always bear a small proportion to the whole number; and that in proportion as the whole number is lessened, the number of men of merit provided for will be lessened also. If it were quite certain that ninety persons would be selected, the most remarkable for conduct, piety, and learning, ninety offices might be sufficient; but out of these ninety are to be taken tutors to Dukes and Marquises, paid in this way by the public; Bishops' Chaplains, running tame about the palace; elegant Clergymen of small understanding, who have made themselves acceptable in the drawing-rooms of the mitre; Billingsgate controversialists, who have tossed and gored an Unitarian. So that there remain but a few rewards for men of real merit—yet these rewards do infinite good; and in this mixed, checkered way human affairs are conducted.

No man at the beginning of the Reform could tell to what excesses the new power conferred upon the multitude would carry them; it was not safe for a Clergyman to appear in the streets. I bought a blue coat, and did not despair in time of looking like a

Layman. All this is passed over. Men are returned to their senses upon the subject of the Church, and I utterly deny that there is any public feeling whatever which calls for the destruction of the resident Prebends. Lord John Russell has pruned the two luxuriant Bishoprics, and has abolished Pluralities: he has made a very material alteration in the state of the Church: not enough to please Joseph Hume, and the tribunes of the people, but enough to satisfy every reasonable and moderate man, and therefore enough to satisfy himself. What another generation may choose to do is another question: I am thoroughly convinced that enough has been done for the present.

Viscount Melbourne declared himself quite satisfied with the Church as it is; but if the public had any desire to alter it, they might do as they pleased. He might have said the same thing of the Monarchy, or of any other of our institutions; and there is in the declaration a permissiveness and good humour which in public men has seldom been exceeded. Carelessness, however, is but a poor imitation of genius, and the formation of a wise and well-reflected plan of Reform conduces more to the lasting fame of a Minister than that affected contempt of duty which every man sees to be mere vanity, and a vanity of no very high description.

But if the truth must be told, our Viscount is somewhat of an impostor. Everything about him seems to betoken careless desolation: any one would suppose from his manner that he was playing at chuck-farthing with human happiness; that he was always on the heel of pastime; that he would giggle away the Great Charter, and decide by the method of tee-totum whether my Lords the Bishops should or should not retain their seats in the House of Lords. All this is the mere vanity of surprising, and making us believe that he can play with kingdoms as other men can with nine-pins. Instead of this lofty nebulo, this miracle of moral and intellectual felicities, he is nothing more than a sensible honest man, who means to do his duty to the Sovereign and to the Country: instead of being the ignorant man he pretends to be, before he meets the deputation of Tallow-Chandlers in the morning, he sits up half the night talking with Thomas Young about melting and skimming, and then, though he has acquired knowledge enough to work off a whole vat of prime Leicester tallow, he pretends next morning not to know the difference between a dip and a mould. In the same way, when he has been employed in reading Acts of Parliament, he would persuade you that he has been reading *Cleghorn on the Beatitudes,* or *Pickler on the Nine Difficult Points.* Neither can I allow to this Minister (however he may be irritated by the denial) the extreme merit of indifference to the consequences of his measures. I believe him to be conscientiously alive to the good or evil that he is doing, and that his caution has more than once arrested the gigantic projects of the Lycurgus of the Lower House. I am sorry to hurt any man's feelings, and to brush away the magnificent fabric of levity and gaiety he has reared; but I accuse our Minister of honesty and diligence: I deny that he is careless or rash: he is nothing more than a man of good understanding, and good principle, disguised in the eternal and somewhat wearisome affectation of a political Roué.

One of the most foolish circumstances attending this destruction of Cathedral property is the great sacrifice of the patronage of the Crown: the Crown gives up eight Prebends of Westminster, two at Worcester, 1500l. per annum at St. Paul's, two Prebends at Bristol, and a great deal of other preferment all over the kingdom; and this at a moment when such extraordinary power has been suddenly conferred upon the people, and when every atom of power and patronage ought to be husbanded for the Crown. A Prebend of Westminster for my second son would soften the Catos of Cornhill, and lull the Gracchi of the Metropolitan Boroughs. Lives there a man so absurd, as to suppose that Government can be carried on without those gentle allurements? You may as well attempt to poultice off the humps of a camel's back as to cure mankind of these little corruptions.

I am terribly alarmed by a committee of Cathedrals now sitting in London, and planning a petition to the Legislature to be heard by counsel. They will take such high ground, and talk a language so utterly at variance with the feelings of the age about Church Property, that I am much afraid they will do more harm than good. In the time of Lord George Gordon's riots, the Guards said they did not care for the mob, if the Gentlemen Volunteers behind would be so good as not to hold their muskets in such a dangerous manner. I don't care for popular clamour, and think it might now be defied; but I confess the Gentlemen Volunteers alarm me. They have unfortunately, too, collected their addresses, and published them in a single volume!!!

I should like to know how many of our institutions at this moment, besides the Cathedrals, are under notice of destruction. I will, before I finish my letter, endeavour to procure a list: in the meantime I will give you the bill of fare with which the last Session opened, and I think that of 1838 will not be less copious. But at the opening of the Session of 1837, when I addressed my first letter to you, this was the state of our intended changes:—The

Law of Copyright was to be re-created by Serjeant Talfourd;
Church Rates abolished by Lord John Russell, and Imprisonment
for Debt by the Attorney-General: the Archbishop of Canterbury
kindly undertook to destroy all the Cathedrals, and Mr. Grote was
to arrange our Voting by Ballot; the Septennial Act was to be
repealed by Mr. Williams, Corn Laws abolished by Mr. Clay, and
the House of Lords reformed by Mr. Ward; Mr. Hume remodelled
County Rates, Mr. Ewart put an end to Primogeniture, and Mr.
Tooke took away the Exclusive Privileges of Dublin, Oxford,
and Cambridge; Thomas Duncombe was to put an end to the
Proxies of the Lords, and Serjeant Prime to turn the Universities
topsy-turvy. Well may it be said that

"Man never continueth in one stay."

See how men accustom themselves to large and perilous
changes. Ten years ago, if a cassock or a hassock had been taken
from the Establishment, the current of human affairs would have
been stopped till restitution had been made. In a fortnight's time,
Lord John Russell is to take possession of, and to repartition all
the Cathedrals in England; and what a prelude for the young
Queen's coronation! what a medal for the august ceremony!—the
fallen Gothic buildings on one side of the gold, the young Protestant Queen on the other:—

Victoria Ecclesiæ Victrix.

And then, when she is full of noble devices, and all sorts en-
chantingly beloved, and amid the solemn swell of music, when her
heart beats happily, and her eyes look Majesty, she turns them on
the degraded Ministers of the Gospel, and shudders to see she is
stalking to the throne of her Protestant ancestors over the broken
altars of God.

Now, remember, I hate to overstate my case. I do not say that
the destruction of Cathedrals will put an end to railroads: I believe
that good mustard and cress, sown after Lord John's Bill is passed,
will, if duly watered, continue to grow. I do not say that the
country has no *right,* after the death of individual incumbents, to
do what they propose to do;—I merely say that it is inexpedient,
uncalled for, and mischievous—that the lower Clergy, for whose
sake it is proposed to be done, do not desire it—that the Bishop-
Commissioners, who proposed it, would be heartily glad if it were
put an end to—that it will lower the character of those who enter
into the Church, and accustom the English people to large and
dangerous confiscations: and I would not have gentlemen of the

money-bags, and of wheat and bean land, forget that the Church means many other things than Thirty-nine Articles, and a discourse of five-and-twenty minutes' duration on the Sabbath. It means a check to the conceited rashness of experimental reasoners—an adhesion to old moral land-marks—an attachment to the happiness we have gained from tried institutions greater than the expectation of that which is promised by novelty and change. The loud cry of ten thousand teachers of justice and worship—that cry which masters the *Borgias* and *Catilines* of the world, and guards from devastation the best works of God—

> Magnâ testantur voce per orbem
> Discite justitiam moniti et non temnere divos.

In spite of his uplifted chess-board, I cannot let my old school-fellow, the Archbishop of Canterbury, off, without harping a little upon his oath which he has taken to preserve the rights and property of the Church of Canterbury: I am quite sure so truly good a man, as from the bottom of my heart I believe him to be, has some line of argument by which he defends himself; but till I know it, I cannot of course say I am convinced by it. The common defence for breaking oaths is, that they are contracts made with another party, which the Creator is called to witness, and from which the swearer is absolved if those for whom the oath is taken choose to release him from his obligation. With whom, then, is the contract made by the Archbishop? Is it with the community at large? If so, nothing but an Act of Parliament (as the community at large have no other organ) could absolve him from his oath; but three years before any act is passed, he puts his name to a plan for taking away two-thirds of the property of the Church of Canterbury. If the contract be not made with the community at large, but with the Church of Canterbury, every member of it is in decided hostility to his scheme. O'Connell takes an oath that he will not injure nor destroy the Protestant Church; but in promoting the destruction of some of the Irish Bishoprics, he may plead that he is sacrificing a part to preserve the whole, and benefiting, not injuring, the Protestant establishment. But the Archbishop does not swear to a general truth, where the principle may be preserved, though there is an apparent deviation from the words; but he swears to a very narrow and limited oath, that he will not alienate the possessions of the Church of Canterbury. A friend of mine has suggested to me that his Grace has perhaps forgotten the oath; but this cannot be, for the first Protestant in Europe of course makes a memorandum in his pocketbook of all the oaths he takes to do, or to abstain. The oath, however, may be less present to the Archbishop's memory, from the fact of his not having taken the oath in person, but by the medium of a gentleman sent down by the coach to take it for him—a practice which, though I believe it to have been long established in the Church, surprised me, I confess, not a little. A proxy to vote, if you please —a proxy to consent to arrangements of estates if wanted; but a proxy sent down in the Canterbury Fly, to take the Creator to witness that the Archbishop, detained in town by business, or pleasure, will never violate that foundation of piety over which he presides—all this seems to me an act of the most extraordinary indolence ever recorded in history. If an Ecclesiastic, not a Bishop, may express any opinion on the reforms of the Church, I recommend that Archbishops and Bishops should take no more oaths by proxy; but, as they do not wait upon the Sovereign or the Prime Minister, or even any of the Cabinet, by proxy, that they should also perform all religious acts in their own person. This practice would have been abolished in Lord John's first Bill, if other grades of Churchmen as well as Bishops had been made Commissioners. But the motto was—

"Peace to the Palaces—war to the Manses."

I have been informed, though I will not answer for the accuracy of the information, that this vicarious oath is likely to produce a scene which would have puzzled the *Ductor Dubitantium*. The attorney who took the oath for the Archbishop is, they say, seized with religious horrors at the approaching confiscation of Canterbury property, and has in vain tendered back his 6s. 8d. for taking the oath. The Archbishop refuses to accept it; and feeling himself light and disencumbered, wisely keeps the saddle upon the back of the writhing and agonised scrivener. I have talked it over with several Clergymen, and the general opinion is, that the scrivener will suffer.

I cannot help thinking that a great opportunity opens itself for improving the discipline of the Church, by means of those Chapters which Lord John Russell * is so anxious to destroy; divide

---

* I only mention Lord John Russell's name so often, because the management of the Church measures devolves upon him. He is beyond all comparison the ablest man in the whole Administration, and to such a degree is he superior, that the Government could not exist a moment without him. If the Foreign Secretary were to retire, we should no longer be nibbling ourselves into disgrace on the coast of Spain. If the amiable Lord Glenelg were to leave us, we should feel secure in our colonial possessions. If Mr. Spring Rice were to go into holy orders, great would be the joy of the

the diocese among the members of the Chapter, and make them responsible for the superintendence and inspection of the Clergy in their various divisions under the supreme control of the Bishop; by a few additions they might be made the Bishop's Council for the trial of delinquent Clergymen. They might be made a kind of college for the general care of education in the diocese, and applied to a thousand useful purposes, which would have occurred to the Commissioners, if they had not been so dreadfully frightened, and to the Government, if their object had been, not to please the Dissenters, but to improve the Church.

The Bishop of Lincoln has lately published a pamphlet on the Church question. His Lordship is certainly not a man full of felicities and facilities, imitating none, and inimitable of any; nor does he work with infinite agitation of wit. His creation has blood without heat, bones without marrow, eyes without speculation. He has the art of saying nothing in many words beyond any man that ever existed; and when he seems to have made a proposition, he is so dreadfully frightened at it, that he proceeds as quickly as possible, in the ensuing sentence, to disconnect the subject and the predicate, and to avert the dangers he has incurred:—but as he is a Bishop, and will be therefore more read than I am, I cannot pass him over. His Lordship tells us, that it was at one time under consideration of the Commissioners whether they should not tax all benefices above a certain value, in order to raise a fund for the improvement of smaller livings; and his Lordship adds, with the greatest innocence, that the considerations which principally weighed with the Commissioners in inducing them not to adopt the plan of taxation was, that they understood the Clergy in general to be decidedly averse to it; so that the plan of the Commission was, that the greater benefices should pay to the little, while the Bishops themselves—the Archbishop of Canterbury with his 15,000*l.* a year, and the Bishop of London with his 10,000*l.* a year—were not to subscribe a single farthing for that purpose.

---

three per cents. A decent good-looking head of the Government might easily enough be found in lieu of Viscount Melbourne; but in five minutes after the departure of Lord John, the whole Whig Government would be dissolved into sparks of liberality and splinters of Reform. There are six remarkable men, who, in different methods and in different degrees, are now affecting the interests of this country—the Duke of Wellington, Lord John Russell, Lord Brougham, Lord Lyndhurst, Sir Robert Peel, and O'Connell. Greater powers than all these are the phlegm of the English people—the great mass of good sense and intelligence diffused among them —and the number of those who have something to lose, and have not the slightest intention of losing it.

Why does John, Bishop of Lincoln, mention these distressing schemes of the Commission, which we are certain would have been met with a general yell of indignation from one end of the kingdom to another? Surely it must have occurred to this excellent Prelate that the Bishops would have been compelled by mere shame to have contributed to the fund which they were about to put upon the backs of the more opulent parochial clergy: surely a moment's reflection must have taught them that the safer method by far was to confiscate Cathedral property.

The idea of abandoning this taxation, because it was displeasing to the Clergy at large, is not unentertaining as applied to a commission who treated the Clergy with the greatest contempt, and did not even notice the Communications from Cathedral bodies upon the subject of the most serious and extensive confiscations.*

---

* Upon this subject I think it right to introduce the following letters, the first of which was published Jan. 23, 1838:—

TO THE EDITOR OF THE TIMES.

"Sir,—

I feel it to be consistent with my duty, as Secretary to the Church Commissioners, to notice a statement emanating from a quarter which would seem to give it authenticity—that, of seven Chapter memorials addressed to the Board, the receipt of one was only acknowledged.

"It is strictly within my province to acknowledge communications made to the Commissioners as a body, either directly or through me; and it is part of their general instructions to me that I should do so in all cases.

"To whatever extent, therefore, the statement may be true, or whatever may be its value, it is clear that it cannot attach to the Commissioners, but that I alone am responsible.

"In the execution of my office I have endeavoured, in the midst of my other duties, to conduct an extensive correspondence in accordance to what I knew to be the feelings and wishes of the Commissioners, and to treat every party in communication with them with attention and respect.

"If, at some period of more than usual pressure, any accidental omission may have occurred, or may hereafter occur, involving an appearance of discourtesy, it is for me to offer, as I now do, explanation and apology.

"I am, Sir, your obedient humble servant,

"C. K. MURRAY.

"Whitehall Place, Jan. 21."

TO THE EDITOR OF THE TIMES.

"Sir,—

A more indiscreet and extraordinary communication than that which appears in your own paper of the 23rd instant, signed by Mr. C. K. Murray, I never read. 'Apparet domus intus.' It is now clear how the Commission has been worked. Where communications from the oldest Ecclesiastical bodies, upon the most important of all subjects to them and to the kingdom,

"The plan of taxation, therefore," says the Bishop, "being abandoned, it was evident that the funds for the augmentation of poor Livings, and for the supply of the spiritual wants of populous districts, must be drawn from the Episcopal and Cathedral revenues; that is, from the revenues from which the Legislature seems to have a peculiar right to draw the funds for the general supply of the religious wants of the people; because they arise from benefices, of which the patronage is either actually in the Crown, or is derivative from the Crown. In the case of the Episcopal revenues, the Commissioners had already carried the principle of re-distribution as far as they thought that it could, with due allowance for the various demands upon the incomes of the Bishops, be carried. The only remaining source, therefore, was to be found in the Cathedral Revenues: and the Commissioners proceeded, in the execution of the duties prescribed to them, to consider in what manner those revenues might be rendered conducive to the efficiency of the Established Church."

This is very good Episcopal reasoning; but is it true? The Bishops and Commissioners wanted a fund to endow small Livings; they did not touch a farthing of their own incomes, only distributed

---

were received by the greatest prelates and noblemen of the land, acting under the King's Commission, I should have thought that answers suitable to the occasion would, in each case, have been dictated by the Commission; that such answers would have been entered on the minutes, and read on the Board-day next ensuing.

"Is Mr. C. K. Murray quite sure that this, which is done at all Boards on the most trifling subjects, was not done at his Board, in the most awful confiscations ever known in England? Is he certain that spoliation was in no instance sweetened by civility, and injustice never varnished by forms? Were all the decencies and proprieties which ought to regulate the intercourse of such great bodies left without a single inquiry from the Commissioner, to a gentleman who seems to have been seized with six distinct fits of oblivion on six separate occasions, any one of which required all that attention to decorum and that accuracy of memory for which secretaries are selected and paid?

"According to Mr. C. K. Murray's account, the only order he received from the Board was, 'If any Prebendary calls, or any Cathedral writes, desiring not to be destroyed, just say the communication has been received;' and even this, Mr. Murray tells us, he has not done, and that no one of the King's Commissioners—Archbishops, Bishops, Marquises, Earls—ever asked him whether he had done it or not—though any one of these great people would have swooned away at the idea of not answering the most trifling communication from any other of these great people.

"Whatever else these Commissioners do, they had better not bring their Secretary forward again. They may feel wind-bound by public opinion, but they must choose, as a sacrifice, a better Iphigenia than Mr. C. K. Murray.
"SYDNEY SMITH."

them a little more equally; and proceeded lustily at once to confiscate Cathedral property. But why was it necessary, if the fund
for small Livings was such a paramount consideration, that the
future Archbishops of Canterbury should be left with two palaces,
and 15,000*l.* per annum? Why is every future Bishop of London
to have a palace in Fulham, a house in St. James's Square, and
10,000*l.* a year? Could not all the Episcopal functions be carried
on well and effectually with the half of these incomes? Is it necessary that the Archbishop of Canterbury should give feasts to
Aristocratic London; and that the domestics of the Prelacy should
stand with swords and bag-wigs round pig, and turkey, and venison, to defend, as it were, the Orthodox gastronome from the
fierce Unitarian, the fell Baptist, and all the famished children of
Dissent? I don't object to all this; because I am sure that the
method of prizes and blanks is the best method of supporting a
Church which must be considered as very slenderly endowed, if
the whole were equally divided among the parishes; but if my
opinion were different—if I thought the important improvement
was to equalise preferment in the English Church—that such a
measure was not the one thing foolish, but the one thing needful
—I should take care, as a mitred Commissioner, to reduce my
own species of preferment to the narrowest limits, before I proceeded to confiscate the property of any other grade of the Church.
I could not, as a conscientious man, leave the Archbishop of
Canterbury with 15,000*l.* a year, and make a fund by annihilating
Residentiaries at Bristol of 500*l.* This comes of calling a meeting
of one species of cattle only. The horned cattle say,—"If you
want any meat, kill the sheep; don't meddle with us, there is no
beef to spare." They said this, however, to the lion; and the cunning animal, after he had gained all the information necessary for
the destruction of the muttons, and learnt how well and widely
they pastured, and how they could be most conveniently eaten
up, turns round and informs the cattle, who took him for their
best and tenderest friend, that he means to eat them up also. Frequently did Lord John meet the destroying Bishops; much did he
commend their daily heap of ruins; sweetly did they smile on
each other, and much charming talk was there of meteorology and
catarrh, and the particular Cathedral they were pulling down at
each time; * till one fine day the Home Secretary, with a voice
more bland, and a look more ardently affectionate, than that which

_____

* "What Cathedral are we pulling down to-day?" was the standing question
at the Commission.

the masculine mouse bestows on his nibbling female, informed them that the Government meant to take all the Church property into their own hands, to pay the rates out of it, and deliver the residue to the rightful possessors. Such an effect, they say, was never before produced by a *coup de théâtre*. The Commission was separated in an instant: London clenched his fist; Canterbury was hurried out by his chaplains, and put into a warm bed; a solemn vacancy spread itself over the face of Gloucester; Lincoln was taken out in strong hysterics. What a noble scene Serjeant Talfourd would have made of this! Why are such talents wasted on *Ion* and the *Athenian Captive?*

But, after all, what a proposition! "You don't make the most of your money: I will take your property into my hands, and see if I cannot squeeze a penny out of it: you shall be regularly paid all you now receive, only if anything more can be made of it, that we will put into our own pockets."—"Just pull off your neckcloth, and lay your head under the guillotine, and I will promise not to do you any harm: just get ready for confiscation; give up the management of all your property; make us the ostensible managers of everything; let us be informed of the most minute value of all, and depend upon it, we will never injure you to the extent of a single farthing."—"Let me get my arms about you," says the bear, "I have not the smallest intention of squeezing you." —"Trust your finger in my mouth," says the mastiff, "I will not fetch blood."

Where is this to end? If Government are to take into their own hands all property which is not managed with the greatest sharpness and accuracy, they may squeeze ⅛ per cent. out of the Turkey Company; Spring Rice would become Director of the Hydroimpervious Association, and clear a few hundreds for the Treasury. The British Roasted Apple Society is notoriously mismanaged, and Lord John and Brother Lister, by a careful selection of fruit, and a judicious management of fuel, would soon get it up to par.

I think, however, I have heard at the Political Economy Club, where I have sometimes had the honour of being a guest, that no trades should be carried on by Governments. That they have enough to do of their own, without undertaking other persons' business. If any savings in the mode of managing Ecclesiastical Leases could be made, great deductions from the savings must be allowed by the jobbing and *Gaspillage* of general Boards, and all the old servants of the Church, displaced by this measure, must receive compensation.

The Whig Government, they will be vexed to hear, would find a great deal of patronage forced upon them by this measure. Their favourite human animal, the Barrister of six years' standing, would be called into action. The whole earth is, in fact, in commission, and the human race saved from the Flood are delivered over to Barristers of six years' standing. The *onus probandi* now lies upon any man who says he is not a Commissioner; the only doubt on seeing a new man among the Whigs is, not whether he is a Commissioner or not, but whether it is Tithes, Poor Laws, Boundaries of Boroughs, Church Leases, Charities, or any of the thousand human concerns which are now worked by Commissioners, to the infinite comfort and satisfaction of mankind, who seem in these days to have found out the real secret of life—the one thing wanting to sublunary happiness—the great principle of Commission, and six years' Barristration.

Then, if there be a better method of working Ecclesiastical Estates—if anything can be gained for the Church—why is not the Church to have it? why is it not applied to Church purposes? what right has the State to seize it? If I give you an estate, I give it you not only in its present state, but I give to you all the improvements which can be made upon it—all that mechanical, botanical, and chemical knowledge, may do hereafter for its improvement—all the ameliorations which care and experience can suggest, in setting, improving, and collecting your rents. Can there be such miserable equivocation as to say—I leave you your property, but I do not leave to you all the improvements which your own wisdom, or the wisdom of your fellow-creatures, will enable you to make of your property? How utterly unworthy of a Whig government is such a distinction as this!

Suppose the same sort of plan had been adopted in the reign of Henry VIII., and the Legislature had said,—You shall enjoy all you now have, but every farthing of improved revenue, after this period, shall go into the pocket of the State—it would have been impossible by this time that the Church could have existed at all; and why may not such a measure be as fatal hereafter to the existence of a Church, as it would have been to the present generation, if it had been brought forward at the time of the Reformation?

There is some safety in dignity. A Church is in danger when it is degraded. It costs mankind much less to destroy it when an institution is associated with mean, and not with elevated, ideas. I should like to see the subject in the hands of H. B. I would entitle the print—

"The Bishops' Saturday Night; or, Lord John Russell at the Pay-Table."

The Bishops should be standing before the pay-table, and receiving their weekly allowance; Lord John and Spring Rice counting, ringing, and biting the sovereigns, and the Bishop of Exeter insisting that the Chancellor of the Exchequer has given him one which was not weight. Viscount Melbourne, in high chuckle, should be standing, with his hat on, and his back to the fire, delighted with the contest; and the Deans and Canons should be in the background, waiting till their turn came, and the Bishops were paid; and among them a Canon, of large composition, urging them on not to give way too much to the Bench. Perhaps I should add the President of the Board of Trade, recommending the truck principle to the Bishops, and offering to pay them in hassocks, cassocks, aprons, shovel-hats, sermon-cases, and such like ecclesiastical gear.

But the madness and folly of such a measure is in the revolutionary feeling which it excites. A Government taking into its hands such an immense value of property! What a lesson of violence and change to the mass of mankind! Do you want to accustom Englishmen to lose all confidence in the permanence of their institutions—to inure them to great acts of plunder—and to draw forth all the latent villainies of human nature? The Whig leaders are honest men, and cannot mean this, but these foolish and inconsistent measures are the horn-book and infantile lessons of revolution; and remember, it requires no great time to teach mankind to rob and murder on a great scale.

I am astonished that these Ministers neglect the common precaution of a foolometer,* with which no public man should be unprovided: I mean, the acquaintance and society of three or four regular British fools as a test of public opinion. Every Cabinet minister should judge of all his measures by his foolometer, as a navigator crowds or shortens sail by the barometer in his cabin. I have a very valuable instrument of that kind myself, which I

---

* Mr. Fox very often used to say, "I wonder what Lord B. will think of this!" Lord B. happened to be a very stupid person, and the curiosity of Mr. Fox's friends was naturally excited to know why he attached such importance to the opinion of such an ordinary common-place person. "His opinion," said Mr. Fox, "is of much more importance than you are aware of. He is an exact representative of all common-place English prejudices, and what Lord B. thinks of any measure, the great majority of English people will think of it." It would be a good thing if every Cabinet of philosophers had a Lord B. among them.

have used for many years; and I would be bound to predict, with the utmost nicety, by the help of this machine, the precise effect which any measure would produce on public opinion. Certainly, I never saw anything so decided as the effects produced upon my machine by the Rate Bill. No man who had been accustomed in the smallest degree to handle philosophical instruments could have doubted of the storm which was coming on, or of the thoroughly un-English scheme, in which the Ministry had so rashly engaged themselves.

I think, also, that it is a very sound argument against this measure of Church Rates, that estates have been bought liable to these payments, and that they have been deducted from the purchase money. And, what, also, if a Dissenter were a Republican as well as a Dissenter—a case which has sometimes happened; and what if our anti-monarchical Dissenter were to object to the expenses of kingly government? Are his scruples to be respected, and his taxes diminished, and the Queen's privy purse to be subjected and exposed to the intervening and economical squeeze of Government Commissioners?

But these lucubrations upon Church Rates are an episode; I must go back to John, Bishop of Lincoln. All other Cathedrals are fixed at four Prebendaries; St. Paul's and Lincoln having only three, are increased to the regulation pattern of four. I call this useless and childish. The Bishop of Lincoln says, there were more Residentiaries before the Reformation; but if for three hundred years three Residentiaries have been found to be sufficient, what a strangely feeble excuse it is for adding another, and diverting 3000*l.* per annum from the Small Living Fund, to say, that there were more Residentiaries three hundred years ago.

Must everything be good and right that is done by Bishops? Is there one rule of right for them, and another for the rest of the world? Now here are two Commissioners, whose express object is to constitute out of the large emoluments of the dignitaries, a Fund for the poorer Parochial Clergy; and in the very heat and fervour of confiscation, they build up two new places, utterly useless and uncalled for, take 3000*l.* from the Charity Fund to pay them, and they give the patronage of these places to themselves. Is there a single epithet in the language of invective which would not have been levelled at Lay Commissioners who had attempted the same thing? If it be necessary to do so much for Archdeacons, why might not one of the three Residentiaries be Archdeacon in virtue of his Prebend? If Government make Bishops, they may surely be trusted to make Archdeacons. I am very willing to ascribe good motives to these Commissioners, who are really worthy and very sensible men, but I am perfectly astonished that they were not deterred from such a measure by appearances, and by the motives which, whether rightly or wrongly, would be imputed to them. In not acting so as to be suspected, the Bishop of London should resemble Cæsar's wife. In other respects, this excellent Prelate would not have exactly suited for the partner for that great and self-willed man; and an idea strikes me, that is not impossible he might have been in the Senate-house instead of Cæsar.

Lord John Russell gives himself great credit for not having confiscated Church property, but merely remodelled and redivided it. I accuse him not of plunder, but I accuse him of taking the Church of England, rolling it about as a cook does a piece of dough with a rolling-pin, cutting a hundred different shapes with all the plastic fertility of a confectioner, and without the most distant suspicion that he can ever be wrong, or ever be mistaken; with a certainty that he can anticipate the consequences of every possible change in human affairs. There is not a better man in England than Lord John Russell; but his worst failure is that he is utterly ignorant of all moral fear; there is nothing he would not undertake. I believe he would perform the operation for the stone—build St. Peter's—or assume (with or without ten minutes' notice) the command of the Channel Fleet; and no one would discover by his manner that the patient had died—the Church tumbled down—and the Channel Fleet been knocked to atoms. I believe his motives are always pure, and his measures often able; but they are endless, and never done with that pedetentous pace and pedetentous mind in which it behoves the wise and virtuous improver to walk. He alarms the wise Liberals; and it is impossible to sleep soundly while he has the command of the watch.*

Do not say, my dear Lord John, that I am too severe upon you. A thousand years have scarce sufficed to make our blessed England what it is; an hour may lay it in the dust: and can you with all your talents renovate its shattered splendour—can you recall back its virtues—can you vanquish time and fate? But, alas! you want to shake the world, and be the Thunderer of the scene!

Now what is the end of what I have written? Why everybody was in a great fright; and a number of Bishops, huddled together, and talking of their great sacrifices, began to destroy other people's property, and to take other people's patronage: and all the fright is over

---

* Another peculiarity of the Russells is, that they never alter their opinions: they are an excellent race, but they must be trepanned before they can be convinced.

now; and all the Bishops are very sorry for what they have done, and regret extremely the destruction of the Cathedral dignitaries, but don't know how to get out of the foolish scrape. The Whig Ministry persevere to please Joseph and his brethren, and the Destroyers; and the good sense of the matter is to fling out the Dean and Chapter Bill, as it now stands, and to bring in another next year—making a fund out of all the Non-resident Prebends, annexing some of the others, and adopting many of the enactments contained in the present Bill.

Third Letter to ARCHDEACON SINGLETON

My dear Sir,

I hope this is the last letter you will receive from me on Church matters. I am tired of the subject; so are you; so is everybody. In spite of many Bishops' charges, I am unbroken; and remain entirely of the same opinion as I was two or three years since—that the mutilation of Deans and Chapters is a rash, foolish, and imprudent measure.

I do not think the charge of the Bishop of London successful, in combating those arguments which have been used against the impending Dean and Chapter Bill; but it is quiet, gentlemanlike, temperate, and written in a manner which entirely becomes the high office and character which he bears.

I agree with him in saying that the Plurality and Residence Bill is, upon the whole, a very good Bill;—nobody, however, knows better than the Bishop of London the various changes it has undergone, and the improvements it has received. I could point out fourteen or fifteen very material alterations for the better since it came out of the hands of the Commission, and all *bearing materially upon the happiness and comfort of the parochial Clergy.* I will mention only a few:—the Bill, as originally introduced, gave the Bishop a power, when he considered the duties of the parish to be improperly performed, to suspend the Clergyman and appoint a Curate with a salary. Some impious person thought it not impossible that occasionally such a power might be maliciously and vindictively exercised, and that some check to it should be admitted into the Bill; accordingly, under the existing act, an Ecclesiastical Jury is to be summoned, and into that jury the defendant Clergyman may introduce a friend of his own.

If a Clergyman, from illness or any other overwhelming necessity, were prevented from having two services, he was exposed to an information, and penalty. In answering the Bishop, he was subjected to two opposite sets of penalties—the one for saying *Yes;* the other for saying *No:* he was amenable to the needless and impertinent scrutiny of a Rural Dean before he was exposed to the scrutiny of the Bishop. Curates might be forced upon him by subscribing parishioners, and the certainty of a schism established in the parish; a Curate might have been forced upon *present* incumbents by the Bishop without any complaint made; upon men who took, or, perhaps, bought, their livings under very different laws;—all these acts of injustice are done away with, but it is not to the *credit* of the framers of the Bill that they were ever admitted, and they completely justify the opposition with which the Bill was received by me and by others. I add, however, with great pleasure, that when these and other objections were made, they were heard with candour, and promised to be remedied by the Archbishop of Canterbury and the Bishop of London and Lord John Russell.

I have spoken of the power to issue a Commission to inquire into the well-being of any parish: a vindictive and malicious Bishop might, it is true, convert this, which was intended for the protection, to the oppression of the Clergy—afraid to dispossess a Clergyman of his own authority, he might attempt to do the same thing under the cover of a jury of his ecclesiastical creatures. But I can hardly conceive such baseness in the prelate, or such infamous subserviency in the agents. An honest and respectable Bishop will remember that the very issue of such a Commission is a serious slur upon the character of a Clergyman; he will do all he can to prevent it by private monition and remonstrance; and if driven to such an act of power, he will of course state to the accused Clergyman the subjects of accusation, the names of his accusers, and give him ample time for his defence. If upon anonymous accusation he subjects a Clergyman to such an investigation, or refuses to him any advantage which the law gives to every accused person, he is an infamous, degraded, and scandalous tyrant: but I cannot believe there is such a man to be found upon the Bench.

There is in this new Bill a very humane clause (though not introduced by the Commission), enabling the widow of the deceased clergyman to retain possession of the parsonage house for two months after the death of the Incumbent. It ought, in fairness, to be extended to the heirs, executors, and administrators of the Incumbent. It is a great hardship that a family settled in a parish for fifty years perhaps, should be torn up by the roots in eight or ten days;

and the interval of two months, allowing time for repairs, might put
to rest many questions of dilapidation.

To the Bishop's power of intruding a Curate without any complaint on the part of the parish that the duty has been inadequately
performed, I retain the same objections as before. It is a power which
without this condition will be unfairly and partially exercised. The
first object I admit is not the provision of the Clergyman, but the
care of the parish: but one way of taking care of parishes is to take
care that clergymen are not treated with tyranny, partiality, and injustice: and the best way of effecting this is to remember that their
superiors have the same human passions as other people; and not
to trust them with a power which may be so grossly abused, and
which (incredible as the Bishop of London may deem it) *has been*,
in some instances, grossly abused.

I cannot imagine what the Bishop means by saying, that the members of Cathedrals do not in virtue of their office bear any part in the
parochial instruction of the people. This is a fine deceitful word, the
word *parochial*, and eminently calculated to coax the public. If he
means simply that Cathedrals do not belong to parishes, that St.
Paul's is not the parish church of Upper Puddicomb, and that the
Vicar of St. Fiddlefrid does not officiate in Westminster Abbey:
all this is true enough, but do they not in the most material points
instruct the people precisely in the same manner as the parochial
Clergy? Are not prayers and sermons the most important means of
spiritual instruction? And are there not eighteen or twenty services
in every Cathedral for one which is heard in parish churches? I have
very often counted in the afternoon of week days in St. Paul's 150
people, and on Sundays it is full to suffocation. Is all this to go for
nothing? and what right has the Bishop of London to suppose that
there is not as much real piety in Cathedrals, as in the most road-
less, postless, melancholy, sequestered hamlet, preached to by the
most provincial, sequestered, bucolic Clergyman in the Queen's
dominions?

A number of little children, it is true, do not repeat a catechism
of which they do not comprehend a word; but it is rather rapid and
wholesale to say, that the parochial Clergy are spiritual instructors
of the people, and that the Cathedral Clergy are only so in a very
restricted sense. I say that in the most material points and acts of
instruction, they are much more laborious and incessant than any
parochial Clergy. It might really be supposed from the Bishop of
London's reasoning, that some other methods of instruction took
place in Cathedrals than prayers and sermons can afford; that lectures were read on chemistry, or lessons given on dancing; or that it

was a Mechanics' Institute, or a vast receptacle for hexameter and pentameter boys. His own most respectable Chaplain, who is often there as a member of the body, will tell him that the prayers are strictly adhered to, according to the rubric, with the difference only that the service is beautifully chanted instead of being badly read; that instead of the atrocious bawling of parish Churches, the Anthems are sung with great taste and feeling; and if the preaching is not good, it is the fault of the Bishop of London, who has the whole range of London preachers from whom to make his selection. The real fact is, that, instead of being something materially different from the parochial Clergy, as the Commissioners wish to make them, the Cathedral Clergy are fellow labourers with the parochial Clergy, outworking them ten to one; but the Commission having provided snugly for the Bishops, have by *the merest accident in the world* entangled themselves in this quarrel with Cathedrals.

"Had the question," says the Bishop, "been proposed to the religious part of the community, Whether, if no other means were to be found, the effective cure of souls should be provided for by the total suppression of those Ecclesiastical Corporations which have no cure of souls, nor bear any part in the parochial labours of the Clergy; that question, I verily believe, would have been carried in the affirmative by an immense majority of suffrages." But suppose no other means could be found for the effective cure of souls than the suppression of Bishops, does the Bishop of London imagine that the majority of suffrages would have been less immense? How idle to put such cases!

A pious man leaves a large sum of money in Catholic times for some purposes which are superstitious, and for others, such as preaching and reading prayers, which are applicable to all times; the superstitious usages are abolished, the pious usages remain: now the Bishop must admit, if you take half or any part of this money from Clergymen to whom it was given, and divide it for similar purposes among Clergy to whom it was not given, you deviate materially from the intentions of the founder. These foundations are made *in loco;* in many of them the *locus* was perhaps the original cause of the gift. A man who founds an almshouse at Edmonton does not mean that the poor of Tottenham should avail themselves of it; and if he could have anticipated such a consequence, he would not have endowed any alms-house at all. Such is the respect for property that the Court of Chancery, when it becomes impracticable to carry the will of the donor into execution, always attend to the *cy pres*, and apply the charitable fund to a purpose as germane as possible to the intention of the founder; but here, when men of Lincoln have left to Lincoln Cathedral, and men of Hereford, to Hereford, the Commissioners seize it all, melt it into a common mass, and disperse it over the kingdom. Surely the Bishop of London cannot contend that this is not a greater deviation from the will of the founder than if the same people remaining in the same place, receiving all the founder gave them, and doing all things not forbidden by the law which the founder ordered, were to do something more than the founder ordered, were to become the guardians of education, the counsel to the Bishop, and the Curators of the Diocese in his old age and decay.

The public are greater robbers and plunderers than any one in the public; look at the whole transaction, it is a mixture of meanness and violence. The country choose to have an established religion, and a resident parochial Clergy, but they do not choose to build houses for their parochial clergy, or to pay them in many instances more than a butler or a coachman receives. How is this deficiency to be supplied? The heads of the Church propose to this public to seize upon estates which never belonged to the public, and which were left for another purpose; and by the seizure of these estates to save that which ought to come out of the public purse.

Suppose Parliament were to seize upon all the alms-houses in England, and apply them to the diminution of the poor-rate, what a number of ingenious arguments might be pressed into the service of this robbery: "Can anything be more revolting than that the poor of Northumberland should be starving, while the poor of the suburban hamlets are dividing the benefactions of the pious dead? *We want for these purposes all that we can obtain from whatever sources derived.*'" I do not deny the right of Parliament to do this, or anything else; but I deny that it would be expedient; because I think it better to make any sacrifices, and to endure any evil, than to gratify this rapacious spirit of plunder and confiscation. Suppose these Commissioner Prelates, firm and unmoved, when we were all alarmed, had told the public that the parochial Clergy were badly provided for, and that it was the duty of that public to provide a proper support for their Ministers;—suppose the Commissioners, instead of leading them on to confiscation, had warned their fellow subjects against the base economy, and the perilous injustice of seizing on that which was not their own;—suppose they had called for water and washed their hands, and said, "We call you all to witness that we are innocent of this great ruin;"—does the Bishop of London imagine that the Prelates who made such a stand would have gone down to posterity less respected and less revered than those men upon whose tombs it must (after all the enumerations of their virtues) be written, *that under their auspices and by their counsels the destruction of the EnglishChurch began?* Pity that the Archbishop of Canterbury had not retained those feelings, when, at the first meeting of Bishops, the Bishop of London proposed this *holy innovation* upon Cathedrals, and the head of our Church declared with vehemence and indignation that nothing in the earth would induce him to consent to it.

Si mens non læva fuisset,
Trojaque nunc stares, Priamique arx alta maneres.

"But," says the Lord Bishop of London, "you admit the principle of confiscation by proposing the confiscation and partition of Prebends in the possession of non-residents." I am thinking of something else, and I see all of a sudden a great blaze of light: I behold a great number of gentlemen in short aprons, neat purple coats, and gold buckles, rushing about with torches in their hands, calling each other "My Lord," and setting fire to all the rooms in the house, and the people below delighted with the combustion: finding it impossible to turn them from their purpose, and finding that they are all what they are, by divine permission; I endeavour to direct their *holy innovations* into another channel; and I say to them, "My Lords, had not you better set fire to the out of door offices, to the barns and stables, and spare this fine library and this noble drawing-room? Yonder are several cow-houses of which no use is made; pray direct your fury against them, and leave this beautiful and venerable mansion as you found it." If I address the divinely permitted in this manner, has the Bishop of London any right to call me a brother incendiary?

Our *holy innovator*, the Bishop of London, has drawn a very affecting picture of *sheep having no shepherd*, and of millions who have no *spiritual food:* our wants, he says, are most imperious; even if we were to tax large Livings we must still have the money of the Cathedrals: no plea will exempt you, nothing can stop us, for the formation of benefices, and the endowment of new ones. We want (and he prints it in italics) for these purposes *"all that we can obtain from whatever sources derived."* I never remember to have been more alarmed in my life than by this passage. I said to myself, the necessities of the Church have got such complete hold of the imagination of this energetic Prelate, who is so captivated by the holiness of his innovations, that all grades and orders of the Church and all present and future interests will be sacrificed to it. I immediately rushed to the acts of Parliament which I always have under my pillow to see at once the worst of what had happened. I found present revenues of the Bishops all safe; that is some comfort, I said to myself:

Canterbury, 24,000*l*. or 25,000*l*. per annum; London, 18,000*l*. or 20,000*l*. I began to feel some comfort: "things are not so bad; the Bishops do not mean to sacrifice to *sheep and shepherd's money* their present revenues; the Bishop of London is less violent and headstrong than I thought he would be." I looked a little further, and found that 15,000*l*. per annum is allotted to the future Archbishop of Canterbury, 10,000*l*. to the Bishop of London, 8000*l*. to Durham, and 8000*l*. each to Winchester and Ely. "Nothing of *sheep and shepherd* in all this," I exclaimed, and felt still more comforted. It was not till after the Bishops were taken care of, and the revenues of the Cathedrals came into full view, that I saw the perfect development of the *sheep and shepherd principle*, the deep and heartfelt compassion for spiritual labourers, and that inward groaning for the destitute state of the Church, and that firm purpose, printed in italics, of taking *for these purposes all that could be obtained from whatever source derived;* and even in this delicious rummage of Cathedral property, where all the fine church feelings of the Bishop's heart could be indulged without costing the poor sufferer a penny, stalls for Archdeacons in Lincoln and St. Paul's are, to the amount of 2000*l*. per annum, taken from the *sheep and shepherd fund*, and the patronage of them divided between two commissioners, the Bishop of London and the Bishop of Lincoln, instead of being paid to additional *labourers in the Vineyard*.

Has there been any difficulty, I would ask, in procuring Archdeacons upon the very moderate pay they now receive? Can any Clergyman be more thoroughly respectable than the present Archdeacons in the see of London? but men bearing such an office in the Church, it may be said, should be highly paid, and Archbishops who could very well keep up their dignity upon 7000*l*. per annum, are to be allowed 15,000*l*. I make no objection to all this; but then what becomes of all these heart-rending phrases of *sheep and shepherd, and drooping vineyards, and flocks without spiritual consolation?* The Bishop's argument is, that the superfluous must give way to the necessary; but in fighting, the Bishop should take great care that his cannons are not seized, and turned against himself. He has awarded to the Bishops of England a superfluity as great as that which he intends to take from the Cathedrals; and then, when he legislates for an order to which he does not belong, begins to remember the distresses of the lower Clergy, paints them with all the colours of impassioned eloquence, and informs the Cathedral institutions that he must have *every farthing he can lay his hand upon*. Is not this as if one affected powerfully by a charity sermon were to put his hands in another man's pocket, and cast, from what he had extracted, a liberal contribution into the plate?

I beg not to be mistaken; I am very far from considering the Bishop of London as a sordid and interested person; but this is a complete instance of how the best of men deceive themselves, where their interests are concerned. I have no doubt the Bishop firmly imagined he was doing his duty; but there should have been men of all grades in the Commission, some one to say a word for Cathedrals and against Bishops.

The Bishop says, "his antagonists have allowed three Canons to be sufficient for St. Paul's, and therefore four must be sufficient for other Cathedrals." Sufficient to read the prayers and preach the sermons, certainly, and so would *one* be; but not sufficient to excite by the hope of increased rank and wealth eleven thousand parochial Clergy.

The most important and cogent arguments against the Dean and Chapter confiscations are passed over in silence in the Bishop's Charge. This, in reasoning, is always the wisest and most convenient plan, and which all young Bishops should imitate after the manner of this wary polemic. I object to the confiscation *because it will throw a great deal more of capital out of the parochial Church than it will bring into it.* I am very sorry to come forward with so homely an argument, which shocks so many Clergymen, and particularly those with the largest incomes, and the best Bishoprics; but the truth is, the greater number of Clergymen go into the Church in order that they may derive a comfortable income *from* the Church. Such men intend to do their duty, and they do it; but the duty is, however, not the motive, but the adjunct. If I were writing in gala and parade, I would not hold this language; but we are in earnest, and on business; and as very rash and hasty changes are founded upon contrary suppositions of the pure disinterestedness and perfect inattention to temporals in the Clergy, we must get down at once to the solid rock, without heeding how we disturb the turf and the flowers above. The parochial Clergy maintain their present decent appearance quite as much by their own capital as by the income they derive from the Church. I will now state the income and capital of seven Clergymen, taken promiscuously in this neighbourhood:—

No. 1. Living 200*l.*, Capital 12,000*l.*;
No. 2. Living 800*l.*, Capital 15,000*l.*;
No. 3. Living 500*l.*, Capital 12,000*l.*;
No. 4. Living 150*l.*, Capital 10,000*l.*;
No. 5. Living 800*l.*, Capital 12,000*l.*;

No. 6. Living 150*l*., Capital   1000*l*.;
No. 7. Living 600*l*., Capital 16,000*l*.

I have diligently inquired into the circumstances of seven Unitarian
and Wesleyan ministers, and I question much if the whole seven could
make up 6000*l*. between them; and the zeal and enthusiasm of this
last division is certainly not inferior to that of the former. Now here is
a capital of 72,000*l*. carried into the Church, which the confiscations
of the Commissioners would force out of it, by taking away the good
things which were the temptation to its introduction. So that by the
old plan of paying by lottery, instead of giving a proper competence
to each, not only do you obtain a parochial Clergy upon much
cheaper terms; but from the gambling propensities of human nature,
and the irresistible tendency to hope that they shall gain the great
prizes, you tempt men into your service who keep up their credit, and
yours, not by your allowance, but by their own capital; and to destroy
this wise and well-working arrangement, a great number of Bishops,
Marquises, and John Russells, are huddled into a chamber, and after
proposing a scheme which will turn the English Church into a collection of consecrated beggars, we are informed by the Bishop of
London that it is a *Holy Innovation*.

I have no manner of doubt, that the immediate effect of passing
the Dean and Chapter Bill will be, that a great number of fathers
and uncles, judging, and properly judging, that the Church is a very
altered and deteriorated profession, will turn the industry and capital of their *élèves* into another channel. My friend, Robert Eden,
says, "This is of the earth earthy:" be it so; I cannot help it, I paint
mankind as I find them, and am not answerable for their defects.
When an argument taken from real life, and the actual condition of
the world, is brought among the shadowy discussions of Ecclesiastics, it always occasions terror and dismay; it is like Æneas stepping
into Charon's boat, which carried only ghosts and spirits.

Gemuit sub pondere cymba Sutilis.

The whole plan of the Bishop of London is a ptochogony—a generation of beggars. He purposes, out of the spoils of the Cathedral,
to create a thousand livings, and to give to the thousand Clergymen
130*l*. per annum each: a Christian Bishop proposing, in cold blood,
to create a thousand livings of 130*l*. per annum each;—to call into
existence a thousand of the most unhappy men on the face of the
earth,—the sons of the poor, without hope, without the assistance
of private fortune, chained to the soil, ashamed to live with their inferiors, unfit for the society of the better classes, and dragging about

the English curse of poverty, without the smallest hope that they can ever shake it off. At present such livings are filled by young men who have better hopes—who have reason to expect good property—who look forward to a college or a family living—who are the sons of men of some substance, and hope so to pass on to something better—who exist under the delusion of being nereafter Deans and Prebendaries—who are paid once by money, and three times by hope. Will the Bishop of London promise to the progeny of any of these thousand victims of the *Holy Innovation* that, if they behave well, one of them shall have his butler's place; another take care of the cedars and hyssops of his garden? Will he take their daughters for his nursery-maids? and may some of the sons of these "labourers of the vineyard" hope one day to ride the leaders from St. James's to Fulham? Here is hope—here is room for ambition—a field for genius, and a ray of amelioration! If these beautiful feelings of compassion are throbbing under the cassock of the Bishop, he ought in common justice to himself to make them known.

If it were a scheme for giving ease and independence to any large bodies of Clergymen, it might be listened to; but the revenues of the English Church are such as to render this wholly and entirely out of the question. If you place a man in a village in the country, require that he should be of good manners and well educated; that his habits and appearance should be above those of the farmers to whom he preaches, if he has nothing else to expect (as would be the case in a Church of equal division); and if upon his village income he is to support a wife and educate a family without any power of making himself known in a remote and solitary situation, such a person ought to receive 500*l.* per annum, and be furnished with a house. There are about 10,700 parishes in England and Wales, whose average income is 285*l.* per annum. Now, to provide these incumbents with decent houses, to keep them in repair, and to raise the income of the incumbent to 500*l.* per annum, would require (if all the incomes of the Bishops, Deans and Chapters of separate dignitaries, of sinecure rectories, were confiscated, and if the excess of all the livings in England above 500*l.* per annum were added to them) a sum of two millions and a half in addition to the present income of the whole Church; and no power on earth could persuade the present Parliament of Great Britain to grant a single shilling for that purpose. Now, is it possible to pay such a Church upon any other principle than that of unequal division? The proposed pillage of the Cathedral and College Churches (omitting all consideration of the separate estate of dignitaries) would amount, divided among all the Benefices in England to about 5*l.* 12*s.* 6½*d.* per man: and this, which would not stop an hiatus in a cassock, and would drive out of the parochial Church ten times as much as it brought into it, is the panacea for pauperism recommended by Her Majesty's Commissioners.

But if this plan were to drive men of capital out of the Church, and to pauperise the English clergy, where would the harm be? Could not all the duties of religion be performed as well by poor Clergymen as by men of good substance? My great and serious apprehension is, that such would not be the case. There would be the greatest risk that your Clergy would be fanatical, and ignorant; that their habits would be low and mean, and that they would be despised.

Then a picture is drawn of a Clergyman with 130*l*. per annum, who combines all moral, physical, and intellectual advantages, a learned man, dedicating himself intensely to the care of his parish—of charming manners and dignified deportment—six feet two inches high, beautifully proportioned, with a magnificent countenance, expressive of all the cardinal virtues and the Ten Commandments,—and it is asked with an air of triumph if such a man as this will fall into contempt on account of his poverty? But substitute for him an average, ordinary, uninteresting Minister; obese, dumpy, neither ill-natured nor good-natured; neither learned nor ignorant, striding over the stiles to Church, with a second-rate wife—dusty and deliquescent—and four parochial children, full of catechism and bread and butter; or let him be seen in one of those Shem-Ham-and-Japhet buggies—made on Mount Ararat soon after the subsidence of the waters, driving in the High Street of Edmonton;*—among all his pecuniary, saponaceous, oleaginous parishioners. Can any man of common sense say that all these outward circumstances of the Ministers of religion have no bearing on religion itself?

I ask the Bishop of London, a man of honour and conscience as he is, if he thinks five years will elapse before a second attack is made upon Deans and Chapters? Does he think, after Reformers have tasted the flesh of the Church, that they will put up with any other diet? Does he forget that Deans and Chapters are but mock turtle—that more delicious delicacies remain behind? Five years hence he will attempt to make a stand, and he will be laughed at and eaten up. In this very charge the Bishop accuses the Lay Commissioners of another intended attack upon the property of the Church,

---

* A parish which the Bishop of London has the greatest desire to divide into little bits; but which appears quite as fit to preserve its integrity as St. James's, St. George's, or Kensington, all in the patronage of the Bishop.

contrary to the clearest and most explicit stipulations (as he says) with the heads of the Establishment.

Much is said of the conduct of the Commissioners, but that is of the least possible consequence. They may have acted for the best, according to the then existing circumstances; they may seriously have intended to do their duty to the country; and I am far from saying or thinking they did not; but without the least reference to the Commissioners, the question is, Is it wise to pass this bill, and to justify such an open and tremendous sacrifice of Church property? Does public opinion *now* call for any such measure? is it a wise distribution of the funds of an ill-paid Church? and will it not force more capital out of the parochial part of the Church than it brings into it? If the bill be bad, it is surely not to pass out of compliment to the feelings of the Archbishop of Canterbury. If the project be hasty, it is not to be adopted to gratify the Bishop of London. The mischief to the Church is surely a greater evil than the stultification of the Commissioners, &c. If the physician have prescribed hastily, is the medicine to be taken to the death or disease of the patient? If the judge have condemned improperly, is the criminal to be hung, that the wisdom of the magistrate may not be impugned? *

But, why are the Commissioners to be stultified by the rejection of the measure? The measure may have been very good when it was recommended, and very objectionable now. I thought, and many men thought, that the Church was going to pieces—that the affections of the common people were lost to the Establishment; and that large sacrifices must be instantly made, to avert the effects of this temporary madness; but those days are gone by—and with them ought to be put aside measures which might have been wise in those days, but are wise no longer.

After all, the Archbishop of Canterbury and the Bishop of London are good and placable men; and will ere long forget and forgive the successful efforts of their enemies in defeating this mis-ecclesiastic law.

Suppose the Commission were now beginning to sit for the first time, will any man living say that they would make such reports as they have made? and that they would seriously propose such a tremendous revolution in Church property? And if they would not, the inference is irresistible, that to consult the feelings of two or three Churchmen, we are complimenting away the safety of the Church. Milton asked where the nymphs were when Lycidas perished? I ask

---

* "After the trouble the Commissioners have taken (says Sir Robert), after the obloquy they have incurred," &c. &c. &c.

where the Bishops are when the remorseless deep is closing over the head of their beloved Establishment? *

You must have read an attack upon me by the Bishop of Gloucester, in the course of which he says that I have not been appointed to my situation as Canon of St. Paul's for my piety and learning, but because I am a scoffer and a jester. Is not this rather strong for a Bishop, and does it not appear to you, Mr. Archdeacon, as rather too close an imitation of that language which is used in the apostolic occupation of trafficking in fish? Whether I have been appointed for my piety or not, must depend upon what this poor man means by piety. He means by that word, of course, a defence of all the tyrannical and oppressive abuses of the Church which have been swept away within the last fifteen or twenty years of my life; the Corporation and Test Acts; the Penal Laws against the Catholics; the Compulsory Marriages of Dissenters, and all those disabling and disqualifying laws which were the disgrace of our Church, and which he has always looked up to as the consummation of human wisdom. If piety consisted in the defence of these—if it was impious to struggle for their abrogation, I have indeed led an ungodly life.

There is nothing pompous gentlemen are so much afraid of as a little humour. It is like the objection of certain cephalic animalcula to the use of small-tooth combs, "Finger and thumb, precipitate powder, or anything else you please; but for heaven's sake no small-tooth combs!" After all, I believe, Bishop Monk has been the cause of much more laughter than ever I have been; I cannot account for it, but I never see him enter a room without exciting a smile on every countenance within it.

Dr. Monk is furious at my attacking the heads of the Church; but how can I help it? If the heads of the Church are at the head of the Mob; if I find the best of men doing that, which has in all times drawn upon the worst enemies of the human race the bitterest curses of History, am I to stop because the motives of these men are pure, and their lives blameless? I wish I could find a blot in their lives, or a vice in their motives. The whole power of the motion is in the character of the movers: feeble friends, false friends, and foolish friends, all cease to look into the measure, and say, Would such a measure have been recommended by such men as the Prelates of Canterbury and London, if it were not for the public advantage? And in this way, the great good of a religious establishment, now rendered moderate and compatible with

* What is the use of publishing separate charges, as the Bishops of Winchester, Oxford, and Rochester have done? Why do not the dissentient Bishops form into a firm phalanx to save the Church and fling out the Bill?

all men's liberties and rights, is sacrificed to names; and the Church destroyed from good breeding and Etiquette! the real truth is, that Canterbury and London have been frightened—they have overlooked the effect of time and delay—they have been betrayed into a fearful and ruinous mistake. Painful as it is to teach men who ought to teach us, the legislature ought, while there is yet time, to awake and read them this lesson.

It is dangerous for a Prelate to write; and whoever does it, ought to be a very wise one. He has speculated why I was made a Canon of St. Paul's. Suppose I were to follow his example, and, going through the bench of Bishops, were to ask for what reason each man had been made a Bishop; suppose I were to go into the county of Gloucester, &c. &c. &c.!!!!!

I was afraid the Bishop would attribute my promotion to the Edinburgh Review; but upon the subject of promotion by Reviews he preserves an impenetrable silence. If my excellent patron Earl Grey had any reasons of this kind, he may at least be sure that the reviews commonly attributed to me were really written *by* me. I should have considered myself as the lowest of created beings to have disguised myself in another man's wit, and to have received a reward to which I was not entitled.*

I presume that what has drawn upon me the indignation of this Prelate, is the observations I have from time to time made on the conduct of the Commissioners; of which he positively asserts himself to have been a member; but whether he was, or was not a member, I utterly acquit him of all possible blame, and of every species of imputation which may attach to the conduct of the Commission. In using that word, I have always meant the Archbishop of Canterbury, the Bishop of London, and Lord John Russell; and have, honestly speaking, given no more heed to the Bishop of Gloucester, than if he had been sitting in a Commission of Bonzes in the Court of Pekin.

To read, however, his Lordship a lesson of good manners, I had prepared for him a chastisement which would have been echoed from the *Seagrave* who banqueteth in the castle, to the idiot who spitteth over the bridge at Gloucester; but the following appeal

---

* I understand that the Bishop bursts into tears every now and then, and says that I have set him the name of Simon, and that all the Bishops now call him Simon. Simon of Gloucester, however, after all, is a real writer, and how could I know that Dr. Monk's name was Simon? When tutor in Lord Carrington's family, he was called by the endearing though somewhat unmajestic name of *Dick;* and if I had thought about his name at all, I should have called him Richard of Gloucester.

struck my eye, and stopped my pen:—"Since that time my inadequate qualifications have sustained an appalling diminution by the affection of my eyes, which have impaired my vision, and the progress of which threatens to consign me to darkness: I beg the benefit of your prayers to the Father of all mercies, that he will restore to me the better use of the visual organs, to be employed on his service; or that he will inwardly illumine the intellectual vision, with a particle of that Divine ray, which his Holy Spirit can alone impart."

It might have been better taste, perhaps, if a mitred invalid, in describing his bodily infirmities before a church full of Clergymen, whose prayers he asked, had been a little more sparing in the abuse of his enemies; but a good deal must be forgiven to the sick. I wish that every Christian was as well aware as this poor Bishop of what he needed from Divine assistance; and in the supplication for the restoration of his sight and the improvement of his understanding, I most fervently and cordially join.

I was much amused with what old Hermann * says of the Bishop of London's Æschylus. "We find," he says, *"a great arbitrariness of proceeding, and much boldness of innovation, guided by no sure principle;"* here it is: *qualis ab incepto.* He begins with Æschylus, and ends with the Church of England; begins with profane and ends with holy innovations—scratching out old readings which every commentator had sanctioned; abolishing ecclesiastical dignities which every reformer had spared; thrusting an anapæst into a verse, which will not bear it; and intruding a Canon into a Cathedral, which does not want it; and this is the Prelate by whom the proposed reform of the Church has been principally planned, and to whose practical wisdom the Legislature is called upon to defer. The Bishop of London is a man of very great ability, humane, placable, generous, munificent; very agreeable, but not to be trusted with great interests where calmness and judgment are required; unfortunately, my old and amiable school-fellow, the Archbishop of Canterbury, has melted away before him, and sacrificed that wisdom on which we all founded our security.

Much writing and much talking are very tiresome; and, above all, they are so to men who, living in the world, arrive at those rapid and just conclusions which are only to be made by living in the world. This bill past, every man of sense acquainted with human affairs must see, that as far as the Church is concerned, the

---

* Ueber die Behandlung der Griechischen Dichter bei den Engländern. Von Gottfried Hermann. Wiemar Jahrbucher, vol. liv. 1831.

thing is at an end. From Lord John Russell, the present improver
of the Church, we shall descend to Hume, from Hume to Roebuck,
and after Roebuck we shall receive our last improvements from
Dr. Wade: plunder will follow after plunder, degradation after
degradation. The Church is gone, and what remains is not life, but
sickness, spasm, and struggle.

Whatever happens, I am not to blame; I have fought my fight.—
Farewell.

Letter to LORD LANSDOWNE

Taunton, Sept. 14th, 1838

Dear Lord Lansdowne,

Do what you like with the Church, it will never make the
slightest alteration in my respect and regard for you. All that I
require is full permission in shilling pamphlets to protest that we
are the most injured, persecuted, and ill-treated persons on the face
of the Earth. Against Lord Holland and you personally I could
not, and would not, write a single syllable, and of course you must
both laugh at such nonsense I put forth from time to time.

After all the Residence and Plurality Bill was (as it came out of
the Commission) a very bad Bill. I could point out eleven or
twelve very material points, bearing strongly upon the happiness of
the parochial clergy, which have been omitted or completely
changed in the passage of the Bill through Parliament; to all of
these I objected, and though I do not of course imagine that I
had weight and authority to produce these changes, yet it shows
that my hostility was not frivolous and vexatious.

The Bill is now a very good Bill. The original Bill was bad, because John Russell, legislating on what it is not likely he could
understand, took his information from bishops, who were sure to
mislead him because they consulted their own power. In the same
way I am sure that his Dean and Chapter Bill may be very materially improved, and that the errors it contains proceed from the
same source.

Many thanks for the venison, which arrived here safely today,
and apparently in good condition. We have had a great run of
blue-stocking ladies here this summer, and are expecting more.
I have had a fit of the gout, which I chased away speedily with
Colchicum. Are you going to make your promised tour to Lynton?
If so, pray come and see us, you and yours.

I am very much obliged by your good-natured and sensible

letter, which gave me great pleasure and satisfaction; for I should have been heartily sorry that my defence of my profession should have been construed into the most distant intention of ill-will and hostility to *you;* and to show you how little I consider the venison as deprecatory, I will put into my next pamphlet any abuse of yourself which you choose to dictate, but decline entirely to insert any of my own.

PART II

Letter to Mrs. M. H. Beach

Winter 1794–5

Madam,

In our conversation about the poor of N. you agreed with me that some of the boys, and girls might possibly be prevented from attending church, or the Sunday School from a want of proper clothing, and you were so good as to add, that you would endeavor in some degree to remove this impediment, if it were found to exist. On Sunday last there were 3 or 4 children with their feet upon the cold stones without any shoes, and one came a perfect *Sans culottes*—or at least only with some grinning remnants of that useful garment, just sufficient to shew that he was so clad from necessity, and not from any ingenious Theory he had taken up against such an useful invention. If the Sunday School had begun, I should have imagined that the poor boy thought it his duty to come ready for whipping, as a fowl is sent from the poulterers, trussed and ready for roasting. In whatsoever manner and to whatsoever extent you may chuse to alleviate this species of misery, be so good as to remember that I am on the spot, and shall be happy to carry your benevolent intentions into execution, in the best manner that I [am] able.

Two Letters to M. H. Beach

LETTER I

April 2, 1795

Dear Sir,

Upon my return from Bath I began to carry into execution your plan of establishing a Sunday School at Netheravon. Andrew Goulter whom you mentioned as a man likely to undertake it, is going to quit the place. Bendall the Blacksmith, Harry Cozens,

taylor, and Cousin to the Clerk, and Giles Harding have all applied
for the appointment. The last I consider as out of the question, his
wife cannot read, and he has no room fit to receive the Children.
Henry Cozens in my opinion is the most eligible he seems to be
the most sensible man of the 2. His wife reads, his Brother reads,
and his apprentice reads. He has a good kitchen, some room in
his Shop and his mother next door has a good kitchen which may
be filled with the overflowings of the School, if it ever should over-
flow. I have mentioned the Salary you arranged with me to the applicants, viz 2 shillings per Sunday and 2 Score of faggots.

The Children will attend Xtmas day, and good Friday; is the
master to be paid for those days? It is impossible to find 2 Rooms
in the same house for boys and girls; if they are put to different
houses, the divided Salary will be too small to induce any reputable
man to accept it.

The Books that are wanted will be, about 60 Spelling Books
(with easy lessons of reading at the end) beginning from the
Letters and going on progressing in Syllables; 20 new Testaments
and 20 prayer Books. Miss Hannah More's Books I think you
will like very much if you look at them; They are 5 shillings per
100; if you will send me down 100 of them, I think I can distribute
them with effect. The people who had sittings in the great pew
have given them up, and Munday is going to fit it up for the children. The people all express a great desire of sending their children to the School. The only farmer I have yet had an opportunity
of speaking to, is Fr. Munday; he will contribute with great cheerfulness. I shall talk to the farmers collectively at the Vestry, and
individually out of it. I am no more judge of hay than I am of
Arabic; if I deal with the farmers, I shall get bad, if I can get any,
and be cheated: If your stock of hay is such that you can supply
me with *perfect convenience* to yourself I should esteem it as a
favor. Your Gardner will keep the acct. and will receive directions
from you what hay he is to send me, but pray deal with me as you
would with a farmer, charge me a good price, a better price than
you did for the clover hay, in which transaction you thought more
of doing me a favor, than of doing justice to yourself. If you wish
at [*the letter is torn here and part of two lines missing*] out of the
sittings in the church, I will. The pews must be coarsely numbered
with white paint. A few forms will be wanting for the Sunday
School; will you empower me to order them; In the very hot
weather why might not the children be instructed in the church
before, and after Service, instead of the little hot room in which

they would otherwise be stuffed. I shall mention it to the church
Wardens with your approbation. . . .

L E T T E R   I I

Edinburgh, June 30th,
Saturday Evening, 1798

My dear Sir,

Anxious as you and Mrs. Beach are for the welfare and
improvement of yr Son, I do not think it fair to keep you much
longer than a fortnight at a time without a Letter, and at about that
interval you may always expect to hear from me.—I can promise
you one thing in my correspondence, I will always tell you the
truth in every thing which concerns yr Son, whether that truth be
likely to give you pleasure, or pain; I have endeavored to make
this my System in life, and (if I understand you right) it is that,
which you yourself have pursued. Our beginning has been very
auspicious; as far as we have hitherto gone, I am extremely
pleased and satisfied with Michael. My first serious conversation
with him, was upon the subject of his toilette, and the very great
portion of time he daily consumed in adorning himself. This Michael
took in high anger, and was extreemly sulky, and upon my renewing the conversation sometime after, he was still more so. Without the smallest appearance of anger, or vexation on my part, I
turned his Sulkiness into ridicule, and compleatly laughed him
into good humor. He acknowledged it was very foolish, and un-
manly to be sulky about anything, promised that he would hear
any future remarks of mine upon his conduct with chearfulness,
and that he would endeavor to dress himself as quickly as he
could, and to these promises he has certainly conformed himself.
Mithoffer was extreemly fond of standing at his elbow while he
was dressing, and reaching him every thing he wanted. This I have
put a stop to; habits of indolence are soon learnt, Michael is a very
apt Scholar in these particulars; Where activity and energy are not
innate they are infused by slow degrees, and by a vigilant attention
to little particulars. Very soon after our arrival here, I checked
his propensity of getting to bed, so very early. He has since then
generally sat up till between 10 and 11, and got up most mornings at about 6. The great apprehension I entertained of Michael
was, that he would hear every thing I said to him with a kind of
torpid Silence, and that I should never be able to learn whether
he acquiesced voluntarily, or from compulsion in my proposals,
or get him by any means to state candidly his objections, and pre-

fer openly and ingenuously his observations. From an entire ignorance of his opinions and disposition, I should then have always been working in the dark. This difficulty however upon a better acquaintance with him has vanished; he talks over a subject boldly with me, and makes his objections like a man.

I have found him very docile in a great many little particulars, and I think very highly of the goodness of his heart, and disposition. I think much better of his understanding than I did. His *acquirements* at Eaton have certainly not been very brilliant; he reads Greek with great difficulty and cannot construe the most easy Latin Book. He spells carelessly, and writes English awkwardly, and ungrammatically. In my attention to his improvement, I shall by no means neglect the 2 latter particulars. I am always for laying a good solid foundation. The plan I have begun with is Latin (very easy) for two hours in the morning, and the history of England for two hours in the afternoon. Twice a week instead of reading Latin, he writes me some English, as an exercise in Style, and when we get into our new Lodgings I mean that a master shall attend him in some thing or other for an hour every day; and then I think his time will be sufficiently employed. He very honestly confesses his love of horses, and hounds and his dislike of study but expresses his great willingness to fag as well as he can, and allows I have not been too hard upon him. In adjusting the time of study, my object was to occupy him fairly, without exciting his disgust; I think I have succeeded. . . .

Letter to FRANCIS JEFFREY

Queen-street, Edinburgh, Burnt Island, Aug. 1802

Dear Jeffrey,

With the inculpative part of *your* criticisms on *mine* I very much agree; and, in particular, am so well aware of that excessive levity into which I am apt to run, that I think I shall soon correct it. I will beg the favour of you to put up Nares review in a little packet for me and to inform your servants where it may be found tomorrow in case the Carrier asks for it, while you are not at home. The levity certainly may be corrected. Of arguments upon the subject of miracles I really do not recollect to have advanced any, but appear to have confined myself to the detection of contradictions, and inconsistencies in his argument. Upon the point of severity I beg you to recollect the facts. That Nares is in point of talents a very stupid and a very contemptible fellow no one pretends to deny. He has been hangman for these ten years to all the poor authors in England, is generally considered to be hired by Government, and has talked about Social Order till he has talked himself into 6 or £700 per annum. That there can be a fairer object for critical severity I cannot conceive; and though he be not notorious in Edinburgh, he is certainly so in London. If he that deserves execution otherwise from anybody deserves it from me in particular, I confess I cannot see why the cumulation of public and private vengeance should not fall upon his head. If you think that the violent attack may induce the generality of readers to sympathize with the sufferer rather than the executioner, in spite of the general recollection that the artificer of death is perishing by his own art, then your objections to my criticism are good for the very opposite reason to that which you have alleged; not because they are too severe, but because, by diminishing the malice of the reader, they do not attain the possible maximum of severity.

As for personalities grant that the man is a proper object of punishment, and in these literary executions I do not care for justice or injustice a fig. My business is to make the archdeacon as ridiculous as possible. The readers to whom I write will allow me some personalities and refuse me others. I could not, and would not, say the man was a bad husband or a cruel father, but nobody (but the very correct few) will be offended with my laughing at his dignities in the church.

You say the readers will probably think my review long. If it is amusing, they will not; and if it is dull, I am sorry for it,—but I can write no better. I am so desirous of attacking this priest, that I cannot consent to omit this article, unless my associates consider their moral or religious character committed by it; at the same time I will with great pleasure attempt to modify it.

I am very much obliged to you for your animadversions on my inaccuracies, and should be obliged to you also to correct them. One of the instances you mention is perhaps rather awkward than incorrect, but had better be amended. I wrote my reviews as you see them; though I certainly made these blunders not in consequence of neglect, but in spite of attention. . . .

Letter to THE FARMER'S MAGAZINE

August, 1819

Sir,

It has been my lot to have passed the greater part of my life in cities.—About six or seven years ago, I was placed in the country, in a situation where I was under the necessity of becoming a farmer; and, amongst the many expensive blunders I have made, I warn those who may find themselves in similar situations, against *Scotch Sheep* and *Oxen for ploughing.* I had heard a great deal of the fine flavour of Scotch mutton, and it was one of the great luxuries I promised myself in farming. A luxury certainly it is; but the price paid for it is such, that I would rather give up the use of animal food altogether, than obtain it by such a system of cares and anxieties. Ten times a day my men were called off from their work to hunt the Scotch sheep out of my own or my neighbour's wheat. They crawled through hedges where I should have thought a rabbit could hardly have found admission; and, where crawling would not do, they had recourse to leaping. Five or six times they all assembled, and set out on their return to the North. My bailiff took a place in the mail, pursued, and overtook them half way to New-castle. Then it was quite impossible to get them fat. They consumed my turnips in winter, and my clover in the summer, without any apparent addition to their weight; 10 or 12 per cent. always died of the rot; and more would have perished in the same manner, if they had not been prematurely eaten out of the way.

My ploughing oxen were an equal subject of vexation. They had a constant purging upon them, which it was impossible to stop. They ate more than twice as much as the same number of horses. They did half as much work as the same number of horses. They could not bear hot weather, nor wet weather, nor go well down hill. It took five men to shoe an ox. They ran against my gate-posts, lay down in the cart whenever they were tired, and ran away at the sight of a stranger.

I have now got into a good breed of English sheep, and useful cart-horses, and am doing very well. I make this statement to guard young gentlemen farmers against listening to the pernicious nonsense of brother gentlemen, for whose advice I am at least poorer by £300, or £400.

ADVICE TO PARISHIONERS

If you begin stealing a little, you will go on from little to much, and soon become a regular thief; and then you will be hanged, or sent over seas to Botany Bay. And give me leave to tell you, transportation is no joke. Up at five in the morning, dressed in a jacket half blue half yellow, chained on to another person like two dogs, a man standing over you with a great stick, weak porridge for breakfast, bread and water for dinner, boiled beans for supper, straw to lie upon; and all this for thirty years; and then you are hanged there by order of the government, without judge or jury. All this is very disagreeable, and you had far better avoid it by making a solemn resolution to take nothing which does not belong to you.

Never sit in wet clothes. Off with them as soon as you can: no constitution can stand it. Look at Jackson, who lives next door to the blacksmith; he was the strongest man in the parish. Twenty different times I warned him of his folly in wearing wet clothes. He pulled off his hat and smiled, and was very civil, but clearly seemed to think it all old woman's nonsense. He is now, as you see, bent double with rheumatism, is living upon parish allowance, and scarcely able to crawl from pillar to post.

Off with your hat when you meet a gentleman. What does it cost? Gentlemen notice these things, are offended if the civility is not paid, and pleased if it is; and what harm does it do you? When first I came to this parish, Squire Tempest wanted a postillion, John Barton was a good, civil fellow; and in thinking over the names of the village, the Squire thought of Barton, remembered his constant civility, sent for one of his sons, made him postillion, then coachman, then bailiff, and he now holds a farm under the Squire of £500 per annum. Such things are constantly happening. . . .

I must positively forbid all poaching; it is absolute ruin to yourself and your family. In the end you are sure to be detected—a hare in one pocket and a pheasant in the other. How are you to pay ten pounds? You have not tenpence beforehand in the world. Daniel's breeches are unpaid for; you have a hole in your hat, and want a new one; your wife, an excellent woman, is about to lie in—and you are, all of a sudden, called upon by the Justice to pay ten pounds. I shall never forget the sight of poor Cranford, hurried to Taunton Jail; a wife and three daughters on their knees to the Justice, who was compelled to do his duty, and commit him. The next day, beds, chairs, and clothes sold, to get the father out of jail. Out of jail he came; but the poor fellow could not bear the sight of his naked cottage, and to see his family pinched with hunger. You know how he ended his days. Was there a dry eye in the church-yard when he was buried? It was a lesson to poachers. It is indeed a desperate and foolish trade. Observe, I am not defending the game-laws, but I am advising you, as long as the game-laws exist, to fear them, and to take care that you and your family are not crushed by them. And then, smart, stout young men hate the game-keeper, and make it a point of courage and spirit to oppose him. Why? The game-keeper is paid to protect the game, and he would be a very dishonest man if he did not do his duty. What right have you to bear malice against him for this? After all, the game in justice belongs to the land-owners, who feed it; and not to you, who have no land at all, and can feed nothing.

I don't like that red nose, and those blear eyes, and that stupid, downcast look. You are a drunkard. Another pint, and one pint more; a glass of gin and water, rum and milk, cider and pepper, a glass of peppermint, and all the beastly fluids which drunkards pour down their throats. It is very possible to conquer it, if you will but be resolute. . . .

It is all nonsense about not being able to work without ale, and gin, and cider, and fermented liquors. Do lions and cart-horses drink ale? It is mere habit. If you have good nourishing food, you can do very well without ale. Nobody works harder than the Yorkshire people, and for years together there are many Yorkshire laborers who never taste ale. I have no objection, you will observe, to a moderate use of ale, or any other liquor you can afford to purchase. My objection is, that you can not afford it; that every penny you spend at the ale-house comes out of the stomachs of the poor children, and strips off the clothes of the wife.

My dear little Nanny, don't believe a word he says. He merely means to ruin and deceive you. You have a plain answer to give: "When I am axed in the church, and the parson has read the service, and all about it is written down in the book, then I will listen to your nonsense, and not before." Am not I a Justice of the Peace, and have not I had a hundred foolish girls brought before me, who have all come with the same story? "Please your worship, he is a false man; he promised me marriage over and over again." I confess I have often wished for the power of hanging these rural lovers. But what use is my wishing? All that can be done with the villain is to make him pay half a crown a week, and you are handed over to the poor-house, and to infamy. Will no example teach you? Look to Mary Willet—three years ago the handsomest and best girl in the village, now a slattern in the poor-house! Look at Harriet Dobson, who trusted in the promises of James Harefield's son, and, after being abandoned by him, went away in despair with a party of soldiers! How can you be such a fool as to surrender your character to the stupid flattery of a plowboy? If the evening is pleasant, and birds sing, and flowers bloom, is that any reason why you are to forget God's Word, the happiness of your family, and your own character? What is a woman worth without character? A profligate carpenter, or a debauched watchmaker, may gain business from their skill; but how is a profligate woman to gain her bread? Who will receive *her?*

A LITTLE MORAL ADVICE

A FRAGMENT ON THE CULTIVATION AND IMPROVEMENT OF THE ANIMAL SPIRITS

It is surprising to see for what foolish causes men hang themselves. The most silly repulse, the most trifling ruffle of temper, or derangement of stomach, anything seems to justify an appeal to the razor or the cord. I have a contempt for persons who destroy themselves. Live on, and look evil in the face; walk up to it, and you will find it less than you imagined, and often you will not find it at all; for it will recede as you advance. Any fool may be a suicide. When you are in a melancholy fit, first suspect the body, appeal to rhubarb and calomel, and send for the apothecary; a little bit of gristle sticking in the wrong place, an untimely consumption of custard, excessive gooseberries, often cover the mind with clouds and bring on the most distressing views of human life.

I start up at two o'clock in the morning, after my first sleep, in an agony of terror, and feel all the weight of life upon my soul. It is impossible that I can bring up such a family of children, my sons and daughters will be beggars; I shall live to see those whom I love exposed to the scorn and contumely of the world!— But stop, thou child of sorrow, and humble imitator of Job, and tell me on what you dined. Was not there soup and salmon, and then a plate of beef, and then duck, blanc-mange, cream cheese, diluted with beer, claret, champagne, hock, tea, coffee, and noyeau? And after all this, you talk of the mind and the evils of life! These kind of cases do not need meditation, but magnesia. Take short views of life. What am I to do in these times with such a family of children? So I argued, and lived dejected and with little hope; but the difficulty vanished as life went on. An uncle died, and left me some money; an aunt died, and left me more; my daughter married well; I had two or three appointments, and before life was half over became a prosperous man. And so will you. Every one has uncles and aunts who are mortal; friends start up out of the earth; time brings a thousand chances in your favour; legacies fall from the clouds. Nothing so absurd as to sit down and wring your hands because all the good which may happen to you in twenty years has not taken place at this precise moment.

The greatest happiness which can happen to any one is to cultivate a love of reading. Study is often dull because it is improperly managed. I make no apology for speaking of myself, for as I write anonymously nobody knows who I am, and if I did not, very few would be the wiser—but every man speaks more firmly when he speaks from his own experience. I read four books at a time; some classical book perhaps on Monday, Wednesday, and Friday mornings. *The History of France,* we will say, on the evenings of the same days. On Tuesday, Thursday, and Saturday, Mosheim or Lardner, and in the evening of those days, Reynolds' *Lectures,* or Burns' *Travels.* Then I have always a standing book of poetry, and a novel to read when I am in the humour to read nothing else. Then I translate some French into English one day, and re-translate it the next; so that I have seven or eight pursuits going on at the same time, and this produces the cheerfulness of diversity, and avoids that gloom which proceeds from hanging a long while over a single book. I do not recommend this as a receipt for becoming a learned man, but for becoming a cheerful one.

Nothing contributes more certainly to the animal spirits than benevolence. Servants and common people are always about you; make moderate attempts to please everybody, and the effort will insensibly lead you to a more happy state of mind. Pleasure is very reflective, and if you give it you will feel it. The pleasure you give by kindness of manner returns to you, and often with compound interest. The receipt for cheerfulness is not to have one motive only in the day for living, but a number of little motives; a man who from the time he rises till bedtime conducts himself like a gentleman, who throws some little condescension into his manner to superiors, and who is always contriving to soften the distance between himself and the poor and ignorant, is always improving his animal spirits, and adding to his happiness.

I recommend lights as a great improver of animal spirits. How is it possible to be happy with two mould candles ill-snuffed? You may be virtuous, and wise, and good, but two candles will not do for animal spirits. Every night the room in which I sit is lighted up like a town after a great naval victory, and in this cereous galaxy and with a blazing fire, it is scarcely possible to be low-spirited, a thousand pleasing images spring up in the mind, and I can see the little blue demons scampering off like parish boys pursued by the beadle.

Letter to LADY GEORGIANA MORPETH

Foston, Feb. 16th, 1820

Dear Lady Georgiana,

. . . Nobody has suffered more from low spirits than I have done—so I feel for you.

1st. Live as well as you dare.

2nd. Go into the shower-bath with a small quantity of water at a temperature low enough to give you a slight sensation of cold, 75° or 80°.

3rd. Amusing books.

4th. Short views of human life—not further than dinner or tea.

5th. Be as busy as you can.

6th. See as much as you can of those friends who respect and like you.

7th. And of those acquaintances who amuse you.

8th. Make no secret of low spirits to your friends, but talk of them freely—they are always worse for dignified concealment.

9th. Attend to the effects tea and coffee produce upon you.

10th. Compare your lot with that of other people.

11th. Don't expect too much from human life—a sorry business at the best.

12th. Avoid poetry, dramatic representations (except comedy), music, serious novels, melancholy sentimental people, and everything likely to excite feeling or emotion not ending in active benevolence.

13th. *Do good,* and endeavour to please everybody of every degree.

14th. Be as much as you can in the open air without fatigue.

15th. Make the room where you commonly sit, gay and pleasant.

16th. Struggle by little and little against idleness.

17. Don't be too severe upon yourself, or underrate yourself, but do yourself justice.

18th. Keep good blazing fires.

19th. Be firm and constant in the exercise of rational religion.

20th. Believe me, dear Lady Georgiana. . . .

Definition of "A NICE PERSON"

A nice person is neither too tall nor too short, looks clean and cheerful, has no prominent feature, makes no difficulties, is never misplaced, sits bodkin, is never foolishly affronted, and is void of affectations.

A nice person helps you well at dinner, understands you, is always gratefully received by young and old, Whig and Tory, grave and gay.

There is something in the very air of a nice person which inspires you with confidence, makes you talk, and talk without fear of malicious misrepresentation; you feel that you are reposing upon a nature which God has made kind, and created for the benefit and happiness of society. It has the effect upon the mind which soft air and a fine climate has upon the body.

A nice person is clear of little, trumpery passions, acknowledges superiority, delights in talent, shelters humility, pardons adversity, forgives deficiency, respects all men's rights, never stops the bottle, is never long and never wrong, always knows the day of the month, the name of every body at table, and never gives pain to any human being.

If any body is wanted for a party, a nice person is the first thought of; when the child is christened, when the daughter is married—all the joys of life are communicated to nice people; the hand of the dying man is always held out to a nice person.

A nice person never knocks over wine or melted butter, does not tread upon the dog's foot, or molest the family cat, eats soup without noise, laughs in the right place, and has a watchful and attentive eye.

Letter to MESSRS. HUNT AND CLARK, Booksellers

Foston, June 30th, 1827

Gentlemen,

I have received from you within these few months some very polite and liberal presents of new publications, and though I was sorry you put yourselves to any expense on my acct, yet was flattered by this mark of respect and goodwill from gentlemen to whom I am personally unknown.

I am quite sure however that you overlooked the purpose and tendency of a work called *Elizabeth Evanshaw,*[1] or that you wd. not have sent it to a clergyman of the Established Church, or to a clergyman of any church. I see also advertised at your house a translation of Voltaire's *Philosophical Dictionary.* I hope you will

---

[1] Written, according to the Preface, "in defence of Deists, not of Deism."

have the goodness to excuse me, and not to attribute what I say to an impertinent, but to a friendly disposition. Let us pass over all higher considerations and look at this point only in a worldly view, as connected with your interests. Is it wise to give to your house the character of Publishers of *Infidel Books?* The English people are a very religious people, and those who are not religious hate the active dissemination of irreligion. The zealots of irreligion are few and insignificant and confined principally to London. You have not a chance of eminence and success in pursuing such a line, and I advise you prudently and quietly to back out of it.

I hate the insolence, persecution and intolerance which so often pass under the name of religion, and (as you know) I have fought against them; *but I have an unaffected horror of irreligion and impiety; and every principle of suspicion and fear wd. be excited in me by a man who professed himself an infidel.*

I write this from respect to you. It is quite a private communication, and I am sure you are too wise and too enlightened to take it in evil part. I shall read all the works and will tell you my opinion of them from time to time.

I was very much pleased with the *Two Months in Ireland,* but did not read the poetical part; the prosaic division of the work is very good.

Letter to——Bedford, Esq.

Foston, Jan. 13th, 1829

Dear Sir,
        I always intended to explain to you why I declined to be Steward to the Sons of the Clergy, but it went out of my head while I was in Bristol. I object to the whole plan of the thing, it appears to me quite ridiculous to desire two men to pay for a charity dinner where actually in many instances less is collected during the dinner than the dinner costs. Men who mean to patronize a charity should dine at their own costs, and the use of a steward would then be to guarantee to the innkeeper that he should not be a loser by providing dinner for a certain number of persons.

If two gentlemen were to give such a guarantee to the extent of 15 or twenty pds. each, this would be a fair tax upon their time, trouble and pocket; but to ask any man to give a dinner for charitable purposes where the guests coming for charitable purposes do not give the value of what they eat and drink is an abuse which I never will countenance. It is in vain to say money is sent after

dinner, so it would be if all paid for their dinner. If ever this alteration is made and I am wanted as steward I will serve or be at the
expense of serving, but not till I have seen the amended plan.

I write this to you not as secretary to the society but as a
neighbour and acquaintance, because, tho' I have a right to say
to the society yes or no, I have no right to criticize their institutions, or to propose to them any change in their plans. My motive
for taking the part I have done, is not only that I have no money
to fling away upon institutions so faulty in their construction (however excellent their principle) but because I believe I am expressing the opinion of many persons who are too timid to express it
themselves, and who would feel the expence as a great and unprofitable burthen.

(You will have the goodness to consider this letter as private.)

Letter to the VESTRY OF HALBERTON [1]

Combe Florey Rectory, Taunton, March 3rd, 1830

Gentlemen,

It has always been a rule with me through life to be as firm
and tenacious in the maintenance of my just rights, as I am willing
to sacrifice those to which I am not entitled. I must in candour
confess that from all the evidence I can collect—and I have employed two active solicitors in the search—I cannot find that the
clergyman of Halberton has been in the habit of nominating a
churchwarden. I shall therefore not attempt to exercise that power
this year at the ensuing Easter. If, from any fresh evidence I can
collect, I should see reason to alter my opinion another year, I
reserve to myself the full right of doing so; but, that I may not
take the parish by surprise, I engage to give two months' notice of
such an intention. In the selection of churchwardens, I submit to
you whether it is not right that they should be members of the
Church of England, and if my wishes were consulted, I should
desire Mr. Manley to be one of them. I have nothing to do, nor
will I ever have anything to do with any dissensions which may
take place in the parish, but Mr. Manley appears to me to be a
gentleman of sense and respectability, and a good Churchman.
However, as I have said before, the choice is with you and not with
me. If I could have satisfied myself that I possessed the right, I
would have contested it at any expense, but I am not so satisfied,
and I give it up as I said I would.

---

[1] S. received this small living with his prebend at Bristol.

Letter to LORD JOHN RUSSELL

November 19th, 1837

My Lord,

I inclose a Copy of the Notice which will forthwith be fixed upon the Cathedral of St. Paul's.

As the Dean and Chapter have now complied entirely and to the utmost extent with your Lordship's request and as they hope now that this question is finally settled they wish to make a few observations at the conclusion of their correspondence with your Lordship.

The Dean and Chapter claim an entire right of shutting the doors of the Church after the services of the Church are finished.

All Churches in England are shut when the service is over, and whoever wishes to see the Church at any other period must find out the Officer of the Church and give him a fee for his trouble.

The same practice obtains in Catholic countries where the Church is kept open much longer than with us because the services are longer but is closed when those services are finished and there entrance is obtained in the same manner by giving a fee to the Officers of the Church.

Fifty new Churches were built by the Nation in the reign of Queen Anne. In the Statutes under which they were erected, as well as in those by the authority of which St. Paul's was built there is no mention of any right to the public to enter those edifices out of the hours of service nor of any legal obligation to their Clergy to provide Doorkeepers for the accommodation of the public. The law remains the same in Churches built by the Country as in those whose founders are unknown or those which have been founded by the piety of known individuals.

The Vergers of the Cathedral are employed for about two hours every day in the service of the Church; if this was the whole of their employment they might carry on some worldly trade at other hours, but now they wait all day to minister to the curiosity of the public and by the Public they ought to be paid.

The public thought fit to erect St. Paul's into a receptacle for national monuments from the erection of which no kind of emolument is derived by the Dean and Chapter, nor is any such emolument thought of or desired; but the public choosing to convert a Church into a School of Art ought surely to defray every expence which proceeds from such an arrangement and not to fling it upon Individuals who have had no other share in the transaction than to give a consent which they might have withholden.

The custom of paying two pence at the doors has existed for more than 100 years; and it is so far from being a tax upon the public that it is a great saving of time and money; for otherwise (unless the doors were kept constantly open) the Officer must be sought at his own residence and would receive a fee six or twelve times as great as that which is now paid to him.

But waiving the extreme injustice of exhibiting a national gallery of Sculpture at the expence of individuals who have (undeservedly perhaps) permitted the Church to which they are the Guardians to be turned to such an use, considerations of a much higher order present themselves to the Dean and Chapter.

There pass by the gates of St. Paul's every day about 100,000 persons and on days of more than ordinary excitement and bustle in the City more than double that number. If the doors of the Church were constantly open such numbers would come in that all idea of performing the service would be entirely out of the question. It has happened that in less than an hour between 2000 and 3000 people have entered the Church, many of them of the lowest description with their hats on laughing talking and making an uproar totally incompatible with any idea of religion.

Of the experiment we tried this summer and of its total failure, I have already informed your Lordship. The whole area of the Church was flung open and the noise of persons walking and talking was so intolerable that from repeated Representations of persons frequenting St. Paul's but determined to frequent it no longer we were forced to revoke our permission and restrict our limits.

If the doors of St. Paul's were flung open the Church would become as it has been in times past, a place of assignation for all the worst characters male and female in the Metropolis; it would be a Royal Exchange for wickedness as the other Royal Exchange is for commerce. Even now with the restricted right of entrance we see beggars, men with burdens, women knitting parties eating luncheon, Dogs, children playing loud laughing and talking and every kind of scenery incompatible with the solemnity of worship, evils in which all sense of religion is destroyed, and in which the interference of the police (as no illegal act is committed) would be rather an aggravation than a remedy from the noisy disputes to which it would give birth. On one side of a line the Congregation are praying; on the other is all the levity, indecorum and tumult of a London mob, squabbling with the Police, looking upon St. Paul's as a gallery of Sculpture, not a house of praying and vindicating their right to be merry and gay if they abstain from crime.

The mischief and indecorum which takes place at St. Paul's is very notorious; the Cathedral is constantly and shamefully polluted with ordure, the pews are sometimes turned into Cabinets d'aisance, and the Prayerbooks torn up; the monuments are scribbled all over and often with the grossest indecency. The inference from these observations is that the right of entry must be restricted or St. Paul's must be opened as a Gallery of Sculpture and shut as a place of worship.

Our duty is to consider the interests of religion as paramount to the interests of art and the gratification of any curiosity upon human subjects however laudable it may be. In complying with your Lordship's request which we have now done to the fullest extent, we have been governed less by our judgment than by that respect which we are always desirous of paying to the wishes of the Sovereign, and to the friendly communications of the Government; but to preserve the decencies of worship is a higher duty than any other. If it shall hereafter appear to be required we shall retrace our steps and resume our original position; but we will not do so without shewing to your Lordship the reasons which have influenced our decisions. If such a necessity should occur we shall feel our opinion strengthened if it should coincide with that of your Lordship, but in a trust so sacred and so well founded on ancient law, the decision must be with ourselves.

These are the sentiments of the Dean and Chapter which the Dean himself would have transmitted to your Lordship if the state of his health had permitted.

The Dean and Chapter beg of your Lordship to accept their sincere good wishes and respect.

PART III

GAME LAWS

THE evil of the Game Laws, in their present state, has long been felt, and of late years has certainly rather increased than diminished. We believe that they cannot long remain in their present state; and we are anxious to express our opinion of those changes which they ought to experience.

We thoroughly acquiesce in the importance of encouraging those field sports which are so congenial to the habits of Englishmen, and which, in the present state of society, afford the only effectual counterbalance to the allurements of great towns. We cannot conceive a more pernicious condition for a great nation, than that its aristocracy should be shut up from one year's end to another in a metropolis, while the mass of its rural inhabitants are left to the management of factors and agents. A great man returning from London to spend his summer in the country diffuses intelligence, improves manners, communicates pleasure, restrains the extreme violence of subordinate politicians, and makes the middling and lower classes better acquainted with, and more attached to their natural leaders. At the same time, a residence in the country gives to the makers of laws an opportunity of studying those interests which they may afterwards be called upon to protect and arrange. Nor is it unimportant to the character of the higher orders themselves, that they should pass a considerable part of the year in the midst of these their larger families; that they should occasionally be thrown among simple, laborious, frugal people, and be stimulated to resist the prodigality of Courts, by viewing with their own eyes the merits and the wretchedness of the poor.

Laws for the preservation of Game are not only of importance, as they increase the amusements of the country, but they may be so constructed as to be perfectly just. The game which my land feeds is certainly mine; or, in other words, the game which all the land feeds certainly belongs to all the owners of the land: and the only practical way of dividing it is, to give to each proprietor what he can take on his own ground. Those who contribute nothing to the support of the animal, can have no possible right to a share in the distribution. To say of animals, that they are *feræ Naturâ* means only, that the precise place of their birth and nature is not known. How they shall be divided, is a matter of arrangement among those whose collected property certainly has produced and fed them: but the case is completely made out against those who have no land at all, and who cannot therefore have been in the slightest degree instrumental to their production. If a large pond were divided by certain marks into four parts, and allotted to that number of proprietors, the fish contained in that pond would be, in the same sense, *feræ Naturâ*. Nobody could tell in which particular division each carp had been born and bred. The owners would arrange their respective rights and pretensions in the best way they could: but the clearest of all possible propositions would be, that the four proprietors, among them, made a complete title to all the fish; and that nobody but them had the smallest title to the smallest share. This we say, in answer to those who contend that there is no foundation for any system of Game Laws; that animals born wild are the property of the public; and that their appropriation is nothing but tyranny and usurpation.

In addition to these arguments, it is perhaps scarcely necessary to add, that nothing which is worth having, which is accessible, and supplied only in limited quantities, could exist at all, if it was not considered as the property of some individual. If everybody might take game wherever they found it, there would soon be an end of every species of game. The advantage would not be extended to fresh classes, but be annihilated for all classes. Besides all this, the privilege of killing game could not be granted, without the privilege of trespassing on landed property;—an intolerable evil, which would entirely destroy the comfort and privacy of a country life.

But though a system of Game Laws is of great use in promoting country amusements, and may, in itself, be placed on a footing of justice, its effects, we are sorry to say, are by no means favourable to the morals of the poor.

It is impossible to make an uneducated man understand in what manner a bird hatched, nobody knows where—to-day living in my field, to-morrow in yours—should be as strictly property as the goose whose whole history can be traced, in the most authentic and satisfactory manner, from the egg to the spit. The arguments upon which this depends are so contrary to the notions of the poor —so repugnant to their passion—and, perhaps, so much above their comprehension, that they are totally unavailing. The same man who would respect an orchard, a garden, or a hen-roost, scarcely thinks he is committing any fault at all in invading the game covers of his richer neighbour; and as soon as he becomes wearied of honest industry, his first resource is in plundering the rich magazine of hares, pheasants, and partridges—the top and bottom dishes, which on every side of his village are running and flying before his eyes. As these things cannot be done with safety in the day, they must be done in the night;—and in this manner a lawless marauder is often formed, who proceeds from one infringement of law and property to another, till he becomes a thoroughly bad and corrupted member of society.

These few preliminary observations lead naturally to the two principal considerations which are to be kept in view, in reforming the Game Laws;—to preserve, as far as is consistent with justice, the amusements of the rich, and to diminish, as much as possible, the temptations of the poor. And these ends, it seems to us, will be best answered,

1. By abolishing qualifications. 2. By giving to every man a property in the game upon his land. 3. By allowing game to be bought by anybody, and sold by its lawful possessors.*

Nothing can be more grossly absurd than the present state of the Game Laws, as far as they concern the qualification for shooting. In England, no man can possibly have a legal right to kill game, who has not 100*l.* a year in land rent. With us in Scotland, the rule is not quite so inflexible, though in principle not very different.—But we shall speak to the case which concerns by far the greatest number; and certainly it is scarcely possible to imagine a more absurd and capricious limitation. For what possible reason is a man, who has only 90*l.* per annum in land, not to kill the game which his own land nourishes? If the Legislature really conceives, as we have heard surmised by certain learned squires, that a person of such a degree of fortune should be confined to profitable pursuits, and debarred from that pernicious idleness into which he would be betrayed by field sports, it would then be expedient to make a qualification for bowls or skittles—to prevent small landowners from going to races, or following a pack of hounds— and to prohibit to men of a certain income, every other species of amusement as well as this. The only instance, however, in which this paternal care is exercised, is that in which the amusement of the smaller landowner is supposed to interfere with those of his richer neighbour. He may do what he pleases, and elect any other

* All this has since been done.

species of ruinous idleness but that in which the upper classes of society are his rivals.

Nay, the law is so excessively ridiculous in the case of small landed proprietors, that on a property of less than 100*l.* per annum, *no human being* has the right of shooting. It is not confined, but annihilated. The lord of the manor may be warned off by the proprietor; and the proprietor may be informed against by anybody who sees him sporting. The case is still stronger in the instance of large farms. In Northumberland, and on the borders of Scotland, there are large capitalists, who farm to the amount of two or three thousand per annum, who have the permission of their distant nonresident landlords to do what they please with the game, and yet who dare not fire off a gun upon their own land. Can anything be more utterly absurd and preposterous, than that the landlord and the wealthy tenant *together* cannot make up a title to the hare which is fattened upon the choicest produce of their land? That the landlord, who can let to farm the fertility of the land for growing wheat cannot let to farm its power of growing partridges? That he may reap by deputy, but cannot on that manor shoot by deputy? Is it possible that any respectable magistrate could fine a farmer for killing a hare upon his own grounds with his landlord's consent, without feeling that he was violating every feeling of common sense and justice?

Since the enactment of the Game Laws, there has sprung up an entirely new species of property, which of course is completely overlooked by their provisions. An Englishman may possess a million of money in funds, or merchandise—may be the *Baring* or the *Hope* of Europe—provide to Government the sudden means of equipping fleets and armies, and yet be without the power of smiting a single partridge, though invited by the owner of the game to participate in his amusement. It is idle to say that the difficulty may be got over, by purchasing land: the question is, upon what principle of justice can the existence of the difficulty be defended? If the right of keeping men-servants were confined to persons who had more than 100*l.* a year in the funds, the difficulty might be got over by every man who could change his landed property to that extent. But what could justify so capricious a partiality to one species of property? There might be some apology for such laws at the time they were made: but there can be none for their not being now accommodated to the changes which time has introduced. If you choose to exclude poverty from this species of amusement, and to open it to wealth, why is it not open to every species of wealth? What amusement can there be morally

lawful to a holder of turnip land, and criminal in a possessor of
Exchequer bills? What delights ought to be tolerated to Long
Annuities, from which wheat and beans should be excluded? What
matters it whether it is scrip or short-horned cattle? If the *locus
quo* is conceded—if the trespass is waived—and if the qualification
for any amusement is wealth, let it be any proveable wealth—

Dives agris, dives positis in fænorenummis.

It will be very easy for any country gentleman who wishes to
monopolise to himself the pleasure of shooting, to let to his tenant
every other right attached to the land, except the right of killing
game; and it will be equally easy, in the formation of a new Game
Act, to give to the landlord a summary process against his tenant,
if such tenant fraudulently exercise the privileges he has agreed to
surrender.

The case which seems most to alarm country gentlemen, is that
of a person possessing a few acres in the heart of a manor, who
might, by planting food of which they are fond, allure the game
into his own little domain, and thus reap a harvest prepared at the
expense of the neighbour who surrounded him. But, under the
present Game Laws, if the smaller possession belong to a qualified
person, the danger of intrusion is equally great as it would be
under the proposed alteration; and the danger from the poacher
would be the same in both cases. But if it be of such great consequence to keep clear from all interference, may not such a piece
of land be rented or bought? Or, may not the food which tempts
game be sown in the same abundance in the surrounding as in the
enclosed land? After all, it is only common justice, that he whose
property is surrounded on every side by a preserver of game,—
whose corn and turnips are demolished by animals preserved for
the amusement of his neighbour, should himself be entitled to that
share of game which plunders upon his land. The complaint which
the landed grandee makes is this. "Here is a man who has only
a twenty-fourth part of the land, and he expects a twenty-fourth
part of the game. He is so captious and litigious, that he will not
be contented to supply his share of the food, without requiring
his share of what the food produces. I want a neighbour who has
talents only for suffering, not one who evinces such a fatal disposition for enjoying." Upon such principles as these, many of the
Game Laws have been constructed, and are preserved. The interference of a very small property with a very large one; the critical
position of one or two fields, is a very serious source of vexation
on many other occasions besides those of game. He who possesses

a field in the middle of my premises may build so as to obstruct my view, and may present to me the hinder parts of a barn, instead of one of the finest landscapes in nature. Nay, he may turn his fields into tea-gardens, and destroy my privacy by the introduction of every species of vulgar company. The Legislature, in all these instances, has provided no remedy for the inconveniences which a small property, by such intermixture, may inflict upon a large one, but has secured the same rights to unequal proportions. It is very difficult to conceive why these equitable principles are to be violated in the case of game alone.

Our securities against that rabble of sportsmen which the abolition of qualifications might be supposed to produce, are, the consent of the owner of the soil, as an indispensable preliminary, guarded by heavy penalties—and the price of a certificate, rendered perhaps greater than it is at present. It is impossible to conceive why the owner of the soil, if the right of game be secured to him, has not a right to sell, or grant the right of killing it to whom he pleases—just as much as he has the power of appointing whom he pleases to kill his ducks, pigeons, and chickens. The danger of making the poor idle, is a mere pretence. It is monopoly calling in the aid of hypocrisy, and tyranny veiling itself in the garb of philosophical humanity. A poor man goes to wakes, fairs, and horse-races, without pain and penalty; a little shopkeeper, when his work is over, may go to a bull-bait, or to the cock-pit; but the idea of his pursuing a hare, even with the consent of the landowner, fills the Bucolic Senator with the most lively apprehensions of relaxed industry, and ruinous dissipation.—The truth is, if a poor man does not offend against morals or religion, and supports himself and his family without assistance, the law has nothing to do with his amusements. The real barriers against increase of sportsmen (if the proposed alteration were admitted) are, as we have before said, the prohibition of the landowner; the tax to the State for a certificate; the necessity of labouring for support.—Whoever violates none of these rights, and neglects none of these duties in his sporting, sports without crime;—and to punish him would be gross and scandalous tyranny.

The next alteration which we would propose is, that game should be made property; that is, that every man should have a right to the game found upon his land—and that the violation of it should be punished as poaching now is, by pecuniary penalties, and summary conviction before magistrates. This change in the Game Laws would be an additional defence of game; for the landed proprietor has now no other remedy against the qualified intruder upon his game, than an action at law for a trespass on the land; and if the trespasser have received no notice, this can hardly be called any remedy at all. It is now no uncommon practice for persons who have the exterior, and perhaps the fortunes of gentlemen, as they are travelling from place to place, to shoot over manors where they have no property, and from which, as strangers, they cannot have been warned. In such case (which, we repeat again, is by no means one of rare occurrence), it would, under the reformed system, be no more difficult for the lord of the soil to protect his game, than it would be to protect his geese and ducks. But though game should be considered as property, it should still be considered as the lowest species of property—because it is in its nature more vague and mutable than any other species of property, and because depredations upon it are carried on at a distance from the dwelling, and without personal alarm to the proprietors. It would be very easy to increase the penalties in proportion to the number of offences committed by the same individual.

The punishments which country gentlemen expect by making game property, are the punishments affixed to offences of a much higher order; but country gentlemen must not be allowed to legislate exclusively on this, more than on any other subject. The very mention of hares and partridges in the country, too often puts an end to common humanity and common sense. Game must be protected; but protected without violating those principles of justice, and that adaptation of punishment to crime which (incredible as it may appear) are of infinitely greater importance than the amusements of country gentlemen.

We come now to the sale of game.—The foundation on which the propriety of allowing this partly rests, is the impossibility of preventing it. There exists, and has sprung up since the Game Laws, an enormous mass of wealth, which has nothing to do with land. Do the country gentlemen imagine, that it is in the power of human laws to deprive the Three-per-cents of pheasants?—that there is upon earth, air, or sea, a single flavour (cost what crime it may to procure it), that mercantile opulence will not procure? Increase the difficulty, and you enlist vanity on the side of luxury; and make that be sought for as a display of wealth, which was before valued only for the gratification of appetite. The law may multiply penalties by reams. Squires may fret and justices commit, and gamekeepers and poachers continue their nocturnal wars. There must be game on Lord Mayor's day, do what you will. You may multiply the crimes by which it is procured; but nothing can arrest its inevitable progress from the wood of the esquire to the spit of the citizen. The late law for preventing the sale of game produced some little temporary difficulty in London at the beginning of the season. The poulterers were alarmed, and came to some resolutions. But the alarm soon began to subside, and the difficulties to vanish. In another season, the law will be entirely nugatory and forgotten. The experiment was tried of increased severity; and a law passed to punish poachers with transportation who were caught poaching in the night-time with arms. What has the consequence been?—Not a cessation of poaching, but a succession of village guerillas;—an internecive war between the gamekeepers and marauders of game;—the whole country flung into brawls and convulsions, for the unjust and exorbitant pleasures of country gentlemen. The poacher hardly believes he is doing any wrong in taking partridges and pheasants. He would admit the justice of being transported for stealing sheep; and his courage in such a transaction would be impaired by a consciousness he was doing wrong: but he has no such feeling in taking game; and the preposterous punishment of transportation makes him desperate and not timid. Single poachers are gathered into large companies for their mutual protection; and go out, not only with the intention of taking game, but of defending that they take with their lives. Such feelings soon produce a rivalry of personal courage, and a thirst of revenge between the villagers and the agents of power. We extract the following passages on this subject from the *Three Letters on the Game Laws.**

"The first and most palpable effect has naturally been, an exaltation of all the savage and desperate features in the poacher's character. The war between him and the gamekeeper has necessarily become a *bellum internecivum*. A marauder may hesitate perhaps at killing his fellowman, when the alternative is only six months' imprisonment in the county gaol; but when the alternative is to overcome the keeper, or to be torn from his family and connections, and sent to hard labour at the Antipodes, we cannot be much surprised that murders and midnight combats have considerably increased this season; or that information such as the following has frequently enriched the columns of the country newspapers.

" 'POACHING.—Richard Barnett was on Tuesday convicted before T. Clutterbuck, Esq., of keeping and using engines or wires

---

* Rest, Fenner, Block & Co., London, 1818.

for the destruction of game in the parish of Dunkerton, and fined 5*l*. He was taken into custody by C. Coates, keeper to Sir Charles Bamfylde, Bart., who found upon him 17 wire-snares. The new act that has just passed against these illegal practices, seems only to have irritated the offenders, and made them more daring and desperate. The following is a copy of an anonymous circular letter, which has been received by several magistrates, and other eminent characters in this neighbourhood.

" 'TAKE NOTICE.—We have lately heard and seen that there is an act passed, and whatever poacher is caught destroying the game, is to be transported for seven years.—*This is English Liberty!*

" 'Now, we do swear to each other, that the first of our company that this law is inflicted on, that there shall not one gentleman's seat in our country escape the rage of fire. We are nine in number, and we will burn every gentleman's house of note. The first that impeaches shall be shot. We have sworn not to impeach. You may think it a threat, but they will find it reality. The Game Laws were too severe before. The Lord of all men sent these animals for the peasants as well as for the prince. God will not let his people be oppressed. He will assist us in our undertaking, and we will execute it with caution.'—(*Bath Paper.*)

" 'DEATH OF A POACHER.—On the evening of Saturday se'en-night, about eight or nine o'clock, a body of poachers, seven in number, assembled by mutual agreement on the estate of the Hon. John Dutton, at Sherborne, Gloucestershire, for the pur-pose of taking hares and other game. With the assistance of two dogs, and some nets and snares which they brought with them, they had succeeded in catching nine hares, and were carrying them away, when they were discovered by the gamekeeper and seven others who were engaged with him in patroling the dif-ferent covers, in order to protect the game from nightly de-predators. Immediately on perceiving the poachers, the keeper summoned them in a civil and peaceable manner to give up their names, the dogs, implements, &c., they had with them, and the game they had taken; at the same time assuring them, that his party had fire-arms (which were produced for the pur-pose of convincing and alarming them), and representing to them the folly of resistance, as, in the event of an affray, they must inevitably be overpowered by superior numbers, even without fire-arms, which they were determined not to resort to unless compelled in self-defence. Notwithstanding this remonstrance of the keeper, the men unanimously refused to give up on any terms, declaring, that if they were followed, they would give them a "brush," and would repel force by force. The poachers then directly took off their great coats, threw them down with the game, &c., behind them, and approached the keepers in an attitude of attack. A smart contest instantly ensued, both parties using only the sticks or bludgeons they carried; and such was the confusion during the battle, that some of the keepers were occasionally struck by their own comrades in mistake for their opponents. After they had fought in this manner about eight or ten minutes, one of the poachers, named Robert Simmons, received a violent blow upon his left temple, which felled him to the ground, where he lay, crying out murder, and asking for mercy. The keepers very humanely desired that all violence might cease on both sides: upon which three of the poachers took to flight and escaped, and the remaining three, together with Simmons, were secured by the keepers. Simmons, by the assistance of the other men, walked to the keeper's house where he was placed in a chair; but he soon after died. His death was no doubt caused by the pressure of blood upon the brain, occasioned by the rupture of a vessel from the blow he had received. The three poachers who had been taken were committed to Northleach prison. The inquest upon the body of Simmons was taken on Monday before W. Trigge, gent., Coroner! and the above account is extracted from the evidence given upon that occasion. The poachers were all armed with bludgeons, except the deceased, who had provided himself with the thick part of a flail, made of firm knotted crabtree, and pointed at the extremity, in order to thrust with, if occasion required. The deceased was an athletic, muscular man, very active, and about twenty-eight years of age. He resided at Bowle, in Oxfordshire, and has left a wife, but no child. The three prisoners were heard in evidence; and all concurred in stating that the keepers were in no way blameable, and attributed their disaster to their own indiscretion and imprudence. Several of the keeper's party were so much beat, as to be now confined to their beds. The two parties are said to be total strangers to each other, consequently no malice prepense could have existed between them; and as it appeared to the jury, after a most minute and deliberate investigation, that the confusion during the affray was so great, that the deceased was as likely to be struck by one of his own party as by the keeper's, they returned a verdict of—*Manslaughter* against some person or persons unknown.'

"Wretched as the first of these productions is, I think it can scarcely be denied, that both its spirit and its probable consequences are wholly to be ascribed to the exasperation naturally consequent upon the severe enactment just alluded to. And the last case is at least a strong proof that severity of enactment is quite inadequate to correct the evil."—(pp. 356-359.)

Poaching will exist in some degree, let the laws be what they may; but the most certain method of checking the poacher seems to be by underselling him. If game can be lawfully sold, the quantity sent to market will be increased, the price lowered, and with that, the profits and temptations of the poacher. Not only would the prices of the poacher be lowered, but we much doubt if he would find any sale at all. Licences to sell game might be confined to real poulterers, and real occupiers of a certain portion of land. It might be rendered penal to purchase it from any but licensed persons; and in this way the facility of the lawful, and the danger of the unlawful trade, would either annihilate the poacher's trade, or reduce his prices so much, that it would be hardly worth his while to carry it on. What poulterer in London, or in any of the large towns, would deal with poachers, and expose himself to indictment for receiving stolen goods, when he might supply his customers at fair prices by dealing with the lawful proprietor of game? Opinion is of more power than law. Such conduct would soon become infamous; and every respectable tradesman would be shamed out of it. The consumer himself would rather buy his game of a poulterer at an increase of price, than pick it up clandestinely, and at a great risk, though a somewhat smaller price, from porters and booth-keepers. Give them a chance of getting it fairly, and they will not get it unfairly. At present, no one has the slightest shame at violating a law which every body feels to be absurd and unjust.

Poultry-houses are sometimes robbed;—but stolen poultry is rarely offered to sale;—at least, nobody pretends that the shops of poulterers, and the tables of moneyed gentlemen, are supplied by these means. Out of one hundred geese that are consumed at Michaelmas, ninety-nine come into the jaws of the consumer by honest means;—and yet, if it had pleased the country gentlemen to have Goose Laws as well as Game Laws;—if goose-keepers had been appointed, and the sale and purchase of this savoury bird prohibited, the same enjoyments would have been procured by the crimes and convictions of the poor; and the periodical gluttony of Michaelmas have been rendered as guilty and criminal, as it is indigestible and unwholesome. Upon this subject we shall quote a passage from the very sensible and spirited Letters before us: —

"In favourable situations, game would be reared and preserved for the express purpose of regularly supplying the market in fair and open competition; which would so reduce its price, that I see no reason why a partridge should be dearer than a rabbit, or a hare and pheasant than a duck or goose. This is about the proportion of price which the animals bear to each other in France, where game can be legally sold, and is regularly brought to market; and where, by the way, game is as plentiful as in any cultivated country in Europe. The price so reduced would never be enough to compensate the risk and penalties of the unlawful poacher, who must therefore be driven out of the market. Doubtless the great poulterers of London and the commercial towns, who are the *principal instigators of poaching,* would cease to have any temptation to continue so, as they could fairly and lawfully procure game for their customers, at a cheaper rate from the regular breeders. They would, as they now do for rabbits and wild fowl, contract with persons to rear and preserve them for the regular supply of their shops, which would be a much more commodious and satisfactory, and less hazardous way for them, than the irregular and dishonest and corrupting methods now pursued. It is not saying very much in favour of human nature to assert, that men in respectable stations of society had rather procure the *same ends* by honest than dishonest means. Thus would all the temptations to offend against the Game Laws, arising from the change of society, together with the long chain of moral and political mischiefs, at once disappear.

"But then, in order to secure a sufficient breed of game for the supply of the market, in fair and open competition, it will be necessary to authorise a certain number of persons, likely to breed game for sale, to take and dispose of it when reared at their expense. For this purpose, I would suggest the propriety of permitting by law, occupiers of land to take and kill game, for sale or otherwise, on their *own occupations only,* unless (if tenants) they are specifically prohibited by agreement with their landlord; reserving the game and the power of taking it to himself (as is now frequently done in leases). This permission, should not, of course, operate during the current leases, unless by agreement With this precaution, nothing could be fairer than such an enactment; for it is certainly at the expense of the *occupier* that the game is raised and maintained: and unless he receive an equivalent for it, either by abatement of rent upon agreement, or by permission to take and dispose of it, he is certainly an injured man; whereas it is perfectly just that the owner of the land should have the option either to increase his rent by leaving the disposal of his game to his tenant, or *vice versâ*. Game would be held to be (as in fact it is) an *outgoing* from the land, like tithe and other burdens, and therefore to be considered in a bargain; and land would either be let *game-free,* or a special reservation of it made by agreement.

"Moreover, since the breed of game must always depend upon the occupier of the land, who may, and frequently does, destroy every head of it, or prevent its coming to maturity, unless it is considered in his rent; the licence for which I am now contending, by affording an inducement to preserve the breed in particular spots, would evidently have a considerable effect in increasing the stock of game in other parts, and in the country at large. There would be introduced a general system of protection, depending upon individual interest, instead of a general system of destruction. I have, therefore, very little doubt that the provision here recommended would, upon the whole, add facilities to the amusements of the sportsman, rather than subtract from them. A sportsman without land might also hire from the occupier of a large tract of land the privilege of shooting over it, which would answer to the latter as well as sending his game to the market. In short, he might in various ways get a fair return, to which he is well entitled for the expense and trouble incurred in rearing and preserving that particular species of stock upon his land."—pp. 337-339.)

There are sometimes 400 or 500 head of game killed in great manors on a single day. We think it highly probable the greater part of this harvest (if the Game Laws were altered) would go to the poulterer, to purchase poultry or fish for the ensuing London season. Nobody is so poor and so distressed as men of very large fortunes, who are fond of making an unwise display to the world; and if they had recourse to these means of supplying game, it is impossible to suppose that the occupation of the poacher could be continued.—The smuggler can compete with the spirit-merchant, on account of the great duty imposed by the revenue; but where there is no duty to be saved, the mere thief—the man who brings the article to market with a halter round his neck—the man of whom it is disreputable and penal to buy,—who hazards life, liberty, and property to procure the articles which he sells; such an adventurer can never be long the rival of him who honestly and fairly produces the articles in which he deals.—Fines, imprisonments, concealment, loss of character, are great deductions from the profits of any trade to which they attach, and great discouragements to its pursuit.

It is not the custom at present for gentlemen to sell their game; but the custom would soon begin, and public opinion soon change. It is not unusual for men of fortune to contract with their gardeners to supply their own table, and to send the residue to market, or to sell their venison; and the same thing might be done with the manor. If game could be bought, it would not be sent in presents:—barn-door fowls are never so sent, precisely for this reason.

The price of game would, under the system of laws of which we are speaking, be further lowered by the introduction of foreign game, the sale of which, at present prohibited, would tend very much to the preservation of English game by underselling the poacher. It would not be just, if it were possible, to confine any of the valuable productions of nature to the use of one class of men, and to prevent them from becoming the subject of barter, when the proprietor wished so to exchange them. It would be just as reasonable that the consumption of salmon should be confined to the proprietors of that sort of fishery—that the use of char should be limited to the inhabitants of the lakes—that maritime Englishmen should alone eat oysters and lobsters, as that every other class of the community than landowners should be prohibited from the acquisition of game.

It will be necessary, whenever the Game Laws are revised, that some of the worst punishments now inflicted for an infringement of these laws should be repealed.—To transport a man for seven years on account of partridges, and to harass a poor wretched peasant in the Crown office, are very preposterous punishments for such offences. Humanity revolts against them—they are grossly tyrannical—and it is disgraceful that they should be suffered to remain on our statute books. But the most singular of all abuses, is the new class of punishments which the Squirarchy have themselves enacted against depredations on game. The law says, that an unqualified man who kills a pheasant shall pay five pounds;

but the squire says he shall be shot;—and accordingly he places a spring-gun in the path of the poacher, and does all he can to take away his life. The more humane and mitigated squire mangles him with traps; and the supra-fine country gentleman only detains him in machines, which prevent his escape, but do not lacerate their captive. Of the gross illegality of such proceedings, there can be no reasonable doubt. Their immorality and cruelty are equally clear. If they are not put down by some declaratory law, it will be absolutely necessary that the Judges, in their invaluable circuits of oyer and terminer, should leave two or three of his Majesty's squires to a fate too vulgar and indelicate to be alluded to in this Journal.

Men have certainly a clear right to defend their property; but then it must be by such means as the law allows:—their houses by pistols, their fields by actions for trespass, their game by information. There is an end of law, if every man is to measure out his punishment for his own wrong. Nor are we able to distinguish between the guilt of two persons,—the one of whom deliberately shoots a man whom he sees in his fields—the other of whom purposely places such instruments as he knows will shoot trespassers upon his fields: better that it should be lawful to kill a trespasser face to face, than to place engines which will kill him. The trespasser may be a child—a woman—a son, or friend:— The spring-gun cannot accommodate itself to circumstances,—the squire or the gamekeeper may.

These, then, are our opinions respecting the alterations in the Game Laws, which, as they now stand, are perhaps the only system which could possibly render the possession of game so very insecure as it now is. We would give to every man an absolute property in the game upon his land, with full power to kill—to permit others to kill—and to sell;—we would punish any violation of that property by summary conviction and pecuniary penalties—rising in value according to the number of offences. This would of course abolish all qualifications; and we sincerely believe it would lessen the profits of selling game illegally, so as very materially to lessen the number of poachers. It would make game, as an article of food, accessible to all classes, without infringing the laws. It would limit the amusements of country gentlemen within the boundaries of justice—and would enable the magistrate cheerfully and conscientiously to execute laws, of the moderation and justice of which he must be thoroughly convinced. To this conclusion, too, we have no doubt we shall come at the last. After

many years of scutigeral folly—loaded prisons *—nightly battles
—poachers tempted—and families ruined, these principles will
finally prevail, and make law once more coincident with reason
and justice.

SPRING GUNS AND MAN TRAPS

WHEN Lord Dacre (then Mr. Brand) brought into the House of
Commons his bill for the amendment of the Game Laws, a system of greater mercy and humanity was in vain recommended to
that popular branch of the Legislature. The interests of humanity,
and the interests of the lord of the manor, were not, however, opposed to each other; nor any attempt made to deny the superior
importance of the last. No such bold or alarming topics were agitated; but it was contended that, if laws were less ferocious, there
would be more partridges—if the lower orders of mankind were
not torn from their families and banished to Botany Bay, hares and
pheasants would be increased in number, or, at least, not diminished. It is not, however, till after long experience, that mankind
ever think of recurring to humane expedients for effecting their
objects. The rulers who ride the people never think of coaxing
and patting till they have worn out the lashes of their whips, and
broken the rowels of their spurs. The legislators of the trigger replied, that two laws had lately passed which would answer their
purpose of preserving game: the one, an act for transporting men
found with arms in their hands for the purposes of killing game in
the night; the other, an act for rendering the buyers of the game
equally guilty with the seller, and for involving both in the same
penalty. Three seasons have elapsed since the last of these laws
was passed; and we appeal to the experience of all the great towns
in England, whether the difficulty of procuring game is in the
slightest degree increased?—whether hares, partridges, and pheasants are not purchased with as much facility as before the passing
this act?—whether the price of such unlawful commodities is even
in the slightest degree increased? Let the Assize and Sessions'
Calendars bear witness, whether the law for transporting poachers
has not had the most direct tendency to encourage brutal assaults

---

* In the course of the last year, no fewer than *twelve hundred* persons were
committed for offences against the game; besides those who ran away
from their families from the fear of commitment. This is no slight quantity
of misery.

and ferocious murders. There is hardly now a jail-delivery in which some gamekeeper has not murdered a poacher—or some poacher a gamekeeper. If the question concerned the payment of five pounds, a poacher would hardly risk his life rather than be taken; but when he is to go to Botany Bay for seven years, he summons together his brother poachers—they get brave from rum, numbers, and despair—and a bloody battle ensues.

Another method by which it is attempted to defeat the depredations of the poacher is, by setting spring guns to murder any person who comes within their reach; and it is to this last new feature in the *supposed* Game Laws, to which, on the present occasion, we intend principally to confine our notice.

We utterly disclaim all hostility to the Game Laws in general. Game ought to belong to those who feed it. All the landowners in England are fairly entitled to all the game in England. These laws are constructed upon a basis of substantial justice; but there is a great deal of absurdity and tyranny mingled with them, and a perpetual and vehement desire on the part of the country gentlemen to push the provisions of these laws up to the highest point of tyrannical severity.

"Is it lawful to put to death by a spring gun, or any other machine, an unqualified person trespassing upon your woods or fields in pursuit of game, and who has received due notice of your intention, and of the risk to which he is exposed?" This, we think, is stating the question as fairly as can be stated. We purposely exclude gardens, orchards, and all contiguity to the dwelling-house. We exclude, also, all felonious intention on the part of the deceased. The object of his expedition shall be proved to be game; and the notice he received of his danger shall be allowed to be as complete as possible. It must also be part of the case, that the spring-gun was placed there for the express purpose of defending the game, by killing or wounding the poacher, or spreading terror, or doing anything that a reasonable man ought to know would happen from such a proceeding.

Suppose any gentleman were to give notice that all other persons must abstain from his manors; that he himself and his servants paraded the woods and fields with loaded pistols and blunderbusses, and would shoot anybody who fired at a partridge; and suppose he were to keep his word, and shoot through the head some rash trespasser who defied this bravado, and was determined to have his sport:—is there any doubt that he would be guilty of murder? We suppose no resistance on the part of the trespasser; but that, the moment he passes the line of demarcation with his dogs and gun, he is shot dead by the proprietor of the land from behind a tree. If this is not murder, what is murder? We will make the case a little better for the homicide squire. It shall be night; the poacher, an unqualified person, steps over the line of demarcation with his nets and snares, and is instantly shot through the head by the pistol of the proprietor. We have no doubt that this would be murder—that it ought to be considered as murder, and punished as murder. We think this so clear, that it would be a waste of time to argue it. There is no kind of resistance on the part of the deceased; no attempt to run away; he is not even challenged: but instantly shot dead by the proprietor of the wood, for no other crime than *the intention* of killing game unlawfully. We do not suppose that any man, possessed of the elements of law and common sense, would deny this to be a case of murder, let the previous notice to the deceased have been as perfect as it could be. It is true, a trespasser in a park may be killed; but then it is when he will not render himself to the keepers, upon a hue and cry to stand to the king's peace. But deer are property, game is not; and this power of slaying deer-stealers is by the 21st Edward I., *de Malefactoribus in Parcis*, and by the 3d and 4th William & Mary, c. 10. So rioters may be killed, house-burners, ravishers, felons refusing to be arrested, felons escaping, felons breaking jail, men resisting a civil process—may all be put to death. All these cases of justifiable homicide are laid down and admitted in our books. But who ever heard that to pistol a poacher was justifiable homicide? It has long been decided, that it is unlawful to kill a dog who is pursuing game in a manor. "To decide the contrary," says Lord Ellenborough, "would outrage reason and sense." (Vere *v.* Lord Cawdor and King, 11 *East*, 386.) Pointers have always been treated by the Legislature with great delicacy and consideration. To *"wish to be a dog, and to bay the moon,"* is not quite so mad a wish as the poet thought it.

If these things are so, what is the difference between the act of firing yourself, and placing an engine which does the same thing? In the one case, your hand pulls the trigger; in the other, it places the wire which communicates with the trigger, and causes the death of the trespasser. There is the same intention of slaying in both cases —there is precisely the same human agency in both cases; only the steps are rather more numerous in the latter case. As to the bad effects of allowing proprietors of game to put trespassers to death at once, or to set guns that will do it, we can have no hesitation in saying, that the first method, of giving the power of life and death to esquires, would be by far the most humane. For, as we have observed in a previous Essay on the Game Laws, a live armigeral spring

gun would distinguish an accidental trespasser from a real poacher
—a woman or a boy from a man—perhaps might spare a friend or
an acquaintance—or a father of a family with ten children—or a
small freeholder who voted for Administration. But this new rural
artillery must destroy, without mercy and selection, every one who
approaches it.

In the case of Ilot *versus* Wilks, Esq., the four judges, Abbot,
Bailey, Holroyd, and Best, gave their opinions *seriatim* on points
connected with this question. In this case, as reported in Chetwynd's
edition of Burn's Justice, 1820, vol. ii. p. 500, Abbot C. J. observes
as follows:—

"I cannot say that repeated and increasing acts of aggression may
not reasonably call for increased means of defence and protection. I believe that many of the persons who cause engines of this
description to be placed in their grounds, do not do so with an
intention to injure any person, but really believe that the publication of notices will prevent any person from sustaining an injury; and that no person having the notice given him will be weak
and foolish enough to expose himself to the perilous consequences
of his trespass. Many persons who place such engines in their
grounds, do so for the purpose of preventing, by means of terror,
injury to their property, rather than from any motive of doing malicious injury."

"Increased means of defence and protection," but increased (his
Lordship should remember) from the payment of five pounds to instant death—and instant death inflicted, not by the arm of law, but
by the arm of the proprietor;—could the Lord Chief Justice of the
King's Bench intend to say, that the impossibility of putting an end to
poaching by other means would justify the infliction of death upon
the offender? Is he so ignorant of the philosophy of punishing, as
to imagine he has nothing to do but to give ten stripes instead of
two, a hundred instead of ten, and a thousand, if a hundred will not
do? to substitute the prison for pecuniary fines, and the gallows instead of the jail? It is impossible so enlightened a Judge can forget,
that the sympathies of mankind must be consulted; that it would be
wrong to break a person upon the wheel for stealing a penny loaf,
and that gradations in punishments must be carefully accommodated
to gradations in crime; that if poaching is punished more than mankind in general think it ought to be punished, the fault will either
escape with impunity, or the delinquent be driven to desperation;
that if poaching and murder are punished equally, every poacher
will be an assassin. Besides, too, if the principle is right in the un-

limited and unqualified manner in which the Chief Justice puts it—
if defence goes on increasing with aggression, the Legislature at least
must determine upon their equal pace. If an act of Parliament made
it a capital offence to poach upon a manor, as it is to commit a
burglary in a dwelling-house, it might then be as lawful to shoot a
person for trespassing upon your manor, as it is to kill a thief for
breaking into your house. But the real question is—and so in sound
reasoning his Lordship should have put it—"If the law at this moment determine the aggression to be in such a state, that it merits
only a pecuniary fine after summons and proof, has any sporadic
squire the right to say, that it shall be punished with death, before
any summons and without any proof?"

It appears to us, too, very singular, to say, that many persons who
cause engines of this description to be placed in their ground, do
not do so with an intention of injuring any person, but really believe
that the publication of notices will prevent any person from sustaining an injury, and that no person, having the notice giving him, will
be weak and foolish enough to expose himself to the perilous consequences of his trespass. But if this be the real belief of the engi-
neer—if he think the mere notice will keep people away—then he
must think it a mere inutility that the guns should be placed at all:
if he think that many will be deterred, and a few come, then he must
mean to shoot those few. He who believes his gun will never be called
upon to do its duty, need set no gun, and trust to rumour of their
being set, or being loaded, for his protection. Against the gun and
the powder we have no complaint; they are perfectly fair and ad-
missible: our quarrel is with the bullets. He who sets a *loaded* gun
means it should go off if it is touched. But what signifies the mere
empty wish that there may be no mischief, when I perform an action
which my common sense tells me may produce the worst mischief?
If I hear a great noise in the street, and fire a bullet to keep people
quiet, I may not perhaps have intended to kill; I may have wished
to have produced quiet, by mere terror, and I may have expressed
a strong hope that my object has been effected without the destruction of human life. Still I have done that which every man of sound
intellect knows is likely to kill; and if any one fall from my act, I
am guilty of murder. "Further" (says Lord Coke), "if there be an
evil intent, though that intent extendeth not to death, it is murder.
Thus, if a man, knowing that many people are in the street, throw
a stone over the wall, intending only to frighten them, or to give
them a little hurt, and thereupon one is killed—this is murder—for
he had an ill intent; though that intent extended not to death, and
though he knew not the party slain." (3 *Inst.* 57.) If a man be not

mad, he must be presumed to foresee common consequences; if he puts a bullet into a spring gun—he must be supposed to foresee that it will kill any poacher who touches the wire—and to that consequence he must stand. We do not suppose all preservers of game to be so bloodily inclined that they would prefer the death of a poacher to his staying away. Their object is to preserve game; they have no objection to preserve the lives of their fellow-creatures also, if both can exist at the same time; if not, the least worthy of God's creatures must fall—the rustic without a soul,—not the Christian partridge—not the immortal pheasant—not the rational woodcock, or the accountable hare.

The Chief Justice quotes the instance of glass and spikes fixed upon walls. He cannot mean to infer from this, because the law connives at the infliction of such small punishments for the protection of property, that it does allow, or ought to allow, proprietors to proceed to the punishment of death. Small means of annoying trespassers may be consistently admitted by the law, though more severe ones are forbidden, and ought to be forbidden; unless it follows, that what is good in any degree, is good in the highest degree. You may correct a servant boy with a switch; but if you bruise him sorely, you are liable to be indicted—if you kill him, you are hanged. A blacksmith corrected his servant with a bar of iron: the boy died, and the blacksmith was executed. (Grey's Case, *Kel.* 64, 65.) A woman kicked and stamped on the belly of her child—she was found guilty of murder. (1 *East, P. C.* 261.) *Si immoderate suo jure utatur, tune reus, homicidii sit.* There is, besides, this additional difference in the two cases put by the Chief Justice, that no publication of notices can be so plain, in the case of the guns, as the sight of the glass or the spikes; for a trespasser may not believe in the notice which he receives, or he may think he shall see the gun, and so avoid it, or that he may have the good luck to avoid it, if he does not see it; whereas, of the presence of the glass or the spikes he can have no doubt; and he has no hope of placing his hand in any spot where they are not. In the one case he cuts his fingers upon full and perfect notice, the notice of his own senses; in the other case, he loses his life after a notice which he may disbelieve, and by an engine which he may hope to escape.

Mr. Justice Bailey observes, in the same case, that it is not an indictable offence to set spring guns: perhaps not. It is not an indictable offence to go about with a loaded pistol, intending to shoot anybody who grins at you: but, if you do it, you are hanged: many inchoate acts are innocent, the consummation of which is a capital offence.

This is not a case where the motto applies of *Volenti non fit injuria*. The man does not will to be hurt, but he wills to get the game; and, with that rash confidence natural to many characters, believes he shall avoid the evil and gain the good. On the contrary, it is a case which exactly arranges itself under the maxim, *Quando aliquid prohibetur ex directo, prohibetur et per obliquum*. Give what notice he may, the proprietor cannot lawfully shoot a trespasser (who neither runs nor resists) with a loaded pistol;—he cannot do it *ex directo;*—how then can he do it *per obliquum*, by arranging on the ground the pistol which commits the murder?

Mr. Justice Best delivers the following opinion. His Lordship concluded as follows:—

> "This case has been discussed at the bar, as if these engines were exclusively resorted to for the protection of game; but I consider them as lawfully applicable to the protection of every species of property against unlawful trespassers. But if even they might not lawfully be used for the protection of game, I, for one, should be extremely glad to adopt such means, if they were found sufficient for that purpose; because I think it a great object that gentlemen should have a temptation to reside in the country, amongst their neighbours and tenantry, whose interests must be materially advanced by such a circumstance. The links of society are thereby better preserved, and the mutual advantage and dependence of the higher and lower classes of society, existing between each other, more beneficially maintained. We have seen, in a neighbouring country, the baneful consequences of the non-residence of the landed gentry; and in an ingenious work, lately published by a foreigner, we learn the fatal effects of a like system on the Continent. By preserving game, gentlemen are tempted to reside in the country; and considering that the diversion of the field is the only one of which they can partake on their estates, I am of opinion that, for the purpose I have stated, it is of essential importance that this species of property should be inviolably protected."

If this speech of Mr. Justice Best be correctly reported, it follows, that a man may put his fellow-creatures to death for any infringement of his property—for picking the sloes and blackberries off his hedges—for breaking a few dead sticks out of them by night or by day—with resistance or without resistance—with warning or without warning;—a strange method this of keeping up the links of society, and maintaining the dependence of the lower upon the higher classes. It certainly is of importance that gentlemen should reside on their estates in the country; but not that gentlemen with such opinions as these should reside. The more *they* are absent from the country, the less strain will there be upon those links to which the learned Judge alludes—the more firm that dependence upon which he places so just a value. In the case of Dean *versus* Clayton, Bart., the Court of Common Pleas were equally divided upon the lawfulness of killing a dog coursing a hare by means of a concealed dog-spear. We confess that we cannot see the least difference between transfixing with a spear, or placing a spear so that it will transfix; and, therefore, if Vere *versus* Lord Cawdor and King is good law, the action could have been maintained in Dean *versus* Clayton; but the solemn consideration concerning the life of the pointer is highly creditable to all the judges. They none of them say that it is lawful to put a trespassing pointer to death under any circumstances, or that they themselves would be glad to do it; they all seem duly impressed with the recollection that they are deciding the fate of an animal faithfully ministerial to the pleasures of the upper classes of society: there is an awful desire to do their duty, and a dread of any rash and intemperate decision. Seriously speaking, we can hardly believe this report of Mr. Justice Best's speech to be correct; yet we take it from a book which guides the practice of nine tenths of all the magistrates of England. Does a Judge—a cool, calm man, in whose hands are the issues of life and death—from whom so many miserable trembling human beings await their destiny—does he tell us, and tell us in a court of justice, that he places such little value on the life of man, that he himself would plot the destruction of his fellow-creatures for the preservation of a few hares and partridges? "Nothing which falls from me" (says Mr. Justice Bailey) "shall have a tendency to encourage the practice."—"I consider them" (says Mr. Justice Best) "as lawfully applicable to the protection of every species of property; but even if they might not lawfully be used for the protection of game, *I, for one, should be extremely glad to adopt them*, if they were found sufficient for that purpose." Can any man doubt to which of these two magistrates he would rather entrust a decision on his life, his liberty, and his possessions? We should be very sorry to misrepresent Mr. Justice Best, and will give to his disavowal of such sentiments, if he do disavow them, all the publicity in our power; but we have cited his very words conscientiously and correctly, as they are given in the Law Report. We have no doubt he meant to do his duty; we blame not his motives, but his feelings and his reasoning.

Let it be observed that, in the whole of this case, we have put every circumstance in favour of the murderer. We have supposed it to be in the night-time; but a many may be shot in the day * by a spring gun. We have supposed the deceased to be a poacher; but he may be a very innocent man, who has missed his way—an unfortunate botanist, or a lover. We have supposed notice; but it is a very possible event that the dead man may have been utterly ignorant of the notice. This instrument, so highly approved of by Mr. Justice Best—this knitter together of the different orders of society —is levelled promiscuously against the guilty or the innocent, the ignorant and the informed. No man who sets such an infernal machine, believes that it can reason or discriminate; it is made to murder all alike, and it does murder all alike.

Blackstone says, that the law of England, like that of every other well-regulated community, is tender of the public peace, and careful of the lives of the subjects; "that it will not suffer with impunity any crime to be prevented by death, *unless the same, if committed, would also be punished by death*." (*Commentaries,* vol. iv. p. 182.) "The law sets so high a value upon the life of a man, that it always intends some misbehaviour in the person who takes it away, unless by the command, or express permission of the law."—"And as to the necessity which excuses a man who kills another *se defendendo,* Lord Bacon calls even that *necessitas culpabilis.*" (*Commentaries,* vol. iv. p. 187.) So far this Luminary of the law.—But the very amusements of the rich are, in the estimation of Mr. Justice Best, of so great importance, that the poor are to be exposed to sudden death who interfere with them. There are other persons of the same opinion with this magistrate respecting the pleasures of the rich. In the last Session of Parliament a bill was passed, entitled "An Act for the summary Punishment, in certain cases, of Persons wilfully or maliciously damaging, or committing Trespasses on public or private Property." *Anno primo*—(a bad specimen of what is to happen) —*Georgii IV. Regis,* cap. 56. In this act it is provided, that "if any person shall wilfully, *or* maliciously, commit any damage, injury, or spoil, upon any building, fence, hedge, gate, stile, guide-post, milestone, tree, wood, underwood, orchard, garden, nursery-ground, crops, vegetables, plants, land, or other matter or thing growing or being therein, or to or upon real or personal property of any nature or kind soever, he may be immediately seized by anybody, without a warrant, taken before a magistrate, and fined, (according to the mischief he has done) to the extent of 5*l.*; or, in default of payment, may be committed to the jail for three months." And at the

---

* Large damages have been given for wounds inflicted by spring guns set in a garden in the day-time, where the party wounded had no notice.

end comes a clause, exempting from the operation of this act *all mischief done in hunting, and by shooters who are qualified*. This is surely the most impudent piece of legislation that ever crept into the statute-book; and, coupled with Mr. Justice Best's declaration, constitutes the following affectionate relation between the different orders of society. Says the higher link to the lower, "If you meddle with my game, I will immediately murder you;—if you commit the slightest injury upon my real or personal property, I will take you before a magistrate, and fine you five pounds. I am in Parliament, and you are not; and I have just brought in an act of Parliament for that purpose. But so important is it to you that my pleasures should not be interrupted, that I have exempted myself and friends from the operation of this act; and we claim the right (without allowing you any such summary remedy) of riding over your fences, hedges, gates, stiles, guide-posts, milestones, woods, underwoods, orchards, gardens, nursery-grounds, crops, vegetables, plants, lands, or other matters or things growing or being thereupon—including your children and yourselves, if you do not get out of the way." Is there, upon earth, such a mockery of justice as an act of Parliament, pretending to protect property, sending a poor hedge-breaker to jail, and specially exempting from its operation the accusing and the judging squire, who, at the tail of the hounds, have that morning, perhaps, ruined as much wheat and seeds as would purchase fuel a whole year for a whole village?

It cannot be urged, in extenuation of such a murder as we have described, that the artificer of death had no particular malice against the deceased; that his object was general, and his indignation levelled against offenders in the aggregate. Everybody knows that there is a malice by implication of law.

"In general, any formal design of doing mischief may be called malice; and, therefore, not such killing only as proceeds from premeditated hatred and revenge against the person killed, but also, in many other cases, such as is accompanied with those circumstances that show the heart to be perversely wicked, is adjudged to be of malice prepense."—(2 *Haw.* c. 31.)

"For, where the law makes use of the term, malice aforethought, as descriptive of the crime of murder, it is not to be understood in that narrow restrained sense in which the modern use of the word *malice* is apt to lead one, a principle of malevolence to particulars; for the law, by the term malice, *malitia*, in this instance meaneth, that the fact hath been attended with such circumstances as are the ordinary symptoms of a wicked heart regardless of social duty, and fatally bent upon mischief."—(*Fost.* 256, 257.)

Ferocity is the natural weapon of the common people. If gentlemen of education and property contend with them at this sort of
warfare, they will probably be defeated in the end. If spring guns
are generally set—if the common people are murdered by them, and
the Legislature does not interfere, the posts of gamekeeper and lord
of the manor will soon be posts of honour and danger. The greatest
curse under heaven (witness Ireland) is a peasantry demoralised by
the barbarity and injustice of their rulers.

It is expected by some persons, that the severe operation of these
engines will put an end to the trade of a poacher. This has always
been predicated of every fresh operation of severity, that it was to
put an end to poaching. But if this argument is good for one thing,
it is good for another. Let the first pickpocket who is taken be hung
alive by the ribs, and let him be a fortnight in wasting to death. Let
us seize a little grammar boy, who is robbing orchards, tie his arms
and legs, throw over him a delicate puff-paste, and bake him in a
bun-pan in an oven. If poaching can be extirpated by intensity of
punishment, why not all other crimes? If racks and gibbets and
tenter-hooks are the best method of bringing back the golden age,
why do we refrain from so easy a receipt for abolishing every species of wickedness? The best way of answering a bad argument is
not to stop it, but to let it go on in its course till it leaps over the
boundaries of common sense. There is a little book called *Beccaria
on Crimes and Punishments*, which we strongly recommend to the
attention of Mr. Justice Best. He who has not read it, is neither fit
to make laws, nor to administer them when made.

As to the idea of abolishing poaching altogether, we will believe
that poaching is abolished when it is found impossible to buy game;
or when they have risen so greatly in price, that none but people of
fortune can buy them. But we are convinced this never can and never
will happen. All the traps and guns in the world will never prevent
the wealth of the merchant and manufacturer from commanding
the game of the landed gentleman. You may, in the pursuit of this
visionary purpose, render the common people savage, ferocious, and
vindictive; you may disgrace your laws by enormous punishments,
and the national character by these new secret assassinations; but
you will never separate the wealthy glutton from his pheasant. The
best way is, to take what you want, and to sell the rest fairly and
openly. This is the real spring gun and steel trap which will annihilate, not the unlawful trade, but the unlawful trade.

There is a sort of horror in thinking of a whole land filled with
lurking engines of death—machinations against human life under
every green tree—traps and guns in every dusky dell and bosky

bourn—the *feræ naturâ*, the lords of manors, eyeing their peasantry as so many butts and marks, and panting to hear the click of the trap and to see the flash of the gun. How any human being, educated in liberal knowledge and Christian feeling, can doom to certain destruction a poor wretch, tempted by the sight of animals that naturally appear to him to belong to one person as well as another, we are at a loss to conceive. We cannot imagine how he could live in the same village, and see the widow and orphans of the man whose blood he had shed for such a trifle. We consider a person who could do this to be deficient in the very elements of morals—to want that sacred regard to human life which is one of the corner stones of civil society. If he sacrifice the life of man for his mere pleasures, he would do so, if he dared, for the lowest and least of his passions. He may be defended, perhaps, by the abominable injustice of the Game Laws—though we think and hope he is not. But there rests upon his head, and there is marked in his account, the deep and indelible sin of *blood-guiltiness*.

Counsel for Prisoners

On the sixth of April, 1824, Mr. George Lamb (a gentleman who is always the advocate of whatever is honest and liberal) presented the following petition from several jurymen in the habit of serving on juries at the Old Bailey:—

"That your petitioners, fully sensible of the invaluable privilege of Jury trials, and desirous of seeing them as complete as human institutions will admit, feel it their duty to draw the attention of the House to the restrictions imposed on the prisoner's counsel, which, they humbly conceive, have strong claims to a legislative remedy. With every disposition to decide justly, the petitioners have found, by experience, in the course of their attendances as jurymen in the Old Bailey, that the opening statements for the prosecution too frequently leave an impression more unfavourable to the prisoner at the bar, than the evidence of itself could have produced; and it has always sounded harsh to the petitioners to hear it announced from the bench, that the counsel, to whom the prisoner has committed his defence, cannot be permitted to address the jury in his behalf, nor reply to the charges which have, or have not, been substantiated by the witnesses. The petitioners have felt their situation peculiarly painful and embarrassing when the prisoner's faculties, perhaps surprised by such an intimation, are too much absorbed in the difficulties of his unhappy circumstances to admit of an effort towards his own justification, against the statements of the prosecutor's counsel, often unintentionally aggravated through zeal or misconception; and it is purely with a view to the attainment of impartial justice, that the petitioners humbly submit to the serious consideration of the House the expediency of allowing every accused person the full benefit of counsel, as in cases of misdemeanour, and according to the practice of the civil courts."

With the opinions so sensibly and properly expressed by these jurymen, we most cordially agree. We have before touched incidentally on this subject; but shall now give to it a more direct and fuller examination.* We look upon it as a very great blot in our overpraised criminal code; and no effort of ours shall be wanting, from time to time, for its removal.

We have now the benefit of discussing these subjects under the government of a Home Secretary of State, whom we may (we believe) fairly call a wise, honest, and high-principled man—as he appears to us, without wishing for innovation, or having any itch for it, not to be afraid of innovation,† when it is gradual and well considered. He is, indeed, almost the only person we remember in his station, who has not considered sound sense to consist in the rejection of every improvement, and loyalty to be proved by the defence of every accidental, imperfect, or superannuated institution.

If this petition of jurymen be a real *bonâ fide* petition, not the result of solicitation—and we have no reason to doubt it—it is a warning which the Legislature cannot neglect, if it mean to avoid the disgrace of seeing the lower and middle orders of mankind making laws for themselves, which the Government is at length compelled to adopt as measures of their own. The Judges and the Parliament would have gone on to this day, hanging, by wholesale, for the forgeries of bank notes, if juries had not become weary of the continual butchery, and resolved to acquit. The proper execution of laws must always depend, in great measure, upon public opinion; and it is undoubtedly most discreditable to any men intrusted with

* *Stockton on the Practice of not allowing Counsel for Prisoners accused of Felony.* 8vo. London. 1826.
† We must always except the Catholic question. Mr. Peel's opinions on this subject (giving him credit for sincerity) have always been a subject of real surprise to us. It must surely be some mistake between the Right Honourable Gentleman and his chaplain! They have been travelling together, and some of the parson's notions have been put up in Mr. Peel's head by mistake. We yet hope he will return them to their rightful owner.

power, when the governed turn round upon their governors, and say, "Your laws are so cruel, or so foolish, we can not, and *will not*, act upon them."

The particular improvement, of allowing counsel to those who are accused of felony, is so far from being unnecessary, from any extraordinary indulgence shown to English prisoners, that we really cannot help suspecting, that not a year elapses in which many innocent persons are not found guilty. How is it possible, indeed, that it can be otherwise? There are seventy or eighty persons to be tried for various offences at the Assizes, who have lain in prison for some months; and fifty of whom, perhaps, are of the lowest order of the people, without friends in any better condition than themselves, and without one single penny to employ in their defence. How are they to obtain witnesses? No attorney can be employed—no subpœna can be taken out; the witnesses are fifty miles off, perhaps—totally uninstructed—living from hand to mouth—utterly unable to give up their daily occupation, to pay for their journey, or for their support when arrived at the town of trial—and, if they could get there, not knowing where to go, or what to do. It is impossible but that a human being, in such a helpless situation, must be found guilty; for as he cannot give evidence for himself, and has not a penny to fetch those who can give it for him, any story told against him must be taken for true (however false); since it is impossible for the poor wretch to contradict it. A brother or a sister may come—and support every suffering and privation themselves in coming; but the prisoner cannot often have such claims upon the persons who have witnessed the transaction, nor any other claims but those which an unjustly accused person has upon those whose testimony can exculpate him —and who probably must starve themselves and their families to do it. It is true, a case of life and death will rouse the poorest persons, every now and then, to extraordinary exertions, and they may tramp through mud and dirt to the Assize town to save a life—though even this effort is precarious enough: but imprisonment, hard labour, or transportation, appeal less forcibly than death—and would often appeal for evidence in vain, to the feeble and limited resources of extreme poverty. It is not that a great proportion of those accused are not guilty—but that some are not—and are utterly without means of establishing their innocence. We do not believe they are often accused from wilful and corrupt perjury; but the prosecutor is himself mistaken—the crime has been committed; and in his thirst for vengeance, he has got hold of the wrong man. The wheat was stolen out of the barn; and, amidst many other collateral circumstances, the witnesses (paid and brought up by a wealthy prosecutor, who is repaid by the county) swear that they saw a man, very like the prisoner, with a sack of corn upon his shoulder, at an early hour of the morning, going from the barn in the direction of the prisoner's cottage! Here is one link, and a very material link, of a long chain of circumstantial evidence. Judge and jury must give it weight, till it is contradicted. In fact, the prisoner did not steal the corn; he was, to be sure, out of his cottage at the same hour—and that also is proved —but travelling in a totally different direction—and was seen to be so travelling by a stage coachman passing by, and by a market gardener. An attorney with money in his pocket, whom every moment of such employ made richer by six-and-eightpence, would have had the two witnesses ready, and at rack and manger, from the first day of the assize; and the innocence of the prisoner would have been established: but by what possible means is the destitute ignorant wretch himself to find or to produce such witnesses? or how can the most humane jury, and the most acute judge, refuse to consider him as guilty, till his witnesses *are* produced? We have not the slightest disposition to exaggerate, and on the contrary, should be extremely pleased to be convinced that our apprehensions were unfounded: but we have often felt extreme pain at the hopeless and unprotected state of prisoners; and we cannot find any answer to our suspicions, or discover any means by which this perversion of justice, under the present state of the law, can be prevented from taking place. Against the prisoner are arrayed all the resources of an angry prosecutor, who has certainly (let who will be the culprit) suffered a serious injury. He has his hand, too, in the public purse; for he prosecutes at the expense of the county. He cannot even relent; for the magistrate has bound him over to indict. His witnesses cannot fail him; for they are all bound over by the same magistrate to give evidence. He is out of prison, too, and can exert himself.

The prisoner, on the other hand, comes into Court, squalid and depressed from long confinement—utterly unable to tell his own story for want of words and want of confidence, and as unable to produce evidence for want of money. His fate accordingly is obvious;—and that there are many innocent men punished every year, for crimes they have not committed, appears to us to be extremely probable. It is indeed, scarcely possible it should be otherwise; and, as if to prove the fact, every now and then, a case of this kind *is* detected. Some circumstances come to light between sentence and execution; immense exertions are made by humane men; time is gained, and the innocence of the condemned person completely established. In Elizabeth Caning's case, two women were capitally convicted, ordered for execution—and at last found innocent, and respited. Such, too, was the case of the men who were sentenced, ten years ago, for the robbery of Lord Cowper's steward. "I have myself (says Mr. Scarlett) *often* seen persons I thought innocent convicted, and the guilty escape, for want of some acute and intelligent counsel to show the bearings of the different circumstances on the conduct and situation of the prisoner."—(*House of Commons Debates, April* 25*th*, 1826.) We are delighted to see, in this last debate, both Mr. Brougham and Mr. Scarlett profess themselves friendly to Mr. Lamb's motion.

But in how many cases has the injustice proceeded without any suspicion being excited? and even if we could reckon upon men being watchful in capital cases, where life is concerned, we are afraid it is in such cases alone that they ever besiege the Secretary of State, and compel his attention. We never remember any such interference to save a man unjustly condemned to the hulks or the tread-mill; and yet there are certainly more condemnations of these minor punishments than to the gallows: but then it is all one—who knows or cares about it? If Harrison or Johnson has been condemned, after regular trial by jury, to six months' tread-mill, because Harrison and Johnson were without a penny to procure evidence—who knows or cares about Harrison or Johnson? how can they make themselves heard? or in what way can they obtain redress? It worries rich and comfortable people to hear the humanity of our penal laws called in question. There is a talk of a society for employing discharged prisoners: might not something be effected by a society instituted for the purpose of providing to poor prisoners a proper defence, and a due attendance of witnesses? But we must hasten on from this disgraceful neglect of poor prisoners, to the particular subject of complaint we have proposed to ourselves.

The proposition is, *That the prisoner accused of felony ought to have the same power of selecting counsel to speak for him as he has in cases of treason and misdemeanour, and as defendants have in all civil actions.*

Nothing can be done in any discussion upon any point of law in England, without quoting Mr. Justice Blackstone. Mr. Justice Blackstone, we believe, generally wrote his Commentaries late in the evening, with a bottle of wine before him; and little did he think, as each sentence fell from the glass and pen, of the immense influence it might hereafter exercise upon the laws and usages of his country. "It is," says this favourite writer, "not at all of a piece with the rest of the humane treatment of prisoners by the English law; for upon what face of reason can that assistance be denied to save the life of a man, which yet is allowed him in prosecutions for every petty trespass?" Nor, indeed, strictly speaking, is it a part of our ancient law; for the Mirror, having observed the necessity of counsel in civil suits, who know how to forward and defend the cause by the rules of law and customs of the realm, immediately subjoins, "and more necessary are they for defence upon indictment and appeals of felony, than upon any other venial crimes." To the authority of Blackstone may be added that of Sir John Hall, in Hollis's case; of Sir Robert Atkyns, in Lord Russell's case; and of Sir Bartholomew Shower, in the arguments for a New Bill of Rights, in 1682. "In the name of God," says this judge, "what harm can accrue to the public in general, or to any man in particular, that, in cases of State-treason, counsel should not be allowed to the accused? What rule of justice is there to warrant its denial, when, in a civil case of a half-penny cake, he may plead either by himself or by his advocate? That the Court is counsel for the prisoner can be no effectual reason; for so they are for each party, that right may be done."—(*Somers' Tracts*, vol. ii. p. 568.) In the trial of Thomas Rosewell, a dissenting clergyman, for high treason, in 1684, *Judge Jeffries*, in summing up, confessed to the jury, "that he thought it a hard case, that a man should have counsel to defend himself for a two-penny trespass, and his witnesses be examined upon oath; but if he stole, committed murder or felony, nay, high treason, where life, estate, honour, and all were concerned, that he should neither have counsel, nor have his witnesses examined upon oath."—(*Howell's State Trials,* vol. x. p. 207.)

There have been two capital errors in the criminal codes of feudal Europe, from which a great variety of mistake and injustice have proceeded: the one, a disposition to confound accusation with guilt; the other, to mistake a defence of prisoners accused by the Crown, for disloyalty and disaffection to the Crown; and from these errors our own code has been slowly and gradually recovering, by all those struggles and exertions which it always costs to remove *folly sanctioned by antiquity*. In the early periods of our history, the accused person could call no evidence:—then for a long time, his evidence against the King could not be examined upon oath; consequently, he might as well have produced none, as all the evidence against him was upon oath. Till the reign of Anne, no one accused of felony could produce witnesses upon oath; and the old practice was vindicated, in opposition to the new one, introduced under the statute of that day, on the grounds of humanity and tenderness to the prisoner! because, as his witnesses were not restricted by an oath, they were at liberty to indulge in simple falsehood as much as they pleased;— so argued the blessed defenders of nonsense in those days. Then it was ruled to be indecent and improper that counsel should be employed against the Crown; and, therefore, the prisoner accused of treason could have no counsel. In like manner, a party accused of felony could have no counsel to assist him in the trial. Counsel might indeed stay in the court, but apart from the prisoner, with whom they could have no communication. They were not allowed to put any question, or to suggest any doubtful point of law; but if the prisoner (likely to be a weak unlettered man) could himself suggest any doubt in matter of law, the Court determined first if the question of law should be entertained, and then assigned counsel to argue it. In those times, too, the jury were punishable if they gave a false verdict against the King, but were *not* punishable if they gave a false verdict against the prisoner. The preamble of the Act of 1696 runs thus:—"Whereas it is expedient that persons charged with high treason should make a full and sufficient defence." Might it not be altered to *persons charged with any species or degree of crime?* All these errors have given way to the force of truth, and to the power of common sense and common humanity—the Attorney and Solicitor General, for the time being, always protesting against each alteration, and regularly and officially prophesying the utter destruction of the whole jurisprudence of Great Britain. There is no man now alive perhaps, so utterly foolish, as to propose, that prisoners should be prevented from producing evidence upon oath, and being heard by their counsel in cases of high treason; and yet it cost a struggle for *seven* sessions to get this measure through the two houses of Parliament. But mankind are much like the children they beget— they always make wry faces at what is to do them good; and it is necessary sometimes to hold the nose, and force the medicine down the throat. They enjoy the health and vigour consequent upon the medicine; but cuff the doctor, and sputter at his stuff!

A most absurd argument was advanced in the honourable House, that the practice of employing counsel would be such an expense to the prisoner!—just as if anything was so expensive as being hanged! What a fine topic for the ordinary! "You are going" (says that exquisite divine) "to be hanged to-morrow, it is true, but consider what a sum you have saved! Mr. Scarlett or Mr. Brougham might certainly have presented arguments to the jury, which would have insured your acquittal; but do you forget that gentlemen of their eminence must be recompensed by large fees, and that, if your life had been saved, you would actually have been out of pocket above 20*l.*? You will now die with the consciousness of having obeyed the dictates of a wise economy; and with a grateful reverence for the laws

of your country, which prevents you from running into such un-
bounded expense—so let us now go to prayers."

It is ludicrous enough to recollect, when the employment of counsel is objected to on account of the expense to the prisoner, that the
same merciful law, which, to save the prisoner's money, has *denied*
him counsel, and produced his conviction, seizes upon all his savings
the moment he is convicted.

Of all false and foolish *dicta,* the most trite and the most absurd
is that which asserts that the Judge is counsel for the prisoner. We
do not hesitate to say that this is merely an unmeaning phrase, invented to defend a pernicious abuse. The Judge *cannot* be counsel
for the prisoner, *ought not* to be counsel for the prisoner, never *is*
counsel for the prisoner. To force an ignorant man into a court of
justice, and to tell him that the Judge is his counsel, appears to us
quite as foolish as to set a hungry man down to his meals, and to
tell him that the table was his dinner. In the first place, a counsel
should always have private and previous communication with the
prisoner, which the Judge, of course, cannot have. The prisoner
reveals to his counsel how far he is guilty, or he is not; states to
him all the circumstances of his case—and might often enable his
advocate, if his advocate were allowed to speak, to explain a long
string of circumstantial evidence in a manner favourable to the
innocence of his client. Of all these advantages, the Judge, if he
had every disposition to befriend the prisoner, is of course deprived. Something occurs to a prisoner in the course of the cause;
he suggests it in a whisper to his counsel, doubtful if it is a wise
point to urge or not. His counsel thinks it of importance, and
would urge it, if his mouth were not shut. Can a prisoner have this
secret communication with a Judge, and take his advice, whether
or not he, the Judge, shall mention it to the jury? The counsel has
(after all the evidence has been given) a bad opinion of his client's
case; but he suppresses that opinion; and it is his duty to do so. He
is not to decide; that is the province of the jury; and in spite of his
own opinion, his client may be innocent. He is brought there (or
would be brought there if the privilege of speech were allowed)
for the express purpose of saying all that could be said on one side
of the question. He is a weight in *one* scale, and some one else
holds the balance. This is the way in which truth is elicited in civil,
and would be in criminal cases. But does *the Judge* ever assume
the appearance of believing a prisoner to be innocent whom he
thinks to be guilty? If the prisoner advances inconclusive or weak
arguments, does not the Judge say they are weak and inconclusive,
and does he not often sum up against his own client? How then is

he counsel for the prisoner? If the counsel for the prisoner were to see a strong point, which the counsel for the prosecution had missed, would he supply the deficiency of his antagonist, and urge what had been neglected to be urged? But is it not the imperious duty of the Judge to do so? How then can these two functionaries stand in the same relation to the prisoner? In fact, the only meaning of the phrase is this, that the Judge will not suffer any undue advantage to be taken of the ignorance and helplessness of the prisoner—that he will point out any evidence or circumstance in his favour—and see that equal justice is done to both parties. But in this sense he is as much the counsel of the prosecutor as of the prisoner. This is all the Judge can do, or even pretends to do; but he can have no previous communication with the prisoner—he can have no confidential communication in court with the prisoner before he sums up; he cannot fling the whole weight of his understanding into the opposite scale against the counsel for the prosecution, and produce that collision of faculties, which, in all other cases but those of felony, is supposed to be the happiest method of arriving at truth. Baron Garrow, in his charge to the grand jury at Exeter, on the 16th of August, 1824, thus expressed his opinion of a Judge being counsel for the prisoner:—
"It has been said, and truly said, that in criminal courts, Judges were counsel for the prisoners. So undoubtedly they were, as far as they could to prevent undue prejudice, to guard against improper influence being excited against prisoners; but it was impossible for them to go further than this; for they could not suggest the course of defence prisoners ought to pursue; for Judges only saw the depositions so short a time before the accused appeared at the bar of their country, that it was quite impossible for them to act fully in that capacity." The learned Baron might have added, that it would be more correct to call the Judge counsel for the prosecution; for his only previous instructions were the depositions for the prosecution, from which, in the absence of counsel, he examined the evidence against the prisoner. On the prisoner's behalf he had no instructions at all

Can anything, then, be more flagrantly and scandalously unjust, than, in a long case of circumstantial evidence, to refuse to a prisoner the benefit of counsel? A foot-mark, a word, a sound, a tool dropped, all gave birth to the most ingenious inferences; and the counsel for the prosecution is so far from being blamable for entering into all these things, that they are all essential to the detection of guilt, and they are all links of a long and intricate chain: but if a close examination into, and a logical statement of, all these circumstances be necessary for the establishment of guilt, is not the same closeness of reasoning, and the same logical statement necessary for the establishment of innocence? If justice cannot be done to society without the intervention of a practised and ingenious mind, who may connect all these links together, and make them clear to the apprehension of a jury, *can* justice be done to the prisoner, unless similar practice and similar ingenuity are employed to detect the flaws of the chain, and to point out the disconnection of the circumstances?

Is there any one gentleman in the House of Commons, who, in yielding his vote to this paltry and perilous fallacy of the Judge being counsel for the prisoner, does not feel, that, were he himself a criminal, he would prefer almost any counsel at the bar, to the tender mercies of the Judge? How strange that any man who could make his election would eagerly and diligently surrender this exquisite privilege, and addict himself to the perilous practice of giving fees to counsel! Nor let us forget, in considering Judges as counsel for the prisoner, that there have been such men as Chief Justice Jeffries, Mr. Justice Page, and Mr. Justice Alybone, and that, in bad times, such men may reappear. "If you do not allow me counsel, my Lords (says Lord Lovat), it is impossible for me to make any defence, by reason of my infirmity. I do not see, I do not hear. I come up to the bar at the hazard of my life. I have fainted several times; I have been up so early, ever since four o'clock this morning. I therefore ask for assistance; and if you do not allow me counsel, or such aid as is necessary, it will be impossible for me to make any defence at all." Though Lord Lovat's guilt was evident, yet the managers of the impeachment felt so strongly the injustice which was done, that, by the hands of Sir W. Young, the chief manager, a bill was brought into Parliament to allow counseling to persons impeached by that House, which was not previously the case; so that the evil is already done away with, in a great measure, to persons of rank: it so happens in legislation, when a gentleman suffers, public attention is awakened to the evil of laws. Every man who makes laws says, "This may be my case:" but it requires the repeated efforts of humane men, or, as Mr. North calls them, dilettanti philosophers, to awaken the attention of law-makers to evils from which they are themselves exempt. We do not say this to make the leaders of mankind unpopular, but to rouse their earnest attention in cases where the poor only are concerned, and where neither good nor evil can happen to themselves.

A great stress is laid upon the moderation of the opening counsel; that is, he does not conjure the farmers in the jury-box, by

the love which they bear to their children—he does not declaim
upon blood-guiltiness—he does not describe the death of Abel by
Cain, the first murderer—he does not describe scattered brains,
ghastly wounds, pale features, and hair clotted with gore—he does
not do a thousand things, which are not in English taste, and
which it would be very foolish and very vulgar to do. We readily
allow all this. But yet, if it be a cause of importance, it is essentially necessary to our counsellor's reputation that this man should
be hung! And accordingly, with a very calm voice, and composed
manner, and with many expressions of candour, he sets himself to
comment astutely upon the circumstances. Distant events are immediately connected; meaning is given to insignificant facts; new
motives are ascribed to innocent actions; farmer gives way after
farmer in the jury-box; and a rope of eloquence is woven round
the prisoner's neck! Every one is delighted with the talents of the
advocate; and, because there has been no noise, no violent action,
and no consequent perspiration, he is praised for his candour and
forbearance, and the lenity of our laws is the theme of universal
approbation. In the meantime, the speech-maker and the prisoner
know better.

We should be glad to know of any one nation in the world,
taxed by kings, or even imagined by poets (except the English),
who have refused to prisoners the benefit of counsel. Why is the
voice of humanity heard everywhere else, and disregarded here?
In Scotland, the accused have not only counsel to speak for them,
but a copy of the indictment, and a list of the witnesses. In France,
in the Netherlands, in the whole of Europe, counsel are allotted as
a matter of course. Everywhere else but here, accusation is considered as unfavourable to the exercise of human faculties. It is
admitted to be that crisis in which, above all others, an unhappy
man wants the aid of eloquence, wisdom, and coolness. In France,
the Napoleon Code has provided not only that counsel should be
allowed to the prisoner, but that, as with us in Scotland, his counsel should have the last word.

It is a most affecting moment in a court of justice when the evidence has all been heard, and the Judge asks the prisoner what
he has to say in his defence. The prisoner, who has (by great exertions, perhaps of his friends) saved up money enough to procure
counsel, says to the Judge, "that he leaves his defense to his counsel." We have often blushed for English humanity to hear the
reply. "Your counsel cannot speak for you, you must speak for
yourself;" and this is the reply given to a poor girl of eighteen—
to a foreigner—to a deaf man—to a stammerer—to the sick—to

the feeble—to the old—to the most abject and ignorant of human beings! It is a reply, we must say, at which common sense and common feeling revolt:—for it is full of brutal cruelty, and of base inattention of those who make laws, to the happiness of those for whom laws were made. We wonder that any juryman can convict under such a shocking violation of all natural justice. The iron age of Clovis and Clottaire can produce no more atrocious violation of every good feeling, and every good principle. Can a sick man find strength and nerves to speak before a large assembly?— can an ignorant man find words?—can a low man find confidence? Is not he afraid of becoming an object of ridicule?—can he believe that his expressions will be understood? How often have we seen a poor wretch, struggling against the agonies of his spirit, and the rudeness of his conceptions, and his awe of better-dressed men and better-taught men, and the shame which the accusation has brought upon his head, and the sight of his parents and children gazing at him in the Court, for the last time, perhaps, and after a long absence! The mariner sinking in the wave does not want a helping hand more than does this poor wretch. But help is denied to all! Age cannot have it, nor ignorance, nor the modesty of women! One hard uncharitable rule silences the defenders of the wretched, in the worst of human evils; and at the bitterest of human moments, mercy is blotted out from the ways of men!

Suppose a crime to have been committed under the influence of insanity; is the insane man, now convalescent, to plead his own insanity?—to offer arguments to show that he must have been mad? —and, by the glimmerings of his returning reason, to prove that at a former period that same reason was utterly extinct? These are the cruel situations into which Judges and Courts of Justice are thrown by the present state of the law.

There is a Judge now upon the Bench, who never took away the life of a fellow-creature without shutting himself up alone, and giving the most profound attention to every circumstance of the case! and this solemn act he always premises with his own beautiful prayer to God, that he will enlighten him with his Divine Spirit in the exercise of this terrible privilege! Now, would it not be an immense satisfaction to this feeling and honourable magistrate, to be sure that every witness on the side of the prisoner had been heard, and that every argument which could be urged in his favour had been brought forward, by a man whose duty it was to see only on one side of the question, and whose interest and reputation were thoroughly embarked in this partial exertion? If a Judge fail to get at the truth, after these instruments of investigation are used, his failure must be attributed to the limited powers of man—not to the want of good inclination, or wise institutions. We are surprised that such a measure does not come into Parliament, with the strong recommendation of the Judges. It is surely better to be a day longer on the circuit, than to murder rapidly in ermine.

It is argued, that, among the various pleas for mercy that are offered, no prisoner has ever urged to the Secretary of State the disadvantage of having no counsel to plead for him; but a prisoner who dislikes to undergo his sentence naturally addresses to those who can reverse it such arguments only as will produce, in the opinion of the referee, a pleasing effect. He does not therefore find fault with the established system of jurisprudence, but brings forward facts and arguments to prove his own innocence. Besides, how few people there are who can elevate themselves from the acquiescence in what *is*, to the consideration of what *ought to be;* and if they could do so, the way to get rid of a punishment is not (as we have just observed) to say, "You have no right to punish me in this manner," but to say, "I am innocent of the offence." The fraudulent baker at Constantinople, who is about to be baked to death in his own oven, does not complain of the severity of baking bakers, but promises to use more flour and less fraud.

Whence comes it (we should like to ask Sir John Singleton Copley, who seems to dread so much the conflicts of talent in criminal cases) that a method of getting at truth which is found so serviceable in civil cases should be so much objected to in criminal cases? Would you have all this wrangling and bickering, it is asked, and contentious eloquence, when the life of a man is concerned? Why not, as well as when his property is concerned? It is either a good means of doing justice, or it is not, that two understandings should be put in opposition to each other, and that a third should decide between them. Does this open every view which can bear upon the question? Does it in the most effectual manner watch the Judge, detect perjury, and sift evidence? If not, why is it suffered to disgrace our civil institutions? If it effect all these objects, why is it not incorporated into our criminal law? Of what importance is a little disgust at professional tricks, if the solid advantage gained be a nearer approximation to truth? Can anything be more preposterous than this preference of taste to justice, and of solemnity to truth? What an eulogium of a trial to say, "I am by no means satisfied that the Jury were right in finding the prisoner guilty; but everything was carried on with the utmost decorum! The verdict was wrong; but there was the most perfect propriety and order in the proceedings. The man will be unfairly hanged; but all was genteel!" If solemnity is what is principally wanted in a court of justice, we had better study the manners of the old Spanish Inquisition; but if battles with the Judge, and battles among the counsel, are the best method, as they certainly are, of getting at the truth, better tolerate this philosophical Billingsgate, than persevere, *because* the life of a man is at stake, in solemn and polished injustice.

Why should it not be just as wise and equitable to leave the defendant without counsel in civil cases—and to tell him that the Judge was his counsel? And if the reply is to produce such injurious effects as are anticipated upon the minds of the Jury in criminal cases, why not in civil cases also? In twenty-eight cases out of thirty, the verdict in civil cases is correct; in the two remaining cases, the error may proceed from other causes than the right of reply; and yet the right of reply has existed in all. In a vast majority of cases, the verdict is for the plaintiff, not because there is a right of reply, but because he who has it in his power to decide whether he will go to law or not, and resolves to expose himself to the expense and trouble of a lawsuit, has probably a good foundation for his claim. Nobody, of course, can intend to say that the majority of verdicts in favour of plaintiffs are against justice, and merely attributable to the advantage of a last speech. If this were the case, the sooner advocates are turned out of court the better—and then the improvement of both civil and criminal law would be an abolition of all speeches; for those who dread the effect of the last word upon the fate of the prisoner must remember that there is at present always a last speech against the prisoner; for, as the counsel for the prosecution cannot be replied to, *his* is the last speech.

There is certainly this difference between a civil and a criminal case—that in one a new trial can be granted, in the other not. But you must first make up your mind whether this system of contentious investigation by opposite advocates is or is not the best method of getting at truth: if it be, the more irremediable the decision, the more powerful and perfect should be the means of deciding; and then it would be a less oppression if the civil defendant were deprived of counsel than the criminal prisoner. When an error has been committed, the advantage is greater to the latter of these persons than to the former;—the criminal is not tried again, but pardoned; while the civil defendant must run the chance of another Jury.

If the effect of reply, and the contention of counsel, have all these baneful consequences in felony, why not also in misdemeanour and high treason? Half the cases at Sessions are cases of misdemeanour, where counsel are employed and half-informed Justices preside instead of learned Judges. There are no complaints of the unfairness of verdicts, though there are every now and then of the severity of punishments. Now, if the reasoning of Mr. Lamb's opponents were true, the disturbing force of the prisoner's counsel must fling everything into confusion. The Court for misdemeanours must be a scene of riot and perplexity; and the detection and punishment of crime must be utterly impossible: and yet in the very teeth of these objections, such courts of justice are just as orderly in one set of offences as the other; and the conviction of a guilty person just as certain and as easy.

The prosecutor (if this system were altered) would have the choice of counsel; so he has now—with this difference, that, at present, his counsel cannot be answered nor opposed. It would be better in all cases, if two men of exactly equal talent could be opposed to each other; but as this is impossible, the system must be taken with its inconvenience; but there can be no inequality between counsel so great as that between any counsel and the prisoner pleading for himself. "It has been lately my lot," says Mr. Denman, "to try two prisoners who were deaf and dumb, and who could only be made to understand what was passing by the signs of their friends. The cases were clear and simple; but if they had been circumstantial cases, in what a situation would the Judge and Jury be placed, when the prisoner could have no counsel to plead for him!"—(*Debates of the House of Commons, April* 25, 1826.)

The folly of being counsel for yourself is so notorious in civil cases, that it has grown into a proverb. But the cruelty of the law compels a man, in criminal cases, to be guilty of a much greater act of folly, and to trust his life to an advocate, who, by the common sense of mankind, is pronounced to be inadequate to defend the possession of an acre of land.

In all cases it must be supposed, that reasonably convenient instruments are selected to effect the purpose in view. A Judge may be commonly presumed to understand his profession, and a Jury to have a fair allowance of common sense; but the objectors to the improvement we recommend appear to make no such suppositions. Counsel are always to make flashy addresses to the passions. Juries are to be so much struck with them, that they are always to acquit or to condemn, contrary to justice; and Judges are always to be so biassed, that they are to fling themselves rashly into the opposite scale against the prisoner. Many cases of misdemeanour consign a man to infamy, and cast a blot upon his posterity. Judges and Juries must feel these cases as strongly as any cases of felony; and yet, in spite of this, and in spite of the free permission of counsel to speak, they preserve their judgment, and command their feelings surprisingly. Generally speaking, we believe none of these evils would take place. Trumpery declamation would be considered as discreditable to the counsel, and would be disregarded by the Jury. The Judge and Jury (as in civil cases) would gain the habit of looking to the facts, selecting the arguments, and coming to reasonable conclusions. It is so in all other countries—and it would be so in this. But the vigilance of the Judge is to relax, if there is counsel for the prisoner. Is, then, the relaxed vigilance of the Judges complained of, in high treason, in misdemeanour, or in civil cases? This appears to us really to shut up the debate, and to preclude reply. *Why* is the practice so good in all other cases, and so pernicious in felony alone? This question has never received even the shadow of an answer. There is no one objection against the allowance of counsel to prisoners in felony, which does not apply to them in all cases. If the vigilance of Judges depend upon this injustice to the prisoner, then, the greater injustice to the prisoner, the more vigilance; and so the true method of perfecting the Bench would be, to deny the prisoner the power of calling witnesses, and to increase as much as possible the disparity between the accuser and the accused. We hope men are selected for *the Judges of Israel* whose vigilance depends upon better and higher principles.

There are three methods of arranging a trial, as to the mode of employing counsel—that both parties should have counsel, or neither—or only one. The first method is the best; the second is preferable to the last; and the last, which is our present system, is the worst possible. If counsel were denied to either of the parties, if it be necessary that any system of jurisprudence should be disgraced by such an act of injustice, they should rather be denied to the prosecutor than to the prisoner.

But the most singular caprice of the law is, that counsel are permitted in very high crimes, and in very small crimes, and denied in crimes of a sort of medium description. In high treason, where you mean to murder Lord Liverpool, and to levy war against the people, and to blow up the two Houses of Parliament, all the lawyers of Westminster Hall may talk themselves dry, and the Jury deaf. Lord Eldon, when at the bar, has been heard for nine hours on such subjects. If, instead of producing the destruction of five thousand people, you are indicted for the murder of one person, here human faculties, from the diminution of guilt, are supposed to be so clear and so unclouded, that the prisoner is quite adequate to make his own defence, and no counsel are allowed. Take it then upon that principle, and let the rule, and the reason of it, pass as sufficient. But if, instead of murdering the man, you have only libelled him, then, for some reason or another, though utterly unknown to us, the original imbecility of faculties in accused persons is respected, and counsel *are* allowed. Was ever such nonsense defended by public men in grave assemblies? The prosecutor, too, (as Mr. Horace Twiss justly observes), can either allow or disallow counsel, by selecting his form of prosecution;—as where a mob had assembled to repeal, by riot and force, some unpopular statute, and certain persons had continued in that assembly for more than an hour after proclamation to disperse. That might be treated as levying war against the King, and then the prisoner would be entitled to receive (as Lord George Gordon did receive) the benefit of counsel. It might also be treated as a seditious rite; then it would be a misdemeanour, and counsel would still be allowed. But if government had a mind to destroy the prisoner effectually, they have only to abstain from the charge of treason, and to introduce into the indictment the aggravation, that the prisoner had continued with the mob for an hour after proclamation to disperse; this is a felony, the prisoner's life is in jeopardy, and counsel are effectually excluded. It produces, in many other cases disconnected with treason, the most scandalous injustice. A receiver of stolen goods, who employs a young girl to rob her master, may be tried for the misdemeanour; the young girl taken afterwards would be tried for the felony. The receiver would be punishable only with fine, imprisonment, or whipping, and he could have counsel to defend him. The girl indicted for felony, and liable to death, would enjoy no such advantage.

In the comparison between felony and treason there are certainly some arguments why counsel should be allowed in felony rather than in treason. Persons accused of treason are generally persons of education and rank, accustomed to assemblies, and to public speaking, while men accused of felony are commonly of the lowest of the people. If it be true, that Judges in cases of high treason are more liable to be influenced by the Crown, and to lean against the prisoner, this cannot apply to cases of misdemeanour, or to the defendants in civil cases; but if it be necessary, that Judges should be watched in political cases, how often are cases of felony connected with political disaffection! Every Judge, too, has his idiosyncrasies, which require to be watched. Some hate Dissenters—some mobs; some have one weakness, some another; and the ultimate truth is, that no court of justice is safe, unless there is some one present whose occupation and interest it is to watch the safety of the prisoner. Till then, no man of right feeling can be easy at the administration of justice, and the punishment of death.

Two men are accused of one offence; the one dexterous, bold, subtle, gifted with speech, and remarkable for presence of mind; the other timid, hesitating, and confused—is there any reason why the chances of these two men for acquittal should be, as they are, so very different? Inequalities there will be in the means of defence under the best system, but there is no occasion the law should make these greater than they are left by chance or nature.

But (it is asked) what practical injustice is done—what practical evil is there in the present system? The great object of all law is, that the guilty should be punished, and that the innocent should be acquitted. A very great majority of prisoners, we admit, are guilty—and so clearly guilty, that we believe they would be found guilty under any system; but among the number of those who are tried, *some* are innocent, and the chance of establishing their innocence is very much diminished by the privation of counsel. In the course of twenty or thirty years, among the whole mass of English prisoners, we believe *many* are found guilty who are innocent, and who would not have been found guilty, if an able and intelligent man had watched over their interest, and represented their case. If this happen only to two or three every year, it is quite a sufficient reason why the law should be altered. That such cases exist we firmly believe; and this is the practical evil—perceptible to men of sense and reflection; but not likely to become the subject of general petition. To ask why there are not petitions —why the evil is not more noticed, is mere parliamentary froth and ministerial juggling. Gentlemen are rarely hung. If they were so, there would be petitions without end for counsel. The creatures exposed to the cruelties and injustice of the law are dumb creatures, who feel the evil without being able to express their feeling. Besides, the question is not, whether the evil is found out, but whether the evil exist. Whoever thinks it is an evil, should vote against it, whether the sufferer from the injustice discover it to be an injustice, or whether he suffer in ignorant silence. When the bill was enacted, which allowed counsel for treason, there was not a petition from one end of England to the other. Can there be a more shocking answer from the Ministerial Bench, than to say, For real evil we care nothing—only for detected evil? We will set about curing any wrong whieh affects our popularity and power: but as to any other evil, we wait till the people find it out; and, in the meantime, commit such evils to the care of Mr. George Lamb, and of Sir James Mackintosh. We are sure so good a man as Mr. Peel can never feel in this manner.

Howard devoted himself to his country. It was a noble example. Let two gentlemen on the Ministerial side of the House (we only ask for two) commit some crimes, which will render their execution a matter of painful necessity. Let them feel, and report to the House, all the injustice and inconvenience of having neither a copy of the indictment, nor a list of witnesses, nor counsel to defend them. We will venture to say, that the evidence of two such persons would do more for the improvement of the criminal law, than all the orations of Mr. Lamb, or the lucubrations of Beccaria. Such evidence would save time, and bring the question to an issue. It is a great duty, and ought to be fulfilled—and in ancient Rome, would have been fulfilled.

The opponents always forget that Mr. Lamb's plan is not to *compel* prisoners to have counsel, but to *allow* them to have counsel, if they choose to do so. Depend upon it, as Dr. Johnson says, when a man is going to be hanged, his faculties are wonderfully concentrated. If it be really true, as the defenders of *Mumpsimus* observe, that the Judge is the best counsel for the prisoner, the prisoner will soon learn to employ him, especially as his Lordship works without fees. All that we want is an option given to the prisoner—that a man, left to adopt his own means of defence in every trifling civil right, may have the same power of selecting his own auxiliaries for higher interests.

But nothing can be more unjust than to speak of Judges, as if they were of one standard, and one heart and head pattern. The great majority of Judges, we have no doubt, are upright and pure; but some have been selected for flexible politics—some are passionate—some are in a hurry—some are violent churchmen— some resemble ancient females—some have the gout—some are eighty years old—some are blind, deaf, and have lost the power of smelling. All one to the unhappy prisoner—he has no choice.

It is impossible to put so gross an insult upon Judges, Jurymen, Grand Jurymen, or any person connected with the administration of justice, as to suppose that the longer time to be taken up by the speeches of counsel constitutes the grand bar to the proposed alteration. If three hours would acquit a man, and he is hanged because he is only allowed two hours for his defence, the poor man is as much murdered as if his throat had been cut before he came into Court. If twelve Judges cannot do the most perfect justice, other twelve must be appointed. Strange administration of criminal law, to adhere obstinately to an inadequate number of Judges, and to refuse any improvement which is incompatible with this arbitrary and capricious enactment. Neither is it quite certain that the proposed alteration would create a greater demand upon the time of the Court. At present the counsel makes a defence by long cross-examinations, and examinations in chief of the witnesses, and the Judge allows a greater latitude than he would do, if the counsel of the prisoner were permitted to speak. The counsel by these oblique methods, and by stating false points of law for the express purpose of introducing facts, endeavours to obviate the injustice of the law, and takes up more time by this oblique, than he would do by a direct defence. But the best answer to this objection of time (which, if true, is no objection at all) is, that as many misdemeanours as felonies are tried in a given time, though counsel are allowed in the former, and not in the latter case.

One excuse for the absence of counsel is, that the evidence upon which the prisoner is convicted is always so clear, that the counsel cannot gainsay it. This is mere absurdity. There is not, and cannot be, any such rule. Many a man has been hung upon a string of circumstantial evidence, which not only very ingenious men, but very candid and judicious men, might criticise and call in question. If no one were found guilty but upon such evidence as would not admit of a doubt, half the crimes in the world would be unpunished. This dictum, by which the present practice has often been defended, was adopted by Lord Chancellor Nottingham. To the lot of this Chancellor, however, it fell to pass sentence of death upon Lord Stafford, whom (as Mr. Denman justly observes) no court of justice, not even the House of Lords (constituted as it was in those days), could have put to death, if he had had counsel to defend him.

To improve the criminal law of England, and to make it really deserving of the incessant eulogium which is lavished upon it, we would assimilate trials for felony to trials for high treason. The prisoner should not only have counsel, but a copy of the indictment and a list of the witnesses, many days antecedent to the trial. It is in the highest degree unjust that I should not see and study the description of the crime with which I am charged, if the most scrupulous exactness be required in that instrument which charges me with crime. If the place *where,* the time *when,* and the manner *how,* and the persons by whom, must all be specified with the most perfect accuracy, if any deviation from this accuracy is fatal, the prisoner, or his legal advisers, should have a full opportunity of judging whether the scruples of the law have been attended to in the formation of the indictment; and they ought not to be confined to the hasty and imperfect consideration which can be given to an indictment exhibited for the first time in Court. Neither is it possible for the prisoner to repel accusation till he knows who is to be brought against him. He may see suddenly, stuck up in the witness's box, a man who has been writing him letters, to extort money from the threat of evidence he could produce. The character of such a witness would be destroyed in a moment, if the letters were produced; and the letters would have been produced, of course, if the prisoner had imagined such a person would have been brought forward by the prosecutor. It is utterly impossible for a prisoner to know in what way he may be assailed, and against what species of attacks he is to guard. Conversations may be brought against him which he has forgotten, and to which he could (upon notice) have given another colour and complexion. Actions are made to bear upon his case, which (if he had known they would have been referred to) might have been explained in the most satisfactory manner. All these modes of attack are pointed out by the list of witnesses transmitted to the prisoner, and he has time to prepare his answer, as it is perfectly just he should have. This is justice, when a prisoner has ample means of compelling the attendance of his witnesses; when his written accusation is put into his hand, and he has time to study it—when he knows in what manner his guilt is to be proved, and when he has a man of practised understanding to state his facts, and prefer his arguments. Then criminal justice may march on boldly. The Judge has no stain of blood on his ermine; and the phrases which English people are so fond of lavishing upon the humanity of their laws will have a real foundation. At present this part of the law is a mere relic of the barbarous injustice by which accusation in the early part of our jurisprudence was always confounded with guilt. The greater part of these abuses have been brushed away, as this cannot fail soon to be. In the meantime it is defended (as every other abuse has been defended) by men who think it their duty to defend everything which *is,* and to dread everything which *is not.* We are told that the Judge does what he does not do, and ought not to do. The most pernicious effects are anticipated in trials of felony, from that which is found to produce the most perfect justice in civil causes, and in cases of treason and misdemeanour: we are called upon to continue a practice without example in any other country, and are required by lawyers to consider that custom as humane, which every one who is not a lawyer pronounces to be most cruel and unjust—and which has not been brought forward to general notice, only because its bad effects are confined to the last and lowest of mankind.*

Too Much Latin and Greek

There are two questions to be asked respecting every new publication—Is it worth buying? Is it worth borrowing? and we would advise our readers to weigh diligently the importance of these interrogations, before they take any decided step as to this work of Mr. Edgeworth; † the more especially as the name carries with it considerable authority, and seems, in the estimation of the unwary, almost to include the idea of purchase. For our own part, we would rather decline giving a direct answer to these questions; and shall content ourselves for the present with making a few such slight observations as may enable the sagacious to conjecture what our direct answer would be, were we compelled to be more explicit.

One great and signal praise we think to be the eminent due of Mr. Edgeworth: in a canting age he does not cant;—at a period when hypocrisy and fanaticism will almost certainly insure the success of any publication, he has constantly disdained to have recourse to any such arts;—without ever having been accused of disloyalty or irreligion, he is not always harping upon Church and King, in order to catch at a little popularity, and sell his books;— he is manly, independent, liberal—and maintains enlightened opinions with discretion and honesty. There is also in this work of Mr. Edgeworth, an agreeable diffusion of anecdote and example, such as a man acquires who reads with a view to talking or writing. With these merits, we cannot say that Mr. Edgeworth is either very new, very profound, or very apt to be right in his opinion. He is active, enterprising, and unprejudiced; but we have not been very much instructed by what he has written, or always satisfied that he has got to the bottom of his subject.

On one subject, however, we cordially agree with this gentleman; and return him our thanks for the courage with which he has combated the excessive abuse of classical learning in England. It is a subject upon which we have long wished for an opportunity

---

* All this nonsense is now put an end to. Council is allowed to the prisoner, and they are permitted to speak in his defence.
† *Essays on Professional Education.* By R. L. Edgeworth, Esq. F.R.S. &c. London. 1809.

of saying something; and one which we consider to be of the very highest importance.

"The principal defect," says Mr. Edgeworth, "in the present system of our great schools, is, that they devote too large a portion of time to Latin and Greek. It is true, that the attainment of classical literature is highly desirable; but it should not, or rather it need not, be the exclusive object of boys during eight or nine years.

"Much less time, judiciously managed, would give them an acquaintance with the classics sufficient for all useful purposes, and would make them as good scholars as gentlemen or professional men need to be. It is not requisite that every man should make Latin or Greek verses; therefore a knowledge of prosody beyond the structure of hexameter and pentameter verses is as worthless an acquisition as any which folly or fashion has introduced amongst the higher classes of mankind. It must indeed be acknowledged that there are some rare exceptions; but even party prejudice would allow, that the persons alluded to must have risen to eminence though they had never written saphics or iambics. Though preceptors, parents, and the public in general, may be convinced of the absurdity of making boys spend so much of life in learning what can be of no use to them; such are the difficulties of making any change in the ancient rules of great establishments, that masters themselves, however reasonable, dare not, and cannot, make sudden alterations.

"The only remedies that can be suggested might be, perhaps, to take those boys, who are not intended for professions in which deep scholarship is necessary, away from school before they reach the highest classes, where prosody and Greek and Latin verses are required.

"In the college of Dublin, where an admirable course of instruction has been long established, where this course is superintended by men of acknowledged learning and abilities, and pursued by students of uncommon industry, such is the force of example, and such the fear of appearing inferior in trifles to English universities, that much pains have been lately taken to introduce the practice of writing Greek and Latin verses, and much solicitude has been shown about the prosody of the learned languages, without any attention being paid to the prosody of our own.

"Boarding houses for the scholars at Eton and Westminster, which are at present mere lodging houses, might be kept by private tutors, who might, during the hours when the boys were not in their public classes, assist them in acquiring general literature, or such knowledge as might be advantageous for their respective professions.

"New schools, that are not restricted to any established routine, should give a fair trial to experiments in education, which afford a rational prospect of success. If nothing can be altered in the old schools, leave them as they are. Destroy nothing—injure none—but let the public try whether they cannot have something better. If the experiment do not succeed, the public will be convinced that they ought to acquiesce in the established methods of instruction, and parents will send their children to the ancient seminaries with increased confidence."—(pp. 47-49.)

We are well aware that nothing very new can remain to be said upon a topic so often debated. The complaints we have to make are at least as old as the time of Locke and Dr. Samuel Clarke; and the evil which is the subject of these complaints has certainly rather increased than diminished since the period of those two great men. A hundred years, to be sure, is a very little time for the duration of a national error; and it is so far from being reasonable to look for its decay at so short a date, that it can hardly be expected, within such limits, to have displayed the full bloom of its imbecility.

There are several feelings to which attention must be paid, before the question of classical learning can be fairly and temperately discussed.

We are apt, in the first place, to remember the immense benefits which the study of the classics once conferred on mankind; and to feel for those models on which the taste of Europe has been formed, something like sentiments of gratitude and obligation. This is all well enough, so long as it continues to be a mere feeling; but as soon as it interferes with action, it nourishes dangerous prejudices about education. Nothing will do in the pursuit of knowledge but the blackest ingratitude;—the moment we have got up the ladder, we must kick it down—as soon as we have passed over the bridge, we must let it rot;—when we have got upon the shoulders of the ancients, we must look over their heads. The man who forgets the friends of his childhood in real life is base; but he who clings to the props of his childhood in literature, must be content to remain as ignorant as he was when a child. His business is to forget, disown, and deny—to think himself above everything which has been of use to him in time past—and to cultivate that exclusively from which he expects future advantage: in short, to do everything for the advancement of his knowledge, which it would be infamous to do for the advancement of his fortune. If mankind still derive advantage from classical literature proportionate to the labour they bestow upon it, let their labour and their study proceed: but the moment we cease to read Latin and Greek for the solid utility we derive from them, it would be a very romantic application of human talents to do so from any feeling of gratitude, and recollection of past service.

To almost every Englishman up to the age of three or four and twenty, classical learning has been the great object of existence; and no man is very apt to suspect, or very much pleased to hear, that what he has done for so long a time was not worth doing. His classical literature, too, reminds every man of the scenes of his childhood, and brings to his fancy several of the most pleasing associations which we are capable of forming. A certain sort of vanity, also, very naturally, grows among men occupied in a common pursuit. Classical quotations are the watchwords of scholars, by which they distinguish each other from the ignorant and the illiterate; and Greek and Latin are insensibly become almost the only test of a cultivated mind.

Some men through indolence, others through ignorance, and most through necessity, submit to the established education of the times; and seek for their children that species of distinction which happens, at the period in which they live, to be stamped with the approbation of mankind. This mere question of convenience every parent must determine for himself. A poor man, who has his fortune to gain, must be a quibbling theologian, or a classical pedant, as fashion dictates; and he must vary his error with the error of the times. But it would be much more fortunate for mankind, if the public opinion, which regulates the pursuits of individuals, were more wise and enlightened than it at present is.

All these considerations make it extremely difficult to procure a candid hearing on this question; and to refer this branch of education to the only proper criterion of every branch of education— its utility in future life.

There are two questions which grow out of this subject: 1st, How far is any sort of classical education useful? 2d, How far is that particular classical education, adopted in this country, useful?

Latin and Greek are, in the first place, useful, as they inure children to intellectual difficulties, and make the life of a young student what it ought to be, a life of considerable labour. We do not, of course, mean to confine this praise exclusively to the study of Latin and Greek; or to suppose that other difficulties might not be found which it would be useful to overcome: but though Latin and Greek have this merit in common with many arts and sciences, still they have it; and, if they do nothing else, they at least secure a solid and vigorous application at a period of life which materially influences all other periods.

To go through the grammar of one language thoroughly is of great use for the mastery of every other grammar; because there obtains, through all languages, a certain analogy to each other in their grammatical construction. Latin and Greek have now mixed themselves etymologically with all the languages of modern Europe—and with none more than our own; so that it is necessary to read these two tongues for other objects than themselves.

The two ancient languages are as mere inventions—as pieces of mechanism incomparably more beautiful than any of the modern languages of Europe; their mode of signifying time and case, by terminations, instead of auxiliary verbs and particles, would of itself stamp their superiority. Add to this the copiousness of the Greek language, with the fancy, majesty, and harmony of its compounds; and there are quite sufficient reasons why the classics should be studied for the beauties of language. Compared to them, merely as vehicles of thought and passion, all modern languages are dull, ill contrived, and barbarous.

That a great part of the Scriptures have come down to us in the Greek language, is of itself a reason, if all others were wanting, why education should be planned so as to produce a supply of Greek scholars.

The cultivation of style is very justly made a part of education. Everything which is written is meant either to please or to instruct. The second object it is difficult to effect, without attending to the first; and the cultivation of style is the acquisition of those rules and literary habits which sagacity anticipates, or experience shows to be the most effectual means of pleasing. Those works are the best which have longest stood the test of time, and pleased the greatest number of exercised minds. Whatever, therefore, our conjectures may be, we cannot be so sure that the best modern writers can afford us as good models as the ancients;—we cannot be certain that they will live through the revolutions of the world, and continue to please in every climate—under every species of government—through every state of civilisation. The moderns have

been well taught by their masters; but the time is hardly yet come
when the necessity for such instruction no longer exists. We may
still borrow descriptive power from Tacitus; dignified perspicuity
from Livy; simplicity from Cæsar; and from Homer some portion
of that light and heat which, dispersed into ten thousand channels,
has filled the world with bright images and illustrious thoughts.
Let the cultivator of modern literature addict himself to the purest
models of taste which France, Italy, and England could supply,
he might still learn from Virgil to be majestic, and from Tibullus
to be tender; he might not yet look upon the face of nature as
Theocritus saw it; nor might he reach those springs of pathos with
which Euripides softened the hearts of his audience. In short, it
appears to us, that there are so many excellent reasons why a certain number of scholars should be kept up in this and in every
civilised country, that we should consider every system of education from which classical education was excluded, as radically erroneous, and completely absurd.

That vast advantages, then, may be derived from classical learning, there can be no doubt. The advantages which are derived
from classical learning by the English manner of teaching, involve
another and a very different question; and we will venture to say,
that there never was a more complete instance in any country of
such extravagant and overacted attachment to any branch of
knowledge, as that which obtains in this country with regard to
classical knowledge. A young Englishman goes to school at six or
seven years old; and he remains in a course of education till
twenty-three or twenty-four years of age. In all that time, his sole
and exclusive occupation is learning Latin and Greek; * he has
scarcely a notion that there is any other kind of excellence; and the
great system of facts with which he is the most perfectly acquainted,
are the intrigues of the Heathen Gods: with whom Pan slept?—
with whom Jupiter?—whom Apollo ravished? These facts the English youth get by heart the moment they quit the nursery; and are
most sedulously and industriously instructed in them till the best
and most active part of life is passed away. Now, this long career
of classical learning, we may, if we please, denominate a foundation; but it is a foundation so far above ground, that there is absolutely no room to put anything upon it. If you occupy a man
with one thing till he is twenty-four years of age, you have exhausted all his leisure time: he is called into the world and com-

---

* Unless he goes to the University of Cambridge; and then classics occupy
him entirely for about ten years; and divide him with mathematics for
four or five more.

pelled to act; or is surrounded with pleasures, and thinks and reads no more. If you have neglected to put other things in him, they will never get in afterwards;—if you have fed him only with words, he will remain a narrow and limited being to the end of his existence.

The bias given to men's minds is so strong, that it is no uncommon thing to meet with Englishmen, whom, but for their grey hairs and wrinkles, we might easily mistake for school-boys. Their talk is of Latin verses; and it is quite clear, if men's ages are to be dated from the state of their mental progress, that such men are eighteen years of age, and not a day older. Their minds have been so completely possessed by exaggerated notions of classical learning, that they have not been able in the great school of the world, to form any other notion of real greatness. Attend, too, to the public feelings—look to all the terms of applause. A learned man!—a scholar!—a man of erudition! Upon whom are these epithets of approbation bestowed? Are they given to men acquainted with the science of government? thoroughly masters of the geographical and commercial relations of Europe: to men who know the properties of bodies, and their action upon each other? No: this is not learning; it is chemistry, or political economy—not learning. The distinguishing abstract term, the epithet of Scholar, is reserved for him who writes on the Æolic reduplication, and is familiar with the Sylburgian method of arranging defectives in ω and μι. The picture which a young Englishman, addicted to the pursuit of knowledge, draws—his *beau idéal,* of human nature—his top and consummation of man's powers—is a knowledge of the Greek language. His object is not to reason, to imagine, or to invent; but to conjugate, decline, and derive. The situations of imaginary glory which he draws for himself, are the detection of an anapæst in the wrong place, or the restoration of a dative case which Cranzius had passed over, and the never-dying Ernesti failed to observe. If a young classic of this kind were to meet the greatest chemist or the greatest mechanician, or the most profound political economist of his time, in company with the greatest Greek scholar, would the slightest comparison between them ever come across his mind?—would he ever dream that such men as Adam Smith and Lavoisier were equal in dignity of understanding to, or of the same utility as, Bentley and Heyne? We are inclined to think, that the feeling excited would be a good deal like that which was expressed by Dr. George about the praises of the great King of Prussia, who entertained considerable doubts whether the King, with all his victories, knew how to conjugate a Greek verb in μι.

Another misfortune of classical learning, as taught in England, is, that scholars have come, in process of time, and from the effects of association, to love the instrument better than the end;— not the luxury which the difficulty encloses, but the difficulty; —not the filbert but the shell;—not what may be read in Greek, but Greek itself. It is not so much the man who has mastered the wisdom of the ancients, that is valued, as he who displays his knowledge of the vehicle in which that wisdom is conveyed. The glory is to show I am a scholar. The good sense and ingenuity I may gain by my acquaintance with ancient authors is matter of opinion; but if I bestow an immensity of pains upon a point of accent or quantity, this is something positive; I establish my pretensions to the name of Scholar, and gain the credit of learning, while I sacrifice all its utility.

Another evil in the present system of classical education is the extraordinary perfection which is aimed at in teaching those languages; a needless perfection; an accuracy which is sought for in nothing else. There are few boys who remain to the age of eighteen or nineteen at a public school, without making above ten thousand Latin verses;—a greater number than is contained in the *Æneid:* and after he has made this quantity of verses in a dead language, unless the poet should happen to be a very weak man indeed, he never makes another as long as he lives. It may be urged, and it is urged, that this is of use in teaching the delicacies of the language. No doubt it is of use for this purpose, if we put out of view the immense time and trouble sacrificed in gaining these little delicacies. It would be of use that we should go on till fifty years of age making Latin verses, if the price of a whole life were not too much to pay for it. We effect our object; but we do it at the price of something greater than our object. And whence comes it, that the expenditure of life and labour is totally put out of the calculation, when Latin and Greek are to be attained? In every other occupation, the question is fairly stated between the attainment and the time employed in the pursuit:—but, in classical learning, it seems to be sufficient if the least possible good is gained by the greatest possible exertion; if the end is anything, and the means everything. It is of some importance to speak and write French; and innumerable delicacies would be gained by writing ten thousand French verses: but it makes no part of our education to write French poetry. It is of some importance that there should be good botanists; but no botanist can repeat by heart the names of all the plants in the known world; nor is any astronomer acquainted with the appellation and magnitude of every star in the map of the heavens. The only department of human knowledge in which there can be no excess, no arithmetic, no balance of profit and loss, is classical learning.

The prodigious honour in which Latin verses are held at public schools is surely the most absurd of all absurd distinctions. You rest all reputation upon doing that which is a natural gift, and which no labour can attain. If a lad won't learn the words of a language, his degradation in the school is a very natural punishment for his disobedience, or his indolence; but it would be as reasonable to expect that all boys should be witty, or beautiful, as that they should be poets. In either case, it would be to make an accidental, unattainable, and not a very important gift of nature, the only, or the principal test of merit. This is the reason why boys, who make a considerable figure at school, so very often make no figure in the world;—and why other lads, who are passed over without notice, turn out to be valuable important men. The test established in the world is widely different from that established in a place which is presumed to be a preparation for the world; and the head of a public school, who is a perfect miracle to his contemporaries, finds himself shrink into absolute insignificance, because he has nothing else to command respect or regard, but a talent for fugitive poetry in a dead language.

The present state of classical education cultivates the imagination a great deal too much, and other habits of mind a great deal too little; and trains up many young men in a style of elegant imbecility, utterly unworthy of the talents with which nature has endowed them. It may be said, there are profound investigations, and subjects quite powerful enough for any understanding, to be met with in classical literature. So there are; but no man likes to add the difficulties of a language to the difficulties of a subject; and to study metaphysics, morals, and politics in Greek, when the Greek alone is study enough without them. In all foreign languages, the most popular works are works of imagination. Even in the French language, which we know so well, for one serious work which has any currency in this country, we have twenty which are mere works of imagination. This is still more true in classical literature; because what their poets and orators have left us is of infinitely greater value than the remains of their philosophy; for, as society advances, men think more accurately and deeply, and imagine more tamely; works of reasoning advance, and works of fancy decay. So that the matter of fact is, that a classical scholar of twenty-three or twenty-four years of age is a man principally conversant with works of imagination. His feelings are quick, his fancy lively, and his taste good. Talents for speculation and original inquiry he has none; nor has he formed the invaluable habit of pushing things up to their first principles, or of collecting dry and unamusing facts as the materials of reasoning. All the solid and masculine parts of his understanding are left wholly without cultivation; he hates the pain of thinking, and suspects every man whose boldness and originality call upon him to defend his opinions and prove his assertions.

A very curious argument is sometimes employed in justification of the learned minutiæ to which all young men are doomed, whatever be their propensities in future life. What are you to do with a young man up to the age of seventeen? Just as if there were such a want of difficulties to overcome, and of important tastes to inspire, that, from the mere necessity of doing something, and the impossibility of doing anything else, you were driven to the expedient of metre and poetry;—as if a young man within that period might not acquire the modern languages, modern history, experimental philosophy, geography, chronology, and a considerable share of mathematics;—as if the memory of things were not more agreeable, and more profitable, than the memory of words.

The great objection is, that we are not making the most of human life, when we constitute such an extensive, and such minute classical erudition, an indispensable article in education. Up to a certain point we would educate every young man in Latin and Greek; but to a point far short of that to which this species of education is now carried. Afterwards, we would grant to classical erudition as high honours as to every other department of knowledge, but not higher. We would place it upon a footing with many other objects of study; but allow to it no superiority. Good scholars would be as certainly produced by these means, as good chemists, astronomers, and mathematicians are now produced, without any direct provision whatsoever for their production. Why are we to trust to the diversity of human tastes, and the varieties of human ambition, in every thing else, and distrust it in classics alone? The passion for languages is just as strong as any other literary passion. There are very good Persian and Arabic scholars in this country. Large heaps of trash have been dug up from Sanscrit ruins. We have seen in our own times, a clergyman of the University of Oxford complimenting their Majesties in Coptic and Syro-phœnician verses; and yet we doubt whether there will be a sufficient avidity in literary men to get at the beauties of the finest writers which the world has yet seen; and though the *Bagvat Gheeta* has (as can be proved) met with human beings to translate, and other human beings to read it, we think that, in order to secure an attention to Homer and Virgil, we must catch up every man—whether he is to be a clergyman or a duke,—begin with him at six years of age, and never quit him till he is twenty; making him conjugate and decline for life and death; and so teaching him to estimate his progress in real wisdom as he can scan the verses of the Greek tragedians.

The English clergy, in whose hands education entirely rests, bring up the first young men of the country as if they were all to keep grammar schools in little country towns; and a nobleman, upon whose knowledge and liberality the honour and welfare of his country may depend, is diligently worried, for half his life, with the small pedantry of longs and shorts. There is a timid and absurd apprehension, on the part of ecclesiastical tutors, of letting out the minds of youth upon difficult and important subjects. They fancy that mental exertion must end in religious scepticism; and, to preserve the principles of their pupils, they confine them to the safe and elegant imbecility of classical learning. A genuine Oxford tutor would shudder to hear his young men disputing upon moral and political truth, forming and pulling down theories, and indulging in all the boldness of youthful discussion. He would augur nothing from it, but impiety to God, and treason to kings. And yet, who vilifies both more than the holy poltroon who carefully averts from them the searching eye of reason, and who knows no better method of teaching the highest duties, than by extirpating the finest qualities and habits of the mind? If our religion is a fable, the sooner it is exploded the better. If our government is bad, it should be amended. But we have no doubt of the truth of the one, or of the excellence of the other; and are convinced that both will be placed on a firmer basis, in proportion as the minds of men are more trained to the investigation of truth. At present, we act with the minds of our young men, as the Dutch did with their exuberant spices. An infinite quantity of talent is annually destroyed in the Universities of England by the miserable jealousy and littleness of ecclesiastical instructors. It is in vain to say we have produced great men under this system. We have produced great men under all systems. Every Englishman must pass half his life in learning Latin and Greek; and classical learning is supposed to have produced the talents which it has not been able to extinguish. It is scarcely possible to prevent great men from rising up under any system of education, however bad. Teach men dæmonology or astrology, and you will still have a certain portion of original genius, in spite of these or any other branches of ignorance and folly.

There is a delusive sort of splendour in a vast body of men pursuing one object, and thoroughly obtaining it; and yet, though it be very splendid, it is far from being useful. Classical literature is the great object at Oxford. Many minds so employed have produced many works, and much fame in that department; but if all liberal arts and sciences useful to human life had been taught there,—if some had dedicated themselves to chemistry, some to mathematics, some to experimental philosophy,—and if every attainment had been honoured in the mixt ratio of its difficulty and utility,—the system of such an University would have been much more valuable, but the splendour of its name something less.

When an University has been doing useless things for a long time, it appears at first degrading to them to be useful. A set of lectures upon political economy would be discouraged in Oxford,* probably despised, probably not permitted. To discuss the enclosure of commons, and to dwell upon imports and exports,—to come so near to common life, would seem to be undignified and contemptible. In the same manner, the Parr, or the Bentley of his day, would be scandalised in an University to be put on a level with the discoverer of a neutral salt; and yet, what other measure is there of dignity in intellectual labour, but usefulness and difficulty? And what ought the term University to mean, but a place where every science is taught which is liberal, and at the same time useful to mankind? Nothing would so much tend to bring classical literature within proper bounds as a steady and invariable appeal to these tests in our appreciation of all human knowledge. The puffed up pedant would collapse into his proper size, and the maker of verses and the rememberer of words, would soon assume that station, which is the lot of those who go up unbidden to the upper places of the feast.

We should be sorry, if what we have said should appear too contemptuous towards classical learning, which we most sincerely hope will always be held in great honour in this country, though we certainly do not wish to it that exclusive honour which it at present enjoys. A great classical scholar is an ornament and an important acquisition to his country; but, in a place of education, we would give to all knowledge an equal chance for distinction; and would trust to the varieties of human disposition, that every science worth cultivation would be cultivated. Looking al-

---

* They have since been established.

ways to real utility as our guide, we should see, with equal pleasure, a studious and inquisitive mind arranging the productions of nature, investigating the qualities of bodies, or mastering the difficulties of the learned languages. We should not care whether he were chemist, naturalist, or scholar, because we know it to be as necessary that matter should be studied, and subdued to the use of man, as that taste should be gratified, and imagination inflamed.

In those who were destined for the church, we would undoubtedly encourage classical learning, more than in any other body of men; but if we had to do with a young man going out into public life, we would exhort him to contemn, or at least not to affect the reputation of a great scholar, but to educate himself for the offices of civil life. He should learn what the constitution of his country really was,—how it had grown into its present state,—the perils that had threatened it,—the malignity that had attacked it,—the courage that had fought for it, and the wisdom that had made it great. We would bring strongly before his mind the characters of those Englishmen who have been the steady friends of the public happiness; and, by their examples, would breathe into him a pure public taste, which should keep him untainted in all the vicissitudes of political fortune. We would teach him to burst through the well paid, and the pernicious cant of indiscriminate loyalty; and to know his Sovereign only as he discharged those duties, and displayed those qualities, for which the blood and the treasure of his people are confided to his hands. We should deem it of the utmost importance, that his attention was directed to the true principles of legislation,—what effect laws can produce upon opinions, and opinions upon laws,—what subjects are fit for legislative interference, and when men may be left to the management of their own interests. The mischief occasioned by bad laws, and the perplexity which arises from numerous laws,—the causes of national wealth,—the relations of foreign trades,—the encouragement of manufactures and agriculture,—the fictitious wealth occasioned by paper credit,—the laws of population,—the management of poverty and mendicity—the use and abuse of monopoly,—the theory of taxation,—the consequences of the public debt. These are some of the subjects, and some of the branches of civil education, to which we would turn the minds of future judges, future senators, and future noblemen. After the first period of life had been given up to the cultivation of the classics, and the reasoning powers were now beginning to evolve themselves, these are some of the propensities in study which we would endeavour to inspire. Great knowledge at such a period of life, we could not convey; but we might fix a decided taste for its acquisition, and a strong disposition to respect it in others. The formation of some great scholars we should certainly prevent, and hinder many from learning what, in a few years, they would necessarily forget; but this loss would be well repaid,—if we could show the future rulers of the country that thought and labour which it requires to make a nation happy,—or if we could inspire them with that love of public virtue, which, after religion, we most solemnly believe to be the brightest ornament of the mind of man.

FEMALE EDUCATION

Mr. Broadhurst is a very good sort of man, who has not written a very bad book * upon a very important subject. His object (a very laudable one) is to recommend a better system of female education than at present prevails in this country—to turn the attention of women from the trifling pursuits to which they are now condemned—and to cultivate faculties which, under the actual system of management, might almost as well not exist. To the examination of his ideas upon these points we shall very cheerfully give up a portion of our time and attention.

A great deal has been said of the original difference of capacity between men and women; as if women were more quick and men more judicious—as if women were more remarkable for delicacy of association, and men for stronger powers of attention. All this, we confess, appears to us very fanciful. That there is a difference in the understandings of the men and the women we every day meet with, everybody, we suppose, must perceive; but there is none surely which may not be accounted for by the difference of circumstances in which they have been placed, without referring to any conjectural difference of original conformation of mind. As long as boys and girls run about in the dirt, and trundle hoops together, they are both precisely alike. If you catch up one half of these creatures, and train them to a particular set of actions and opinions, and the other half to a perfectly opposite set, of course their understandings will differ, as one or the other sort of occupations has called this or that talent into action. There is surely no occasion to go into any deeper or more abstruse reasoning, in order to explain so very simple a phenomenon. Taking it, then, for granted, that nature has been as bountiful of understanding to one

---

* *Advice to Young Ladies on the Improvement of the Mind.* By Thomas Broadhurst. 8vo. London, 1808.

sex as the other, it is incumbent on us to consider what are the principal objections commonly made against the communication of a greater share of knowledge to women than commonly falls to their lot at present: for though it may be doubted whether women should learn all that men learn, the immense disparity which now exists between their knowledge we should hardly think could admit of any rational defence. It is not easy to imagine that there can be any just cause why a woman of forty should be more ignorant than a boy of twelve years of age. If there be any good at all in female ignorance, this (to use a very colloquial phrase) is surely too much of a good thing.

Something in this question must depend, no doubt, upon the leisure which either sex enjoys for the cultivation of their understandings:—and we cannot help thinking, that women have fully as much, if not more, idle time upon their hands than men. Women are excluded from all the serious business of the world; men are lawyers, physicians, clergymen, apothecaries, and justices of the peace—sources of exertion which consume a great deal more time than producing and suckling children; so that if the thing is a thing that ought to be done—if the attainments of literature are objects really worthy the attention of females, they cannot plead the want of leisure as an excuse for indolence and neglect. The lawyer who passes his day in exasperating the bickerings of Roe and Doe, is certainly as much engaged as his lady, who has the whole of her morning before her to correct the children and pay the bills. The apothecary, who rushes from an act of phlebotomy in the western parts of the town to insinuate a bolus in the east, is surely as completely absorbed as that fortunate female who is darning the garment or preparing the repast of her Æsculapius at home; and in every degree and situation of life, it seems that men must necessarily be exposed to more serious demands upon their time and attention, than can possibly be the case with respect to the other sex. We are speaking always of the fair demands which ought to be made upon the time and attention of women; for, as the matter now stands, the time of women is considered as worth nothing at all. Daughters are kept to occupations in sewing, patching, mantua-making, and mending, by which it is impossible they can earn tenpence a day. The intellectual improvement of women is considered to be of such subordinate importance, that twenty pounds paid for needle-work would give to a whole family leisure to acquire a fund of real knowledge. They are kept with nimble fingers and vacant understandings, till the season for improvement is utterly past away, and all chance of forming more important habits completely lost. We do not therefore say that .women have more leisure than men, if it be necessary they should lead the life of artisans; but we make this assertion only upon the supposition that it is of some importance women should be instructed; and that many ordinary occupations, for which a little money will find a better substitute should be sacrificed to this consideration.

We bar, in this discussion, any objection which proceeds from the mere novelty of teaching women more than they are already taught. It may be useless that their education should be improved, or it may be pernicious; and these are the fair grounds on which the question may be argued. But those who cannot bring their minds to consider such an unusual extension of knowledge, without connecting with it some sensation of the ludicrous, should remember, that, in the progress from absolute ignorance, there is a period when cultivation of the mind is new to every rank and description of persons. A century ago, who would have believed that country gentlemen could be brought to read and spell with the ease and accuracy which we now so frequently remark,—or supposed that they could be carried up even to the elements of ancient and modern history? Nothing is more common, or more stupid, than to take the actual for the possible— to believe that all which is, is all which can be; first to laugh at every proposed deviation from practice as impossible—then, when it is carried into effect, to be astonished that it did not take place before.

It is said, that the effect of knowledge is to make women pedantic and affected; and that nothing can be more offensive, than to see a woman stepping out of the natural modesty of her sex, to make an ostentatious display of her literary attainments. This may be true enough; but the answer is so trite and obvious, that we are almost ashamed to make it. All affectation and display proceed from the supposition of possessing something better than the rest of the world possesses. Nobody is vain of possessing two legs and two arms;— because that is the precise quantity of either sort of limb which every body possesses. Who ever heard a lady boast that she understood French?—for no other reason, that we know of, but because everybody in these days does understand French; and though there may be some disgrace in being ignorant of that language, there is little or no merit in its acquisition. Diffuse knowledge generally among women, and you will at once cure the conceit which knowledge occasions while it is rare. Vanity and conceit we shall of course witness in men and women as long as the world endures:—but by multiplying the attainments upon which these feelings are founded, you increase the difficulty of indulging them, and render them much more tolerable, by making them the proofs of a much higher merit. When learning ceases to be uncommon among women, learned women will cease to be affected. A great many of the lesser and more obscure duties of life necessarily devolve upon the female sex. The arrangement of all household matters, and the care of children in their early infancy, must of course depend upon them. Now, there is a very general notion, that the moment you put the education of women upon a better footing than it is at present, at that moment there will be an end of all domestic economy: and that, if you once suffer women to eat of the tree of knowledge, the rest of the family will very soon be reduced to the same kind of aërial and unsatisfactory diet. These, and all such opinions are referable to one great and common cause of error;—that man does everything, and that nature does nothing; and that everything we see, is referable to positive institution, rather than to original feeling. Can anything, for example, be more perfectly absurd than to suppose, that the care and perpetual solicitude which a mother feels for her children depends upon her ignorance of Greek and Mathematics; and that she would desert an infant for a quadratic equation? We seem to imagine, that we can break in pieces the solemn institutions of nature by the little laws of a boarding-school; and that the existence of the human race depends upon teaching women a little more or a little less;—that Cimmerian ignorance can aid parental affection, or the circle of arts and sciences produce its destruction. In the same manner, we forget the principles upon which the love of order, arrangement, and all the arts of economy depend. They depend not upon ignorance nor idleness; but upon the poverty, confusion, and ruin which would ensue from neglecting them. Add to these principles the love of what is beautiful and magnificent, and the vanity of display;—and there can surely be no reasonable doubt but that the order and economy of private life is amply secured from the perilous inroads of knowledge.

We would fain know, too, if knowledge is to produce such baneful effects upon the material and the household virtues, why this influence has not already been felt? Women are much better educated now than they were a century ago; but they are by no means less remarkable for attention to the arrangements of their household, or less inclined to discharge the offices of parental affection. It would be very easy to show, that the same objection has been made at all times to every improvement in the education of both sexes, and all ranks—and been as uniformly and completely refuted by experience. A great part of the objections made to the education of women are rather objections made to human nature than to the female sex: for it is surely true, that knowledge, where it produces any bad effects at all, does as much mischief to one sex as to the other,—and gives birth to fully as much arrogance, inattention to common affairs, and eccentricity among men, as it does among women. But it by no means follows, that you get rid of vanity and self-conceit, because you get rid of learning. Self-complacency can never want an excuse; and the best way to make it more tolerable, and more useful, is to give to it as high and as dignified an object as possible. But, at all events, it is unfair to bring forward against a part of the world an objection which is equally powerful against the whole. When foolish women think they have any distinction, they are apt to be proud of it; so are foolish men. But we appeal to any one who has lived with cultivated persons of either sex, whether he has not witnessed as much pedantry, as much wrongheadedness, as much arrogance, and certainly a great deal more rudeness, produced by learning in men than in women: therefore, we should make the accusation general—or dismiss it altogether; though, with respect to pedantry, the learned are certainly a little unfortunate, that so very emphatic a word, which is occasionally applicable to all men embarked eagerly in any pursuit, should be reserved exclusively for them: for, as pedantry is an ostentatious obtrusion of knowledge, in which those who hear us cannot sympathise, it is a fault of which soldiers, sailors, sportsmen, gamesters, cultivators, and all men engaged in a particular occupation, are quite as guilty as scholars; but they have the good fortune to have the vice only of pedantry,—while scholars have both the vice and the name for it too.

Some persons are apt to contrast the acquisition of important knowledge with what they call simple pleasures; and deem it more becoming that a woman should educate flowers, make friendships with birds, and pick up plants, than enter into more difficult and fatiguing studies. If a woman have no taste and genius for higher occupations, let her engage in these, rather than remain destitute of any pursuit. But why are we necessarily to doom a girl, whatever be her taste or her capacity, to one unvaried line of petty and frivolous occupation? If she be full of strong sense and elevated curiosity, can there be any reason why she should be diluted and enfeebled down to a mere culler of simples, and fancier of birds?—why books of history and reasoning are to be torn out of her hand, and why she is to be sent, like a butterfly, to hover over the idle flowers of the field? Such amusements are innocent to those whom they can occupy; but they are not innocent to those who have too powerful understandings to be occupied by them. Light broths and fruits are innocent food only to weak or to infant stomachs; but they are poison to that organ in its perfect and mature state. But the great charm appears to be in the word *simplicity*—simple pleasure! If by a simple pleasure is meant an innocent pleasure, the observation is best answered by showing, that the pleasure which results from the acquisition of important knowledge is quite as innocent as any pleasure whatever: but if by a simple pleasure is meant one, the cause of which can be easily analysed, or which does not last long, or which in itself is very faint; then simple pleasures seem to be very nearly synonymous with small pleasures; and if the simplicity were to be a little increased, the pleasure would vanish altogether.

As it is impossible that every man should have industry or activity sufficient to avail himself of the advantages of education, it is natural that men who are ignorant themselves, should view, with some degree of jealousy and alarm, any proposal for improving the education of women. But such men may depend upon it, however the system of female education may be exalted, that there will never be wanting a due proportion of failures; and that after parents, guardians, and preceptors have done all in their power to make everybody wise, there will still be a plentiful supply of women who have taken special care to remain otherwise; and they may rest assured, if the utter extinction of ignorance and folly be the evil they dread, that their interests will always be effectually protected, in spite of every exertion to the contrary.

We must in candour allow, that those women who begin, will have something more to overcome than may probably hereafter be the case. We cannot deny the jealousy which exists among pompous and foolish men, respecting the education of women. There is a class of pedants, who would be cut short in the estimation of the world a whole cubit, if it were generally known that a young lady of eighteen could be taught to decline the tenses of the middle voice, or acquaint herself with the Æolic varieties of that celebrated language. Then women have, of course, all ignorant men for enemies to their instruction, who being bound (as they think), in point of sex to know more, are not well pleased, in point of fact, to know less. But, among men of sense and liberal politeness, a woman who has successfully cultivated her mind, without diminishing the gentleness and propriety of her manners, is always sure to meet with a respect and attention bordering upon enthusiasm.

There is in either sex a strong and permanent disposition to appear agreeable to the other: and this is the fair answer to those who are fond of supposing, that a higher degree of knowledge would make women rather the rivals than the companions of men. Presupposing such a desire to please, it seems much more probable, that a common pursuit should be a fresh source of interest than a cause of contention. Indeed, to suppose that any mode of education can create a general jealousy and rivalry between the sexes, is so very ridiculous, that it requires only to be stated in order to be refuted. The same desire of pleasing secures all that delicacy and reserve which are of such inestimable value to women. We are quite astonished, in hearing men converse on such subjects, to find them attributing such beautiful effects to ignorance. It would appear, from the tenor of such objections, that ignorance had been the great civiliser of the world. Women are delicate and refined only because they are ignorant;—they manage their household, only because they are ignorant;—they attend to their children, only because they know no better. Now, we must really confess, we have all our lives been so ignorant, as not to know the value of ignorance. We have always attributed the modesty and the refined manners of women, to their being well taught in moral and religious duty,—to the hazardous situation in which they are placed,—to that perpetual vigilance which it is their duty to exercise over thought, word, and action,—and to that cultivation of the mild virtues, which those who cultivate the stern and magnanimous virtues expect at their hands. After all, let it be remembered, we are not saying there are no objections to the diffusion of knowledge among the female sex. We would not hazard such a proposition respecting anything; but we are saying, that, upon the whole, it is the best method of employing time; and that there are fewer objections to it than to any other method. There are, perhaps, 50,000 females in Great Britain, who are exempted by circumstances from all necessary labour: but every human being must do something with their existence; and the pursuit of knowledge is, upon the whole, the most innocent, the most dignified, and the most useful method of filling up that idleness, of which there is always so large a portion in nations far advanced in civilisation. Let any man reflect, too, upon the solitary situation in which women are placed, —the ill treatment to which they are sometimes exposed, and which they must endure in silence, and without the power of complaining,—and he must feel convinced that the happiness of a woman will be materially increased in proportion as education has given to her the habit and the means of drawing her resources from herself.

There are a few common phrases in circulation, respecting the duties of women, to which we wish to pay some degree of attention, because they are rather inimical to those opinions which we have advanced on this subject. Indeed, independently of this, there is nothing which requires more vigilance than the current phrases of the day, of which there are always some resorted to in every dispute, and from the sovereign authority of which it is often vain to make

any appeal. "The true theatre for a woman is the sick chamber;"—
"Nothing so honourable to a woman as not to be spoken of at all."
These two phrases, the delight of *Noodledom*, are grown into
commonplaces upon the subject; and are not unfrequently employed
to extinguish that love of knowledge in women, which, in our humble
opinion, it is of so much importance to cherish. Nothing, certainly,
is so ornamental and delightful in women as the benevolent affections; but time cannot be filled up, and life employed, with high and
impassioned virtues. Some of these feelings are of rare occurrence
—all of short duration—or nature would sink under them. A scene
of distress and anguish is an occasion where the finest qualities of
the female mind may be displayed; but it is a monstrous exaggeration to tell women that they are born only for scenes of distress and
anguish. Nurse father, mother, sister, and brother, if they want it;—
it would be a violation of the plainest duties to neglect them. But,
when we are talking of the common occupations of life, do not let
us mistake the accidents for the occupations;—when we are arguing
how the twenty-three hours of the day are to be filled up, it is idle
to tell us of those feelings and agitations above the level of common
existence, which may employ the remaining hour. Compassion, and
every other virtue, are the great objects we all ought to have in view;
but no man (and no woman) can fill up the twenty-four hours by
acts of virtue. But one is a lawyer, and the other a ploughman, and
the third a merchant; and then, acts of goodness, and intervals of
compassion and fine feeling, are scattered up and down the common
occupations of life. We know women are to be compassionate; but
they cannot be compassionate from eight o'clock in the morning till
twelve at night:—and what are they to do in the interval? This is
the only question we have been putting all along, and is all that can
be meant by literary education.

Then, again, as to the notoriety which is incurred by literature.—
The cultivation of knowledge is a very distinct thing from its publication; nor does it follow that a woman is to become an author,
merely because she has talent enough for it. We do not wish a lady
to write books,—to defend and reply,—to squabble about the tomb
of Achilles, or the plain of Troy,—any more than we wish her to
dance at the opera, to play at a public concert, or to put pictures in
the Exhibition, because she has learned music, dancing, and drawing. The great use of her knowledge will be that it contributes to
her private happiness. She may make it public: but it is not the
principal object which the friends of female education have in view.
Among men, the few who write bear no comparison to the many
who read. We hear most of the former, indeed, because they are, in

general, the most ostentatious part of literary men; but there are innumerable persons who, without ever laying themselves before the public, have made use of literature to add to the strength of their understandings, and to improve the happiness of their lives. After all, it may be an evil for ladies to be talked of: but we really think those ladies who are talked of only as Mrs. Marcet, Mrs. Somerville, and Miss Martineau are talked of, may bear their misfortunes with a very great degree of Christian patience.

Their exemption from all the necessary business of life is one of the most powerful motives for the improvement of education in women. Lawyers and physicians have in their professions a constant motive to exertion; if you neglect their education, they must in a certain degree educate themselves by their commerce with the world; they must learn caution, accuracy, and judgment, because they must incur responsibility. But if you neglect to educate the mind of a woman, by the speculative difficulties which occur in literature, it can never be educated at all: if you do not effectually rouse it by education, it must remain for ever languid. Uneducated men may escape intellectual degradation; uneducated women cannot. They have nothing to do; and if they come untaught from the schools of education, they will never be instructed in the school of events.

Women have not their livelihood to gain by knowledge; and that is one motive for relaxing all those efforts which are made in the education of men. They certainly have not; but they have happiness to gain, to which knowledge leads as probably as it does to profit; and that is a reason against mistaken indulgence. Besides, we conceive the labour and fatigue of accomplishments to be quite equal to the labour and fatigue of knowledge; and that it takes quite as many years to be charming as it does to be learned.

Another difference of the sexes is, that women are attended to, and men attend. All acts of courtesy and politeness originate from the one sex, and are received by the other. We can see no sort of reason, in this diversity of condition, for giving to women a trifling and insignificant education; but we see in it a very powerful reason for strengthening their judgment, and inspiring them with the habit of employing time usefully. We admit many striking differences in the situation of the two sexes, and many striking differences of understanding, proceeding from the different circumstances in which they are placed; but there is not a single difference of this kind which does not afford a new argument for making the education of women better than it is. They have nothing serious to do;—is that a reason why they should be brought up to do nothing but what is trifling? They are exposed to greater dangers;—is that a reason why their faculties are to be purposely and industriously weakened? They are to form the characters of future men;—is that a cause why their own characters are to be broken and frittered down as they now are? In short, there is not a single trait in that diversity of circumstances, in which the two sexes are placed, that does not decidedly prove the magnitude of the error we commit in neglecting (as we do neglect) the education of women.

If the objections against the better education of women could be overruled, one of the great advantages that would ensue would be the extinction of innumerable follies. A decided and prevailing taste for one or another mode of education there must be. A century past, it was for housewifery—now it is for accomplishments. The object now is, to make women artists,—to give them an excellence in drawing, music, painting, and dancing,—of which, persons who make these pursuits the occupation of their lives, and derive from them their subsistence, need not be ashamed. Now, one great evil of all this is, that it does not last. If the whole of life were an Olympic game,—if we could go on feasting and dancing to the end,—this might do; but it is in truth merely provision for the little interval between coming into life and settling in it; while it leaves a long and dreary expanse behind, devoid both of dignity and cheerfulness. No mother, no woman who has passed over the few first years of life, sings, or dances, or draws, or plays upon musical instruments. These are merely means for displaying the grace and vivacity of youth, which every woman gives up, as she gives up the dress and the manners of eighteen: she has no wish to retain them; or, if she has, she is driven out of them by diameter and derision. The system of female education, as it now stands, aims only at embellishing a few years of life, which are in themselves so full of grace and happiness, that they hardly want it; and then leaves the rest of existence a miserable prey to idle insignificance. No woman of understanding and reflection can possibly conceive she is doing justice to her children by such kind of education. The object is, to give to children resources that will endure as long as life endures—habits that time will ameliorate, not destroy,—occupations that will render sickness tolerable, solitude pleasant, age venerable, life more dignified and useful, and therefore death less terrible: and the compensation which is offered for the omission of all this, is a short-lived blaze,—a little temporary effect, which has no other consequence than to deprive the remainder of life of all taste and relish. There may be women who have a taste for the fine arts, and who evince a decided talent for drawing, or for music. In that case, there can be no objection to the cultivation of these arts; but the error is, to make such things the grand

and universal object,—to insist upon it that every woman is to sing, and draw, and dance,—with nature, or against nature,—to bind her apprentice to some accomplishment, and if she cannot succeed in oil or water colours, to prefer gilding, varnishing, burnishing, box-making, to real and solid improvement in taste, knowledge, and understanding.

A great deal is said in favour of the social nature of the fine arts. Music gives pleasure to others. Drawing is an art, the amusement of which does not centre in him who exercises it, but is diffused among the rest of the world. This is true; but there is nothing, after all, so social as a cultivated mind. We do not mean to speak slightingly of the fine arts, or to depreciate the good humour with which they are sometimes exhibited; but we appeal to any man, whether a little spirited and sensible conversation—displaying, modestly, useful acquirements—and evincing rational curiosity, is not well worth the highest exertions of musical or graphical skill. A woman of accomplishments may entertain those who have the pleasure of knowing her for half an hour with great brilliancy; but a mind full of ideas, and with that elastic spring which the love of knowledge only can convey, is a perpetual source of exhilaration and amusement to all that come within its reach;—not collecting its force into single and insulated achievements, like the efforts made in the fine arts—but diffusing, equally over the whole of existence, a calm pleasure— better loved as it is longer felt—and suitable to every variety and every period of life. Therefore, instead of hanging the understanding of a woman upon walls, or hearing it vibrate upon strings,—instead of seeing it in clouds, or hearing it in the wind, we would make it the first spring and ornament of society, by enriching it with attainments upon which alone such power depends.

If the education of women were improved, the education of men would be improved also. Let any one consider (in order to bring the matter more home by an individual instance) of what immense importance to society it is, whether a nobleman of first-rate fortune and distinction is well or ill brought up;—what a taste and fashion he may inspire for private and for political vice!—and what misery and mischief he may produce to the thousand human beings who are dependent on him! A country contains no such curse within its bosom. Youth, wealth, high rank, and vice, form a combination which baffles all remonstrance and beats down all opposition. A man of high rank who combines these qualifications for corruption, is almost the master of the manners of the age, and has the public happiness within his grasp. But the most beautiful possession which a country can have is a noble and rich man who loves virtue and knowledge;—

who without being feeble or fanatical is pious—and who without being factious is firm and independent;—who, in his political life, is an equitable mediator between king and people; and, in his civil life, a firm promoter of all which can shed a lustre upon his country, or promote the peace and order of the world. But if these objects are of the importance which we attribute to them, the education of women must be important, as the formation of character for the first seven or eight years of life seems to depend almost entirely upon them. It is certainly in the power of a sensible and well educated mother to inspire, within that period, such tastes and propensities as shall nearly decide the destiny of the future man; and this is done, not only by the intentional exertions of the mother, but by the gradual and insensible imitation of the child; for there is something extremely contagious in greatness and rectitude of thinking, even at that age; and the character of the mother with whom he passes his early infancy is always an event of the utmost importance to the child. A merely accomplished woman cannot infuse her tastes into the minds of her sons; and, if she could, nothing could be more unfortunate than her success. Besides, when her accomplishments are given up, she has nothing left for it but to amuse herself in the best way she can; and, becoming entirely frivolous, either declines altogether the fatigue of attending to her children, or, attending to them, has neither talents nor knowledge to succeed; and, therefore, here is a plain and fair answer to those who ask so triumphantly, Why should a woman dedicate herself to this branch of knowledge? or, why should she be attached to such science?—Because, by having gained information on these points, she may inspire her son with valuable tastes, which may abide by him through life, and carry him up to all the sublimities of knowledge;—because she cannot lay the foundation of a great character if she is absorbed in frivolous amusements, nor inspire her child with noble desires when a long course of trifling has destroyed the little talents which were left by a bad education.

It is of great importance to a country that there should be as many understandings as possible actively employed within it. Mankind are much happier for the discovery of barometers, thermometers, steam-engines, and all the innumerable inventions in the arts and sciences. We are every day and every hour reaping the benefit of such talent and ingenuity. The same observation is true of such works as those of Dryden, Pope, Milton, and Shakespeare. Mankind are much happier that such individuals have lived and written; they add every day to the stock of public enjoyment—and perpetually gladden and embellish life. Now, the number of those who exercise their understandings to any good purpose is exactly in proportion to those who exercise it at all; but as the matter stands at present, half the talent in the universe runs to waste, and is totally unprofitable. It would have been almost as well for the world, hitherto, that women, instead of possessing the capacities they do at present, should have been born wholly destitute of wit, genius, and every other attribute of mind of which men make so eminent an use: and the ideas of use and possession are so united together, that, because it has been the custom in almost all countries to give to women a different and a worse education than to men, the notion has obtained, that they do not possess faculties which they do not cultivate. Just as, in breaking up a common, it is sometimes very difficult to make the poor believe it will carry corn, merely because they have been hitherto accustomed to see it produce nothing but weeds and grass—they very naturally mistake present condition for general nature. So completely have the talents of women been kept down, that there is scarcely a single work, either of reason or imagination, written by a woman, which is in general circulation, either in the English, French, or Italian literature;—scarcely one that has crept even into the ranks of our minor poets.

If the possession of excellent talents is not a conclusive reason why they should be improved, it at least amounts to a very strong presumption; and, if it can be shown that women may be trained to reason and imagine as well as men, the strongest reasons are certainly necessary to show us why we should not avail ourselves of such rich gifts of nature; and we have a right to call for a clear statement of those perils which make it necessary that such talent should be totally extinguished, or, at most, very partially drawn out. The burthen of proof does not lie with those who say. Increase the quantity of talent in any country as much as possible—for such a proposition is in conformity with every man's feelings: but it lies with those who say, Take care to keep that understanding weak and trifling which nature has made capable of becoming strong and powerful. The paradox is with them, not with us. In all human reasoning, knowledge must be taken for a good, till it can be shown to be an evil. But now, Nature makes to us rich and magnificent presents; and we say to her—You are too luxuriant and munificent—we must keep you under, and prune you;—we have talents enough in the other half of the creation; and, if you will not stupify and enfeeble the minds of women to our hands, we ourselves must expose them to a narcotic process, and educate away that fatal redundance with which the world is afflicted, and the order of sublunary things deranged.

One of the greatest pleasures of life is conversation;—and the pleasures of conversation are of course enhanced by every increase of knowledge: not that we should meet together to talk of alkalis and angles, or to add to our stock of history and philology,—though a little of these things is no bad ingredient in conversation; but let the subject be what it may, there is always a prodigious difference between the conversation of those who have been well educated and those who have not enjoyed this advantage. Education gives fecundity of thought, copiousness of illustration, quickness, vigour, fancy, words, images, and illustrations;—it decorates every common thing, and gives the power of trifling without being undignified and absurd. The subjects themselves may not be wanted upon which the talents of an educated man have been exercised; but there is always a demand for those talents which his education has rendered strong and quick. Now, really, nothing can be further from our intention than to say anything rude and unpleasant; but we must be excused for observing, that it is not now a very common thing to be interested by the variety and extent of female knowledge, but it is a very common thing to lament that the finest faculties in the world have been confined to trifles utterly unworthy of their richness and their strength.

The pursuit of knowledge is the most innocent and interesting occupation which can be given to the female sex; nor can there be a better method of checking a spirit of dissipation, than by diffusing a taste for literature. The true way to attack vice, is by setting up something else against it. Give to women, in early youth, something to acquire, of sufficient interest and importance to command the application of their mature faculties, and to excite their perseverance in future life;—teach them, that happiness is to be derived from the acquisition of knowledge, as well as the gratification of vanity; and you will raise up a much more formidable barrier against dissipation, than an host of invectives and exhortations can supply.

It sometimes happens that an unfortunate man gets drunk with very bad wine—not to gratify his palate but to forget his cares: he does not set any value on what he receives, but on account of what it excludes;—it keeps out something worse than itself. Now, though it were denied that the acquisition of serious knowledge is of itself important to a woman, still it prevents a taste for silly and pernicious works of imagination; it keeps away the horrid trash of novels; and, in lieu of that eagerness for emotion and adventure which books of that sort inspire, promotes a calm and steady temperament of mind.

A man who deserves such a piece of good fortune, may generally find an excellent companion for all the vicissitudes of his life; but it is not so easy to find a companion for his understanding, who has similar pursuits with himself, or who can comprehend the pleasure he derives from them. We really can see no reason why it should not be otherwise; nor comprehend how the pleasures of domestic life can be promoted by diminishing the number of subjects in which persons who are to spend their lives together take a common interest.

One of the most agreeable consequences of knowledge, is the respect and importance which it communicates to old age. Men rise in character often as they increase in years;—they are venerable from what they have acquired, and pleasing from what they can impart. If they outlive their faculties, the mere frame itself is respected for what it once contained; but women (such is their unfortunate style of education) hazard everything upon one cast of the die;—when youth is gone, all is gone. No human creature gives his admiration for nothing; either the eye must be charmed, or the understanding gratified. A woman must talk wisely or look well. Every human being must put up with the coldest civility, who has neither the charms of youth nor the wisdom of age. Neither is there the slightest commiseration for decayed accomplishments;—no man mourns over the fragments of a dancer, or drops a tear on the relics of musical skill. They are flowers destined to perish; but the decay of great talents is always the subject of solemn pity; and, even when their last memorial is over, their ruins and vestiges are regarded with pious affection.

There is no connection between the ignorance in which women are kept, and the preservation of moral and religious principle; and yet certainly there is, in the minds of some timid and respectable persons, a vague, indefinite dread of knowledge, as if it were capable of producing these effects. It might almost be supposed, from the dread which the propagation of knowledge has excited, that there was some great secret which was to be kept in impenetrable obscurity, that all moral rules were a species of delusion and imposture, the detection of which, by the improvement of the understanding, would be attended with the most fatal consequences to all, and particularly to women. If we could possibly understand what these great secrets were, we might perhaps be disposed to concur in their preservation; but believing that all the salutary rules which are imposed on women are the result of true wisdom, and productive of the greatest happiness, we cannot understand how they are to become less sensible of this truth in proportion as their power of discovering truth in general is increased, and the habit of viewing questions with accuracy and comprehension established by education. There are men, indeed, who are always exclaiming against every species of power, because it is connected with danger: their dread of abuses is so much stronger than their admiration of uses, that they would cheerfully give up the use of fire, gunpowder, and printing, to be freed from robbers, incendiaries, and libels. It is true, that every increase of knowledge may possibly render depravity more depraved, as well as it may increase the strength of virtue. It is in itself only power; and its value depends on its application. But, trust to the natural love of good where there is no temptation to be bad—it operates nowhere more forcibly than in education. No man, whether he be tutor, guardian, or friend, ever contents himself with infusing the mere ability to acquire; but giving the power, he gives with it a taste for the wise and rational exercise of that power; so that an educated person is not only one with stronger and better faculties than others, but with a more useful propensity—a disposition better cultivated— and associations of a higher and more important class.

In short, and to recapitulate the main points upon which we have insisted,—Why the disproportion in knowledge between the two sexes should be so great, when the inequality in natural talents is so small; or why the understanding of women should be lavished upon trifles, when nature has made it capable of higher and better things, we profess ourselves not able to understand. The affectation charged upon female knowledge is best cured by making that knowledge more general: and the economy devolved upon women is best secured by the ruin, disgrace, and inconvenience which proceeds from neglecting it. For the care of children, nature has made a direct and powerful provision; and the gentleness and elegance of women is the natural consequence of that desire to please which is productive of the greatest part of civilisation and refinement, and which rests upon a foundation too deep to be shaken by any such modifications in education as we have proposed. If you educate women to attend to dignified and important subjects, you are multiplying, beyond measure, the chances of human improvement, by preparing and *medicating* those early impressions, which always come from the mother; and which, in a great majority of instances, are quite decisive of character and genius. Nor is it only in the business of education that women would influence the destiny of men.—If women knew more, men must learn more—for ignorance would then be shameful —and it would become the fashion to be instructed. The instruction of women improves the stock of national talents, and employs more minds for the instruction and amusement of the world;—it increases the pleasures of society, by multiplying the topics upon which the two sexes take a common interest,—and makes marriage an intercourse of understanding as well as of affection, by giving dignity and importance to the female character. The education of women favours

public morals; it provides for every season of life, as well as for the
brightest and the best; and leaves a woman when she is stricken by
the hand of time, not as she now is, destitute of everything, and
neglected by all; but with the full power and the splendid attractions
of knowledge,—diffusing the elegant pleasures of polite literature,
and receiving the just homage of learned and accomplished men.

THE SOCIETY FOR THE SUPPRESSION OF VICE

A society, that holds out as its object the suppression of vice,* must
at first sight conciliate the favour of every respectable person; and
he who objects to an institution calculated apparently to do so much
good, is bound to give very clear and satisfactory reasons for his
dissent from so popular an opinion. We certainly have, for a long
time, had doubts of its utility; and now think ourselves called upon
to state the grounds of our distrust.

Though it were clear that individual informers are useful auxiliaries to the administration of the laws, it would by no means follow
that these informers should be allowed to combine,—to form themselves into a body,—to make a public purse,—and to prosecute
under a common name. An informer, whether he is paid by the week,
like the agents of this society—or by the crime, as in common cases,
—is, in general, a man of a very indifferent character. So much fraud
and deception are necessary for carrying on his trade—it is so odious
to his fellow-subjects,—that no man of respectability will ever undertake it. It is evidently impossible to make such a character otherwise than odious. A man who receives weekly pay for prying into
the transgressions of mankind, and bringing them to consequent punishment, will always be hated by mankind; and the office must fall
to the lot of some man of desperate fortunes and ambiguous character. The multiplication, therefore, of such officers, and the extensive
patronage of such characters, may by the management of large and
opulent societies, become an evil nearly as great as the evils they
would suppress. The alarm which a private and disguised accuser
occasions in the neighbourhood, is known to be prodigious, not only

* *Statement of the Proceedings of the Society for the Suppression of Vice,
from July 9 to November 12, read at their General Meeting, held November 12, 1804. With an Appendix, containing the Plan of the Society, &c.
&c. &c. London. 1804.
An Address to the Public from the Society for the Suppression of Vice,
instituted in London, 1802. Part the Second. Containing an Account of the
Proceedings of the Society from its original Institution. London. 1804.*

to the guilty, but to those who may be at once innocent, and ignorant, and timid. The destruction of social confidence is another evil, the consequence of information. An informer gets access to my house or family,—worms my secret out of me,—and then betrays me to the magistrate. Now, all these evils may be tolerated in a small degree, while, in a greater degree, they would be perfectly intolerable. Thirty or forty informers roaming about the metropolis, may frighten the mass of offenders a little, and do some good: ten thousand informers would either create an insurrection, or totally destroy the confidence and cheerfulness of private life. Whatever may be said, therefore, of the single and insulated informer, it is quite a new question when we come to a corporation of informers supported by large contributions. The one may be a good, the other a very serious evil; the one legal the other wholly out of the contemplation of law,—which often, and very wisely, allows individuals to do, what it forbids to many individuals assembled.

If once combination is allowed for the suppression of vice, where are its limits to be? Its capital may as well consist of 100,-000*l. per annum,* as of a thousand: its numbers may increase from a thousand subscribers, which this society, it seems, had reached in its second year, to twenty thousand: and in that case, what accused person of an inferior condition of life would have the temerity to stand against such a society? Their mandates would very soon be law; and there is no compliance into which they might not frighten the common people, and the lower orders of tradesmen. The idea of a society of gentlemen, calling themselves an Association for the Suppression of Vice, would alarm any small offender, to a degree that would make him prefer any submission to any resistance. He would consider the very fact of being accused by them as almost sufficient to ruin him.

An individual accuser accuses at his own expense; and the risk he runs is a good security that the subject will not be harassed by needless accusations,—a security which, of course, he cannot have against such a society as this, to whom pecuniary loss is an object of such little consequence. It must never be forgotten, that this is not a society for *punishing* people who have been found to transgress the law, but for *accusing* persons of transgressing the law; and that before trial, the accused person is to be considered as innocent, and is to have every fair chance of establishing his innocence. He must be no common defendant, however, who does not contend against such a society with very fearful odds;— the best counsel engaged for his opponents,—great practice in the particular court and particular species of cause,—witnesses thoroughly hackneyed in a court of justice,—and an unlimited command of money. It by no means follows, that the legislature, in allowing individuals to be informers, meant to subject the accused person to the superior weight and power of such societies. The very influence of names must have a considerable weight with the jury. Lord Dartmouth, Lord Radstock, and the Bishop of Durham, *versus* a Whitechapel butcher or a publican! Is this a fair contest before a jury? It is not so even in London; and what must it be in the country, where a society for the suppression of vice may consist of all the principal persons in the neighbourhood? These societies are now established in York, in Reading, and in many other large towns. Wherever this is the case, it is far from improbable that the same persons at the Quarter or Town Sessions, may be both judges and accusers; and still more fatally so, if the offence is tried by a special jury. This is already most notoriously the case in societies for the preservation of game. They prosecute a poacher;—the jury is special; and the poor wretch is found guilty by the very same persons who have accused him.

If it be lawful for respectable men to combine for the purpose of turning informers, it is lawful for the lowest and most despicable race of informers, to do the same thing; and then it is quite clear that every species of wickedness and extortion would be the consequence. We are rather surprised that no society of perjured attorneys and fraudulent bankrupts has risen up in this metropolis for the suppression of vice. A chairman, deputy-chairman, subscriptions, and an annual sermon, would give great dignity to their proceedings; and they would soon begin to take some rank in the world.

It is true that it is the duty of grand juries to inform against vice; but the law knows the probable number of grand jurymen, the times of their meeting, and the description of persons of whom they consist. Of voluntary societies it can know nothing,—their numbers, their wealth, or the character of their members. It may therefore trust to a grand jury what it would by no means trust to an unknown combination. A vast distinction is to be made, too, between official duties and voluntary duties. The first are commonly carried on with calmness and moderation; the latter often characterised, in their execution, by rash and intemperate zeal.

The present Society receives no members but those who are of the Church of England. As we are now arguing the question generally, we have a right to make any supposition. It is equally free, therefore, upon general principles, for a society of sectarians to combine and exclude members of the Church of England; and the suppression of vice may thus come in aid of Methodism, Jacobinism, or of any set of principles, however perilous, either to Church or State. The present Society may perhaps consist of persons whose sentiments on these points are rational and respectable. Combinations, however, of this sort may give birth to something far different; and such a supposition is the fair way of trying the question.

We doubt if there be not some mischief in averting the fears and hopes of the people from the known and constituted authorities of the country to those self-created powers;—a Society that punishes in the Strand, another which rewards at Lloyd's Coffee-house! If these things get to any great height, they throw an air of insignificance over those branches of the government to whom these cares properly devolve, and whose authority is by these means assisted, till it is superseded. It is supposed that a project must necessarily be good, because it is intended for the aid of law and government. At this rate, there should be a society in aid of the government, for procuring intelligence from foreign parts, with accredited agents all over Europe. There should be a voluntary transport board, and a gratuitous victualling office. There should be a duplicate, in short, of every department of the State,—the one appointed by the King, and the other by itself. There should be a real Lord Glenbervie in the woods and forests,—and with him a monster, a voluntary Lord Glenbervie, serving without pay, and guiding *gratis,* with secret counsel, the axe of his prototype. If it be asked, who are the constituted authorities who are legally appointed to watch over morals, and whose functions the Society usurp? our answer is, that there are in England about 12,000 clergy, not unhandsomely paid for persuading the people, and about 4000 justices, 30 grand juries, and 40,000 constables, whose duty and whose inclination it is to compel them to do right. Under such circumstances, a voluntary moral society does indeed seem to be the purest result of volition; for there certainly is not the smallest particle of necessity mingled with its existence.

It is hardly possible that a society for the suppression of vice can ever be kept within the bounds of good sense and moderation. If there are many members who have really become so from a feeling of duty, there will necessarily be some who enter the Society to hide a bad character, and others whose object it is to recommend themselves to their betters by a sedulous and bustling inquisition into the immoralities of the public. The loudest and noisiest suppressors will always carry it against the more prudent part of the community; the most violent will be considered as the most moral; and those who see the absurdity will, from the fear of being thought to encourage vice, be reluctant to oppose it.

It is of great importance to keep public opinion on the side of virtue. To their authorised and legal correctors, mankind are, on common occasions; ready enough to submit; but there is something in the self-erection of a voluntary magistracy which creates so much disgust that it almost renders vice popular, and puts the offence at a premium. We have no doubt but that the immediate effect of a voluntary combination for the suppression of vice, is an involuntary combination in favour of the vices to be suppressed; and this is a very serious drawback from any good of which such societies may be the occasion; for the state of morals, at any one period, depends much more upon opinion than law; and to bring odious and disgusting auxiliaries to the aid of virtue, is to do the utmost possible good to the cause of vice. We regret that mankind are as they are; and we sincerely wish that the species at large were as completely devoid of every vice and infirmity as the President, Vice-President, and Committee of the Suppressing Society; but, till they are thus regenerated, it is of the greatest consequence to teach them virtue and religion in a manner which will not make them hate both the one and the other. The greatest delicacy is required in the application of violence to moral and religious sentiment. We forget, that the object is, not to produce the outward compliance, but to raise up the inward feeling, which secures the outward compliance. You may drag men into church by main force, and prosecute them for buying a pot of beer,—and cut them off from the enjoyment of a leg of mutton;—and you may do all this, till you make the common people hate Sunday, and the clergy, and religion, and everything which relates to such subjects. There are many crimes, indeed, where persuasion cannot be waited for, and where the untaught feelings of all men go along with the violence of the law. A robber and a murderer must be knocked on the head like mad dogs; but we have no great opinion of the possibility of indicting men into piety, or of calling in the Quarter Sessions to the aid of religion. You may produce outward conformity by these means; but you are so far from producing (the only thing worth producing) the inward feeling, that you incur a great risk of giving birth to a totally opposite sentiment.

The violent modes of making men good, just alluded to, have been resorted to at periods when the science of legislation was not so well understood as it now is; or when the manners of the age have been peculiarly gloomy or fanatical. The improved knowledge, and the improved temper of later times, push such laws into the back ground, and silently repeal them. A Suppressing Society, hunting everywhere for penalty and information, has a direct tendency to revive ancient ignorance and fanaticism,—and to re-enact laws which, if ever they ought to have existed at all, were certainly calculated for a very different style of manners, and a very different degree of information. To compel men to go to church under a penalty appears to us to be absolutely absurd. The bitterest enemy of religion will necessarily be that person who is driven to a compliance with its outward ceremonies, by informers and justices of the peace. In the same manner, any constable who hears another swear an oath has a right to seize him, and carry him before a magistrate, where he is to be fined so much for each execration. It is impossible to carry such laws into execution; and it is lucky that it is impossible,—for their execution would create an infinitely greater evil than it attempted to remedy. The common sense, and common feeling of mankind, if left to themselves, would silently repeal such laws; and it is one of the evils of these societies, that they render absurdity eternal, and ignorance indestructible. Do not let us be misunderstood: upon the object to be accomplished, there can be but one opinion;—it is only upon the means employed, that there can be the slightest difference of sentiment. To go to church is a duty of the greatest possible importance; and on the blasphemy and vulgarity of swearing, there can be but one opinion. But such duties are not the objects of legislation; they must be left to the general state of public sentiment; which sentiment must be influenced by example, by the exertions of the pulpit and the press, and, above all, by education. The fear of God can never be taught by constables, nor the pleasures of religion be learnt from a common informer.

Beginning with the best intentions in the world, such societies must in all probability degenerate into a receptacle for every species of tittle-tattle, impertinence, and malice. Men whose trade is rat-catching, love to catch rats; the bug-destroyer seizes on his bug with delight; and the suppressor is gratified by finding his vice. The last soon becomes a mere tradesman like the others; none of them moralise, or lament that their respective evils should exist in the world. The public feeling is swallowed up in the pursuit of a daily occupation, and in the display of a technical skill. Here, then, is a society of men, who invite accusation,—who receive it (almost unknown to themselves) with pleasure,—and who, if they hate dulness and inoccupation, can have very little pleasure in the innocence of their fellow-creatures. The natural consequence of all this is, that (besides that portion of rumour which every member con-

THE SOCIETY FOR THE SUPPRESSION OF VICE

tributes at the weekly meeting) their table must be covered with anonymous lies against the characters of individuals. Every servant discharged from his master's service,—every villain who hates the man he has injured,—every cowardly assassin of character,—now knows where his accusations will be received, and where they cannot fail to produce some portion of the mischievous effects which he wishes. The very first step of such a Society should be, to declare, in the plainest manner, that they would never receive any anonymous accusation. This would be the only security to the public, that they were not degrading themselves into a receptacle for malice and falsehood. Such a declaration would inspire some species of confidence; and make us believe that their object was neither the love of power, nor the gratification of uncharitable feelings. The Society for the Suppression, however, have done no such thing. They request, indeed, the signature of the informers whom they invite; but they do not (as they ought) make that signature an indispensable condition.

Nothing has disgusted us so much in the proceedings of this Society, as the control which they exercise over the amusements of the poor. One of the specious titles under which this legal meanness is gratified is, *Prevention of Cruelty to Animals.*

Of cruelty to animals, let the reader take the following specimens:

Running an iron hook in the intestines of an animal; presenting this first animal to another as his food; and then pulling this second creature up and suspending him by the barb in his stomach.

Riding a horse till he drops, in order to see an innocent animal torn to pieces by dogs.

Keeping a poor animal upright for many weeks, to communicate a peculiar hardness to his flesh.

Making deep incisions into the flesh of another animal while living, in order to make the muscles more firm.

Immersing another animal, while living, in hot water.

Now we do fairly admit, that such abominable cruelties as these are worthy the interference of the law: and that the Society should have punished them, cannot be matter of surprise to any feeling mind.—But stop, gentle reader! these cruelties are the cruelties of the Suppressing Committee, not of the poor. You must not think of punishing these.—The first of these cruelties passes under the pretty name of *angling;*—and therefore there can be no harm in it—the more particularly as the President himself has one of the best preserved trout streams in England.—The next is *hunting;*—and as many of the Vice-Presidents and of the Committee hunt, it is not possible there can be any cruelty in hunting.* The next is, a process for making *brawn*—a dish never tasted by the poor, and therefore not to be disturbed by indictment. The fourth is the mode of *crimping* cod; and the fifth, of boiling lobsters; all high-life cruelties, with which a justice of the peace has no business to meddle. The real thing which calls forth the sympathies, and harrows up the soul, is to see a number of boisterous artisans baiting a bull, or a bear; not a savage hare, or a carnivorous stag,—but a poor, innocent, timid bear;—not pursued by magistrates, and deputy lieutenants, and men of education,—but by those who must necessarily seek their relaxation in noise and tumultuous merriment,—by men whose feelings are blunted, and whose understanding is wholly devoid of refinement. The Society detail, with symptoms of great complacency, their detection of a bear-baiting in Blackboy Alley, Chick Lane, and the prosecution of the offenders before a magistrate. It appears to us, that nothing can be more partial and unjust than this kind of proceedings. A man of ten thousand a year may worry a fox as much as he pleases,—may encourage the breed of a mischievous animal on purpose to worry it; and a poor labourer is carried before a magistrate for paying sixpence to see an exhibition of courage between a dog and a bear! Any cruelty may be practised to gorge the stomachs of the rich,—none to enliven the holidays of the poor. We venerate these feelings which really protect creatures susceptible of pain, and incapable of complaint. But heaven-born pity, now-a-days, calls for the income-tax, and the court guide; and ascertains the rank and fortune of the tormentor before she weeps for the pain of the sufferer. It is astonishing how the natural feelings of mankind are distorted by false theories. Nothing can be more mischievous than to say, that the pain inflicted by the dog of a man of quality is not (when the strength of the two animals is the same) equal to that produced

---

* "How reasonable creatures," says the Society, "can enjoy a pastime which is the cause of such sufferings to brute animals, or how they can consider themselves entitled, for their own amusement, to stimulate those animals, by means of the antipathies which Providence has thought proper to place between them, to worry and tear, and often to destroy each other, it is difficult to conceive. So inhuman a practice, by a retribution peculiarly just, tends obviously to render the human character brutal and ferocious," &c. &c. (*Address,* pp. 71, 72.) We take it for granted, that the reader sees clearly that no part of this description can possibly apply to the case of *hunting.*

by the cur of a butcher. Haller, in his Pathology, expressly says, *that the animal bitten knows no difference in the quality of the biting animal's master;* and it is now the universal opinion among all enlightened men, that the misery of the brawner would be very little diminished, if he could be made sensible that he was to be eaten up only by persons of the first fashion. The contrary supposition seems to us to be absolute nonsense; it is the desertion of the true *Baconian* philosophy, and the substitution of mere unsupported conjecture in its place. The trespass, however, which calls forth all the energies of a suppressor, is the sound of a fiddle. That the common people are really enjoying themselves, is now beyond all doubt: and away rush Secretary, President, and Committee, to clap the cotillon into the Compter, and to bring back the life of the poor to its regular standard of decorous gloom. The gambling houses of St. James's remain untouched. The peer ruins himself and his family with impunity; while the Irish labourer is privately whipped for not making a better use of the excellent moral and religious education which he has received in the days of his youth!

It is not true, as urged by the Society, that the vices of the poor are carried on in houses of public resort, and those of the rich in their own houses. The Society cannot be ignorant of the innumerable gambling houses resorted to by men of fashion. Is there one they have suppressed, or attempted to suppress? Can anything be more despicable than such distinctions as these? Those who make them seem to have for other persons' vices all the rigour of the ancient Puritans—without a particle of their honesty or their courage. To suppose that any society will ever attack the vices of people of fashion, is wholly out of the question. If the Society consisted of tradesmen, they would infallibly be turned off by the vicious customers whose pleasures they interrupted: and what gentleman so fond of suppressing, as to interfere with the vices of good company, and inform against persons who were really genteel? He knows very well that the consequence of such interference would be a complete exclusion from elegant society; that the upper classes could not, and would not, endure it; and that he must immediately lose his rank in the world, if his zeal subjected fashionable offenders to the slightest inconvenience from the law. Nothing, therefore, remains, but to rage against the Sunday dinners of the poor, and to prevent a bricklayer's labourer from losing, on the seventh day, that beard which has been augmenting the other six. We see at the head of this Society the names of several noblemen, and of other persons moving in the fashionable world. Is it possible they can be ignorant of the innumerable offences against the law and morality which are committed by their own acquaintances and connections? Is there one single instance where they have directed the attention of the Society to this higher species of suppression, and sacrificed men of consideration to that zeal for virtue which watches so acutely over the vices of the poor? It would give us very little pleasure to see a duchess sent to the Poultry Compter; but if we saw the Society flying at such high game, we should at least say they were honest and courageous, whatever judgment we might form of their good sense. At present they should denominate themselves a Society for suppressing the vices of persons whose income does not exceed 500*l. per annum;* and then, to put all classes upon an equal footing, there must be another society of barbers, butchers, and bakers, to return to the higher classes that moral character, by which they are so highly benefited.

To show how impossible it is to keep such societies within any kind of bounds, we shall quote a passage respecting circulating libraries, from their Proceedings.

"Your Committee have good reasons for believing, that the circulation of their notices among the printsellers, warning them against the sale or exhibition of indecent representations, has produced, and continues to produce, the best effects.

"But they have to lament that the extended establishments of circulating libraries, however useful they may be, in a variety of respects, to the easy and general diffusion of knowledge, are extremely injurious to morals and religion, by the indiscriminate admission which they give to works of a prurient and immoral nature. It is a toilsome task to any virtuous and enlightened mind, to wade through the catalogues of these collections, and much more to select such books from them as have only an apparent bad tendency. But your Committee being convinced that their attention ought to be directed to those institutions which possess such powerful and numerous means of poisoning the minds of young persons, and especially of the female youth, have therefore begun to make some endeavours towards their better regulation."—*Statement of the Proceedings for* 1804, pp. 11, 12.

In the same spirit we see them writing to a country magistrate in Devonshire, respecting a wake advertised in the public papers.

Nothing can be more presumptuous than such conduct, or produce, in the minds of impartial men, a more decisive impression against the Society.

The natural answer from the members of the Society (the only answer they have ever made to the enemies of their institution) will be, that we are lovers of vice,—desirous of promoting indecency, of destroying the Sabbath, and of leaving mankind to the unrestrained gratification of their passions. We have only very calmly to reply, that we are neither so stupid nor so wicked as not to concur in every scheme which has for its object the preservation of rational religion and sound morality;—but the scheme must be well concerted,—and those who are to carry it into execution must deserve our confidence, from their talents and their character. Upon religion and morals depends the happiness of mankind;—but the fortune of knaves and the power of fools is sometimes made to rest on the same apparent basis; and we will never (if we can help it) allow a rogue to get rich, or a blockhead to get powerful, under the sanction of these awful words. We do not by any means intend to apply these contemptuous epithets to the Society for the Suppression. That there are among their numbers some very odious hypocrites, is not impossible; that many men who believe they come there from the love of virtue, do really join the Society from the love of power, we do not doubt: but we see no reason to doubt that the great mass of subscribers consists of persons who have very sincere intentions of doing good. That they have, in some instances, done a great deal of good, we admit with the greatest pleasure. We believe, that in the hands of truly honest, intrepid, and, above all, discreet men, such a society might become a valuable institution, improve in some degree the public morals, and increase the public happiness. So many qualities, however, are required to carry it on well,—the temptations to absurdity and impertinence are so very great,—that we ever despair of seeing our wishes upon this subject realised. In the present instance, our object has been to suppress the arrogance of suppressers,—to keep them within due bounds,—to show them that to do good requires a little more talent and reflection than they are aware of,—and, above all, to impress upon them that true zeal for virtue knows no distinction between the rich and the poor; and that the cowardly and the mean can never be the true friends of morality, and the promoters of human happiness. If they attend to these rough doctrines they will ever find in the writers of this Journal their warmest admirers, and their most sincere advocates and friends.

CHIMNEY SWEEPERS

AN excellent and well-arranged dinner is the most pleasing occurrence, and a great triumph of civilised life. It is not only the descending morsel, and the enveloping sauce—but the rank, wealth, wit, and beauty which surround the meats—the learned management of light and heat—the silent and rapid services of the attendants—the smiling and sedulous host, proffering gusts and relishes —the exotic bottles—the embossed plate—the pleasant remarks— the handsome dresses—the cunning artifices in fruit and farina! The hour of dinner, in short, includes every thing of sensual and intellectual gratification which a great nation glories in producing.

In the midst of all this, who knows that the kitchen chimney caught fire half an hour before dinner!—and that a poor little wretch of six or seven years old, was sent up in the midst of the flames to put it out? We could not, previous to reading this evidence, have formed a conception of the miseries of these poor wretches, or that there should exist, in a civilised country, a class of human beings destined to such extreme and varied distress. We will give a short epitome of what is developed in the evidence before the two Houses of Parliament.

Boys are made chimney sweepers at the early age of five or six. *Little boys for small flues,* is a common phrase in the cards left at the door by itinerant chimney sweepers. Flues made to ovens and coppers are often less than nine inches square; and it may be easily conceived, how slender the frame of that human body must be, which can force itself through such an aperture.

"What is the age of the youngest boys who have been employed in this trade, to your knowledge? About five years of age: I know one now between five and six years old; it is the man's own son in the Strand: now there is another at Somers Town, I think, said he was between four and five, or about five; Jack Hall, a little lad, takes him about.—Did you ever know any female children employed? Yes, I know one now. About two years ago there was a woman told me she had climbed scores of times, and there is one at Paddington now, whose father taught her to climb; but I have often heard talk of them when I was apprentice, in different places.—What is the smallest-sized flue you have ever met with in the course of your experience? About eight inches by nine; these they are always obliged to climb in this posture (*describing it*), keeping the arms up straight; if they slip their arms down, they get jammed in; unless they get their arms close over their head, they cannot climb." —(*Lords Minutes,* No. 1. p. 8.)

The following is a specimen of the manner in which they are taught this art of climbing chimneys.

"Do you remember being taught to climb chimneys? Yes.— What did you feel upon the first attempt to climb a chimney? The first chimney I went up, they told me there was some plum-pudding and money up at the top of it, and that is the way they enticed me up; and when I got up I would not let the other boy get from under me to get at it, I thought he would get it; I could not get up, and shoved the pot and half the chimney down into the yard.—Did you experience any inconvenience to your knees, or your elbows? Yes, the skin was off my knees and elbows too, in climbing up the new chimneys they forced me up.—How did they force you up? When I got up, I cried out about my sore knees.—Were you beat or compelled to go up by any violent means? Yes, when I went to a narrow chimney, if I could not do it, I durst not go home; when I used to come down, my master would well beat me with the brush; and not only my master, but when we used to go with the journeymen, if we could not do it, they used to hit us three or four times with the brush."—(*Lords' Minutes,* No. 1. p. 5.)

In practising the art of climbing, they are often crippled.

"You talked of the pargetting of chimneys; are many chimneys pargetted? There used to be more than are now; we used to have to go and sit all a-twist to parge them, according to the floors, to keep the smoke from coming out; then I could not straighten my legs; and that is the reason that many are cripples, —from parging and stopping the holes."—(*Lords' Minutes,* No. 1. p. 17.)

They are often stuck fast in a chimney, and, after remaining there many hours, are cut out.

"Have you known, in the course of your practice, boys stick in chimneys at all? Yes, frequently.—Did you ever know an instance of a boy being suffocated to death? No; I do not recollect any one at present, but I have assisted in taking boys out when they have been nearly exhausted.—Did you ever know an instance of its being necessary to break open a chimney to take the boy out? O yes.—*Frequently? Monthly I might say;* it is done with a cloak, if possible, that it should not be discovered: a master in general wishes it not to be known, and therefore speaks to the people belonging to the house not to mention it, for it was merely the boy's neglect; they often say that it was the boy's neglect.—Why do they say that? The boy's climbing shirt is often very bad; the boy coming down, if the chimney be very narrow, and numbers of them are only nine inches, gets his shirt rumpled underneath him, and he has no power after he is fixed in that way (*with his hand up*).— Does a boy frequently stick in the chimney? Yes; I have known more instances of that the last twelvemonth than before.—Do you ever have to break open in the inside of a room? Yes, I have helped to break through into a kitchen chimney in a dining-room."—(*Lords' Minutes*, p. 34.)

To the same effect is the evidence of John Daniels (*Minutes*, p. 100), and of James Ludford (*Lords' Minutes*, p. 147).

"You have swept the Penitentiary? I have.—Did you ever know a boy stick in any of the chimneys there? Yes, I have.—Was it one of your boys? It was—Was there one or two that stuck? Two of them.—How long did they stick there? Two hours.— How were they got out? They were cut out.—Was there any danger while they were in that situation? It was the core from the pargetting of the chimney, and the rubbish that the labourers had thrown down, that stopped them, and when they got it aside them, they could not pass.—They both stuck together? Yes."—(*Lords' Minutes*, p. 147.)

One more instance we shall give, from the Evidence before the Commons.

"Have you heard of any accidents that have recently happened to climbing-boys in the small flues? Yes; I have *often* met with accidents myself when I was a boy; there was lately one in Mary-le-bone where the boy *lost his life* in a flue, a boy of the name of Tinsey (his father was of the same trade); that boy I think was about eleven or twelve years old.—Was there a coroner's inquest sat on the body of that boy you mentioned? Yes, there was; he was an apprentice of a man of the name of Gay. —How many accidents do you recollect, which were attended with loss of life to the climbing boys? I have heard talk of many more than I know of; I never knew of more than three since I have been at the trade, but I have heard talk of many more.—

Of twenty or thirty? I cannot say; I have been near losing my own life several times."—(*Commons' Report,* p. 53.)

We come now to burning little chimney sweepers. A large party are invited to dinner—a great display is to be made;—and about an hour before dinner, there is an alarm that the kitchen chimney is on fire! It is impossible to put off the distinguished personages who are expected. It gets very late for the soup and fish, the cook is frantic—all eyes are turned upon the sable consolation of the master chimney sweeper—and up into the midst of the burning chimney is sent one of the miserable little infants of the brush! There is a positive prohibition of this practice, and an enactment of penalties in one of the acts of Parliament, which respect chimney sweepers. But what matter acts of Parliament, when the pleasures of genteel people are concerned? Or what is a toasted child compared to the agonies of the mistress of the house with a deranged dinner?

"Did you ever know a boy get burnt up a chimney? Yes.—Is that usual? Yes, I have been burnt myself, and have got the scars on my legs; a year ago I was up a chimney in Liquor Pond Street; I have been up *more than forty chimneys where I have been burnt.*—Did your master or the journeymen ever direct you to go up a chimney that is on fire? Yes, it is a general case. —Do they compel you to go up a chimney that is on fire? Oh yes, it was the general practice for two of us to stop at home on Sunday to be ready in case of a chimney being a-fire.—You say it is general to compel the boys to go up chimneys on fire? Yes, boys get very ill treated if they do not go up."—(*Lords' Minutes,* p. 34.)
"Were you ever forced up a chimney on fire? Yes, I was forced up once, and, because I could not do it, I was taken home and well hided with a brush by the journeyman.—Have you frequently been burnt in ascending chimneys on fire? Three times. —Are such hardships as you have described common in the trade with other boys? Yes, they are."—(*Ibid.* p. 100.)
"What is the price for sending a boy up a chimney badly on fire? The price allowed is five shillings, but most of them charge half a guinea.—Is any part of that given to the boy? No, but very often the boy gets half a crown; and then the journeyman has half, and his mistress takes the other part to take care of against Sunday.—Have you never seen water thrown down from the top of a chimney when it is on fire? Yes.—Is not that generally done? Yes; I have seen that done twenty times, and the

boy in the chimney; at the time when the boy has hallooed out,
'It is so hot I cannot go any further'; and then the expression
is, with an oath 'Stop, and I will heave a pail of water down.' "
—(*Ibid.* p. 39.)

Chimney sweepers are subject to a peculiar sort of cancer, which
often brings them to a premature death.

"He appeared perfectly willing to try the machines everywhere?
I must say the man appeared perfectly willing; he had a fear that
he and his family would be ruined by them; but I must say of
him, that he is very different from other sweeps I have seen; he
attends very much to his own business; he was as black as any
boy he had got, and unfortunately in the course of conversation
he told me he had got a cancer; he was a fine healthy strong-
looking man; he told me he dreaded having an operation performed, but his father died of the same complaint, and that his
father was sweeper to King George the Second."—(*Lords'*
Minutes, p. 84.)

"What is the nature of the particular diseases? The diseases that
we particularly noticed, to which they were subject, were of a
cancerous description.—In what part? The scrotum in particular, &c.—Did you ever hear of cases of that description that
were fatal? No, I do not think them as being altogether fatal,
unless they will not submit to the operation; they have such a
dread of the operation that they will not submit to it, and if
they do not let it be perfectly removed, they will be liable to the
return of it.—To what cause do you attribute that disease? I
think it begins from a want of care: the scrotum being in so
many folds or crevices, the soot lodges in them and creates an
itching, and I conceive that, by scratching it and tearing it, the
soot gets in and creates the irritability; which disease we know
by the name of the chimney-sweeper's cancer, and is always
lectured upon separately as a distinct disease.—Then the Committee understands that the physicians who are entrusted with
the care and management of those hospitals think that disease of
such common occurrence, that it is necessary to make it a part
of surgical education? Most assuredly; I remember Mr. Cline
and Mr. Cooper were particular on that subject.—Without an
operation there is no cure? I conceive not; I conceive without the
operation it is death; for cancers are of that nature that unless
you extirpate them entirely, they will never be cured."—(*Com-*
mons' Rep. pp. 60, 61.)

In addition to the life they lead as chimney sweepers, is super-added the occupation of nightmen.

"(*By a Lord.*) Is it generally the custom that many masters are likewise nightmen? Yes; I forgot that circumstance, which is very grievous; I have been tied round the middle and let down several privies, for the purpose of fetching watches and such things; it is generally made the practice to take the smallest boy, to let him through the hole without taking up the seat, and to paddle about there until he finds it; they do not take a big boy, because it disturbs the seat."—(*Lords' Minutes,* p. 38.)

The bed of these poor little wretches is often the soot they have swept in the day.

"How are the boys generally lodged; where do they sleep at night? Some masters may be better than others, but I know I have slept on the soot that was gathered in the day myself.— Where do boys generally sleep? Never on a bed; I never slept on a bed myself while I was apprentice.—Do they sleep in cellars? Yes, very often; I have slept in the cellar myself on the sacks I took out.—What had you to cover you? The same.— Had you any pillow? No further than my breeches and jacket under my head.—How were you clothed? When I was apprentice we had a pair of leather breeches and a small flannel jacket. —Any shoes and stockings? Oh dear no; no stockings.—Had you any other clothes for Sunday? Sometimes we had an old bit of a jacket, that we might wash out ourselves, and a shirt."— (*Lords' Minutes,* p. 40.)

Girls are occasionally employed as chimney sweepers.

"Another circumstance, which has not been mentioned to the Committee, is, that there are several little girls employed; there are two of the name of Morgan at Windsor, daughters of the chimney sweeper who is employed to sweep the chimneys of the Castle; another instance at Uxbridge, and at Brighton, and at Whitechapel (which was some years ago), and at Hadley near Barnet, and Witham in Essex, and elsewhere."—(*Commons' Report,* p. 71.)

Another peculiar danger to which chimney sweepers are exposed, is the rottenness of the pots at the top of chimneys;—for they must ascend to the very summit, and show their brushes above them, or there is no proof that the work is properly completed. These chimney-pots, from their exposed situation, are very subject to decay; and when the poor little wretch has worked his way up to the top, pot and boy give way together and are both shivered to atoms. There are many instances of this in the evidence before both Houses. When they outgrow the power of going up a chimney, they are fit for nothing else. The miseries they have suffered lead to nothing. They are not only enormous, but unprofitable; having suffered in what is called the happiest part of life, every misery which a human being can suffer, they are then cast out to rob and steal, and given up to the law.

Not the least of their miseries, while their trial endures, is their exposure to cold. It will easily be believed that much money is not expended on the clothes of a poor boy stolen from his parents, or sold by them for a few shillings, and constantly occupied in dirty work. Yet the nature of their occupations renders chimney sweepers peculiarly susceptible of cold. And as chimneys must be swept very early, at four or five o'clock of a winter morning, the poor boys are shivering at the door, and attempting by repeated ringings to rouse the profligate footman; but the more they ring, the more the footman does not come.

"Do they go out in the winter time without stockings? Oh yes. —Always? I never saw one go out *with* stockings; I have known masters make their boys pull off their leggings, and cut off the feet, to keep their feet warm when they have chilblains.—Are chimney sweepers' boys peculiarly subject to chilblains? Yes; I believe it is owing to the weather: they often go out at two or three in the morning, and their shoes are generally very bad.— Do they go out at that hour at Christmas? Yes; a man will have twenty jobs at four, and twenty more at five or six.—Are chimneys generally swept much about Christmas time? Yes; they are in general; it is left to the Christmas week.—Do you suppose it is frequent that, in the Christmas week, boys are out from three o'clock in the morning to nine or ten? Yes, further than that; I have known that a boy has been only in and out again directly all day till five o'clock in the evening.—Do you consider the journeymen and masters treat those boys generally with greater cruelty than other apprentices in other trades are treated? They do, most horrid and shocking."—(*Lords' Minutes,* p. 33.)

The following is the reluctant evidence of a master.

"At what hour in the morning did your boys go out upon their employment? According to orders.—At any time? To be sure; suppose a nobleman wished to have his chimney done before

four or five o'clock in the morning, it was done, or how were
the servants to get their things done?—Supposing you had an
order to attend at four o'clock in the morning in the month of
December, you sent your boy? I was generally with him, or had
a careful follower with him.—Do you think those early hours
beneficial for him? I do: and I have heard that 'early to bed
and early to rise, is the way to be healthy, wealthy, and wise.'—
Did they always get in as soon as they knocked? No; it would
be pleasant to the profession if they could.—How long did they
wait? *Till the servants please to rise.*—How long might that be?
According how heavy they were to sleep.—How long was that?
It is impossible to say; ten minutes at one house, and twenty at
another.—Perhaps half an hour? *We cannot see in the dark how
the minutes go.*—Do you think it healthy to let them stand
there twenty minutes at four o'clock in the morning in the winter time? He has a cloth to wrap himself in like a mantle, and
keep himself warm."—(*Lords' Minutes,* pp. 138, 139.)

We must not forget sore eyes. Soot lodges on their eyelids, produces irritability, which requires friction; and the friction of dirty
hands of course increases the disease. The greater proportion of
chimney sweepers are in consequence blear-eyed. The boys are
very small, but they are compelled to carry heavy loads of soot.

"Are you all lame yourself? No; but I am 'knapped-kneed'
with carrying heavy loads when I was an apprentice.—That was
the occasion of it? It was.—In general, are persons employed
in your trade either stunted or knock-kneed by carrying heavy
loads during their childhood? It is owing to their masters a great
deal; and when they climb a great deal it makes them weak."—
(*Commons' Report,* p. 58.)

In climbing a chimney, the great hold is by the knees and elbows. A young child of six or seven years old, working with knees
and elbows against hard bricks, soon rubs off the skin from these
bony projections, and is forced to climb high chimneys with raw
and bloody knees and elbows.

"Are the boys' knees and elbows rendered sore when they first
begin to learn to climb? Yes, they are, and pieces out of them.
—Is that almost generally the case? It is; *there is not one out
of twenty who is not;* and they are sure to take the scars to their
grave: I have some now.—Are they usually compelled to continue climbing while those sores are open? *Yes;* the way they
use to make them hard is that way.—Might not this severity

be obviated by the use of pads in learning to climb? Yes; but they consider in the business, learning a boy, that he is never thoroughly learned until the boy's knees are hard after being sore; then they consider it necessary to put a pad on, from seeing the boys have bad knees; the children generally walk stiff-kneed.—Is it usual among the chimney sweepers to teach their boys to learn by means of pads? No; they learn them with nearly naked knees.—Is it done in one instance in twenty? No, nor one in fifty."—(*Lords' Minutes,* p. 32.)

According to the humanity of the master, the soot remains upon the bodies of the children, unwashed off, for any time from a week to a year.

"Are the boys generally washed regularly? No, unless they wash themselves.—Did not your master take care you were washed? No.—Not once in three months? No, *not once a year.*—Did not he find you soap? No; I can take my oath on the Bible that he never found me one piece of soap during the time I was apprentice."—(*Lords' Minutes,* p. 41.)

The life of these poor little wretches is so miserable, that they often lie sulking in the flues, unwilling to come out.

"Did you ever see severity used to boys that were not obstinate and perverse? Yes.—Very often? Yes, very often. The boys are rather obstinate; some of them are; some of them will get halfway up the chimney, and will not go any further, and then the journeymen will swear at them to come down, or go on; but the boys are too frightened to come down; they halloo out, we cannot get up, and they are afraid to come down; sometimes they will send for another boy, and drag them down; sometimes get up to the top of the chimney, and throw down water, and drive them down; then, when they get them down, they will begin to drag, or beat, or kick them about the house; then, when they get home, the master will beat them all round the kitchen afterwards, and give them no breakfast perhaps."—(*Lords' Minutes,* pp. 9, 10.)

When a chimney boy has done sufficient work for the master, he must work for the man; and he thus becomes for several hours after his morning's work a perquisite to the journeyman.

"It is frequently the perquisite of the journeyman, when the first labour of the day on account of the master is finished, to 'call the streets,' in search of employment on their own account, with the apprentices, whose labour is thus unreasonably extended, and whose limbs are weakened and distorted by the weights which they have to carry, and by the distance which they have to walk. John Lawless says, 'I have known a boy to climb from twenty to thirty chimneys for his master in the morning; he has then been sent out instantly with the journeyman, who has kept him out till three or four o'clock, till he has accumulated from six to eight bushels of soot.' "—(*Lords' Report,* p. 24.)

The sight of a little chimney sweeper often excites pity; and they have small presents made to them at the houses where they sweep. These benevolent alms are disposed of in the following manner:—

"Do the boys receive little presents of money from people often in your trade? Yes, it is in general the custom.—Are they allowed to keep that for their own use? Not the whole of it,—the journeymen take what they think proper. The journeymen *are entitled to half* by the master's orders; and whatever a boy may get, if two boys and one journeyman are sent to a large house to sweep a number of chimneys, and after they have done, there should be a shilling, or eighteen-pence given to the boys, the journeyman has his full half, and the two boys in general have the other.—Is it usual or customary for the journeyman to play at chuck farthing or other games with the boys? Frequently.— Do they win the money from the boys? Frequently; the children give their money to the journeymen to screen for them.—What do you mean by screening? Such a thing as sifting the soot. The child is tired, and he says, 'Jem, I will give you twopence if you will sift my share of the soot'; there is sometimes twenty or thirty bushels to sift.—Do you think the boys retain one quarter of that given them for their own use? No."—(*Lords' Minutes,* p. 35.)

To this most horrible list of calamities is to be added the dreadful deaths by which chimney sweepers are often destroyed. Of these we once thought of giving two examples; one from London, the other from our own town of Edinburgh: but we confine ourselves to the latter.

"James Thompson, chimney sweeper.—One day in the beginning of June, witness and panel (that is, the master, the party accused), had been sweeping vents together. About *four* o'clock in the afternoon, the panel proposed to go to Albany Street, where the panel's brother was cleaning a vent, with the assistance of Fraser, whom he had borrowed from the panel for the occasion. When witness and panel got to the house in Albany Street, they found Fraser, who had gone up the vent, *between eleven and twelve* o'clock, not yet come down. On entering the house they found a mason making a hole in the wall. Panel said, what was he doing? I suppose he has taken a lazy fit. The panel called to the boy, 'What are you doing? what's keeping you?' The boy answered that he could not come. The panel worked a long while, sometimes persuading him, sometimes threatening and swearing at the boy, to get him down. Panel then said, 'I will go to a hardware shop, and get a barrel of gunpowder, and blow you and the vent to the devil, if you do not come down.' Panel then began to slap at the wall—witness then went up a ladder, and spoke to the boy through a small hole in the wall previously made by the mason—but the boy did not answer. Panel's brother told witness to come down, as the boy's master knew best how to manage him. Witness then threw off his jacket, and put a handkerchief about his head, and said to the panel, 'Let me go up the chimney to see what's keeping him.' The panel made no answer, but pushed witness away from the chimney, and continued bullying the boy. At this time the panel was standing on the grate, so that witness could not go up the chimney; witness then said to panel's brother, 'There is no use for me here,' meaning that panel would not permit him to use his services. He prevented the mason making the hole larger, saying, Stop, and I'll bring him down in five minutes' time. Witness then put on his jacket, and continued an hour in the room, *during all which time, the panel continued bullying the boy.* Panel then desired witness to go to Reid's house to get the loan of his boy Alison. Witness went to Reid's house, and asked Reid to come and speak to panel's brother. Reid asked if panel was there? Witness answered he was; Reid said he would send his boy to the panel, but not to the panel's brother. Witness and Reid went to Albany Street; and when they got into the room, panel took his head out of the chimney and asked Reid if he would lend him his boy; Reid agreed: witness then returned to Reid's house for his boy, and Reid called after him, 'Fetch down a set of ropes with you.' By this time witness had been ten minutes in the room, during which time panel was swearing, and asking, 'What's keeping you, you scoundrel?' When witness returned with the boy and ropes, Reid took hold of the rope, and, having loosed it, gave Alison one end, and directed him to go up the chimney, saying, 'Do not go farther than his feet, and when you get there fasten it to his foot.' Panel said nothing all this time. Alison went up, and having fastened the rope, Reid desired him to come down; Reid took the rope and pulled, but did not bring down the boy; the rope broke! Alison was sent up again with the other end of the rope, which was fastened to the boy's foot. When Reid was pulling the rope, panel said, 'You have not the strength of a cat'; he took the rope into his own hands, *pulling as strong as he could.* Having pulled *about a quarter of an hour,* panel and Reid fastened the rope round a crow bar, which they applied to the wall as a lever, and both *pulled with all their strength for about a quarter of an hour longer,* when it broke. During this time witness heard the boy cry, and say, 'My God Almighty!' Panel said, 'If I had you here, I would God Almighty you.' Witness thought the cries were in agony. The master of the house brought a new piece of rope, and the panel's brother spliced an eye on it. Reid expressed a wish to have it fastened on both thighs, to have greater purchase. Alison was sent up for this purpose, but came down, and said he could not get it fastened. Panel then began to slap at the wall. After striking a long while at the wall he got out a large stone; he then put in his head and called to Fraser, 'Do you hear, you sir?' but got no answer: he then put in his hands, and drew down deceased's breeches. He then came down from the ladder. At this time the panel was in a state of perspiration: he sat down on a stool, and the master of the house gave him a dram. Witness did not hear panel make any remarks as to the situation of the boy Fraser. Witness thinks, that, from panel's appearance, he knew the boy was dead."—(*Commons' Report,* pp. 136-138.)

We have been thus particular in stating the case of the chimney sweepers, and in founding it upon the basis of facts, that we may make an answer to those profligate persons who are always ready to fling an air of ridicule upon the labours of humanity, because they are desirous that what they have not virtue to do themselves, should appear to be foolish and romantic when done by others. A still higher degree of depravity than this, is to want every sort of compassion for human misery, when it is accompanied by filth, poverty, and ignorance,—to regulate humanity by the income tax, and to deem the bodily wretchedness and the dirty tears of the poor a fit subject for pleasantry and contempt. We should have been loth to believe, that such deep-seated and disgusting immorality existed in these days; but the notice of it is forced upon us. Nor must we pass over a set of marvellously weak gentlemen, who discover democracy and revolution in every effort to improve the condition of the lower orders, and to take off a little of the load of misery from those points where it presses the hardest. Such are the men into whose heart Mrs. Fry has struck the deepest terror,—who abhor Mr. Bentham and his penitentiary; Mr. Bennet and his hulks; Sir James Mackintosh and his bloodless assizes; Mr. Tooke and his sweeping machines,—and every other human being who is great and good enough to sacrifice his quiet to his love for his fellow-creatures. Certainly we admit that humanity is sometimes the veil of ambition or of faction; but we have no doubt that there are a great many excellent persons to whom it is misery to see misery, and pleasure to lessen it; and who, by calling the public attention to the worst cases, and by giving birth to judicious legislative enactments for their improvement, have made, and are making, the world somewhat happier than they found it. Upon these principles we join hands with the friends of the chimney sweepers, and most heartily wish for the diminution of their numbers, and the limitation of their trade.

We are thoroughly convinced there are many respectable master chimney sweepers; though we suspect their numbers have been increased by the alarm which their former tyranny excited, and by the severe laws made for their coercion: but even with good masters the trade is miserable,—with bad ones it is not to be endured; and the evidence already quoted shows us how many of that character are to be met with in the occupation of sweeping chimneys.

After all, we must own that it was quite right to throw out the bill for prohibiting the sweeping of chimneys by boys—because humanity is a modern invention; and there are many chimneys in old houses which cannot possibly be swept in any other manner. But the construction of chimneys should be attended to in some new building act; and the treatment of boys be watched over with the most severe jealousy of the law. Above all, those who have chimneys accessible to machinery, should encourage the use of machines, and not think it beneath their dignity to take a little trouble, in order to do a great deal of good. We should have been very glad to have seconded the views of the Climbing Society *, and to have pleaded for the complete abolition of climbing boys, if we could conscientiously have done so. But such a measure, we are convinced from the evidence, could not be carried into execution without great injury to property, and great increased risk of

_____

* *Account of the Proceedings of the Society for superseding the Necessity of Climbing Boys*. Baldwin, &c. London. 1816.

fire. The Lords have investigated the matter with the greatest patience, humanity, and good sense; and they do not venture, in their Report, to recommend to the House the abolition of climbing boys.

"LOCKING IN" ON RAILWAYS

LETTER I

To the Editor of the Morning Chronicle.

SIR,

IT falls to my lot to travel frequently on the Great Western Railway, and I request permission, through the medium of your able and honest journal, to make a complaint against the directors of that company.

It is the custom on that railway to lock the passengers in on both sides—a custom which, in spite of the dreadful example at Paris, I have every reason to believe they mean to continue without any relaxation.

In the course of a long life I have no recollection of any accident so shocking as that on the Paris railway—a massacre so sudden, so full of torment—death at the moment of pleasure—death aggravated by all the amazement, fear, and pain which can be condensed into the last moments of existence.

Who can say that the same scene may not be acted over again on the Great Western Railroad? That in the midst of their tunnel of three miles' length the same scene of slaughter and combustion may not scatter dismay and alarm over the whole country?

It seems to me perfectly monstrous that a board of ten or twelve monopolists can read such a description, and say to the public, "You must run your chance of being burnt or mutilated. We have arranged our plan upon the locking-in system, and we shall not incur the risk and expense of changing it."

The plea is, that rash or drunken people will attempt to get out of the carriages which are not locked, and that this measure really originates from attention to the safety of the public; so that the lives of two hundred persons who are not drunk and are not rash, are to be endangered for the half-yearly preservation of some idiot, upon whose body the coroner is to sit, and over whom the sudden-death man is to deliver his sermon against the directors.

The very fact of locking the doors will be a frequent source of accidents. Mankind, whatever the directors may think of that process, are impatient of combustion. The Paris accident will never be forgotten. The passengers will attempt to escape through the windows, and ten times more of mischief will be done than if they had been left to escape by the doors in the usual manner.

It is not only the locking of the doors which is to be deprecated; but the effects which it has upon the imagination. Women, old people, and the sick, are all forced to travel by the railroad; and for 200 miles they live under the recollection not only of impending danger, but under the knowledge that escape is impossible—a journey comes to be contemplated with horror. Men cannot persuade the females of their family to travel by the railroad; it is inseparably connected with abominable tyranny and perilous imprisonment.

Why does the necessity of locking both doors exist only on the Great Western? Why is one of the doors left open on all other railways?

The public have a right to every advantage under permitted monopoly which they would enjoy under free competition; and they are unjust to themselves if they do not insist upon this right. If there were two parallel railways, the one locking you in, and the other not, is there the smallest doubt which would carry away all the business? Can there be any hesitation in which timid women, drunken men, sages, philosophers, bishops, and all combustible beings, would place themselves.

I very much doubt the legality of locking doors, and refusing to open them. I arrive at a station where others are admitted; but I am not suffered to get out, though perhaps at the point of death. In all other positions of life there is egress where there is ingress. Man is universally the master of his own body, except he chooses to go from Paddington to Bridgewater: there only the Habeas Corpus is refused.

Nothing, in fact, can be more utterly silly or mistaken than this over-officious care of the public; as if every man who was not a railway director was a child or a fool. But why stop here? Why are not strait-waistcoats used? Why is not the accidental traveller strapped down? Why do contusion and fracture still remain physically possible?

Is not this extreme care of the public new? When first mail coaches began to travel twelve miles an hour, the *outsides* (if I remember rightly) were never tied to the roof. In packets, landsmen are not locked into the cabin to prevent them from tumbling overboard. This affectionate nonsense prevails only on the Great Western. It is there only that men, women, and children (seeking the only mode of transit which remains) are by these tender-hearted monopolists immediately committed to their locomotive prisons. Nothing can, in fact, be so absurd as all this officious zeal. It is the duty of the directors to take all reasonable precautions to warn the public of danger—to make it clear that there is no negligence on the part of the railroad directors; and then, this done, if a fool-hardy person choose to expose himself to danger, so be it. Fools there will be on roads of iron and on roads of gravel, and they must suffer for their folly; but why are Socrates, Solon, and Solomon to be locked up?

But is all this, which appears so philanthropical, mere philanthropy? Does not the locking of the doors save servants and policemen? Does not economy mingle with these benevolent feelings? Is it to save a few fellow-creatures, or a few pounds, that the children of the West are to be hermetically sealed in the locomotives? I do not say it is so; but I say it deserves a very serious examination whether it be so or not. Great and heavy is the sin of the directors of this huge monopoly, if they repeat upon their own iron the tragedy of Paris, in order to increase their dividends a few shillings per cent.

The country has (perhaps inevitably) given way to this great monopoly. Nothing can make it tolerable for a moment but the most severe and watchful jealousy of the manner in which its powers are exercised. We shall have tyrannical rules, vexatious rules, ill temper, pure folly, and meddling and impertinent paternity. It is the absolute duty of Lord Ripon and Mr. Gladstone (if the directors prove themselves to be so inadequate to the new situation in which they are placed) to restrain and direct them by law; and if these two gentlemen are afraid of the responsibility of such laws, they are deficient in the moral courage which their office requires, and the most important interests of the public are neglected.

May 21, 1842.

LETTER II

To the Editor of the Morning Chronicle.

SIR,

SINCE the letter upon railroads, which you were good enough to insert in your paper, I have had some conversation with two gentlemen officially connected with the Great Western. Though nothing could be more courteous than their manner, nor more intelligible than their arguments, I remain unshaken as to the necessity of keeping the doors open.

There is, in the first place, the effect of imagination, the idea that all escape is impossible, that (let what will happen) you must sit quiet in first class No. 2, whether they are pounding you into a jam, or burning you into a cinder, or crumbling you into a human powder. These excellent directors, versant in wood and metal, seem to require that the imagination should be sent by some other conveyance, and that only loads of unimpassioned, unintellectual flesh and blood should be darted along on the Western rail; whereas, the female *homo* is a screaming, parturient, interjectional, hysterical animal, whose delicacy and timidity, monopolists (even much as it may surprise them) must be taught to consult. The female, in all probability, never would jump out; but she thinks she may jump out when she pleases; and this is intensely comfortable.

There are two sorts of dangers which hang over railroads. The one retail dangers, where individuals only are concerned; the other, wholesale dangers, where the whole train, or a considerable part of it, is put in jeopardy. For the first danger there is a remedy in the prudence of individuals; for the second, there is none. No man need be drunk, nor need he jump out when the carriage is in motion; but in the present state of science it is impossible to guard effectually against the fracture of the axle-tree, or the explosion of the engine; and if the safety of the one party cannot be consulted but by the danger of the other, if the foolish cannot be restrained but by the unjust incarceration of the wise, the prior consideration is due to those who have not the remedy for the evil in their own hands.

But the truth is—and so (after a hundred monopolising experiments on public patience) the railroad directors will find it—there can be no other dependence for the safety of the public than the care which every human being is inclined to take of his own life and limbs. Everything beyond this is the mere lazy tyranny of monopoly, which makes no distinction between human beings and brown paper parcels. If riding were a monopoly, as travelling in carriages is now become, there are many gentlemen whom I see riding in the Park upon such false principles, that I am sure the cantering and galloping directors would strap them, in the ardour of their affection, to the saddle, padlock them to the stirrups, or compel them to ride behind a policeman of the stable; and nothing but a motion from O'Brien, or an order from Gladstone, could release them.

Let the company stick up all sorts of cautions and notices within their carriages and without; but, after that, no doors locked. If one door is allowed to be locked, the other will soon be so too; there is no other security to the public than absolute prohibition of the practice. The directors and agents of the Great Western are individually excellent men; but the moment men meet in public boards, they cease to be collectively excellent. The fund of morality becomes less, as the individual contributors increase in number. I do not accuse such respectable men of any wilful violation of truth, but the memoirs which they are about to present will be, without the scrupulous cross-examination of a committee of the House of Commons, mere waste paper.

But the most absurd of all legislative enactments is this hemiplegian law—an act of Parliament to protect one side of the body and not the other. If the wheel comes off on the right, the open door is uppermost, and every one is saved. If, from any sudden avalanche on the road, the carriage is prostrated to the left, the locked door is uppermost, all escape is impossible, and the railroad martyrdom begins.

Leave me to escape in the best way I can, as the fire-offices very kindly permit me to do. I know very well the danger of getting out on the off-side; but escape is the affair of a moment; suppose a train to have passed at that moment, I know I am safe from any other trains for twenty minutes or half an hour; and if I do get out on the off-side, I do not remain in the valley of death between the two trains, but am over to the opposite bank in an instant—only half-roasted, or merely browned, certainly not done enough for the Great Western directors.

On Saturday morning last, the wheel of the public carriage, in which a friend of mine was travelling, began to smoke, but was pacified by several buckets of water, and proceeded. After five more miles, the whole carriage was full of smoke, the train was with difficulty stopped, and the flagrant vehicle removed. The axle was nearly in two, and in another mile would have been severed.

Railroad travelling is a delightful improvement of human life. Man is become a bird; he can fly longer and quicker than a Solan goose. The mamma rushes sixty miles in two hours to the aching finger of her conjugating and declining grammar boy. The early Scotchman scratches himself in the morning mists of the North, and has his porridge in Piccadilly before the setting sun. The Puseyite priest, after a rush of 100 miles, appears with his little volume of nonsense at the breakfast of his bookseller. Everything is near, everything is immediate—time, distance, and delay are abolished. But, though charming and fascinating as all this is, we must not shut our eyes to the price we shall pay for it. There will be every three or four years some dreadful massacre—whole trains will be hurled down a precipice, and 200 or 300 persons will be killed on the spot. There will be every now and then a great combustion of human bodies, as there has been at Paris; then all the newspapers up in arms—a thousand regulations, forgotten as soon as the directors dare—loud screams of the velocity whistle—monopoly locks and bolts, as before.

The locking plea of directors is philanthrophy; and I admit that to guard men from the commission of moral evil is as philanthropical as to prevent physical suffering. There is, I allow, a strong propensity in mankind to travel on railroads without paying; and to lock mankind in till they have completed their share of the contract is benevolent, because it guards the species from degrading and immoral conduct, but to burn or crush a whole train merely to prevent a few immoral insides from not paying, is I hope a little more than Ripon or Gladstone will bear.

We have been, up to this point, very careless of our railway regulations. The first person of rank who is killed will put everything in order, and produce a code of the most careful rules. I hope it will not be one of the bench of bishops; but should it be so destined, let the burnt bishop—the unwilling Latimer—remember that, however painful gradual concoction by fire may be, his death will produce unspeakable benefit to the public. Even Sodor and Man will be better than nothing. From that moment the bad effects of the monopoly are destroyed; no more fatal deference to the directors; no despotic incarceration, no barbarous inattention to the anatomy and physiology of the human body; no commitment to locomotive prisons with warrant. We shall then find it possible

"Voyager libre sans mourir."

June 7, 1842.

MODERN CHANGES

"The good of ancient times let others state,
I think it lucky I was born so late."

IT is of some importance at what period a man is born. A young man, alive at this period, hardly knows to what improvements of human life he has been introduced; and I would bring before his notice the following eighteen changes which have taken place in

England since I first began to breathe in it the breath of life—a period amounting now to nearly seventy-three years.

Gas was unknown: I groped about the streets of London in all but the utter darkness of a twinkling oil lamp, under the protection of watchmen in their grand climacteric, and exposed to every species of depredation and insult.

I have been nine hours in sailing from Dover to Calais before the invention of steam. It took me nine hours to go from Taunton to Bath before the invention of railroads, and I now go in six hours from Taunton to London! In going from Taunton to Bath, I suffered between 10,000 and 12,000 severe contusions, before stone-breaking Macadam was born.

I paid 15*l.* in a single year for repairs of carriage-springs on the pavement of London; and I now glide without noise or fracture, on wooden pavements.

I can walk, by the assistance of the police, from one end of London to the other, without molestation; or, if tired, get into a cheap and active cab, instead of those cottages on wheels, which the hackney coaches were at the beginning of my life.

I had no umbrella! They were little used, and very dear. There were no waterproof hats, and *my* hat has often been reduced by rains into its primitive pulp.

I could not keep my smallclothes in their proper place, for braces were unknown. If I had the gout, there was no colchicum. If I was bilious, there was no calomel. If I was attacked by ague, there was no quinine. There were filthy coffee-houses instead of elegant clubs. Game could not be bought. Quarrels about uncommuted tithes were endless. The corruption of Parliament, before Reform, infamous. There were no banks to receive the savings of the poor. The Poor Laws were gradually sapping the vitals of the country; and whatever miseries I suffered, I had no post to whisk my complaints for a single penny to the remotest corners of the empire; and yet, in spite of all these privations, I lived on quietly, and am now ashamed that I was not more discontented, and utterly surprised that all these changes and inventions did not occur two centuries ago.

I forgot to add, that as the basket of stage coaches, in which luggage was then carried, had no springs, your clothes were rubbed all to pieces; and that even in the best society one-third of the gentlemen at least were always drunk.

PART IV

Letter to FRANCIS JEFFREY

January 30th, 1806

My dear Jeffrey,

The change in administration (tho' I am not ordinarily a great politician) has made me extremely happy both because I believe the War will not be protracted longer than honor and safety require, and because the Law and the Church will be refreshed by the elevation of men of Whig principles under which appellation I find as I see more of the World all the truly honest and able men (who are of any party at all) ranging themselves. I cannot describe to you how disgusted I am by the set of canting rascals who have crept into all kinds of power during the profligate reign of Mr. Pitt, who patronised hypocrisy, folly, fraud and anything else which contributed to his power—peace to his ashes and from them, but whatever feelings and proprieties it violates I must say he was one of the most luminous eloquent blunderers with which any people was ever afflicted. For 15 years I have found my income dwindling away under his eloquence, and regularly in every Session of Parliament he has charmed every classical feeling and stript me of every guinea I possess. At the close of every brilliant display an expedition failed or a Kingdom fell, and by the time that his Style had gained the summit of perfection Europe was degraded to the lowest abyss of Misery. God send us a stammerer, a tongueless man, let Moses come for this heaven-born Aaron has failed. . . .

Letter to JOHN ALLEN

March 10th, 1814

Dear Allen,

I cannot at all enter into your feelings about the Bourbons, nor can I attend to so remote an evil as the encouragement of super-

321

stitious attachment to kings, when the present evil of a military Monarchy, or of thirty years more of war, is before my eyes. I want to get rid of this great disturber of human happiness, and I scarcely know any price too great to effect it. If you were sailing from Alicant to Aleppo in a storm, and if (after the sailors had held up the image of a Saint and prayed to it) the storm were to abate, you would be more sorry for the encoragement of superstition than rejoiced for the preservation of your life,—and so would every other man born, and bred in Edinburgh.

My view of the matter would be much shorter and coarser; I should be so glad to find myself alive that I should not care a farthing if the storm had generated a thousand new, and revived as many old Saints. How can any man stop in the midst of the stupendous joy of getting rid of Buonaparte, and prophesy the little piddling evils that will result from restoring the Bourbons? Nor am I quite certain that I don't wish Paris burnt and France laid waste by Cossacks for revenge, and for security. The most important of all objects is the independence of Europe: it has been twice very nearly destroyed by the French; it is menaced from no other quarter; and the people must be identified with their sovereign. There is no help for it; it will teach them in future to hang kings who set up for conquerors. I will not believe that the Bourbons have no party in France. My only knowledge of politics is from the York paper; yet nothing shall convince me that the people are not heartily tired of Buonaparte, and ardently wish for the cessation of the conscription; that is, for the Bourbons. . . .

Letter to LORD GREY

Foston, York, Dec. 3rd, 1819

My dear Lord Grey,

I entirely agree with you in that mere force alone without some attempts at conciliation will not do. Readers are fourfold in number compared with what they were before the beginning of the French war; and demagogues will of course address to them every species of disaffection. As the violence of restraint increases there will be private presses as there are private stills. Juries will acquit, being themselves Jacobins. It is possible for able men to do a great deal of mischief in libels, which it is extremely difficult to punish as libels; and the worst of it all is that a considerable portion of what these rascals say is so very true. Their remedies are worse than their evils; but when they state to the people how they are bought and sold and the abuses entailed upon the country by so corrupted a Parliament it is not easy to answer them, or to hang them. What I want to see the State do is to lessen in these sad times some of their numerous enemies. Why not do something for the Catholics and scratch them off the list? Then come the Protestant Dissenters. Then of measures,—a mitigation of the game-laws—commutation of tithes—granting to such towns as Birmingham and Manchester the seats in Parliament taken from the rottenness of Cornwall—revision of the Penal Code—sale of the Crown lands—sacrifice of the Droits of Admiralty against a new war;—anything that would show the Government to the people in some other attitude than that of taxing, punishing, and restraining. I believe what Tierney said to be strictly true that the House of Commons is falling into contempt with the people. Democracy has many more friends among tradesmen and persons of that class of life than is known or supposed commonly. I believe the feeling is most rapidly increasing and that Parliament in two or three years' time will meet under much greater circumstances of terror than those under which it is at present assembled. . . .

Letter to LADY GREY

Foston, York, Feb. 19th, 1823

My dear Lady Grey,

In seeing my handwriting again so soon, you will say that your attack upon me for my indisposition to letter-writing has been more successful than you wished it to be; but I cannot help saying a word about war.

For God's sake, do not drag me into another war! I am worn down, and worn out, with crusading and defending Europe, and protecting mankind; I *must* think a little of myself. I am sorry for the Spaniards—I am sorry for the Greeks—I deplore the fate of the Jews; the people of the Sandwich Islands are groaning under the most detestable tyranny; Bagdad is oppressed; I do not like the present state of the Delta; Thibet is not comfortable. Am I to fight for all these people? The world is bursting with sin and sorrow. Am I to be champion of the Decalogue, and to be eternally raising fleets and armies to make all men good and happy? We have just done saving Europe, and I am afraid the consequence will be, that we shall cut each other's throats. No war, dear Lady Grey!—no eloquence; but apathy, selfishness, common sense, arithmetic; I beseech you, secure Lord Grey's swords and pistols, as the housekeeper did Don Quixote's armour. If there is another war, life will not be worth having. I will go to war with the King of Denmark if he is impertinent to you, or does any injury to Howick; but for no other cause.

"May the vengeance of Heaven" overtake all the Legitimates of Verona! but, in the present state of rent and taxes, they must be *left* to the vengeance of Heaven. I allow fighting in such a cause to be a luxury; but the business of a prudent, sensible man, is to guard against luxury. . . .

Letter to MR. SWING

The wool your coat is made of is spun by machinery, and this machinery makes your coat two or three shillings cheaper—perhaps six or seven. Your white hat is made by machinery at half price. The coals you burn are pulled out of the pit by machinery, and are sold to you much cheaper than they could be if they were pulled out by hand. You do not complain of *these* machines, because they do you good, though they throw many artisans out of work. But what right have you to object to fanning machines, which make bread cheaper to the artisans, and to avail yourselves of *other* machines which make manufactures cheaper to you?

If all machinery were abolished, every thing would be so dear that you would be ten times worse off than you now are. Poor people's cloth would get up to a guinea a yard. Hats could not be sold for less than eighteen shillings. Coals would be three shillings per hundred. It would be quite impossible for a poor man to obtain any comfort.

If you begin to object to machinery in farming, you may as well object to a plow, because it employs fewer men than a spade. You may object to a harrow, because it employs fewer men than a rake. You may object even to a spade, because it employs fewer men than fingers and sticks, with which savages scratch the ground in Otaheite. If you expect manufacturers to turn against machinery, look at the consequence. They may succeed, perhaps, in driving machinery out of the town they live in, but they often drive the manufacturer *out* of the town also. He sets up his trade in some distant part of the country, gets new men, and the disciples of Swing are left to starve in the scene of their violence and folly. In this way the lace manufacture traveled in the time of Ludd, Swing's grandfather, from Nottingham to Tiverton. Suppose a free importation of corn to be allowed, as it ought to be, and will be. If you will not allow farmers to grow corn here as cheap as they can, more corn will come from America; for every thrashing-machine that is destroyed, more *Americans* will be employed, not more Englishmen.

Swing! Swing! you are a stout fellow, but you are a bad adviser. The law is up, and the Judge is coming. Fifty persons in Kent are already transported, and will see their wives and children no more. Sixty persons will be hanged in Hampshire. There are two hundred for trial in Wiltshire—all scholars of Swing! I am no farmer: I have not a machine bigger than a pepper-mill. I am a sincere friend to the poor, and I think every man should live by his labour: but it cuts me to the very heart to see honest husbandmen perishing by that worst of all machines, the gallows—under the guidance of that most fatal of all leaders—Swing!

Dec. 8, 1830

Four Speeches on the Reform Bill *

I.

Mr. Bailiff,—This is the greatest measure which has ever been before Parliament in my time, and the most pregnant with good or

---

* I was a sincere friend to Reform; I am so still. It was a great deal too violent—but the only justification is, that you cannot reform as you wish, by degrees; you must avail yourself of the few opportunities that present themselves. The Reform carried, it became the business of every honest man to turn it to good, and to see that the people (drunk with their new power) did not ruin our ancient institutions. We have been in considerable danger, and that danger is not over. What alarms me most is the large price paid by both parties for popular favour. The yeomanry were put down: nothing could be more grossly absurd—the people were rising up against the poor laws, and such an excellent and permanent force was abolished because they were not deemed a proper force to deal with popular insurrections. You may just as well object to put out a fire with pond water because pump water is better for the purpose: I say, put out the fire with the first water you can get;—but the truth is, Radicals don't like armed yeomen: they have an ugly homicide appearance. Again,—a million of revenue is given up in the nonsensical penny-post scheme, to please my old, excellent, and universally dissentient friend, Noah Warburton. I admire the Whig Ministry, and think they have done more good things than all the ministries since the Revolution; but these concessions are sad and un evil to the country; and though I seldom meddle with political meetings, I could not reconcile it to my conscience to be absent from this.

Every year for this half century the question of Reform has been pressing upon us, till it has swelled up at last into this great and awful combination; so that almost every City and every Borough in England are at this moment assembled for the same purpose, and are doing the same thing we are doing. It damps the ostentation of argument and mitigates the pain of doubt, to believe (as I believe) that the measure is inevitable; the consequences may be good or bad, but done it must be; I defy the most determined enemy of popular influence, either now, or a little time from now, to prevent a Reform in Parliament. Some years ago, by timely concession, it might have been prevented. If Members had been granted to Birmingham, Leeds, and Manchester, and other great towns as opportunities occurred, a spirit of conciliation would have been evinced, and the people might have been satisfied with a Reform, which though remote would have been gradual; but with the customary blindness and insolence of human beings, the day of adversity was forgotten, the rapid improvement of the people was not noticed; the object of a certain class of politicians was to please the Court and to gratify their own arrogance by treating every attempt to expand the representation, and to increase the popular influence, with every species of contempt and obloquy: the golden opportunity was lost; and now proud lips must swallow bitter potions.

The arguments and the practices (as I remember to have heard Mr. Huskisson say) which did very well twenty years ago, will not do now. The people read too much, think too much, see too many newspapers, hear too many speeches, have their eyes too intensely fixed upon political events. But if it were possible to put off Parliamentary Reform a week ago, is it possible now? When a Monarch (whose amiable and popular manners have, I verily believe, saved us from a Revolution) approves the measure—when a Minister of exalted character plans and fashions it—when a Cabinet of such varied talent and disposition protects it—when such a body of the Aristocracy vote for it—when the hundred-horse power of the Press is labouring for it;—who does not know after this (whatever be the decision of the present Parliament) that the measure is virtually car-

worthy marks of weakness, and fill reasonable men with just alarm. All this folly has taken place since they have become ministers upon principles of chivalry and gallantry; and the Tories, too, for fear of the people, have been much too quiet. There is only one principle of public conduct—*Do what you think right and take place and power as an accident.* Upon any other plan, office is shabbiness, labour, and sorrow.

ried—and that all the struggle between such annunciation of such a plan, and its completion, is tumult, disorder, disaffection, and (it may be) political ruin?

An Honourable Member of the Honourable House, much connected with this town, and once its representative, seems to be amazingly surprised, and equally dissatisfied, at this combination of King, Ministers, Nobles, and People, against his opinion—like the gentleman who came home from serving on a jury very much disconcerted, and complaining he had met with eleven of the most obstinate people he had ever seen in his life, whom he found it absolutely impossible by the strongest arguments to bring over to his way of thinking.

They tell you, gentlemen, that you have grown rich and powerful with these rotten boroughs, and that it would be madness to part with them, or to alter a constitution which had produced such happy effects. There happens, gentlemen, to live near my parsonage a labouring man, of very superior character and understanding to his fellow-labourers; and who has made such good use of that superiority, that he has saved what is (for his station in life) a very considerable sum of money, and if his existence be extended to the common period, he will die rich. It happens, however, that he is (and long has been) troubled with violent stomachic pains, for which he has hitherto obtained no relief, and which really are the bane and torment of his life. Now, if my excellent labourer were to send for a physician, and to consult him respecting this malady, would it not be very singular language if our doctor were to say to him, "My good friend, you surely will not be so rash as to attempt to get rid of these pains in your stomach. Have you not grown rich with these pains in your stomach? have you not risen under them from poverty to prosperity? has not your situation, since you were first attacked, been improving every year? You surely will not be so foolish and so indiscreet as to part with the pains in your stomach?"—Why, what would be the answer of the rustic to this nonsensical monition? "Monster of Rhubarb! (he would say) I am not rich in consequence of the pains in my stomach, but in spite of the pains in my stomach; and I should have been ten times richer, and fifty times happier, if I had never had any pains in my stomach at all." Gentlemen, these rotten boroughs are your pains in the stomach—and you would have been a much richer and greater people if you had never had them at all. Your wealth and your power have been owing, not to the debased and corrupted parts of the House of Commons, but to the many independent and honourable Members, whom it has always contained within its walls. If there had been a few more of these very valuable members for close boroughs, we should, I verily believe, have been by this time about as free as Denmark, Sweden, or the Germanised States of Italy.

They tell you of the few men of name and character who have sat for boroughs; but nothing is said of those mean and menial men who are sent down every day by their aristocratic masters to continue unjust and unnecessary wars, to prevent inquiring into profligate expenditure, to take money out of your pockets, or to do any other bad or base thing which the Minister of the day may require at their unclean hands. What mischief, it is asked, have these boroughs done? I believe there is not a day of your lives in which you are not suffering in all the taxed commodities of life from the accumulation of bad votes of bad men. But, Mr. Bailiff, if this *were otherwise*, if it really were a great political invention, that cities of 100,000 men should have no representatives, because those representatives were wanted for political ditches, political walls, and political parks; that the people should be bought and sold like any other commodity; that a retired merchant should be able to go into the market and buy ten shares in the government of twenty millions of his fellow-subjects; yet, can such asseverations be made openly before the people? Wise men, men conversant with human affairs, may whisper such theories to each other in retirement; but can the People ever be taught that it is right they should be bought and sold? Can the vehemence of eloquent democrats be met with such arguments and theories? Can the doubts of honest and limited men be met by such arguments and theories? The moment such a government is looked at by all the people, it is lost. It is impossible to explain, defend, and recommend it to the mass of mankind. And true enough it is, that as often as misfortune threatens us at home, or imitation excites us from abroad, political Reform is clamoured for by the people—there it stands, and ever will stand, in the apprehension of the multitude—Reform, the cure of every evil—Corruption, the source of every misfortune—famine, defeat, decayed trade, depressed agriculture, will all lapse into the question of Reform. Till that question is set at rest (and it may be set at rest) all will be disaffection, tumult, and perhaps (which God avert!) destruction.

But democrats and agitators (and democrats and agitators there are in the world) will not be contented with this Reform. Perhaps not, Sir; I never hope to content men whose game is never to be contented—but if they are not contented, I am sure their discontent will then comparatively be of little importance. I am afraid of them now; I have no arguments to answer them: but I shall not be afraid of them after this Bill, and would tell them boldly, in the middle of their mobs, that there was no longer cause for agitation and excitement, and that they were intending wickedly to the people. You may depend upon it such a measure would destroy their trade, as the repeal of duties would destroy the trade of the smuggler; their functions would be carried on faintly, and with little profit; you would soon feel that your position was stable, solid, and safe.

All would be well, it is urged, if they would but let the people alone. But what chance is there, I demand of these wise politicians, that the people will ever be let alone; that the orator will lay down his craft, and the demagogue forget his cunning? If many things were let alone, which never will be let alone, the aspect of human affairs would be a little varied. If the winds would let the waves alone, there would be no storms. If gentlemen would let ladies alone, there would be no unhappy marriages, and deserted damsels. If persons who can reason no better than this, would leave speaking alone, the school of eloquence might be improved. I have little hopes, however, of witnessing any of these acts of forbearance, particularly the last, and so we must (however foolish it may appear) proceed to make laws for a people who we are sure will not be let alone.

We might really imagine, from the objections made to the plan of Reform, that the great mass of Englishmen were madmen, robbers, and murderers. The Kingly power is to be destroyed, the House of Lords is to be annihilated, the Church is to be ruined, estates are to be confiscated. I am quite at a loss to find in these perpetrators of crimes—in this mass of pillagers and lunatics—the steady and respectable tradesmen and farmers, who will have votes to confer, and the steady and respectable country gentlemen, who will probably have votes to receive;—it may be true of the tradesmen of *Mauritania*, it may be just of the country gentlemen of *Fez*—it is anything but true of the English people. The English are a tranquil, phlegmatic, money-loving, money-getting people, who want to be quiet—and would be quiet if they were not surrounded by evils of such magnitude, that it would be baseness and pusillanimity not to oppose to them the strongest constitutional resistance.

Then it is said that there is to be a lack of talent in the new Parliament: it is to be composed of ordinary and inferior persons, who will bring the government of the country into contempt. But the best of all talents, gentlemen, is to conduct our affairs honestly, diligently, and economically—and this talent will, I am sure, abound as much in the new Parliament as in many previous Parliaments. Parliament is not a school for rhetoric and declamation, where a stranger would go to hear a speech, as he would go to the Opera to hear a song; but if it were otherwise—if eloquence be a necessary ornament of, and an indispensable adjunct to popular assemblies— can it ever be absent from popular assemblies? I have always found that all things, moral or physical, grow in the soil best suited for them. Show me a deep and tenacious earth—and I am sure the oak will spring up in it. In a low and damp soil I am equally certain of the alder and the willow. Gentlemen, the free Parliament of a free People is the native soil of eloquence—and in that soil will it ever flourish and abound—there it will produce those intellectual effects which drive before them whole tribes and nations of the human race, and settle the destinies of man. And, gentlemen, if a few persons of a less elegant and aristocratic description were to become members of the House of Commons, where would be the evil? They would probably understand the common people a great deal better, and in this way the feelings and interests of all classes of people would be better represented. The House of Commons thus organised will express more faithfully the opinions of the people.

The people are sometimes, it is urged, grossly mistaken; but are Kings never mistaken? Are the higher orders never mistaken?— never wilfully corrupted by their own interests? The people have at least this superiority, that they always intend to do what is right.

The argument of fear is very easily disposed of: he who is afraid of a knock on the head or a cut on the cheek is a coward; he who is afraid of entailing greater evils on the country by refusing the remedy than by applying it, and who acts in pursuance of that conviction, is a wise and prudent man—nothing can be more different than personal and political fear; it is the artifice of our opponents to confound them together.

The right of disfranchisement, gentlemen, must exist somewhere, and where but in Parliament? If not, how was the Scotch Union, how was the Irish Union, effected? The Duke of Wellington's Administration disfranchised at one blow 200,000 Irish voters—for no fault of theirs, and for no other reason than the best of all reasons, that public expediency required it. These very same politicians are now looking in an agony of terror at the disfranchisement of Corporations containing twenty or thirty persons, sold to their representatives, who are themselves perhaps sold to the Government: and to put an end to these enormous abuses is called *Corporation robbery,* and there are some persons wild enough to talk of compensation. This principle of compensation you will consider perhaps in the following instance to have been carried as far as sound discretion permits. When I was a young man, the place in England I remember as most notorious for highwaymen and their exploits was Finchley Common, near the metropolis; but Finchley Common, gentlemen, in the progress of improvement, came to be enclosed, and the highwaymen lost by these means the opportunity of exercising their gallant vocation. I remember a friend of mine proposed to draw up for them a petition to the House of Commons for compensation, which ran in this manner—"We, your loyal highwaymen of Finchley Common and its neighbourhood, having, at great expense, laid in a stock of blunderbusses, pistols, and other instruments for plundering the public, and finding ourselves impeded in the exercise of our calling by the said enclosure of the said Common of Finchley, humbly petition your Honourable House will be pleased to assign to us such compensation as your Honourable House in its wisdom and justice may think fit."—Gentlemen, I must leave the application to you.

An Honourable Baronet says, if Parliament is dissolved, I will go to my Borough with the bill in my hand, and will say, "I know of no crime you have committed, I found nothing proved against you: I voted against the bill, and am come to fling myself upon your kindness, with the hope that my conduct will be approved, and that you will return me again to Parliament." That Honourable Baronet may, perhaps, receive from his Borough an answer he little expects —"We are above being bribed by such a childish and unworthy artifice; we do not choose to consult our own interest at the expense of the general peace and happiness of the country; we are thoroughly convinced a Reform ought to take place; we are very willing to sacrifice a privilege we ought never to have possessed to the good of the community, and we will return no one to Parliament who is not deeply impressed with the same feeling." This, I hope, is the answer that gentlemen will receive; and this, I hope, will be the noble and generous feeling of every Borough in England.

The greater part of human improvements, gentlemen, I am sorry to say, are made after war, tumult, bloodshed, and civil commotion: mankind seem to object to every species of gratuitous happiness, and to consider every advantage as too cheap, which is not purchased by some calamity. I shall esteem it as a singular act of God's providence, if this great nation, guided by these warnings of history, not waiting till tumult for Reform, nor trusting Reform to the rude hands of the lowest of the people, shall amend their decayed institutions at a period when they are ruled by a popular Monarch, guided by an upright Minister, and blest with profound peace.

II.

MR. CHAIRMAN,—I am particularly happy to assist on this occasion, because I think that the accession of the present King is a marked and important era in English history. Another coronation has taken place since I have been in the world, but I never assisted at its celebration. I saw in it a change of masters, not a change of system. I did not understand the joy which it occasioned. I did not feel it, and I did not counterfeit what I did not feel.

I think very differently of the accession of his present Majesty. I believe I see in that accession a great probability of serious improvement, and a great increase of public happiness. The evils which have been long complained of by bold and intelligent men are now universally admitted. The public feeling, which has been so often appealed to, is now intensely excited. The remedies which have so often been called for are now at last, vigorously, wisely, and faithfully applied. I admire, gentlemen, in the present King, his love of peace—I admire in him his disposition to economy, and I admire in him, above all, his faithful and honourable conduct to those who happen to be his ministers. He was, I believe, quite as faithful to the Duke of Wellington as to Lord Grey, and would, I have no doubt, be quite as faithful to the political enemies of Lord Grey (if he thought fit to employ them) as he is to Lord Grey himself. There is in this reign no secret influence, no double ministry—on whomsoever he confers the office, to him he gives that confidence without which the office cannot be holden with honour, nor executed with effect. He is not only a peaceful King, and an economical King, but he is an honest King. So far, I believe, every individual of this company will go with me. There is another topic of eulogium, on which, before I sit down, I should like to say a few words—I mean the willingness of our present King to investigate abuses, and to reform them. If this subject be not unpleasant, I will offer upon it a very few observations—a few, because the subject is exhausted, and because, if it were not, I have no right, from my standing or my situation in this county, to detain you long upon that or any other subject.

In criticising this great question of Reform, I think there is some injustice done to its authors. Men seem to suppose that a minister can sit down and make a plan of reform with as much ease and as much exactness, and with as complete a gratification of his own will, as an architect can do in building or altering a house. But a minister of state (it should be in justice observed) works in the midst of hatred, injustice, violence, and the worst of human passions—his works are not the works of calm and unembarrassed wisdom—they are not the best that a dreamer of dreams can imagine. It is enough if they are the best plans which the passions, parties, and prejudices of the times in which he acts will permit. In passing a Reform Bill the minister overthrows the long and deep interest which powerful men have in existing abuses—he subjects himself to the deepest hatred, and encounters the bitterest opposition. Auxiliaries he must have, and auxiliaries he can only find among the people—not the mob—but the great mass of those who have opinions worth hearing, and property worth defending—a greater mass, I am happy to say, in this country than exists in any other country on the face of the earth. Now, before the middling orders will come forward with one great impulse, they must see that something is offered them worth the price of contention; they must see that the object is great and the gain serious. If you call them in at all, it must not be to displace one faction at the expense of another, but to put down all factions—to substitute purity and principle for corruption—to give to the many that political power which the few have unjustly taken to themselves—to get rid of evils so ancient and so vast that any other arm than the public arm would be lifted up against them in vain. This, then, I say, is one of the reasons why ministers have been compelled to make their measure a little more vigorous and decisive than a speculative philosopher, sitting in his closet, might approve of. They had a mass of opposition to contend with, which could be encountered only by a general exertion of public spirit—they had a long suffering and an often deceived public to appeal to, who were determined to suffer no longer, and to be deceived no more. The alternative was to continue the ancient abuses, or to do what they have done—and most firmly do I believe that you and I, and the latest posterity of us all, will rejoice in the decision they have made. Gradation has been called for in reform: we might, it is said, have taken thirty or forty years to have accomplished what we have done in one year. "It is not so much the magnitude of what you are doing we object to, as the suddenness." But was not gradation tendered? Was it not said by the friends of reform—"Give us Birmingham and Manchester, and we will be satisfied"? and what was the answer? "No Manchester, no Birmingham, no reform in any degree—all abuses as they are—all perversions as we have found them—the corruptions which our fathers bequeathed us we will hand down un-impaired and unpurified to our children." But I would say to the graduate philosopher,—"How often does a reforming minister oc-cur?" and if such are so common that you can command them when you please, how often does a reforming monarch occur? and how often does the conjunction of both occur? Are you sure that a people, bursting into new knowledge, and speculating on every public event, will wait for your protracted reform? Strike while the iron is hot—up with the arm and down with the hammer, and up again with the arm, and down again with the hammer. The iron is hot— the opportunity exists now—if you neglect it, it may not return for a hundred years to come.

There is an argument I have often heard, and that is this—Are we to be afraid?—is this measure to be carried by intimidation?—is the House of Lords to be overawed? But this style of argument proceeds from confounding together two sets of feelings which are entirely distinct—personal fear and political fear. If I am afraid of voting against this bill, because a mob may gather about the House of Lords—because stones may be flung at my head—because my house may be attacked by a mob, I am a poltroon, and unfit to meddle with public affairs; but I may rationally be afraid of producing great public agitation—I may be honourably afraid of flinging people into secret clubs and conspiracies—I may be wisely afraid of making the aristocracy hateful to the great body of the people. This surely has no more to do with fear than a loose identity of name; it is in fact prudence of the highest order; the deliberate reflection of a wise man, who does not like what he is going to do, but likes still less the consequences of not doing it, and who of two evils chooses the least.

There are some men much afraid of what is to happen: my lively hope of good is, I confess, mingled with very little apprehension; but of one thing I must be candid enough to say that I am much afraid, and that is of the opinion now increasing, that the people are become indifferent to reform; and of that opinion I am afraid, because I believe in an evil hour it may lead some misguided members of the Upper House of Parliament to vote against the bill. As for the opinion itself, I hold it in the utmost contempt. The people are waiting in virtuous patience for the completion of the bill, because they know it is in the hands of men who do not mean to deceive them. I do not believe they have given up one atom of reform—I do not believe that a great people were ever before so firmly bent upon any one measure. I put it to any man of common sense, whether he believes it possible, after the King and Parliament have acted as they have done, that the people will ever be content with much less than the present bill contains. If a contrary principle be acted upon, and the bill attempted to be got rid of altogether, I confess I tremble for the consequences, which I believe will be of the worst and most painful description; and this I say deliberately, after the most diligent and extensive inquiry. Upon that diligent inquiry, I repeat again my firm conviction, that the desire of reform has increased, not diminished; that the present repose is not indifference, but the calmness of victory, and the tranquillity of success. When I see all the wishes and appetites of created beings changed, when I see an eagle, that, after long confinement, has escaped into the air, come back to his cage and his chain,—when I see the emancipated negro asking again for the hoe which has broken down his strength, and the lash which has tortured his body, I will then, and not till then, believe that the English people will return to their ancient degradation—that they will hold out their repentant hands for those manacles which at this moment lie broken into links at their feet.

III.

The Reverend Sydney Smith rose and said:—Mr. Bailiff, I have spoken so often on this subject, that I am sure both you and the gentlemen here present will be obliged to me for saying but little, and that favour I am as willing to confer, as you can be to receive it. I feel most deeply the event which has taken place, because, by putting the two Houses of Parliament in collision with each other, it will impede the public business, and diminish the public prosperity. I feel it as a churchman, because I cannot but blush to see so many dignitaries of the Church arrayed against the wishes and happiness of the people. I feel it more than all, because I believe it will sow the seeds of deadly hatred between the aristocracy and the great mass of the people. The loss of the bill I do not feel, and for the best of all possible reasons—because I have not the slightest idea that it *is* lost. I have no more doubt, before the expiration of the winter, that this bill will pass, than I have that the annual tax bills will pass, and greater certainty than this no man can have, for Franklin tells us, there are but two things certain in this world —death and taxes. As for the possibility of the House of Lords preventing ere long a reform of Parliament, I hold it to be the most absurd notion that ever entered into human imagination. I do not mean to be disrespectful, but the attempt of the Lords to stop the progress of reform, reminds me very forcibly of the great storm of Sidmouth, and of the conduct of the excellent Mrs. Partington on that occasion. In the winter of 1824, there set in a great flood upon that town—the tide rose to an incredible height-- the waves rushed in upon the houses, and everything was threatened with destruction. In the midst of this sublime and terrible storm, Dame Partington, who lived upon the beach, was seen at the door of her house with mop and pattens, trundling her mop, squeezing out the sea-water, and vigorously pushing away the Atlantic Ocean. The Atlantic was roused. Mrs. Partington's spirit was up; but I need not tell you that the contest was unequal. The Atlantic Ocean beat Mrs. Partington. She was excellent at a slop, or a puddle, but she should not have meddled with a tempest. Gentlemen, be at your ease—be quiet and steady. You will beat Mrs. Partington.

They tell you, gentlemen, in the debates by which we have been lately occupied, that the bill is not justified by experience. I do not think this true; but if it were true, nations are sometimes compelled to act without experience for their guide, and to trust to their own sagacity for the anticipation of consequences. The instances where this country has been compelled thus to act have been so eminently successful, that I see no cause for fear, even if we were acting in the manner imputed to us by our enemies. What precedents and what experience were there at the Reformation, when the country, with one unanimous effort, pushed out the Pope, and his grasping and ambitious clergy?—What experience, when at the Revolution we drove away our ancient race of kings, and chose another family, more congenial to our free principles?—And yet to those two events, contrary to experience, and unguided by precedents, we owe all our domestic happiness, and civil and religious freedom— and having got rid of corrupt priests, and despotic kings, by our sense and our courage, are we now to be intimidated by the awful danger of extinguishing Boroughmongers, and shaking from our neck the ignominious yoke which their baseness has imposed upon it? Go on, they say, as you have done for these hundred years last past. I answer it is impossible: five hundred people now write and read, where one hundred wrote and read fifty years ago. The iniquities and enormities of the borough system are now known to the meanest of the people. You have a different sort of men to deal with—you must change because the beings whom you govern are changed. After all, and to be short, I must say that it has always appeared to me to be the most absolute nonsense that we cannot be a great, or a rich and happy nation, without suffering ourselves to be bought and sold every five years like a pack of negro slaves. I hope I am not a very rash man, but I would launch boldly into this experiment without any fear of consequences, and I believe there is not a man here present who would not cheerfully embark with me. As to the enemies of the bill, who pretend to be reformers, I know them, I believe, better than you do, and I earnestly caution you against them. You will have no more of reform than they

are compelled to grant—you will have no reform at all, if they can
avoid it—you will be hurried into a war to turn your attention from
reform. They do not understand you—they will not believe in the
improvement you have made—they think the English of the present day are as the English of the times of Queen Anne or George
the First. They know no more of the present state of their own
country, than of the state of the Esquimaux Indians. Gentlemen, I
view the ignorance of the present state of the country with the most
serious concern, and I believe they will one day or another waken
into conviction with horror and dismay. I will omit no means of
rousing them to a sense of their danger;—for this object, I cheerfully sign the petition proposed by Dr. Kinglake, which I consider
to be the wisest and most moderate of the two.

IV.

STICK to the Bill—it is your Magna Charta, and your Runnymede.
King John made a present to the Barons. King William has made
a similar present to you. Never mind; common qualities good in
common times. If a man does not vote for the Bill, he is unclean—
the plague-spot is upon him—push him into the lazaretto of the
last century, with Wetherell and Sadler—purify the air before you
approach him—bathe your hands in Chloride of Lime, if you have
been contaminated by his touch.

So far from its being a merely theoretical improvement, I put it
to any man, who is himself embarked in a profession, or has sons
in the same situation, if the unfair influence of Boroughmongers
has not perpetually thwarted him in his lawful career of ambition
and professional emolument? "I have been in three general en-
gagements at sea," said an old sailor—"have been twice wounded;
—I commanded the boats when the French frigate, the ASTROLABE,
was cut out so gallantly." "Then you are made a Post Captain?"
"No. I was very near it; but—Lieutenant Thompson cut me out,
as I cut out the French frigate; his father is Town Clerk of the
Borough for which Lord F—— is Member, and there my chance
was finished." In the same manner, all over England, you will find
great scholars rotting on curacies—brave captains starving in gar-
rets—profound lawyers decayed and mouldering in the Inns of
Court, because the parsons, warriors, and advocates of Boroughmongers must be crammed to saturation, before there is a morsel
of bread for the man who does not sell his votes, and put his country up to auction; and though this is of every day occurrence, the
Borough system, we are told, is no practical evil.

Who can bear to walk through a slaughter-house? blood, garbage, stomachs, entrails, legs, tails, kidneys, horrors—I often walk
a mile about to avoid it. What a scene of disgust and horror is an
election—the base and infamous traffic of principles—a candidate of high character reduced to such means—the perjury and
evasion of agents—the detestable rapacity of voters—the ten days'
dominion of mammon, and Belial. The Bill lessens it—begins the
destruction of such practices—affords some chance, and some
means of turning public opinion against bribery, and of rendering
it infamous.

But the thing I cannot, and will not bear, is this;—what right
has *this* Lord, or *that* Marquis, to buy ten seats in Parliament, in
the shape of Boroughs, and then to make laws to govern me? And
how are these masses of power redistributed? The eldest son of my
Lord is just come from Eton—he knows a good deal about Æneas
and Dido, Apollo and Daphne—and that is all; and to this boy his
father gives a six-hundredth part of the power of making laws, as
he would give him a horse or a double-barrelled gun. Then Vellum,
the steward, is put in—an admirable man:—he has raised the estates—watched the progress of the family Road and Canal Bills—
and Vellum shall help to rule over the people of Israel. A neigh-
bouring country gentleman, Mr. Plumpkin, hunts with my Lord—
opens him a gate or two, while the hounds are running—dines with
my Lord—agrees with my Lord—wishes he could rival the South-
Down sheep of my Lord—and upon Plumpkin is conferred a portion of the government. Then there is a distant relation of the
same name, in the County Militia, with white teeth, who calls up
the carriage at the Opera, and is always wishing O'Connell was
hanged, drawn, and quartered—then a barrister, who has written
an article in the Quarterly, and is very likely to speak, and refute
M'Culloch; and these five people, in whose nomination I have no
more agency than I have in the nomination of the toll-keepers of
the Bosphorus, are to make laws for me and my family—to put
their hands in my purse, and to sway the future destinies of this
country; and when the neighbours step in, and beg permission to
say a few words before these persons are chosen, there is an universal cry of ruin, confusion, and destruction;—we have become
a great people under Vellum and Plumpkin—under Vellum and
Plumpkin our ships have covered the ocean—under Vellum and
Plumpkin our armies have secured the strength of the Hills—to
turn out Vellum and Plumpkin is not Reform, but Revolution.

Was there ever such a Ministry? Was there ever before a real
Ministry of the people? Look at the condition of the country when

it was placed in their hands: the state of the house when the in-
coming tenant took possession: windows broken, chimneys on fire,
mobs round the house threatening to pull it down, roof tumbling,
rain pouring in. It was courage to occupy it; it was a miracle to
save it; it will be the glory of glories to enlarge and expand it, and
to make it the eternal palace of wise and temperate freedom.

Proper examples have been made among the unhappy and misguided disciples of Swing: a rope has been carried round O'Connell's legs, and a ring inserted in Cobbett's nose. Then the Game
Laws!!! Was ever conduct so shabby as that of the two or three
governments which preceded that of Lord Grey? The cruelties and
enormities of this code had been thoroughly exposed; and a general
conviction existed of the necessity of a change. Bills were brought
in by various gentlemen, containing some trifling alteration in this
abominable code, and even these were sacrificed to the tricks and
manoeuvres of some noble Nimrod, who availed himself of the
emptiness of the town in July, and flung out the Bill. Government
never stirred a step. The fulness of the prisons, the wretchedness
and demoralisation of the poor, never came across them. The humane and considerate Peel never once offered to extend his ægis
over them. It had nothing to do with the state of party; and some
of their double-barrelled voters might be offended. In the meantime, for every ten pheasants which fluttered in the wood, one English peasant was rotting in gaol. No sooner is Lord Althorp Chancellor of the Exchequer, than he turns out of the house a trumpery
and (perhaps) an insidious Bill for the improvement of the Game
Laws; and in an instant offers the assistance of Government for the
abolition of the whole code.

Then look at the gigantic Brougham, sworn in at 12 o'clock,
and before 6 has a bill on the table, abolishing the abuses of a
Court which has been the curse of the people of England for centuries. For twenty-five long years did Lord Eldon sit in that Court,
surrounded with misery and sorrow, which he never held up a finger to alleviate. The widow and the orphan cried to him as vainly
as the town crier cries when he offers a small reward for a full
purse; the bankrupt of the Court became the lunatic of the Court,
estates moulded away, and mansions fell down; but the fees came
in, and all was well. But in an instant the iron mace of Brougham
shivered to atoms this house of fraud and of delay; and this is the
man who will help to govern you; who bottoms his reputation on
doing good to you; who knows, that to reform abuses is the safest
basis of fame, and the surest instrument of power; who uses the
highest gifts of reason, and the most splendid efforts of genius, to

rectify those abuses, which all the genius and talent of the profession * have hitherto been employed to justify, and to protect.
Look to Brougham, and turn you to that side where he waves his
long and lean finger; and mark well that face which nature has
marked so forcibly—which dissolves pensions—turns jobbers into
honest men—scares away the plunderer of the public—and is a
terror to him who doeth evil to the people. But, above all, look
to the Northern Earl, victim, before this honest and manly reign,
of the spitefulness of the Court. You may now, for the first time,
learn to trust in the professions of a Minister; you are directed by
a man who prefers character to place, and who has given such un-
equivocal proofs of honesty and patriotism, that his image ought
to be amongst your household gods, and his name to be lisped by
your children: two thousand years hence it will be a legend like
the fable of Perseus and Andromeda: Britannia chained to a
mountain—two hundred rotten animals menacing her destruction, till a tall Earl, armed with Schedule A., and followed by his
page Russell, drives them into the deep, and delivers over Britannia in safety to crowds of ten-pound renters, who deafen the air
with their acclamations. Forthwith, Latin verses upon this—school
exercises—boys whipt, and all the usual absurdities of education.
Don't part with the Administration composed of Lord Grey and
Lord Brougham; and not only these, but look at them all—the mild
wisdom of Lansdowne—the genius and extensive knowledge of
Holland, in whose bold and honest life there is no varying nor
shadow of change—the unexpected and exemplary activity of
Lord Melbourne—and the rising parliamentary talents of Stanley.
You are ignorant of your best interests, if every vote you can be-
stow is not given to such a ministry as this.

You will soon find an alteration of behaviour in the upper orders when elections become real. You will find that you are raised
to the importance to which you ought to be raised. The merciless
ejector, the rural tyrant, will be restrained within the limits of
decency and humanity, and will improve their own characters, at
the same time that they better your condition.

It is not the power of aristocracy that will be destroyed by these
measures, but the *unfair* power. If the Duke of Newcastle is kind
and obliging to his neighbours, he will probably lead his neighbours; if he is a man of sense, he will lead them more certainly,
and to a better purpose. All this is as it should be; but the Duke

---

* Lord Lyndhurst is an exception; I firmly believe he had no wish to perpetuate the abuses of the Court of Chancery.

of Newcastle, at present, by buying certain old houses, could govern his neighbours and legislate for them, even if he had not five grains of understanding, and if he were the most churlish and brutal man under heaven. The present state of things renders unnecessary all those important virtues, which rich and well-born men, under a better system, would exercise for the public good. The Duke of Newcastle (I mention him only as an instance), Lord Exeter will do as well, but either of those noblemen, depending not upon walls, arches, and abutments, for their power—but upon mercy, charity, forbearance, indulgence, and example—would pay this price, and lead the people by their affections; one would be the God of Stamford, and the other of Newark. This union of the great with the many is the real healthy state of a country; such a country is strong to invincibility—and this strength the Borough system entirely destroys.

Cant words creep in, and affect quarrels; the changes are rung between Revolution and Reform; but, first settle whether a wise government ought to attempt the measure—whether anything is wanted—whether less would do—and, having settled this, mere nomenclature becomes of very little consequence. But, after all, if it be Revolution, and not Reform, it will only induce me to receive an old political toast in a twofold meaning, and with twofold pleasure. When King William and the great and glorious Revolution are given, I shall think not only of escape from bigotry, but exemption from corruption; and I shall thank Providence, which has given us a second King William for the destruction of vice, as the other of that name was given us for the conservation of freedom.

All former political changes, proposed by these very men, it is said, were mild and gentle, compared to this: true, but are you on Saturday night to seize your apothecary by the throat, and to say to him, "Subtle compounder, fraudulent posologist, did not you order me a drachm of this medicine on Monday morning, and now you declare, that nothing short of an ounce can do me any good?" "True enough," would he of the phials reply, *"but you did not take the drachm on Monday morning*—that makes all the difference, my dear Sir; if you had done as I advised you at first, the small quantity of medicine would have sufficed; and, instead of being in a night-gown and slippers upstairs, you would have been walking vigorously in Piccadilly. Do as you please—and die if you please; but don't blame me because you despised my advice, and by your own ignorance and obstinacy have entailed upon yourself tenfold rhubarb and unlimited infusion of senna."

Now see the consequences of having a manly Leader, and a manly Cabinet. Suppose they had come out with a little ill-fashioned seven months' reform; what would have been the consequence? The same opposition from the Tories—that would have been quite certain—and not a single Reformer in England satisfied with the measure. You have now a real Reform, and a fair share of power delegated to the people.

The Anti-Reformers cite the increased power of the press—this is the very reason why I want an increased power in the House of Commons. The Times, Herald, Advertiser, Globe, Sun, Courier, and Chronicle, are a heptarchy, which govern this country, and govern it because the people are so badly represented. I am perfectly satisfied, that with a fair and honest House of Commons the power of the press would diminish—and that the greatest authority would centre in the highest place.

Is it possible for a gentleman to get into Parliament, at present, without doing things he is utterly ashamed of—without mixing himself up with the lowest and basest of mankind? Hands, accustomed to the scented lubricity of soap, are defiled with pitch, and contaminated with filth. Is there not some inherent vice in a Government, which cannot be carried on but with such abominable wickedness, in which no gentleman can mingle without moral degradation, and the practice of crimes, the very imputation of which, on other occasions, he would repel at the hazard of his life?

What signifies a small majority in the House? The miracle is, that there should have been any majority at all; that there was not an immense majority on the other side. It was a very long period before the Courts of Justice in Jersey could put down smuggling; and why? The Judges, Counsel, Attorneys, Crier of the Court, Grand and Petty Jurymen, were all smugglers, and the High Sheriff and Constables were running goods every moonlight night.

How are you to do without a government? And what other government, if this Bill be ultimately lost, could possibly be found? How could any country defray the ruinous expense of protecting, with troops and constables, the Duke of Wellington and Sir Robert Peel, who literally would not be able to walk from the Horse Guards to Grosvenor Square, without two or three regiments of foot to screen them from the mob; and in these hollow squares the Hero of Waterloo would have to spend his political life? By the whole exercise of his splendid military talents, by strong batteries, at Bootle's and White's, he might, on nights of great debate, reach the House of Lords; but Sir Robert would probably be cut off, and nothing could save Twiss and Lewis.

The great majority of persons returned by the new Boroughs would either be men of high reputation for talents, or persons of fortune known in the neighbourhood; they have property and character to lose. Why are they to plunge into mad and revolutionary projects of pillaging the public creditor? It is not the interest of any such man to do it; he would lose more by the destruction of public credit than he would gain by a remission of what he paid for the interest of the public debt. And if it is not the interest of any one to act in this manner, it is not the interest of the mass. How many, also, of these new legislators would there be, who were not themselves creditors of the State? Is it the interest of such men to create a revolution, by destroying the constitutional power of the House of Lords, or of the King? Does there exist in persons of that class any disposition for such changes? Are not all their feelings, and opinions, and prejudices, on the opposite side? The majority of the new members will be landed gentlemen: their genus is utterly distinct from the revolutionary tribe; they have Molar teeth; they are destitute of the carnivorous and incisive jaws of political adventurers.

There will be mistakes at first, as there are in all changes. All young Ladies will imagine (as soon as this Bill is carried) that they will be instantly married. Schoolboys believe that Gerunds and Supines will be abolished, and that Currant Tarts must ultimately come down in price; the Corporal and Sergeant are sure of double pay; bad Poets will expect a demand for their Epics; Fools will be disappointed, as they always are; reasonable men, who know what to expect, will find that a very serious good has been obtained.

What good to the hewer of wood and the drawer of water? How is he benefited, if Old Sarum is abolished and Birmingham Members created? But if you ask this question of Reform, you must ask it of a great number of other great measures? How is he benefited by Catholic Emancipation, by the repeal of the Corporation and Test Act, by the Revolution of 1688, by any great political change? by a good government? In the first place, if many are benefited, and the lower orders are not injured, this alone is reason enough for the change. But the hewer of wood and the drawer of water *are* benefited by reform. Reform will produce economy and investigation; there will be fewer jobs, and a less lavish expenditure; wars will not be persevered in for years after the people are tired of them; taxes will be taken off the poor, and laid upon the rich; demotic habits will be more common in a country where the rich are forced to court the poor for political power; cruel and oppressive punishments (such as those for night poaching) will be abolished. If you steal a pheasant you will be punished as you ought to be, but not sent away from your wife and children for seven years. Tobacco will be 2*d*. per lb. cheaper. Candles will fall in price. These last results of an improved government will be felt. We do not pretend to abolish poverty, or to prevent wretchedness; but if peace, economy, and justice, are the results of Reform, a number of small benefits, or rather of benefits which appear small to us, but not to them, will accrue to millions of the people; and the connection between the existence of John Russell, and the reduced price of bread and cheese, will be as clear as it has been the object of his honest, wise, and useful life to make it.

Don't be led away by such nonsense; all things are dearer under a bad government, and cheaper under a good one. The real question they ask you is, What difference can any change of government make to you? They want to keep the bees from buzzing and stinging, in order that they may rob the hive in peace.

Work well! How does it work well, when every human being indoors and out (with the exception of the Duke of Wellington) says it must be made to work better, or it will soon cease to work at all? It is little short of absolute nonsense to call a government good, which the great mass of Englishmen would, before twenty years were elapsed, if Reform were denied, rise up and destroy. Of what use have all the cruel laws been of Perceval Eldon, and Castlereagh, to extinguish Reform? Lord John Russell, and his abettors, would have been committed to gaol twenty years ago for half only of his present Reform; and now relays of the people would drag them from London to Edinburgh; at which latter city we are told, by Mr. Dundas, that there is no eagerness for Reform. Five minutes before Moses struck the rock, this gentleman would have said that there was no eagerness for water.

There are two methods of making alterations: the one is to despise the applicants, to begin with refusing every concession, then to relax by making concessions which are always too late; by offering in 1831 what is then too late, but would have been cheerfully accepted in 1830—gradually to O'Connellise the country, till at last, after this process has gone on for some time, the alarm becomes too great, and everything is conceded in hurry and confusion. In the meantime fresh conspiracies have been hatched by the long delay, and no gratitude is expressed for what has been extorted by fear. In this way peace was concluded with America, and Emancipation granted to the Catholics; and in this way the war of complexion will be finished in the West Indies. The other method is, to see at a distance that the thing must be done, and to do it effectually, *and at once;* to take it out of the hands of the common people, and to carry the measure in a manly liberal manner, so as to satisfy the great majority. The merit of this belongs to the Administration of Lord Grey. He is the only Minister I know of who has begun a great measure in good time, conceded at the beginning of twenty years what would have been extorted at the end of it, and prevented that folly, violence, and ignorance, which emanate from a long denial and extorted concession of justice to great masses of human beings. I believe the question of Reform, or any dangerous agitation of it, is set at rest for thirty or forty years; and this is an eternity in politics.

Boroughs are not the power proceeding from wealth. Many men who have no Boroughs are infinitely richer than those who have—but it is the artifice of wealth in seizing hold of certain localities. The Boroughmonger is like rheumatism, which owes its power not so much to the intensity of the pain as to its peculiar position; a little higher up, or a little lower down, the same pain would be trifling; but it fixes in the joints, and gets into the head-quarters of motion and activity. The Boroughmonger knows the importance of arthritic positions; he disdains muscle, gets into the joints, and lords it over the whole machine by felicity of place. Other men are as rich—but those riches are not fixed in the critical spot.

I live a good deal with all ranks and descriptions of people; I am thoroughly convinced that the party of Democrats and Republicans is very small and contemptible; that the English love their institutions—that they love not only this King, (who would not love him?) but the kingly office—that they have no hatred to the Aristocracy. I am not afraid of trusting English happiness to English Gentlemen. I believe that the half million of new voters will choose much better for the public, than the twenty or thirty Peers, to whose usurped power they succeed.

If any man doubt of the power of Reform, let him take these two memorable proofs of its omnipotence. First, but for the declaration against it, I believe the Duke of Wellington might this day have been in office; and, secondly, in the whole course of the debates at County Meetings and in Parliament, there are not twenty men who have declared against Reform. Some advance an inch, some a foot, some a yard—but nobody stands still—nobody says, We ought to remain just where we were—everybody discovers that he is a Reformer, and has long been so—and appears infinitely delighted with this new view of himself. Nobody appears without the cockade—bigger or less—but always the cockade.

An exact and elaborate census is called for—vast information should have been laid upon the table of the House—great time should have been given for deliberation. All these objections, being turned into English, simply mean, that the chances of another year should have been given for defeating the Bill. In that time the Poles may be crushed, the Belgians organised, Louis Philippe dethroned; war may rage all over Europe—the popular spirit may be diverted to other objects. It is certainly provoking that the Ministry foresaw all these possibilities and determined to model the iron while it was red and glowing.

It is not enough that a political institution works well practically: it must be defensible; it must be such as will bear discussion, and not excite ridicule and contempt. It might work well for aught I know, if, like the savages of Onelashka, we sent out to catch a king: but who could defend a coronation by chase? who can defend the payment of 40,000*l.* for the three-hundredth part of the power of Parliament, and the resale of this power to Government for places to the Lord Williams and Lord Charles's, and others of the Anglophagi? Teach a million of the common people to read—and such a government (work it ever so well) must perish in twenty years. It is impossible to persuade the mass of mankind that there are not other and better methods of governing a country. It is so complicated, so wicked, such envy and hatred accumulate against the gentlemen who have fixed themselves on the joints, that it cannot fail to perish, and to be driven, as it *is* driven, from the country by a general burst of hatred and detestation. I meant, gentlemen, to have spoken for another half hour, but I am old and tired. Thank me for ending—but, gentlemen, bear with me for another moment; one word before I end. I am old, but I thank God I have lived to see more than my observations on human nature taught me I had any right to expect. I have lived to see an honest King, in whose word his Ministers can trust; who disdains to deceive those men whom he has called to the public service, but makes common cause with them for the common good; and exercises the highest powers of a ruler for the dearest interests of the State. I have lived to see a King with a good heart, who, surrounded by Nobles, thinks of common men; who loves the great mass of English people, and wishes to be loved by them; who knows that his real power, as he feels that his happiness, is founded on their affection. I have lived to see a King, who, without pretending to the pomp of superior intellect, has the wisdom to see, that the decayed institutions of human policy require amendment; and who, in spite of clamour, interest, prejudice, and fear, has the manliness to carry these wise changes into immediate execution. Gentlemen, farewell: shout for the King.

BALLOT

It is possible, and perhaps not very difficult, to invent a machine, by the aid of which electors may vote for a candidate, or for two or three candidates, out of a greater number, without its being discovered for whom they vote; it is less easy than the rabid and foaming Radical supposes; but I have no doubt it may be accomplished. In Mr. Grote's dagger ballot box, which has been carried around the country by eminent patriots, you stab the card of your favorite candidate with a dagger. I have seen another, called the mouse-trap ballot box, in which you poke your finger into the trap of the member you prefer, and are caught and detained till the trap-clerk below (who knows by means of a wire when you are caught) marks your vote, pulls the liberator, and releases you. Which may be the most eligible of these two methods I do not pretend to determine, nor do I think my excellent friend Mr. Babbage has as yet made up his mind on the subject; but, by some means or another, I have no doubt the thing may be done.

Landed proprietors imagine they have a right to the votes of their tenants; and instances, in every election, are numerous where tenants have been dismissed for voting contrary to the wishes of their landlords. In the same manner strong combinations are made against tradesmen who have chosen to think, and act for themselves in political matters, rather than yield their opinions to the solicitations of their customers. There is a great deal of tyranny and injustice in all this. I should no more think of asking what the political opinions of a shopkeeper were, than of asking whether he was tall or short, or large or small: for a difference of 2½ per cent. I would desert the most aristocratic butcher that ever existed, and deal with one who

"Shook the arsenal, and fulmin'd over Greece."

On the contrary, I would not adhere to the man who put me in uneasy habiliments, however great his veneration for trial by jury, or however ardent his attachment to the liberty of the subject. A tenant I never had; but I firmly believe that if he had gone through certain pecuniary formalities twice a year, I should have thought it a gross act of tyranny to have interfered either with his political or his religious opinions.

I distinctly admit that every man has a right to do what he pleases with his own. I cannot, by law, prevent any one from discharging his tenants, and changing his tradesmen, for political reasons; but I may judge whether that man exercises his right to the public detriment, or for the public advantage. A man has a right to refuse dealing with any tradesman who is not five feet eleven inches high; but if he act upon this rule, he is either a madman or a fool. He has a right to lay waste his own estate, and to make it utterly barren; but I have also a right to point him out as one who exercises his right in a manner very injurious to society. He may set up a religious or a political test for his tradesmen; but admitting his right, and deprecating all interference with law, I must tell him he is making the aristocracy odious to the great mass, and that he is sowing the seeds of revolution. His purse may be full, and his fields may be wide; but the moralist will still hold the rod of public opinion over his head, and tell the money-bloated blockhead that he is shaking those laws of property which it has taken ages to extort from the wretchedness and rapacity of mankind; and that what he calls his own will not long be his own, if he tramples too heavily on human patience.

All these practices are bad; but the facts and the consequences are exaggerated.

In the first place, the plough is not a political machine: the loom and the steam-engine are furiously political, but the plough is not. Nineteen tenants out of twenty care nothing about their votes, and pull off their opinions as easily to their landlords as they do their hats. As far as the great majority of tenants are concerned, these histories of persecution are mere declamatory nonsense; they have no more predilection for whom they vote than the organ pipes have for what tunes they are to play. A tenant dismissed for a fair and just cause often attributes his dismissal to political motives, and endeavours to make himself a martyr with the public: a man who ploughs badly, or who pays badly, says he is dismissed for his vote. No candidate is willing to allow that he has lost his election by his demerits; and he seizes hold of these stories, and circulates them with the greatest avidity: they are stated in the House of Commons; John Russell and Spring Rice fall a crying: there is lamentation of Liberals in the land; and many groans for the territorial tyrants.

A standing reason against the frequency of dismissal of tenants

is that it is always injurious to the pecuniary interests of the landlord to dismiss a tenant: the property always suffers in some degree by a going-off tenant; and it is therefore always the interest of
a landlord not to change when the tenant does his duty as an agri-
culturalist.

To part with tenants for political reasons always makes a landlord unpopular. The Constitutional, price 4*d*.; the Cato, at 3½*d*.;
and the Lucius Junius Brutus, at 2*d.*, all set upon the unhappy
scutiger; and the squire, unused to be pointed at, and thinking that
all Europe and part of Asia are thinking of him and his farmers,
is driven to the brink of suicide and despair. That such things are
done is not denied, that they are scandalous when they are done is
equally true; but these are reasons why such acts are less frequent
than they are commonly represented to be. In the same manner,
there are instances of shopkeepers being materially injured in their
business from the votes they have given; but the facts themselves,
as well as the consequences, are grossly exaggerated. If shopkeepers lose Tory they gain Whig customers; and it is not always
the vote which does the mischief, but the low vulgar impertinence,
and the unbridled scurrility of a man, who thinks that by dividing
to mankind their rations of butter and of cheese he has qualified himself for legislation, and that he can hold the rod of empire because he
has wielded the yard of mensuration. I detest all inquisition
into political opinions, but I have very rarely seen a combination against any tradesman who modestly, quietly, and conscientiously took his own line in politics. But Brutus and butterman,
cheesemonger and Cato, do not harmonise well together; good
taste is offended, the coxcomb loses his friends, and general disgust is mistaken for combined oppression. Shopkeepers, too, are
very apt to cry out before they are hurt: a man who sees after an
election one of his customers buying a pair of gloves on the opposite side of the way roars out that his honesty will make him a
bankrupt, and the county papers are filled with letters from Brutus,
Publicola, Hampden, and Pym.

This interference with the freedom of voting, bad as it is, produces no political deliberation; it does not make the Tories stronger
than the Whigs, nor the Whigs than the Tories, for both are equally
guilty of this species of tyranny; and any particular system of
measures fails or prevails, much as if no such practice existed. The
practice had better not be at all; but if a certain quantity of the
evil does exist, it is better that it should be equally divided among
both parties, than that it should be exercised by one, for the de-
pression of the other. There are politicians always at a white heat,

who suppose that there are landed tyrants only on one side of
the question; but human life has been distressingly abridged by the
flood: there is no time to spare,—it is impossible to waste it upon
such senseless bigotry.

If a man be sheltered from intimidation, is it at all clear that
he would vote from any better motive than intimidation? If you
make so tremendous an experiment, are you sure of attaining your
object? The landlord has perhaps said a cross word to the tenant;
the candidate for whom the tenant votes in opposition to his landlord has taken his second son for a footman, or his father knew
the candidate's grandfather: how many thousand votes, sheltered
(as the ballotists suppose) from intimidation, would be given from
such silly motives as these? how many would be given from the
mere discontent of inferiority? or from that strange simious school-
boy passion of giving pain to others, even when the author cannot
be found out?—motives as pernicious as any which could proceed
from intimidation. So that all voters screened by ballot would not
be screened for any public good.

The Radicals, (I do not use this word in any offensive sense,
for I know many honest and excellent men of this way of thinking,)—but the Radicals praise and admit the lawful influence of
wealth and power. They are quite satisfied if a rich man of popular
manners gains the votes and affections of his dependants; but why
is not this as bad as intimidation? The real object is to vote for the
good politician, not for the kind-hearted or agreeable man: the
mischief is just the same to the country whether I am smiled into
a corrupt choice, or frowned into a corrupt choice,—what is it to
me whether my landlord is the best of landlords, or the most agreeable of men? I must vote for Joseph Hume, if I think Joseph more
honest than the Marquis. The more mitigated Radical may pass
over this, but the real carnivorous variety of the animal should declaim as loudly against the fascinations as against the threats of the
great. The man who possesses the land should never speak to the
man who tills it. The intercourse between landlord and tenant
should be as strictly guarded as that of the sexes in Turkey. A
funded duenna should be placed over every landed grandee.—
And then intimidation! Is intimidation confined to the aristocracy?
Can anything be more scandalous and atrocious than the intimidation of mobs? Did not the mob of Bristol occasion more ruin,
wretchedness, death, and alarm than all the ejection of tenants,
and combinations against shopkeepers, from the beginning of the
century? and did not the Scotch philosophers tear off the clothes
of the Tories in Mintoshire? or at least such clothes as the cus-

toms of the country admit of being worn?—and did not they, without any reflection at all upon the customs of the country, wash the Tory voters in the river?

Some sanguine advocates of the ballot contend that it would put an end to all canvassing: why should it do so? Under the ballot, I canvass (it is true) a person who may secretly deceive me. I cannot be sure he will not do so—but I am sure it is much less likely he will vote against me, when I have paid him all the deference and attention which a representative bestows on his constitutents, than if I had totally neglected him: to any other objections he may have against me, at least I will not add that of personal incivility.

Scarcely is any great virtue practised without some sacrifice; and the admiration which virtue excites seems to proceed from the contemplation of such sufferings, and of the exertions by which they are endured: a tradesman suffers some loss of trade by voting for his country; is he not to vote? he might suffer some loss of blood in fighting for his country; is he not to fight? Every one would be a good Samaritan, if he were quite sure his compassion would cost him nothing. We should all be heroes, if it were not for blood and fractures; all saints, if it were not for the restrictions and privations of sanctity; all patriots, if it were not for the losses and misrepresentations to which patriotism exposes us. The ballotists are a set of Englishmen glowing with the love of England and the love of virtue, but determined to hazard the most dangerous experiments in politics, rather than run the risk of losing a penny in defence of their exalted feelings.

An abominable tyranny exercised by the ballot is, that it compels those persons to conceal their votes, who hate all concealment, and who glory in the cause they support. If you are afraid to go in at the front door, and to say in a clear voice what you have to say, go in at the back door, and say it in a whisper—but this is not enough for you; you make me, who am bold and honest, sneak in at the back door as well as yourself: because you are afraid of selling a dozen or two of gloves less than usual, you compel me, who have no gloves to sell, or who would dare and despise the loss if I had, to hide the best feelings of my heart, and to lower myself down to your mean morals. It is as if a few cowards, who could only fight behind walls and houses, were to prevent the whole regiment from showing a bold front in the field: what right has the coward to degrade me who am no coward, and put me in the same shameful predicament with himself? If ballot be established, a zealous voter cannot do justice to his cause; there will be so many false Hampdens, and spurious Catos, that all men's actions and

motives will be mistrusted. It is in the power of any man to tell
me that my colours are false, that I declaim with simulated warmth,
and canvass with fallacious zeal; that I am a Tory, though I call
Russell for ever, or a Whig, in spite of my obstreperous panegyrics
of *Peel*. It is really a curious condition that all men must imitate the
defects of a few, in order that it may not be known who have the
natural imperfection, and who put it on from conformity. In this
way in former days, to hide the grey hairs of the old, everybody
was forced to wear powder and pomatum.

It must not be forgotten that, in the ballot, concealment must
be absolutely *compulsory*. It would never do to let one man vote
openly, and another secretly. You may go to the edge of the box
and say, "I vote for A.," but who knows that your ball is not put
in for B.? There must be a clear plain opportunity for telling an
undiscoverable lie, or the whole invention is at an end. How
beautiful is the progress of man!—printing has abolished ignorance
—gas put an end to darkness—steam has conquered time and distance—it remained for Grote and his box to remove the encumbrance of truth from human transactions. May we not look now
for more little machines to abolish the other cardinal virtues?

But if all men are suspected; if things are so contrived that it is
impossible to know what men really think, a serious impediment
is created to the formation of good public opinion in the multitude.
There is a town (No. 1.) in which live two very clever and respectable men, Johnson and Pelham, small tradesmen, men always
willing to run some risk for the public good, and to be less rich,
and more honest than their neighbours. It is of considerable consequence to the formation of opinion in this town, as an example,
to know how Johnson and Pelham vote. It guides the affections,
and directs the understandings, of the whole population, and materially affects public opinion in this town; and in another borough
(No. 2.), it would be of the highest importance to public opinion
if it were certain how Mr. Smith, the ironmonger, and Mr. Rogers,
the London carrier, voted; because they are both thoroughly honest
men, and of excellent understanding for their condition of life.
Now, the tendency of ballot would be to destroy all the Pelhams,
Johnsons, Rogers's, and Smiths, to sow a universal mistrust, and
to exterminate the natural guides and leaders of the people: political influence, founded upon honour and ancient honesty in politics,
could not grow up under such a system. No man's declaration
could get believed. It would be easy to whisper away the character
of the best men; and to assert that, in spite of all his declarations,

which are nothing but a blind, the romantic Rogers has voted on the other side, and is in secret league with our enemies.

"Who brought that mischievous profligate villain into Parliament? Let us see the names of his real supporters. Who stood out against the strong and uplifted arm of power? Who discovered this excellent and hitherto unknown person? Who opposed the man whom we all know to be one of the first men in the country?" Are these fair and useful questions to be veiled hereafter in impenetrable mystery? Is this sort of publicity of no good as a restraint? Is it of no good as an incitement to and a reward for exertions? Is not public opinion formed by such feelings? and is it not a dark and demoralising system to draw this veil over human actions, to say to the mass, be base, and you will not be despised; be virtuous, and you will not be honoured? Is this the way in which Mr. Grote would foster the spirit of a bold and indomitable people? Was the liberty of that people established by fraud? Did America lie herself into independence? Was it treachery which enabled Holland to shake off the yoke of Spain? Is there any instance since the beginning of the world where human liberty has been established by little systems of trumpery and trick? These are the weapons of monarchs against the people, not of the people against monarchs. With their own right hand, and with their mighty arm, have the people gotten to themselves the victory, and upon them may they ever depend; and then comes Mr. Grote, a scholar and a gentleman, and knowing all the histories of public courage, preaches cowardice and treachery to England; tells us that the bold cannot be free, and bids us seek for liberty by clothing ourselves in the mask of falsehood, and trampling on the cross of truth.*

If this shrinking from the performance of duties is to be tolerated, voters are not the only persons who would recur to the accommodating convenience of ballot. A member of Parliament who votes against Government can get nothing in the army, navy, or Church, or at the bar, for his children or himself: they are placed on the north wall, and starved for their honesty. Judges, too, suffer for their unpopularity—Lord Kilwarden was murdered, Lord Mansfield burnt down! but voters, forgetting that they are only trustees for those who have no vote, require that they themselves should be virtuous with impunity, and that all the penalties of austerity and Catonism should fall upon others. I am aware that

---

* Mr. Grote is a very worthy, honest, and able man; and if the world were a chessboard, would be an important politician.

it is of the greatest consequence to the constituent that he should be made acquainted with the conduct of his representative; but I maintain, that to know, without the fear of mistake, what the conduct of individuals has been in their fulfilment of the great trust of electing members of Parliament, is also of the greatest importance in the formation of public opinion; and that, when men acted in the dark, the power of distinguishing between the bad and good would be at an end.

To institute ballot is to apply a very dangerous innovation to a temporary evil; for it is seldom, but in very excited times, that these acts of power are complained of which the ballot is intended to remedy. There never was an instance in this country where parties were so nearly balanced; but all this will pass away, and, in a very few years, either Peel will swallow Lord John, or Lord John will pasture upon Peel; parties will coalesce, the Duke of Wellington and Viscount Melbourne meet at the same board, and the lion lie down with the lamb. In the meantime a serious and dangerous political change is resorted to for the cure of a temporary evil, and we may be cursed with ballot when we do not want it, and cannot get rid of it.

If there be ballot there can be no scrutiny, the controlling power of Parliament is lost, and the members are entirely in the hands of returning officers.

An election is hard run—the returning officer lets in twenty votes which he ought to have excluded, and the opposite candidate is unjustly returned. I petition, and as the law now stands, the return would be amended, and I, who had the legitimate majority, should be seated in Parliament. But how could justice be done if the ballot obtained, and if the returning officer were careless or corrupt? Would you put all the electors upon their oath? Would it be advisable to accept any oath where detection was impossible? and could any approximation to truth be expected under such circumstances, from such an inquisition? It is true, the present committees of the House of Commons are a very unfair tribunal, but that tribunal may and will be amended; and bad as that tribunal is, nobody can be insane enough to propose that we are to take refuge in the blunders or the corruptions of 600 returning officers, 100 of whom are Irish.

It is certainly in the power of a committee, when incapacity or villany of the returning officer has produced an unfair return, to annul the whole election and to proceed again *de novo;* but how is this just? or what satisfaction is this to me, who have unquestionably a lawful majority, and who ask of the House of Commons to examine the votes, and to place in their house the man who has combined the greatest number of suffrages? The answer of the House of Commons is, "One of you is undoubtedly the rightful member, but we have so framed our laws of election, that it is impossible to find out which that man is; the loss and penalties ought only to fall upon one, but they must fall upon both; we put the well-doer and the evil-doer precisely in the same situation, there shall be no election;" and this may happen ten times running.

Purity of election, the fair choice of representatives, must be guarded either by the coercing power of the House of Commons exercised upon petitions, or it must be guarded by the watchful jealousy of opposite parties at the registrations; but if (as the Radicals suppose) ballot gives a power of perfect concealment, whose interest is it to watch the registrations? If I despair of distinguishing my friends from my foes, why should I take any trouble about registrations? Why not leave everything to that great *primum mobile* of all human affairs, the barrister of six years' standing?

The answer of the excellent Benthamites to all this is, "What you say may be true enough in the present state of registrations, but we have another scheme of registration to which these objections will not apply." There is really no answering this Paulopost legislation. I reason now upon registration and reform which are in existence, which I have seen at work for several years. What new improvements are in the womb of time, or (if time have no womb) in the more capacious pockets of the followers of Bentham, I know not: when I see them tried I will reason upon them. There is no end to these eternal changes; we have made an enormous revolution within the last ten years,—let us stop a little and secure it, and prevent it from being turned into ruin; I do not say the Reform Bill is final, but I want a little time for breathing; and if there are to be any more changes, let them be carried into execution hereafter by those little legislators who are now receiving every day after dinner a cake or a plum, in happy ignorance of Mr. Grote and his ballot. I long for the quiet times of *Log,* when all the English common people are making calico, and all the English gentlemen are making long and short verses, with no other interruption of their happiness than when false quantities are discovered in one or the other.

What is to become of petitions if ballot is established? Are they to be open as they now are, or are they to be conducted by ballot? Are the radical shopkeepers and the radical tenant to be exposed (as they say) to all the fury of incensed wealth and power, and is that protection to be denied to them in petitions, which is so loudly demanded in the choice of representatives? Are there to be two distinct methods of ascertaining the opinions of the people, and these completely opposed to each other? A member is chosen this week by a large majority of voters who vote in the dark, and the next week, when men vote in the light of day, some petition is carried totally opposite to all those principles for which the member with invisible votes was returned to Parliament. How, under such a system, can Parliament ever ascertain what the wishes of the people really are? The representatives are Radicals, the petitioners eminently conservative; the voice is the voice of Jacob, but the hands are the hands of Esau.

And if the same protection be adopted for petitions as is given in elections, and if both are conducted by ballot, how are the House of Commons to deal with petitions? When it is intended particularly that a petition should attract the attention of the House of Commons, some member bears witness to the respectability or the futility of the signatures; and how is it possible, without some guides of this kind, that the House could form any idea of the value and importance of the petition?

These observations apply with equal force to the communications between the representative and the constituent. It is the Radical doctrine that a representative is to obey the instructions of his constituents. He has been elected under the ballot by a large majority; an open meeting is called, and he receives instructions in direct opposition to all those principles upon which he has been elected. Is this the real opinion of his constituents? and if he receive his instructions for a ballot meeting, who are his instructors? The lowest men in the town, or the wiseet and the best?—But if ballot be established for elections only, and all communications between the constituents on one side, and Parliament and the representatives on the other, are carried on in open meetings, then are there two publics according to the Radical doctrines, essentially differing from each other; the one acting under the influence of the rich and powerful, the other free; and if all political petitions are to be carried on by ballot, how are Parliament to know who petitions, or the member to know who instructs?

I have hitherto spoken of ballot, as if it were, as the Radicals suppose it to be, a mean of secrecy; their very cardinal position is, that landlords, after the ballot is established, will give up in despair all hopes of commanding the votes of their tenants. I scarcely ever heard a more foolish and gratuitous assumption. Given up? Why should they be given up? I can give many reasons why landlords should never exercise this unreasonable power, but I can give no possible reason why a man determined to do so should be baffled by the ballot. When two great parties in the empire are combating for the supreme power, does Mr. Grote imagine, that the man of woods, forests, and rivers,—that they who have the strength of the hills,—are to be baffled by bumpkins thrusting a little pin into a little card in a little box? that England is to be governed by political acupunctuation?

A landlord who would otherwise be guilty of the oppression will not change his purpose, because you attempt to outwit him by the invention of the ballot; he will become, on the contrary, doubly vigilant, inquisitive, and severe. "I am a professed Radical," said the tenant of a great duke to a friend of mine, "and the duke knows it; but if I vote for his candidates, he lets me talk as I please, live with whom I please, and does not care if I dine at a Radical dinner every day in the week. If there was a ballot, nothing could persuade the duke, or the duke's master, the steward, that I was not deceiving them, and I should lose my farm in a week." This is the real history of what would take place. The single lie on the hustings would not suffice; the concealed democrat who voted against his landlord must talk with the wrong people, subscribe to the wrong club, huzza at the wrong dinner, break the wrong head, lead (if he wished to escape from the watchful jealousy of his land-lord) a long life of lies between every election; and he must do this, not only *eundo,* in his calm and prudential state, but *redeundo* from the market, warmed with beer, and expanded by alcohol; and he must not only carry on his seven years of dissimulation before the world, but in the very bosom of his family, or he must expose himself to the dangerous garrulity of wife, children, and servants, from whose indiscretion every kind of evil report would be carried to the ears of the watchful steward. And when once the ballot is established, mere gentle, quiet lying will not do to hide the tenant who secretly votes against his landlord: the quiet passive liar will be suspected, and he will find, if he does not wave his bonnet and strain his throat in furtherance of his bad faith, and lie loudly, that he has put in a false ball in the dark to very little purpose. I con-sider a long concealment of political opinion from the landlord to be nearly impossible for the tenant: and if you conceal from the landlord the only proof he can have of his tenant's sincerity, you are taking from the tenant the only means he has of living quietly upon his farm. You are increasing the jealousy and irascibility of the tyrant, and multipl ing instead of lessening the number of his victims.

Not only you do not protect the tenant who wishes to deceive his landlord, by promising one way and voting another, but you expose all the other tenants who have no intention of deceiving, to all the evils of mistake and misrepresentation. The steward hates a tenant, and a rival wants his farm; they begin to whisper him out of favour, and to propagate rumours of his disaffection to the blue or the yellow cause; as matters now stand he can refer to the poll-book and show how he has voted. Under the ballot his security is gone, and he is exposed in common with his deceitful neighbour, to that suspicion from which none can be exempt when all vote in secret. If ballot then answered the purpose for which it was intended, the number of honest tenants whom it exposed to danger would be as great as the number of deceitful tenants whom it screened.

But if landlords could be prevented from influencing their tenants in voting, by threatening them with the loss of farms;—if public opinion were too strong to allow of such threats, what would prevent a landlord from refusing to take, as a tenant, a man whose political opinion did not agree with his own? what would prevent him from questioning, long before the election, and cross-examining his tenant, and demanding certificates of his behaviour and opinions, till he had, according to all human probability, found a man who felt as strongly as himself upon political subjects, and who would adhere to those opinions with as much firmness and tenacity? What would prevent, for instance, an Orange landlord from filling his farms with Orange tenants, and from cautiously rejecting every Catholic tenant who presented himself plough in hand? But if this practice were to obtain generally, of cautiously selecting tenants from their political opinion, what would become of the sevenfold shield of the ballot? Not only this tenant is not continued in the farm he already holds, but he finds, from the severe inquisition into which men of property are driven by the invention of ballot, that it is extremely difficult for a man whose principles are opposed to those of his landlord, to get any farm at all.

The noise and jollity of a ballot mob must be such as the very devils would look on with delight. A set of deceitful wretches wearing the wrong colours, abusing their friends, pelting the man for whom they voted, drinking their enemies' punch, knocking down persons with whom they entirely agreed, and roaring out eternal duration to principles they abhorred. A scene of wholesale bacchanalian fraud, a *posse comitatus* of liars, which would disgust any man with a free government, and make him sigh for the monocracy of Constantinople.

All the arguments which apply to suspected tenants apply to suspected shopkeepers. Their condition under the ballot would be infinitely worse than under the present system; the veracious shopkeeper would be suspected, perhaps without having his vote to appeal to for his protection, and the shopkeeper who meant to deceive must prop up his fraud, by accommodating his whole life to the first deceit, or he would have told a disgraceful falsehood in vain. The political persecutors would not be baffled by the ballot: customers who think they have a right to persecute tradesmen now, would do it then; the only difference would be that more would be persecuted then on suspicion, than are prosecuted now from a full knowledge of every man's vote. Inquisitors would be exasperated by this attempt of their victims to become invisible, and the search for delinquents would be more sharp and incessant.

A state of things may (to be sure) occur where the aristocratic part of the voters may be desirous, by concealing their votes, of protecting themselves from the fury of the multitude; but precisely the same objection obtains against ballot, whoever may be the oppressor or the oppressed. It is no defence; the single falsehood at the hustings will not suffice. Hypocrisy for seven years is impossible; the multitude will be just as jealous of preserving the power of intimidation, as aristocrats are of preserving the power of property, and will in the same way redouble their vicious activity from the attempt at destroying their empire by ballot.

Ballot could not prevent the disfranchisement of a great number of voters. The shopkeeper, harassed by men of both parties, equally consuming the articles in which he dealt, would seek security in not voting at all, and, of course, the ballot could not screen the disobedient tenant whom the landlord requested to stay away from the poll. Mr. Grote has no box for this; but a remedy for securing the freedom of election, which has no power to prevent the voter from losing the exercise of his franchise altogether, can scarcely be considered as a remedy at all. There is a method, indeed, by which this might be remedied, if the great soul of Mr. Grote will stoop to adopt it. Why are the acts of concealment to be confined to putting in a ball? Why not vote in a domino, taking off the vizor to the returning officer only? or as tenant Jenkins or tenant Hodge might be detected by their stature, why not poll in sedan chairs with the curtains closely drawn, choosing the chairman by ballot?

What a flood of deceit and villany comes in with ballot! I admit there are great moral faults under the present system. It is a serious violation of duty to vote for A. when you think B. the more worthy representative; but the open voter, acting under the influence of his landlord, commits only this one fault, great as it is:—if he vote for his candidate, the landlord is satisfied, and asks no other sacrifice of truth and opinion; but if the tenant vote against his landlord under the ballot, he is practising every day some fraud to conceal his first deviation from truth. The present method may produce a vicious act, but the ballot establishes a vicious habit; and then it is of some consequence, that the law should not range itself on the side of vice. In the open voting, the law leaves you fairly to choose between the dangers of giving an honest, or the convenience of giving a dishonest vote; but the ballot law opens a booth and asylum for fraud, calling upon all men to lie by beat of drum, forbidding open honesty, promising impunity for the most scandalous deceit, and encouraging men to take no other view of virtue than whether it pays or does not pay; for it must always be remembered and often repeated, and said and sung to Mr. Grote, that it is to the degraded liar only that the box will be useful. The man who performs what he promises needs no box. The man who refuses to do what he is asked to do despises the box. The liar, who says he will do what he never means to do, is the only man to whom the box is useful, and for whom this leaf out of the punic Pandects is to be inserted in our statute book; the other vices will begin to look up, and to think themselves neglected, if falsehood obtains such flattering distinction, and is thus defended by the solemn enactments of law.

Old John Randolph, the American orator, was asked one day at a dinner party in London, whether the ballot prevailed in his state of Virginia—"I scarcely believe," he said, "we have such a fool in all Virginia, as to mention even the vote by ballot; and I do not hesitate to say that the adoption of the ballot *would make any nation a nation of scoundrels if it did not find them so."* John Randolph was right; he felt that it was not necessary that a people should be false in order to be free; universal hypocrisy would be the consequence of ballot: we should soon say on deliberation what David only asserted in his haste, *that all men were liars.*

This exclamation of old Randolph applied to the method of popular elections, which I believe has always been by open voice in Virginia; but the assemblies voted, and the Judges were chosen by ballot; and in the year 1830, upon a solemn review of their institutions, ballot was entirely abolished in every instance throughout the State, and open voting substituted in its place.

Not only would the tenant under ballot be constantly exposed to the suspicions of the landlord, but the landlord would be exposed to the constant suspicions and the unjust misrepresentation of the tenant. Every tenant who was dismissed for a fair and a just cause, would presume he was suspected, would attribute his dismissal to political motives, and endeavour to make himself a martyr with the public; and in this way violent hatred would be by the ballot disseminated among classes of men on whose agreement the order and happiness of England depends.

All objections to ballot which are important in England, apply with much greater force to Ireland, a country of intense agitation, fierce passions, and quick movements. Then how would the ballot box of Mr. Grote harmonise with the confessional box of Father O'Leary?

I observe Lord John Russell, and some important men as well as him, saying, "We hate ballot, but if these practices continue, we shall be compelled to vote for it." What! vote for it, if ballot be no remedy for these evils? Vote for it, if ballot produce still greater evils than it cures? That is (says the physician), if fevers increase in this alarming manner, I shall be compelled to make use of some medicine which will be of no use to fevers, and will at the same time bring on diseases of a much more serious nature. I shall be under the absolute necessity of putting out your eyes, because I cannot prevent you from being lame. In fact, this sort of language is utterly unworthy of the sense and courage of Lord John; he gives hopes where he *ought* to create absolute despair. This is that hovering between two principles which ruins political strength by lowering political character, and creates a notion that his enemies need not fear such a man, and that his friends cannot trust him. No opinion could be more unjust as applied to Lord John; but such an opinion will grow if he begin to value himself more upon his dexterity and finesse, than upon those fine manly historico-Russell qualities he most undoubtedly possesses. There are two beautiful words in the English language,—Yes and No; he must pronounce them boldly and emphatically; stick to Yes and No to the death; for Yes and No lay his head down upon the scaffold, where his ancestors have laid their heads before, and cling to his Yes and No in spite of Robert Peel and John Wilson, and Joseph, and Daniel, and Fergus, and Stephens himself. He must do as the Russells always have done, advance his firm foot on the field of honour, plant it on the line marked out by justice, and determine in that cause to perish or to prevail.

In clubs, ballot preserves secrecy; but in clubs, after the barrister has blackballed the colonel, he most likely never hears of the colonel again: he does not live among people who are calling out for seven years *the colonel for ever;* nor is there any one who, thinking he has a right to the barrister's suffrage, exercises the most incessant vigilance to detect whether or not he has been defrauded of it. I do not say that ballot can never in any instance be made a mean of secrecy and safety, but that it cannot be so in popular elections. Even in elections, a consummate hypocrite who was unmarried, and drank water, might perhaps exercise his timid patriotism with impunity; but the instances would be so rare, as to render ballot utterly inefficient as a general protection against the abuses of power.

In America, ballot is nearly a dead letter; no protection is wanted: if the ballot protects any one it is the master, not the man. Some of the States have no ballot—some have exchanged the ballot for open voting.

Bribery carried on in any town now, would probably be carried on with equal success under the ballot. The attorney (if such a system prevailed) would say to the candidate, "There is my list of promises: if you come in I will have 5000*l.*, and if you do not, you shall pay me nothing." To this list, to which I suppose all the venal rabble of the town to have put their names, there either is an opposition bribery list, or there is not: if there is not, the promisers, looking only to make money by their vote, have every inducement to keep their word. If there be an opposite list, the only trick which a promiser can play is to put down his name upon both lists: but this trick would be so easily detected, so much watched and suspected, and would even in the vote market render a man so infamous, that it never would be attempted to any great extent. At present, if a man promise his vote to A., and votes for B., because he can get more money by it, he does not become infamous among the bribed, because they lose no money by him; but where a list is found, and a certain sum of money is to be divided among that list, every interloper lessens the receipts of all the rest; it becomes their interest to guard against fraudulent intrusion; and a man who puts his name upon more lists than the votes he was entitled to give, would soon be hunted down by those he had robbed. Of course there would be no pay till after the election, and the man who having one vote had put himself down on two lists, or having two votes had put himself down on three lists, could hardly fail to be detected, and would, of course, lose his political *aceldama.* There must be honour among thieves; the mob regularly inured to bribery under the canopy of the ballot, would for their own sake soon introduce rules for the distribution of the plunder, and infuse with their customary energy, the morality of not being sold more than once at every election.

If ballot were established, it would be received by the upper classes with the greatest possible suspicion, and every effort would be made to counteract it and to get rid of it. Against those attacks the inferior orders would naturally wish to strengthen themselves, and the obvious means would be by extending the number of voters; and so comes on universal suffrage. The ballot would fail: it would be found neither to prevent intimidation nor bribery. Universal suffrage would cure both, as a teaspoonful of prussic acid is a certain cure for the most formidable diseases; but universal suffrage would in all probability be the next step. "The 200 richest voters of Bridport shall not beat the 400 poorest voters. Everybody who has a house shall vote, or everybody who is twenty-one shall vote, and then the people will be sure to have their way—we will blackball every member standing for Bridgewater who does not promise to vote for universal suffrage."

The ballot and universal suffrage are never mentioned by the Radicals without being coupled together. Nobody ever thinks of separating them. Any person who attempted to separate them at torchlight or sunlight meetings would be hooted down. It is professedly avowed that ballot is only wanted for ulterior purposes, and no one makes a secret of what those ulterior purposes are: not only would the gift of ballot, if universal suffrage were refused, not be received with gratitude, but it would be received with furious indignation and contempt, and universal suffrage be speedily extorted from you.

There would be this argument also for universal suffrage, to which I do not think it very easy to find an answer. The son of a man who rents a house of ten pounds a year is often a much cleverer man than his father; the wife more intelligent than the husband. Under the system of open voting, these persons are not excluded from want of intellect, but for want of independence, for they would necessarily vote with their principal; but the moment the ballot is established, according to the reasoning of the Grote school, one man is as independent as another, because all are concealed, and so all are equally entitled to offer their suffrages. This cannot sow dissensions in families; for how, ballotically reasoning, can the father find it out? or, if he did find it out, how has any father, ballotically speaking, a right to control the votes of his family?

I have often drawn a picture in my own mind of a Balloto-Grotical family voting and promising under the new system. There is one vacancy, and three candidates, Tory, Whig, and Radical. Walter

Wiggins, a small artificer of shoes, for the moderate gratuity of five pounds, promises his own vote, and that of the chaste Arabella his wife, to the Tory candidate; he, Walter Wiggins, having also sold, for one sovereign, the vote of the before-named Arabella to the Whigs. Mr. John Wiggins, a tailor, the male progeny of Walter and Arabella, at the solicitation of his master, promises his vote to the Whigs, and persuades his sister Honoria to make a similar promise in the same cause. Arabella, the wife, yields implicitly to the wishes of her husband. In this way, before the election, stand committed the highly moral family of Mr. Wiggins. The period for lying arrives, and the mendacity machine is exhibited to the view of the Wigginses. What happens? Arabella, who has in the interim been chastised by her drunken husband, votes secretly for the Radicals, having been sold both to Whig and Tory. Mr. John Wiggins, pledged beyond redemption to Whigs, votes for the Tory; and Honoria, extrinsically furious in the cause of Whigs, is persuaded by her lover to vote for the Radical member. The following Table exhibits the state of this moral family, before and after the election:

> Walter Wiggins sells himself once and his wife twice.
> Arabella Wiggins, sold to Tory and Whig, votes for Radical.
> John Wiggins, promised to Whig, votes for Tory.
> Honoria Wiggins, promised to Whig, votes for Radical.

In this way the families of the poor, under the legislation of Mr. Grote, will become schools for good faith, openness, and truth! What are Chrysippus and Crantor, and all the moralists of the whole world, compared to Mr. Grote?

It is urged that the lower order of voters, proud of such a distinction, will not be anxious to extend it to others: but the lower order of voters will often find that they possess this distinction in vain— that wealth and education are too strong for them; and they will call in the multitude as auxiliaries, firmly believing that they can curb their inferiors and conquer their superiors. Ballot is a mere illusion, but universal suffrage is not an illusion. The common people will get nothing by the one, but they will gain everything, and *ruin* everything, by the last.

Some members of Parliament who mean to vote for ballot, in the fear of losing their seats, and who are desirous of reconciling to their conscience such an act of disloyalty to mankind, are fond of saying that ballot is harmless; that it will neither do the good nor the evil that is expected from it; and that the people may fairly be indulged in such an innocent piece of legislation. Never was such folly and madness as this: ballot will be the cause of interminable hatred and jealousy among the different orders of mankind; it will familiarise the English people to a long tenor of deceit; it will not answer its purpose of protecting the independent voter, and the people, exasperated and disappointed by the failure, will indemnify themselves by insisting upon unlimited suffrage. And then it is talked of as an experiment, as if men were talking of acids and alkalies, and the galvanic pile; as if Lord John could get on the hustings and say, "Gentlemen, you see this ballot does not answer; do me the favour to give it up, and to allow yourselves to be replaced in the same situation as the ballot found you." Such, no doubt, is the history of nations and the march of human affairs; and, in this way, the error of a sudden and foolish largess of power to the people might, no doubt, be easily retrieved! The most unpleasant of all bodily feelings is a cold sweat: nothing brings it on so surely as perilous nonsense in politics. I lose all warmth from the bodily frame when I hear the ballot talked of as an *experiment*.

I cannot at all understand what is meant by this indolent opinion. Votes are coerced now; if votes are free, will the elected be the same? if not, will the difference of the elected be unimportant? Will not the ballot stimulate the upper orders to fresh exertions? and is their increased jealousy and interference of no importance? If ballot, after all, be found to hold out a real protection to the voter, is universal lying of no importance? I can understand what is meant by calling ballot a great good, or a great evil; but, in the mighty contention for power which is raging in this country, to call it indifferent, appears to me extremely foolish in all those in whom it is not extremely dishonest.

If the ballot did succeed in enabling the lower order of voters to conquer their betters, so much the worse. In a town consisting of 700 voters, the 300 most opulent and powerful (and therefore probably the best instructed) would make a much better choice than the remaining 400; and the ballot would, in that case, do more harm than good. In nineteen cases out of twenty, the most numerous party would be in the wrong. If this be the case, why give the franchise to all? why not confine it to the first division? *because even with all the abuses which occur, and in spite of them, the great mass of the people are much more satisfied with having a vote occasionally controlled, than with having none.* Many agree with their superiors, and therefore feel no control. Many are persuaded by their superiors, and not controlled. Some are indifferent which way they exercise the power, though they would not like to be utterly deprived of it. Some guzzle away their vote, some sell it, some brave their superiors, if they are threatened and controlled. The election, in different ways, is affected by the superior influence of the upper orders; and the great mass (occasionally and justly complaining) are, beyond all doubt, better pleased than if they had no votes at all. The lower orders always have it in their power to rebel against their superiors; and occasionally they will do so, and have done so, and occasionally and justly carried elections * against gold, and birth, and education. But it is madness to make laws of society which attempt to shake off the great laws of nature. As long as men love bread, and mutton, and broad cloth, wealth, in a long series of years, must have enormous effects upon human affairs, and the strong box will beat the ballot box. Mr. Grote has both, but he miscalculates their respective powers. Mr. Grote knows the relative values of gold and silver; but by what moral rate of exchange is he able to tell us the relative values of liberty and truth?

It is hardly necessary to say anything about universal suffrage, as there is no act of folly or madness which it may not in the beginning produce. There would be the greatest risk that the monarchy, as at present constituted, the funded debt, the established church, titles, and hereditary peerage, would give way before it. Many really honest men may wish for these changes; I know, or at least believe, that wheat and barley would grow if there were no Archbishop of Canterbury, and domestic fowls would breed if our Viscount Melbourne was again called Mr. Lamb; but they have stronger nerves than I have who would venture to bring these changes about. So few nations have been free, it is so difficult to guard freedom from kings, and mobs, and patriotic gentlemen; and we are in such a very tolerable state of happiness in England, that I think such changes would be very rash; and I have an utter mistrust in the sagacity and penetration of political reasoners who pretend to foresee all the consequences to which they would give birth. When I speak of the tolerable state of happiness in which we live in England, I do not speak merely of nobles, squires, and canons of St. Paul's, but of drivers of coaches, clerks in offices, carpenters, blacksmiths, butchers, and bakers, and most men who do not marry upon nothing, and become burdened with large families before they have arrived at years of maturity. The earth is not sufficiently fertile for this:

Difficilem victum fundit durissima tellus.

After all, the great art in politics and war is to choose a good position for making a stand. The Duke of Wellington examined and fortified the lines of Torres Vedras a year before he had any occa-

---

* The 400 or 500 voting against the 200 are right about as often as juries are right in differing from judges; and that is very seldom.

sion to make use of them, and he had previously marked out Waterloo as the probable scene of some future exploit. The people seem
to be hurrying on through all the well known steps to anarchy; they
must be stopped at some pass or another: the first is the best and
the most easily defended. The people have a right to ballot or to
anything else which will make them happy; and they have a right
to *nothing which will make them unhappy.* They are the best judges
of their immediate gratifications, and the worst judges of what would
best conduce to their interests for a series of years. Most earnestly
and conscientiously wishing their good, I say,

No BALLOT.

PART V

AMERICA

There is a set of miserable persons in England, who are dreadfully afraid of America and everything American—whose great delight is to see that country ridiculed and vilified—and who appear to imagine that all the abuses which exist in this country acquire additional vigour and chance of duration from every book of travels which pours forth its venom and falsehood on the United States. We shall from time to time call the attention of the public to this subject, not from any party spirit, but because we love truth, and praise excellence wherever we find it; and because we think the example of America will in many instances tend to open the eyes of Englishmen to their true interests.

The *Economy* of America is a great and important object for our imitation. The salary of Mr. Bagot, our late Ambassador, was, we believe, rather higher than that of the President of the United States. The Vice-President receives rather less than the second Clerk of the House of Commons; and all salaries, civil and military, are upon the same scale; and yet no country is better served than America! Mr. Hume has at last persuaded the English people to look a little into their accounts, and to see how sadly they are plundered. But we ought to suspend our contempt for America, and consider whether we have not a very momentous lesson to learn from this wise and cautious people on the subject of economy.

A lesson on the importance of Religious Toleration, we are determined, it would seem, *not* to learn,—either from America, or from any other quarter of the globe. The high sheriff of New York, last year, was a Jew. It was with the utmost difficulty that a bill was carried this year to allow the first duke of England to carry a gold stick before the King—because he was a Catholic!—and yet we think ourselves entitled to indulge in impertinent sneers at America,—as if civilisation did not depend more upon making wise laws for the promotion of human happiness, than in having good inns, and post-horses, and civil waiters. The circumstances of the Dissenters' Marriage Bill are such as would excite the contempt of a Chictaw or

Cherokee, if he could be brought to understand them. A certain class of Dissenters beg they may not be compelled to say that they marry in the name of the Trinity, because they do not believe in the Trinity. Never mind, say the corruptionists, you must go on saying you marry in the name of the Trinity whether you believe in it or not. We know that such a protestation from you will be false: but, unless you make it, your wives shall be concubines, and your children illegitimate. Is it possible to conceive a greater or more useless tyranny than this?

"In the religious freedom which America enjoys, I see a more unquestioned superiority. In Britain we enjoy toleration, but here they enjoy liberty. If Government has a right to grant toleration to any particular set of religious opinions, it has also a right to take it away; and such a right with regard to opinions exclusively religious I would deny in all cases, because totally inconsistent with the nature of religion, in the proper meaning of the word, and equally irreconcilable with civil liberty, rightly so called. God has given to each of us his inspired word, and a rational mind to which that word is addressed. He has also made known to us, that each for himself must answer at his tribunal for his principles and conduct. What man, then, or body of men, has a right to tell me, 'You do not think aright on religious subjects, but we will tolerate your error?' The answer is a most obvious one, 'Who gave you authority to dictate?—or what exclusive claim have you to infallibility?' If my sentiments do not lead me into conduct inconsistent with the welfare of my fellow-creatures, the question as to their accuracy or fallacy is one between God and my own conscience; and, though a fair subject for argument, is none for compulsion.

"The Inquisition undertook to regulate astronomical science, and kings and parliaments have with equal propriety presumed to legislate upon questions of theology. The world has outgrown the former, and it will one day be ashamed that it has been so long of outgrowing the latter. The founders of the American republic saw the absurdity of employing the attorney-general to refute deism and infidelity, or of attempting to influence opinion on abstract subjects by penal enactment; they saw also the injustice of taxing the whole to support the religious opinions of the few, and have set an example which older governments will one day or other be compelled to follow.

"In America the question is not, 'What is his creed?'—but, 'What is his conduct?' Jews have all the privileges of Christians; Episcopalians, Presbyterians, and Independents, meet on common ground. No religious test is required to qualify for public office, except in some cases a mere verbal assent to the truth of the Christian religion; and, in every court throughout the country, it is optional whether you give your affirmation or your oath." —(*Duncan's Travels,* Vol. II, pp. 328–330.)*

In fact, it is hardly possible for any nation to show a greater superiority over another than the Americans, in this particular, have done over this country. They have fairly and completely, and probably for ever, extinguished that spirit of religious persecution which has been the employment and the curse of mankind for four or five centuries,—not only that persecution which imprisons and scourges for religious opinions, but the tyranny of incapacitation, which, by disqualifying from civil offices, and cutting a man off from the lawful objects of ambition, endeavours to strangle religious freedom in silence, and to enjoy all the advantages, without the blood, and noise, and fire of persecution. What passes in the mind of one mean blockhead is the general history of all persecution. "This man pretends to know better than me—I cannot subdue him by argument; but I will take care he shall never be mayor or alderman of the town in which he lives; I will never consent to the repeal of the Test Act or to Catholic Emancipation; I will teach the fellow to differ from me in religious opinions!" So says the Episcopalian to the Catholic—and so the Catholic says to the Protestant. But the wisdom of America keeps them all down—secures to them all their just rights—gives to each of them their separate pews, and bells, and steeples—makes them all aldermen in their turns—and quietly extinguishes the faggots which each is preparing for the combustion of the other. Nor is this indifference to religious subjects in the American people, but pure civilisation—a thorough comprehension of what is best calculated to secure the public happiness and peace—and a determination that this happiness and peace shall not be violated by the insolence of any human being, in the garb, and under the sanction, of religion. In this particular, the Americans are at the head of all the nations of the world: and at the same time they are, especially in the Eastern and Midland States, so far from being indifferent on subjects of religion, that they may be most justly characterised as a very religious people, but they are devout without being unjust (the great problem in religion); a higher proof of civilisation than·painted teacups, water-proof leather, or broad cloth at two guineas a yard.

---

* *Travels through Part of the United States and Canada, in* 1818 *and* 1819. By John M. Duncan, A.B. Glasgow. 1823.

America is exempted, by its very newness as a nation, from many
of the evils of the old governments of Europe. It has no mischievous
remains of feudal institutions, and no violations of political economy
sanctioned by time, and older than the age of reason. If a man find
a partridge upon his ground eating his corn, in any part of Kentucky
or Indiana, he may kill it, even if his father be not a Doctor of
Divinity. The Americans do not exclude their own citizens from any
branch of commerce which they leave open to all the rest of the
world.

"One of them said, that he was well acquainted with a British
subject, residing at Newark, Upper Canada, who annually smuggled from 500 to 1000, chests of tea into that province from the
United States. He mentioned the name of this man, who he said
was growing very rich in consequence; and he stated the manner
in which the fraud was managed. Now, as all the tea ought to be
brought from England, it is of course very expensive; and therefore the Canadian tea dealers, after buying one or two chests at
Montreal or elsewhere, which have the Custom-house mark upon
them, fill them up ever afterwards with tea brought from the
United States. It is calculated that near 10,000 chests are annually consumed in the Canadas, of which not more than 2000 or
3000 come from Europe. Indeed, when I had myself entered
Canada, I was told that of every fifteen pounds of tea sold there
thirteen were smuggled. The profit upon smuggling this article is
from 50 to 100 per cent., and, with an extensive and wild frontier
like Canada, cannot be prevented. Indeed it every year increases,
and is brought to a more perfect system. But I suppose that the
English Government, which is the perfection of wisdom, will never
allow the Canadian merchants to trade direct to China, in order
that (from pure charity) the whole profit of the tea trade may be
given up to the United States."—(*Excursion*, pp. 394, 395.) *
"You will readily conceive, that it is with no small mortification
that I hear these American merchants talk of sending their ships
to London and Liverpool, to take in goods or specie, with which
to purchase tea for the supply of European ports almost within
sight of our own shores. They often taunt me, by asking me what
our government can possibly mean by prohibiting us from en-
gaging in a profitable trade, which is open to them and to all the
world? or where can be our boasted liberties, while we tamely
submit to the infraction of our natural rights, to supply a mo-

---

* *An Excursion through the United States and Canada, during the Years
1822–3.* By an English Gentleman. London. 1824.

nopoly as absurd as it is unjust, and to honour the caprice of a company who exclude their fellow-subjects from a branch of commerce which they do not pursue themselves, but leave to the enterprise of foreigners, or commercial rivals? On such occasions I can only reply, that both our government and people are growing wiser; and that if the charter of the East India Company be renewed, when it next expires, I will allow them to infer, that the people of England have little influence in the administration of their own affairs."—(*Hodgson's Letters,* Vol. II, pp. 128, 129.) *

Though America is a confederation of republics, they are in many cases much more amalgamated than the various parts of Great Britain. If a citizen of the United States can make a shoe, he is at liberty to make a shoe anywhere between Lake Ontario and New Orleans,—he may sole on the Mississippi,—heel on the Missouri,—measure Mr. Birkbeck on the little Wabash, or take (which our best politicians do not find an easy matter) the length of Mr. Munro's foot on the banks of the Potowmac. But woe to the cobbler, who, having made Hessian boots for the aldermen of Newcastle, should venture to invest with these coriaceous integuments the leg of a liege subject at York. A yellow ant in a nest of red ants—a butcher's dog in a fox kennel—a mouse in a bee-hive,—all feel the effects of untimely intrusion;—but far preferable their fate to that of the misguided artisan, who, misled by sixpenny histories of England, and conceiving his country to have been united at the Heptarchy, goes forth from his native town to stitch freely within the sea-girt limits of Albion. Him the mayor, him the alderman, him the recorder, him the quarter sessions would worry. Him the justices before trial would long to get into the tread-mill,† and would much lament that, by

---

* *Letters from North America, written during a Tour in the United States and Canada.* By Adam Hodgson. London. 1824.
† This puts us in mind of our friend Mr. Headlam, who, we hear, has written an answer to our Observations on the Tread-mill before Trial. It would have been a very easy thing for us to have hung Mr. Headlam up as a spectacle to the United Kingdoms of England, Scotland, and Ireland, the principality of Wales, and the town of Berwick-on-Tweed; but we have no wish to make a worthy and respectable man appear ridiculous. For these reasons we have not even looked at his pamphlet, and we decline entering into a controversy upon a point, where among men of sense and humanity (who had not heated themselves in the dispute), there cannot possibly be any difference of opinion. All members of both Houses of Parliament were unanimous in their condemnation of the odious and nonsensical practice of working prisoners in the tread-mill before trial. It had not one single advocate. Mr. Headlam and the magistrates of the North Riding, in their eagerness to save a relic of their prison system, forgot themselves so far as to petition to be intrusted with the power of putting prisoners to work

a recent act, they could not do so, even with the intruding tradesman's consent; but the moment he was tried, they would push him
in with redoubled energy, and leave him to tread himself into a
conviction of the barbarous institutions of his corporation-divided
country.

Too much praise cannot be given to the Americans for their great
attention to the subject of Education. All the public lands are sur-
veyed according to the direction of Congress. They are divided into
townships of six miles square, by lines running with the cardinal
points, and consequently crossing each other at right angles. Every
township is divided into 36 sections, each a mile square, and containing 640 acres. One section in each township is reserved, and
given in perpetuity for the benefit of common schools. In addition
to this the states of Tennessee and Ohio have received grants for
the support of colleges and academies. The appropriation generally
in the new States for seminaries of the higher orders, amount to one
fifth of those for common schools. It appears from Seybert's Statistical Annals, that the land, in the states and territories on the east
side of the Mississippi, in which appropriations have been made,
amounts to 237,300 acres; and according to the ratio above mentioned, the aggregate on the east side of the Mississippi is 7,900,000.
The same system of appropriation applied to the west, will make,
for schools and colleges, 6,600,000; and the total appropriation for
literary purposes, in the new states and territories, 14,500,000 acres,
which, at two dollars per acre, would be 29,000,000 dollars. These
facts are very properly quoted by Mr. Hodgson; and it is impossible to speak too highly of their value and importance. They quite
put into the back-ground everything which has been done in the Old
World for the improvement of the lower orders, and confer deserv-
edly upon the Americans the character of a wise, a reflecting, and
a virtuous people.

It is rather surprising that such a people, spreading rapidly over
so vast a portion of the earth, and cultivating all the liberal and useful arts so successfully, should be so extremely sensitive and touchy
as the Americans are said to be. We really thought at one time they
would have fitted out an armament against the Edinburgh and Quar-

---

before trial, *with their own consent*—the answer of the Legislature was,
"We will not trust you,"—the severest practical rebuke ever received by
any public body. We will leave it to others to determine whether it was
deserved. We have no doubt the great body of magistrates meant well. They
must have meant well—but they have been sadly misled, and have thrown
odium on the subordinate administration of justice, which it is far from
deserving on other occasions, in their hands. This strange piece of nonsense is, however, now well ended.—*Requiescat in pace!*

terly Reviews, and burnt down Mr. Murray's and Mr. Constable's shops, as we did the American Capitol. We, however, remember no other anti-American crime of which we were guilty, than a preference of Shakspeare and Milton over Joel Barlow and Timothy Dwight. That opinion we must still take the liberty of retaining. There is nothing in Dwight comparable to the finest passages of Paradise Lost, nor is Mr. Barlow ever humorous or pathetic, as the great Bard of the English stage is humorous and pathetic. We have always been strenuous * advocates for, and admirers of, America— not taking our ideas from the over-weening vanity of the weaker part of the Americans themselves, but from what we have observed of their real energy and wisdom. It is very natural that we Scotch, who live in a little shabby scraggy corner of a remote island, with a climate which cannot ripen an apple, should be jealous of the aggressive pleasantry of more favoured people; but that Americans, who have done so much for themselves, and received so much from nature, should be flung into such convulsions by English Reviews and Magazines, is really a sad specimen of Columbian juvenility. We hardly dare to quote the following account of an American rout, for fear of having our motives misrepresented,—and strongly suspect that there are but few Americans who could be brought to admit that a Philadelphia or Boston concern of this nature is not quite equal to the most brilliant assemblies of London or Paris.

"A tea party is a serious thing in this country; and some of those at which I have been present in New York and elsewhere, have been on a very large scale. In the modern houses the two principal apartments are on the first floor, and communicate by large folding-doors, which on gala days throw wide their ample portals, converting the two apartments into one. At the largest party which I have seen, there were about thirty young ladies present, and more than as many gentlemen. Every sofa, chair, and footstool were occupied by the ladies, and little enough room some of them appeared to have after all. The gentlemen were obliged to be con-

---

* Ancient women, whether in or out of breeches, will of course imagine that we are the enemies of the institutions of our country, because we are the admirers of the institutions of America: but circumstances differ. American institutions are too new, English institutions are ready made to our hands. If we were to build the house afresh, we might perhaps avail ourselves of the improvements of a new plan; but we have no sort of wish to pull down an excellent house, strong, warm, and comfortable, because, upon second trial, we might be able to alter and amend it,—a principle which would perpetuate demolition and construction. Our plan, where circumstances are tolerable, is to sit down and enjoy ourselves.

tent with walking up and down, talking now with one lady, now with another. Tea was brought in by a couple of blacks, carrying large trays, one covered with cups, the other with cake. Slowly making the round, and retiring at intervals for additional supplies, the ladies were gradually gone over; and after much patience the gentlemen began to enjoy the beverage 'which cheers but not inebriates;' still walking about, or leaning against the wall, with the cup and saucer in their hand.

"As soon as the first course was over, the hospitable trays again entered, bearing a chaos of preserves—peaches, pine-apples, ginger, oranges, citrons, pears, &c. in tempting display. A few of the young gentlemen now accompanied the revolution of the trays, and sedulously attended to the pleasure of the ladies. The party was so numerous that the period between the commencement and the termination of the round was sufficient to justify a new solicitation; and so the ceremony continued, with very little intermission, during the whole evening. Wine succeeded the preserves, and dried fruit followed the wine; which, in its turn, was supported by sandwiches in the name of supper, and a forlorn hope of confectionary and frost work. I pitied the poor blacks who, like Tantalus, had such a profusion of dainties the whole evening at their finger ends, without the possibility of partaking of them. A little music and dancing gave variety to the scene; which to some of us was a source of considerable satisfaction; for when a number of ladies were on the floor, those who cared not for the dance had the pleasure of getting a seat. About eleven o'clock I did myself the honour of escorting a lady home, and was well pleased to have an excuse for escaping."—(*Duncan's Travels*, Vol. II, pp. 279, 280.)

The coaches must be given up; so must the roads, and so must the inns. They are of course what these accommodations are in all new countries; and much like what English great-grandfathers talk about as existing in this country at the first period of their recollection. The great inconvenience of American inns, however, in the eyes of an Englishman, is one which more sociable travellers must feel less acutely—we mean the impossibility of being alone, of having a room separate from the rest of the company. There is nothing which an Englishman enjoys more than the pleasure of sulkiness,—of not being forced to hear a word from anybody which may occasion to him the necessity of replying. It is not so much that Mr. Bull disdains to talk, as that Mr. Bull has nothing to say. His forefathers have been out of spirits for six or seven hundred years, and seeing nothing but fog and vapour, he is out of spirits too; and when there is no selling or buying, or no business to settle, he prefers being alone and looking at the fire. If any gentleman were in distress, he would willingly lend a helping hand; but he thinks it no part of neighbourhood to talk to a person because he happens to be near him. In short, with many excellent qualities, it must be acknowledged that the English are the most disagreeable of all the nations of Europe,—more surly and morose, with less disposition to please, to exert themselves for the good of society, to make small sacrifices, and to put themselves out of their way. They are content with Magna Charter and Trial by Jury; and think they are not bound to excel the rest of the world in small behaviour, if they are superior to them in great institutions.

We are terribly afraid that some Americans spit upon the floor, even when that floor is covered by good carpets. Now all claims to civilisation are suspended till this secretion is otherwise disposed of. No English gentleman has spit upon the floor since the Heptarchy.

The curiosity for which the Americans are so much laughed at, is not only venial, but laudable. Where men live in woods and forests, as is the case, of course, in remote American settlements, it is the duty of every man to gratify the inhabitants by telling them his name, place, age, office, virtues, crimes, children, fortune, and remarks: and with fellow-travellers it seems to be almost a matter of necessity to do so. When men ride together for 300 or 400 miles through woods and prairies, it is of the greatest importance that they should be able to guess at subjects most agreeable to each other, and to multiply their common topics. Without knowing who your companion is, it is difficult to know both what to say and what to avoid. You may talk of honour and virtue to an attorney, or contend with a Virginian planter that men of a fair colour have no right to buy and sell men of a dusky colour. The following is a lively description of the rights of interrogation, as understood and practised in America.

"As for the *Inquisitiveness* of the Americans, I do not think it has been at all exaggerated.—They certainly are, as they profess to be, a very inquiring people; and if we may sometimes be disposed to dispute the claims of their *love of knowing* to the character of a liberal curiosity, we must at least admit that they make a most liberal use of every means in their power to gratify it. I have seldom, however, had any difficulty in repressing their home questions, if I wished it, and without offending them; but I more frequently amused myself by putting them on the rack, civilly, and apparently unconsciously, eluded their inquiries for a time, and then awakening their gratitude by such a discovery of myself as I might choose to make. Sometimes a man would place himself at my side in the wilderness, and ride for a mile or two without the smallest communication between us, except a slight nod of the head. He would then, perhaps, make some grave remark on the weather, and if I assented, in a monosyllable, he would stick to my side for another mile or two, when he would commence his attack. 'I reckon, stranger, you do not belong to these parts?'—'No, sir; I am not a native of Alabama.'—'I guess you are from the north?'—'No, Sir; I am not from the north.'—'I guess you found the roads mighty muddy, and the creeks swimming. You are come a long way, I guess?'—'No, not so very far; we have travelled a few hundred miles since we turned our faces westward.'—'I guess you have seen Mr. ———, or General ———?' (mentioning the names of some well-known individuals in the Middle and Southern States, who were to serve as guide-posts to detect our route); but 'I have not the pleasure of knowing any of them,' or, 'I have the pleasure of knowing all,' equally defeated his purpose, but not his hopes. 'I reckon, stranger, you have had a good crop of cotton this year?'—'I am told, sir, the crops have been unusually abundant in Carolina and Georgia.'—'You grow tobacco, then, I guess?' (to track me to Virginia).—'No; I do not grow tobacco.' Here a modest inquirer would give up in despair, and trust to the chapter of accidents to develope my name and history; but I generally rewarded his modesty, and excited his gratitude, by telling him I would torment him no longer.

"The courage of a thorough-bred Yankee * would rise with his difficulties; and after a decent interval, he would resume: 'I hope no offence, sir; but you know we Yankees lose nothing for want of asking. I guess, stranger, you are from the old country?'— 'Well, my friend, you have guessed right at last, and I am sure you deserve something for your perseverance: and now I suppose it will save us both trouble if I proceed to the second part of the story, and tell you where I am going. I am going to New Orleans.' This is really no exaggeration picture: dialogues, not indeed in these very words, but *to this effect,* occurred continually, and some of them more minute and extended than I can venture upon in a letter. I ought, however, to say, that many questions lose much of their familiarity when travelling in the wilderness.

---

* In America, the term Yankee is applied to the natives of New England only, and is generally used with an air of pleasantry.

'Where are you from?' and, 'Whither are you bound?' do not appear impertinent interrogations at sea; and often in the western wilds I found myself making inquiries which I should have thought very free and easy at home."—(*Hodgson's Letters,* Vol. II, pp. 32–35.)

In all new and distant settlements the forms of law must, of course, be very limited. No justice's warrant is current in the Dismal Swamp; constables are exceedingly puzzled in the neighbourhood of the Mississippi; and there is no tread-mill, either before or after trial, on the Little Wabash. The consequence of this is, that the settlers take the law into their own hands, and give notice to a justice-proof delinquent to quit the territory. If this notice is disobeyed, they assemble and whip the culprit, and this failing, on the second visit, they cut off his ears. In short, Captain Rock has his descendants in America. Mankind cannot live together without some approximation to justice; and if the actual government will not govern well, or cannot govern well, is too wicked or too weak to do so—then men prefer Rock to anarchy. The following is the best account we have seen of this system of irregular justice.

"After leaving Carlyle, I took the Shawnee town road that branches off to the S.E., and passed the Walnutt Hills, and Moore's Prairie. These two places had a year or two before been infested by a notorious gang of robbers and forgers, who had fixed themselves in these wild parts in order to avoid justice. As the country became more settled, these desperadoes became more and more troublesome. The inhabitants therefore took that method of getting rid of them that had been adopted not many years ago in Hopkinson and Henderson counties, Kentucky, and which is absolutely necessary in new and thinly settled districts, where it is almost impossible to punish a criminal according to legal forms. "On such occasions, therefore, all the quiet and industrious men of a district form themselves into companies, under the name of 'Regulators.' They appoint officers, put themselves under their orders, and bind themselves to assist and stand by each other. The first step they then take is to send notice to any notorious vagabonds, desiring them to quit the State in a certain number of days, under the penalty of receiving a domiciliary visit. Should the person who receives the notice refuse to comply, they suddenly assemble, and when unexpected, go in the night time to the rogue's house, take him out, tie him to a tree, and give him a severe whipping, every one of the party striking him a certain number of times.

"This discipline is generally sufficient to drive off the culprit; but should he continue obstinate, and refuse to avail himself of another warning, the Regulators pay him a second visit, inflict a still severer whipping, with the addition probably of cutting off both his ears. No culprit has ever been known to remain after a second visit. For instance, an old man, the father of a family, all of whom he educated as robbers, fixed himself at Moore's Prairie, and committed numerous thefts, &c. &c. He was hardy enough to remain after the first visit, when both he and his sons received a whipping. At the second visit the Regulators punished him very severely, and cut off his ears. This drove him off, together with his whole gang; and travellers can now pass in perfect safety where it was once dangerous to travel alone.

"There is also a company of Regulators near Vincennes, who have broken up a notorious gang of coiners and thieves who had fixed themselves near that place. These rascals, before they were driven off, had parties settled at different distances in the woods, and thus held communication and passed horses and stolen goods from one to another, from the Ohio to Lake Erie, and from thence into Canada or the New England States. Thus it was next to impossible to detect the robbers, or to recover the stolen property.

"This practice of *Regulating* seems very strange to an European. I have talked with some of the chief men of the Regulators, who all lamented the necessity of such a system. They very sensibly remarked, that when the country became more thickly settled, there would no longer be any necessity for such proceedings, and that they should all be delighted at being able to obtain justice in a more formal manner. I forgot to mention that the rascals punished have sometimes prosecuted the Regulators for an assault. The juries, however, knowing the bad character of the prosecutors, would give but trifling damages, which, divided among so many, amounted to next to nothing for each individual."—(*Excursion*, pp. 233–236.)

This same traveller mentions his having met at table three or four American ex-kings—presidents who had served their time, and had retired into private life; he observes also upon the effect of a democratical government in preventing mobs. Mobs are created by opposition to the wishes of the people;—but when the wishes of the people are consulted so completely as they are consulted in America—all motives for the agency of mobs are done away.

"It is, indeed, entirely a government of opinion. Whatever the people wish is done. If they want any alteration of laws, tariffs,

&c., they inform their representatives, and if there be a majority that wish it, the alteration is made at once. In most European countries there is a portion of the population denominated the *mob*, who, not being acquainted with real liberty, give themselves up to occasional fits of licentiousness. But in the United States there is no *mob*, for every man feels himself free. At the time of Burr's conspiracy, Mr. Jefferson said, that there was little to be apprehended from it, as every man felt himself a part of the general sovereignty. The event proved the truth of this assertion; and Burr, who in any other country would have been hanged, drawn, and quartered, is at present leading an obscure life in the city of New York, despised by every one."—(*Excursion, p. 70.*)

It is a real blessing for America to be exempted from that vast burthen of taxes, the consequences of a long series of foolish just and necessary wars, carried on to please kings and queens, or the waiting-maids and waiting-lords or gentlemen who have always governed kings and queens in the Old World. The Americans owe this good to the newness of their government; and though there are few classical associations or historical recollections in the United States, this barrenness is well purchased by the absence of all the feudal nonsense, inveterate abuses, and profligate debts of an old country.

"The good effects of a free government are visible throughout the whole country. There are no tithes, no poor-rates, no excise, no heavy internal taxes, no commercial monopolies. An American can make candles if he have tallow, can distil brandy if he have grapes or peaches, and can make beer if he have malt and hops, without asking leave of any one, and much less with any fear of incurring punishment. How would a farmer's wife there be astonished, if told that it was contrary to law for her to make soap out of the potass obtained on the farm, and of the grease she herself had saved! When an American has made these articles, he may build his little vessel, and take them without hinderance to any part of the world; for there is no rich company of merchants that can say to him, 'You shall not trade to India; and you shall not buy a pound of tea of the Chinese; as, by so doing, you would infringe upon our privileges.' In consequence of this freedom, all the seas are covered with their vessels, and the people at home are active and independent. I never saw a beggar in any part of the United States; nor was I ever asked for charity but once— and that was by an Irishman."—(*Excursion, pp. 70, 71.*)

America is so differently situated from the old governments of Europe, that the United States afford no political precedents that are exactly applicable to our old governments. There is no idle and discontented population. When they have peopled themselves up to the Mississippi, they cross to the Missouri, and will go on till they are stopped by the Western Ocean; and then, when there are a number of persons who have nothing to do, and nothing to gain, no hope for lawful industry and great interest in promoting changes, we may consider their situation as somewhat similar to our own, and their example as touching us more nearly. The changes in the constitution of the particular States seem to be very frequent, very radical, and to us very alarming;—they seem, however, to be thought very little of in that country, and to be very little heard of in Europe. Mr. Duncan, in the following passage, speaks of them with European feelings.

"The other great obstacle to the prosperity of the American nation, universal suffrage,* will not exhibit the full extent of its evil tendency for a long time to come; and it is possible that ere that time some antidote may be discovered, to prevent or alleviate the mischief which we might naturally expect from it. It does, however, seem ominous of evil, that so little ceremony is at present used with the constitutions of the various States. The people of Connecticut, not contented with having prospered abundantly under their old system, have lately assembled a convention, composed of delegates from all parts of the country, in which the former order of things has been condemned entirely, and a completely new constitution manufactured; which, among other things, provides for the same process being again gone through as soon as the *profanum vulgus* takes it into its head to desire it.† A sorry legacy the British Constitution would be to us, if it were at the mercy of a meeting of delegates, to be summoned whenever a majority of the people took a fancy for a new one; and I am afraid that if the Americans continue to cherish a fondness for such repairs, the Highlandman's pistol with its new stock, lock, and barrel, will bear a close resemblance to what is ultimately produced."—(*Duncan's Travels,* Vol. II, pp. 335, 336.)

In the Excursion there is a list of the American navy, which, in conjunction with the navy of France, will one day or another, we

---

* In the greater number of the States, every white person, 21 years of age, who has paid taxes for one year, is a voter; in others, some additional qualifications are required, but they are not such as materially to limit the privilege.
† The people of the State of New York have subsequently taken a similar fancy to *clout the cauldron.* (1822.)

fear, settle the Catholic question in a way not quite agreeable to the Earl of Liverpool for the time being, nor very creditable to the wisdom of those ancestors of whom we hear, and from whom we suffer so much. The regulations of the American navy seem to be admirable. The States are making great exertions to increase this navy; and since the capture of so many English ships, it has become the favourite science of the people at large. Their flotillas on the lakes completely defeated ours during the last war.

Fanaticism of every description seems to rage and flourish in America, which has no Establishment, in about the same degree which it does here under the nose of an Established Church;— they have their prophets and prophetesses, their preaching encampments, female preachers, and every variety of noise, folly, and nonsense, like ourselves. Among the most singular of these fanatics, are the Harmonites. Rapp, their founder, was a dissenter from the Lutheran Church, and therefore, of course, the Lutheran clergy of Stutgard (near to which he lived) began to put Mr. Rapp in white sheets, to prove him guilty of theft, parricide, treason, and all the usual crimes of which men dissenting from established churches are so often guilty,—and delicate hints were given respecting faggots! Stutgard abounds with underwood and clergy; and—away went Mr. Rapp to the United States, and, with a great multitude of followers, settled about twenty-four miles from our countryman Mr. Birkbeck. His people have here built a large town, and planted a vineyard, where they make very agreeable wine. They carry on also a very extensive system of husbandry, and are the masters of many flocks and herds. They have a distillery, brewery, tannery, make hats, shoes, cotton and woollen cloth, and everything necessary to the comfort of life. Every one belongs to some particular trade. But in bad weather, when there is danger of losing their crops, Rapp blows a horn, and calls them all together. Over every trade there is a head man, who receives the money, and gives a receipt, signed by Rapp, to whom all the money collected is transmitted. When any of these workmen wants a hat or a coat, Rapp signs him an order for the garment, for which he goes to the store, and is fitted. They have one large store where these manufactures are deposited. This store is much resorted to by the neighbourhood, on account of the goodness and cheapness of the articles. They have built an excellent house for their founder, Rapp,—as it might have been predicted they would have done. The Harmonites profess equality, community of goods, and celibacy, for the men and women (let Mr. Malthus hear this) live separately, and are not allowed the slightest intercourse. In order to keep up their numbers, they have once or twice sent over for a supply of Germans, as they admit no Americans, of any intercourse with whom they are very jealous. The Harmonites dress and live plainly. It is a part of their creed that they should do so. Rapp, however, and the head men have no such particular creed for themselves; and indulge in wine, beer, grocery, and other irreligious diet. Rapp is both governor and priest,—preaches to them in church, and directs all their proceedings in their working hours. In short, Rapp seems to have made use of the religious propensities of mankind, to persuade one or two thousand fools to dedicate their lives to his service; and if they do not get tired, and fling their prophet into a horse-pond, they will in all probability disperse as soon as he dies.

Unitarians are increasing very fast in the United States, not being kept down by charges from bishops and archdeacons, their natural enemies.

The author of the Excursion remarks upon the total absence of all games in America. No cricket, foot-ball, nor leap-frog—all seems solid and profitable.

"One thing that I could not help remarking with regard to the Americans in general, is the total want of all those games and sports that obtained for our country the appellation of 'Merry England.' Although children usually transmit stories and sports from one generation to another, and although many of our nursery games and tales are supposed to have been imported into England in the vessels of Hengist and Horsa, yet our brethren in the United States seem entirely to have forgotten the childish amusements of our common ancestors. In America I never saw even the schoolboys playing at any game whatsoever. Cricket, foot-ball, quoits, &c. appear to be utterly unknown; and I believe that if an American were to see grown-up men playing at cricket, he would express as much astonishment as the Italians did when some Englishmen played at this finest of all games in the Casina at Florence. Indeed, that joyous spirit which, in our country, animates not only childhood, but also maturer age, can rarely or never be seen among the inhabitants of the United States."—(*Excursion,* pp. 502, 503.)

These are a few of the leading and prominent circumstances respecting America, mentioned in the various works before us: of which works we can recommend the Letters of Mr. Hodgson, and the Excursion into Canada, as sensible, agreeable books, written in a very fair spirit.

America seems, on the whole, to be a country possessing vast advantages, and little inconveniences; they have a cheap government, and bad roads; they pay no tithes, and have stage coaches without springs. They have no poor-laws, and no monopolies—but their inns are inconvenient, and travellers are teased with questions. They have no collections in the fine arts; but they have no Lord Chancellor, and they can go to law without absolute ruin. They cannot make Latin verses, but they expend immense sums in the education of the poor. In all this the balance is prodigiously in their favour: but then comes the great disgrace and danger of America—the existence of slavery, which, if not timously corrected, will one day entail (and ought to entail) a bloody servile war upon the Americans—which will separate America into slave States and States disclaiming slavery, and which remains at present as the foulest blot in the moral character of that people. A high-spirited nation, who cannot endure the slightest act of foreign aggression, and who revolt at the very shadow of domestic tyranny, beat with cart-whips, and bind with chains, and murder for the merest trifles, wretched human beings, who are of a more dusky colour than themselves; and have recently admitted in their Union a new State, with the express permission of ingrafting this atrocious wickedness into their constitution! No one can admire the simple wisdom and manly firmness of the Americans more than we do, or more despise the pitiful propensity which exists among Government runners to vent their small spite at their character; but on the subject of slavery, the conduct of America is, and has been, most reprehensible. It is impossible to speak of it with too much indignation and contempt; but for it we should look forward with unqualified pleasure to such a land of freedom, and such a magnificent spectacle of human happiness.

On American Debts

The Humble Petition of the Rev. Sydney Smith of the House of Congress at Washington.

I petition your honourable House to institute some measures for the restoration of American credit, and for the repayment of debts incurred and repudiated by several of the States. Your Petitioner lent to the State of Pennsylvania a sum of money, for the purpose of some public improvement. The amount, though small, is to him important, and is a saving from a life income, made with difficulty and privation. If their refusal to pay (from which a very large number of English families are suffering) had been the result of war, produced by the unjust aggression of powerful enemies; if it had arisen from civil discord; if it had proceeded from an improvident application of means in the first years of self-government: if it were the act of a poor State struggling against the barrenness of nature—every friend of America would have been contented to wait for better times; but the fraud is committed in the profound peace of Pennsylvania, by the richest State in the Union, after the wise investment of the borrowed money in roads and canals, of which the repudiators are every day reaping the advantage. It is an act of bad faith which (all its circumstances considered) has no parallel, and no excuse.

Nor is it only the loss of property which your Petitioner laments; he laments still more that immense power which the bad faith of America has given to aristocratical opinions, and to the enemies of free institutions, in the old world. It is in vain any longer to appeal to history, and to point out the wrongs which the many have received from the few. The Americans, who boast to have improved the institutions of the old world, have at least equalled its crimes. A great nation, after trampling under foot all earthly tyranny, has been guilty of a fraud as enormous as ever disgraced the worst king of the most degraded nation of Europe.

It is most painful to your Petitioner to see that American citizens excite, wherever they may go, the recollection that they belong to a dishonest people, who pride themselves on having tricked and pillaged Europe; and this mark is fixed by their faithless legislators on some of the best and most honourable men in the world, whom every Englishman has been eager to see and proud to receive.

It is a subject of serious concern to your Petitioner that you are losing all that power which the friends of freedom rejoiced that you possessed, looking upon you as the ark of human happiness, and the most splendid picture of justice and of wisdom that the world had yet seen. Little did the friends of America expect it, and sad is the spectacle to see you rejected by every State in Europe, as a nation with whom no contract can be made, because none will be kept; unstable in the very foundations of social life, deficient in the elements of good faith, men who prefer any load of infamy however great, to any pressure of taxation however light.

Nor is it only this gigantic bankruptcy for so many degrees of longitude and latitude which your Petitioner deplores, but he is alarmed also by that total want of shame with which these things have been done; the callous immorality with which Europe has been plundered, that deadness of the moral sense which seems to preclude all return to honesty, to perpetuate this new infamy, and to threaten its extension over every State of the Union.

To any man of real philanthropy, who receives pleasure from the improvements of the world, the repudiation of the public debts of America, and the shameless manner in which it has been talked of and done, is the most melancholy event which has happened during the existence of the present generation. Your Petitioner sincerely prays that the great and good men still existing among you may, by teaching to the United States the deep disgrace they have incurred in the whole world, restore them to moral health, to that high position they have lost, and which, for the happiness of mankind, it is so important they should ever maintain; for the United States are now working out the greatest of all political problems, and upon that confederacy the eyes of thinking men are intensely fixed, to see how far the mass of mankind can be trusted with the management of their own affairs, and the establishment of their own happiness.

May 18, 1843.

LETTER I.

To the Editor of the Morning Chronicle

Sir,

You did me the favour, some time since, to insert in your valuable journal a petition of mine to the American Congress, for the repayment of a loan made by me, in common with many other unwise people, to the State of Pennsylvania. For that petition I have been abused in the grossest manner by many of the American papers. After some weeks' reflection, I see no reason to alter my opinions, or to retract my expressions. What I then said was not wild declamation, but measured truth. I repeat again, that no conduct was ever more profligate than that of the State of Pennsylvania. History cannot pattern it: and let no deluded being imagine that they will ever repay a single farthing—their people have tasted of the dangerous luxury of dishonesty, and they will never be brought back to the homely rule of right. The money transactions of the Americans are become a by-word among the nations of Europe. In every grammar-school of the old world *ad Græcas Calendas* is translated—the American dividends.

I am no enemy to America. I loved and admired honest America when she respected the laws of pounds, shillings, and pence; and I thought the United States the most magnificent picture of human happiness: I meddle now in these matters because I hate fraud—because I pity the misery it has occasioned—because I mourn over the hatred it has excited against free institutions.

Among the discussions to which the moral lubricities of this insolvent people have given birth, they have arrogated to themselves the right of sitting in judgment upon the property of their creditors—of deciding who among them is rich, and who poor, and who are proper objects of compassionate payment; but in the name of Mercury, the great god of thieves, did any man ever hear of debtors alleging the wealth of the lender as a reason for eluding the payment of the loan? Is the Stock Exchange a place for the tables of the money-lenders; or is it a school of moralists, who may amerce the rich, exalt the poor, and correct the inequalities of fortune. Is *Biddle* an instrument in the hand of Providence to exalt the humble, and send the rich empty away? Does American Providence work with such instruments as *Biddle?*

But the only good part of this bad morality is not acted upon. The rich are robbed, but the poor are not paid: they growl against the dividends of Dives, and don't lick the sores of Lazarus. They seize with loud acclamations on the money bags of Jones Loyd, Rothschild, and Baring, but they do not give back the pittance of the widow, and the bread of the child. Those knaves of the setting sun may call me rich, for I have a twentieth part of the income of the Archbishop of Canterbury; but the curate of the next parish is a wretched soul, bruised by adversity; and the three hundred pounds for his children, which it has taken his life to save, is eaten and drunken by the mean men of Pennsylvania—by men who are always talking of the virtue and honour of the United States—by men who soar above others in what they say, and sink below all nations in what they do—who, after floating on the heaven of declamation, fall down to feed on the offal and garbage of the earth.

Persons who are not in the secret are inclined to consider the abominable conduct of the repudiating States to proceed from exhaustion—"They don't pay because they cannot pay"; whereas, from estimates which have just now reached this country, this is the picture of the finances of the insolvent States. Their debts may be about 200 millions of dollars; at an interest of 6 per cent., this makes an annual charge of 12 millions of dollars, which is little more than 1 per cent. of their income in 1840, and may be presumed to be less than 1 per cent. of their present income; but if they were all to provide funds for the punctual payment of interest, the debt could readily be converted into a 4 or 5 per cent. stock, and the excess, converted into a sinking fund, would discharge the debt in less than thirty years. The debt of Pennsylvania, estimated at 40 millions of dollars, bears, at 5 per cent., an annual interest of 2 millions. The income of this State was, in 1840, 131 millions of dollars, and is probably at this time not less than 150 millions: a nett revenue of only 1½ per cent. would produce the two millions required. So that the price of national character in Pennsylvania is 1½ per cent. on the nett income; and if this market price of morals were established here, a gentleman of a thousand a year would deliberately and publicly submit to infamy for 15*l.* per annum; and a poor man, who by laborious industry had saved one hundred a year, would incur general disgrace and opprobrium for thirty shillings by the year. There really should be lunatic asylums for nations as well as for individuals.

But they begin to feel all this: their tone is changed; they talk with bated breath and whispering apology, and allay with some cold drops of modesty their skipping spirit. They strutted into this miserable history, and begin to think of sneaking out.

And then the subdolous press of America contends that the English under similar circumstances would act with their own debt in the same manner; but there are many English constituencies where are thousands not worth a shilling, and no such idea has been broached among them, nor has any petition to such effect been presented to the legislature. But what if they did act in such a manner, would it be a conduct less wicked than that of the Americans? Is there not one immutable law of justice—is it not written in the book? Does it not beat in the heart?—are the great guide-marks of life to be concealed by such nonsense as this? I deny the fact on which the reasoning is founded; and if the facts were true, the reasoning would be false.

I never meet a Pennsylvanian at a London dinner without feeling a disposition to seize and divide him;—to allot his beaver to one sufferer and his coat to another—to appropriate his pocket-handkerchief to the orphan, and to comfort the widow with his silver watch, Broadway rings, and the London Guide, which he always carries in his pockets. How such a man can set himself down at an English table without feeling that he owes two or three pounds to every man in company I am at a loss to conceive: he has no more right to eat with honest men than a leper has to eat with clean men. If he have a particle of honour in his composition he should shut himself up, and say, "I cannot mingle with you, I belong to a degraded people—I must hide myself—I am a plunderer from Pennsylvania."

Figure to yourself a Pennsylvanian receiving foreigners in his own country, walking over the public works with them, and showing them Larcenous Lake, Swindling Swamp, Crafty Canal, and Rogues' Railway, and other dishonest works. "This swamp we gained (says the patriotic borrower) by the repudiated loan of 1828. Our canal robbery was in 1830; we pocketed your good people's money for the railroad only last year." All this may seem very smart to the Americans; but if I had the misfortune to be born among such a people, the land of my fathers should not retain me a single moment after the act of repudiation. I would appeal from my fathers to my forefathers. I would fly to Newgate for greater purity of thought, and seek in the prisons of England for better rules of life.

This new and vain people can never forgive us for having preceded them 300 years in civilisation. They are prepared to enter into the most bloody wars in England, not on account of Oregon, or boundaries, or right of search, but because our clothes and carriages are better made, and because Bond Street beats Broadway. Wise Webster does all he can to convince the people that these are not lawful causes of war; but wars, and long wars, they will one day or another produce; and this, perhaps, is the only advantage of repudiation. The Americans cannot gratify their avarice and ambition at once; they cannot cheat and conquer at the same time. The warlike power of every country depends on their Three per Cents. If Cæsar were to reappear upon earth, Wettenhall's list would be more important than his Commentaries; Rothschild would open and shut the temple of Janus; Thomas Baring, or Bates, would probably command the Tenth Legion, and the soldiers would march to battle with loud cries of Scrip and Omnium reduced, Consols, and Cæsar! Now, the Americans have cut themselves off from all resources of credit. Having been as dishonest as they can be, they are prevented from being as foolish as they wish to be. In the whole habitable globe they cannot borrow a guinea, and they cannot draw the sword because they have not money to buy it.

If I were an American of any of the honest States, I would never rest till I had compelled Pennsylvania to be as honest as myself. The bad faith of that State brings disgrace on all; just as common snakes are killed because vipers are dangerous. I have a general feeling, that by that breed of men I have been robbed and ruined, and I shudder and keep aloof. The pecuniary credit of every State is affected by Pennsylvania. Ohio pays; but with such a bold bankruptcy before their eyes how long will Ohio pay? The truth is, that the eyes of all capitalists are averted from the United States. The finest commercial understandings will have nothing to do with them. Men rigidly just, who penetrate boldly into the dealings of nations, and work with vigour and virtue for honourable wealth—great and high-minded merchants—will loathe, and are now loathing, the name of America: it is becoming, since its fall, the common-sewer of Europe, and the native home of the needy villain.

And now, drab-coloured men of Pennsylvania, there is yet a moment left: the eyes of all Europe are anchored upon you—

"Surrexit mundus justis furiis:"

start up from that trance of dishonesty into which you are plunged; don't think of the flesh which walls about your life, but of that sin which has hurled you from the heaven of character, which hangs over you like a devouring pestilence, and makes good men sad, and ruffians dance and sing. It is not for Gin Sling and Sherry Cobbler alone that man is to live, but for those great principles against which no argument can be listened to—principles which give to every power a double power above their functions and their offices, which are the books, the arts, the academies that teach, lift up, and nourish the world—principles (I am quite serious in what I say) above cash, superior to cotton, higher than currency,—principles, without which it is better to die than to live, which every servant of God, over every sea and in all lands, should cherish—*usque ad abdita spiramenta animæ.*

Nov. 3, 1843.

LETTER II.

To the Editor of the Morning Chronicle.

Sir,

Having been unwell for some days past, I have had no opportunity of paying my respects to General Duff Green, who (whatever be his other merits), has certainly not shown himself a Washington in defence of his country. The General demands, with a beautiful simplicity, *"Whence this morbid hatred of America?"* But this question, all-affecting as it is, is stolen from Pilpay's fables:—"A fox," says Pilpay, "caught by the leg in a trap near the farm-yard, uttered the most piercing cries of distress: forthwith all the birds of the yard gathered round him, and seemed to delight in his misfortune; hens chuckled, geese hissed, ducks quacked, and chanticleer with shrill cockadoodles rent the air. 'Whence,' said the fox, limping forward with infinite gravity, 'whence this morbid hatred of the fox? What have I done? Whom have I injured? I am overwhelmed with astonishment at these symptoms of aversion.' 'Oh! you old villain,' the poultry exclaimed, 'Where are our ducklings? Where are our goslings? Did not I see you running away yesterday with my mother in your mouth? Did you not eat up all my relations last week? You ought to die the worst of deaths—to be pecked into a thousand pieces.' " Now hence, General Green, comes the morbid hatred of America, as you term it— because her conduct has been predatory—because she has ruined so many helpless children, so many miserable women, so many aged men—because she has disturbed the order of the world, and rifled those sacred treasures which human virtue had hoarded for human misery. Why is such hatred morbid? Why, is it not just, inevitable, innate? Why, is it not disgraceful to want it? Why, is it not honourable to feel it?

Hate America!!! I have loved and honoured America all my life; and in the *Edinburgh Review,* and at all opportunities which my trumpery sphere of action has afforded, I have never ceased to praise and defend the United States; and to every American to whom I have had the good fortune to be introduced, I have proffered all the hospitality in my power. But I cannot shut my eyes to enormous dishonesty; nor, remembering their former state, can I restrain myself from calling on them (though I copy Satan) to spring up from the gulf of infamy in which they are rolling,—

"Awake, arise, or be for ever fallen."

I am astonished that the honest States of America do not draw a *cordon sanitaire* round their unpaying brethren—that the truly mercantile New Yorkers, and the thoroughly honest people of Massachusetts, do not in their European visits wear an uniform with "S. S., or Solvent States," worked in gold letters upon the coat, and receipts in full of all demands tamboured on their waistcoats, and "our own property" figured on their pantaloons.

But the General seemed shocked that I should say the Americans cannot go to war without money: but what do I mean by war? Not irruptions into Canada—not the embodying of militia in Oregon; but a long, tedious, maritime war of four or five years' duration. Is any man so foolish as to suppose that Rothschild has nothing to do with such wars as these? and that a bankrupt State, without the power of borrowing a shilling in the world, may not be crippled in such a contest? We all know that the Americans can fight. Nobody doubts their courage. I see now in my mind's eye a whole army on the plains of Pennsylvania in battle array, immense corps of insolvent light infantry, regiments of heavy horse debtors, battalions of repudiators, brigades of bankrupts, with *Vivre sans payer, ou mourir,* on their banners, and *ære alieno* on their trumpets: all these desperate debtors would fight to the death for their country, and probably drive into the sea their invading creditors. Of their courage, I repeat again, I have no doubt. I wish I had the same confidence in their wisdom. But I believe they will become intoxicated by the flattery of unprincipled orators; and, instead of entering with us into a noble competition in making calico (the great object for which the Anglo-Saxon race appears to have been created), they will waste their happiness and their money (if they can get any) in years of silly, bloody, foolish, and accursed war, to prove to the world that Perkins is a real fine gentleman, and that the carronades of the Washington steamer will carry further than those of the Britisher Victoria, or the Robert Peel vessel of war.

I am accused of applying the epithet repudiation to States which have not repudiated. Perhaps so; but then these latter States have not paid. But what is the difference between a man who says, "I don't owe you anything, and will not pay you," and another who says, "I do owe you a sum," and who, having admitted the debt, never pays it? There seems in the first to be some slight colour of right; but the second is broad, blazing, refulgent, meridian fraud.

It may be very true that rich and educated men in Pennsylvania wish to pay the debt, and that the real objectors are the Dutch and German agriculturists, who cannot be made to understand the effect of character upon clover. All this may be very true, but it is a domestic quarrel. Their churchwardens of reputation must make a private rate of infamy for themselves—we have nothing to do with this rate. The real quarrel is the Unpaid World *versus* the State of Pennsylvania.

And now, dear Jonathan, let me beg of you to follow the advice of a real friend, who will say to you what Wat Tyler had not the virtue to say, and what all speakers in the eleven recent Pennsylvanian elections have cautiously abstained from saying,— "Make a great effort; book up at once, and pay." You have no conception of the obloquy and contempt to which you are exposing yourselves all over Europe. Bull is naturally disposed to love you, but he loves nobody who does not pay him. His imaginary paradise is some planet of punctual payment, where ready money prevails, and where debt and discount are unknown. As for me, as soon as I hear that the last farthing is paid to the last creditor, I will appear on my knees at the bar of the Pennsylvanian Senate in the plumeopicean robe of American controversy. Each Conscript Jonathan shall trickle over me a few drops of tar, and help to decorate me with those penal plumes in which the vanquished reasoner of the transatlantic world does homage to the physical superiority of his opponents. And now, having eased my soul of its indignation, and sold my stock at 40 per cent. discount, I sulkily retire from the subject, with a fixed intention of lending no more money to free and enlightened republics, but of employing my money henceforth in buying up Abyssian bonds, and purchasing into the Turkish Fours, or the Tunis three-and-a-half per cent funds.

November 22, 1843.

.

Printed in Great Britain
by Amazon